The Ozarks

THE OZARKS
Land and Life

Milton D. Rafferty

University of Oklahoma Press : Norman

Library of Congress Cataloging in Publication Data

Rafferty, Milton D. 1932–
The Ozarks, land and life.

Includes bibliographies and index.
1. Ozark Mountain region—History. 2. Ozark Mountain region—Description and travel. I. Title.
F147.09R17 976.7′1 79–4738
ISBN 0-8061-1582-3

Manufactured in the U.S.A.
First edition.

Contents

Illustrations

Figures

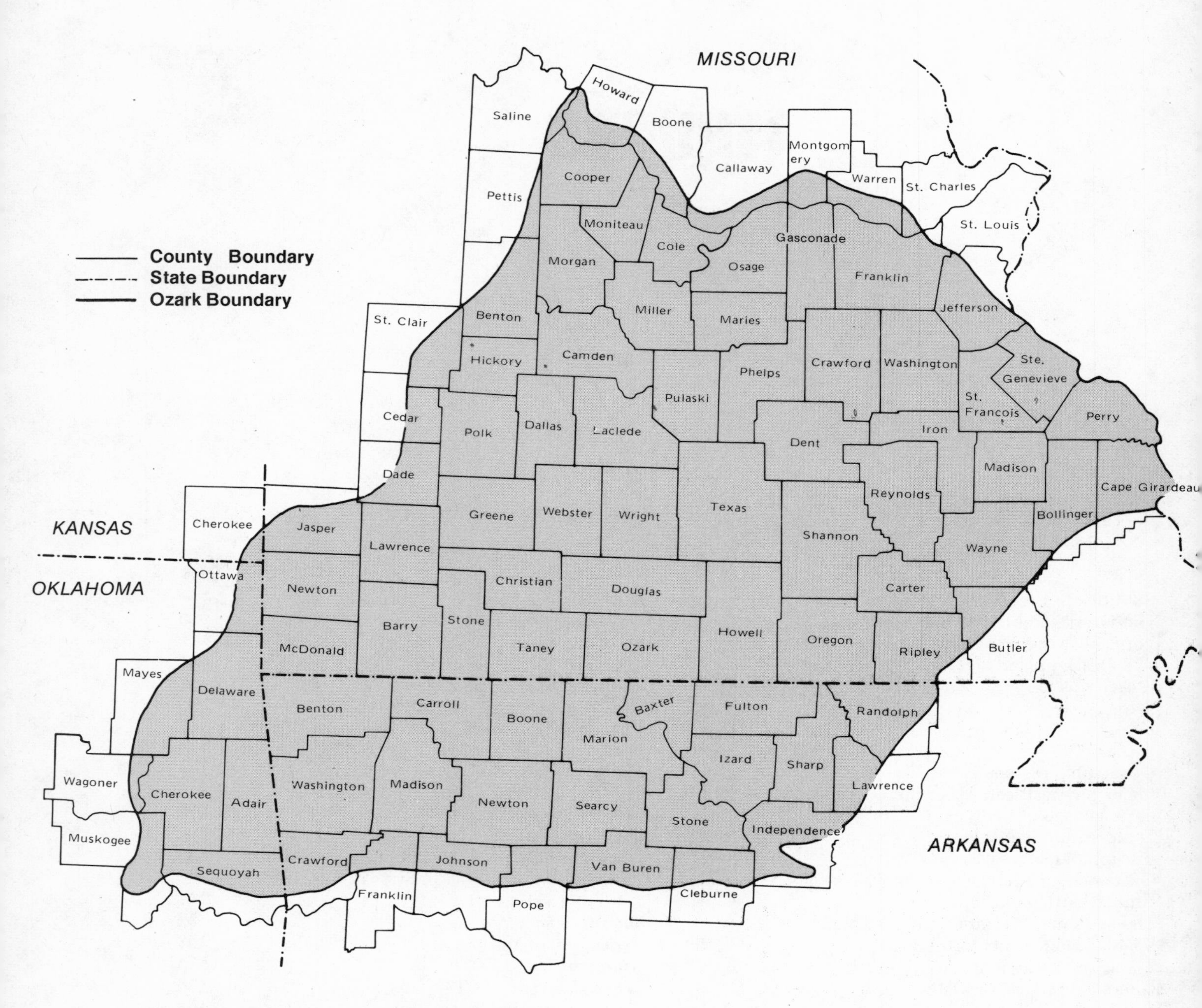

Figure 0-1. Counties in the Ozark Region.

Preface

This volume is a study in the geography of the Ozarks, with emphasis on historical development and contemporary conditions of life. Its purpose is to provide an explanation of the land and people at a time when the region is experiencing unprecedented population growth and environmental change. In at least one sense, it is a pioneer effort because heretofore there has been no treatise on either the geography or history of the Ozark region of Missouri, Arkansas, Oklahoma, and Kansas.

Rather than advocate theories or plead for policies, I have chosen to present information that will educate the reader and provide background for the Ozark scene. The selection of material and its organization reflects my professional training and personal interests. Like that of any geographer, my view is imperfect and subject to the limitations of personal impressions; but intimate firsthand acquaintance is, at best, the beginning of thorough understanding. The geographer can only hope to meld the little he has learned about the lives of people with material he has observed in the field or found in the record. I hope I have helped to make sense of the geographic aspects of human experience in the Ozarks.

A central theme throughout this book is that of persistence versus change in the relationships of man and land. In large part, it is a story of constant adjustment of man-land relations. Different peoples (Indians, French, Americans, European immigrant groups and present-day immigrants), have in different times opted for contrasting systems of land and resource use and have produced an evolving series of cultural landscapes. Man's adjustments have been mainly in terms of natural resources and cultural preferences, as is attested by the sites selected for settlement by the pioneers and by the first systems of agriculture that were used. The first wave of pioneers had scarcely put down roots when the Civil War broke out and the Ozarks became a major battlefield and stage for guerrilla warfare in the western campaigns. After the war, far-reaching innovations and adjustments were made when railroads were constructed and people from the Northern states entered the region. Commercial agriculture, mining, and forest exploitation progressed rapidly, and, all too frequently, little attention was given to the wise use of natural resources.

In more recent years, several man-induced factors have worked to reshape the economy and geography of the Ozarks. Among the more important are these: development of an integrated and fully serviceable network of roads; depletion of mineral deposits and discovery of new ore bodies; a shift from animal power to mechanical power in agriculture; growth and acceptance of a multitude of federal assistance programs in agriculture, commerce, trade, and social services; establishment of electrical utilities and improved communications; improved educational opportunities; construction of a dozen large reservoirs; and development of alternative and part-time employment, particularly in manufacturing and the tourism-recreation business.

The region's future involves unforseeables that cannot be predicted reliably from present trends. However, I have attempted to identify patterns that seem to be established and to point out potential problems that should be of concern to everyone interested in stewardship of land and resources.

The first draft of this book was written for use in a course, "Land and Life in the Ozarks," taught at Southwest Missouri State University and filmed and telecast by KOZK, Channel 21, the Public Broadcasting System station in Springfield, Missouri. Favorable responses from students and other viewers of the television lectures encouraged me to expand and publish my material.

Acknowledgement is made to many people who have given generously of their time in explaining points of difficulty and in assisting in many other ways. To Professor Leslie Hewes, my mentor at the University of Nebraska, I am indebted for introducing me to the study of the Ozarks and for impressing upon me the fact that research, teaching, and learning are all part of the same process.

My colleagues in the Department of Geography and Geology at Southwest Missouri State University have always been ready with helpful advice. Professor Russel Gerlach has shared with me an abiding interest in the Ozarks over the past ten years. Professor William Cheek provided valuable counsel on the manufacturing and recreational geography of the Ozarks. Professor Burl E. Self, Director of the Southwest Missouri State University Center for Resource Planning and Management, provided recent information from original research about Ozarkers' attitudes and preferences regarding land use and environmental problems. Michael Fuller, research associate for the Southwest Missouri State University Center for Archeological Research, provided information and references dealing with the prehistoric Indian population. Professors Robert Cooley, Robert Flanders, Donald Holliday, Carol Mock, and Lloyd Young, all members of the Ozark Studies Faculty at Southwest Missouri State University, provided new insights into the human experience in the Ozarks that otherwise would have gone unnoticed. Nancy Schanda, my coworker in the Department of Geography and Geology, provided cheerful and competent assistance throughout the project. Finally, I am greatly indebted to those alert students whose critical discussions in the classroom and keen observations in the field have helped me to appreciate new values in Ozark geography.

MILTON RAFFERTY

Springfield, Missouri

The Ozarks

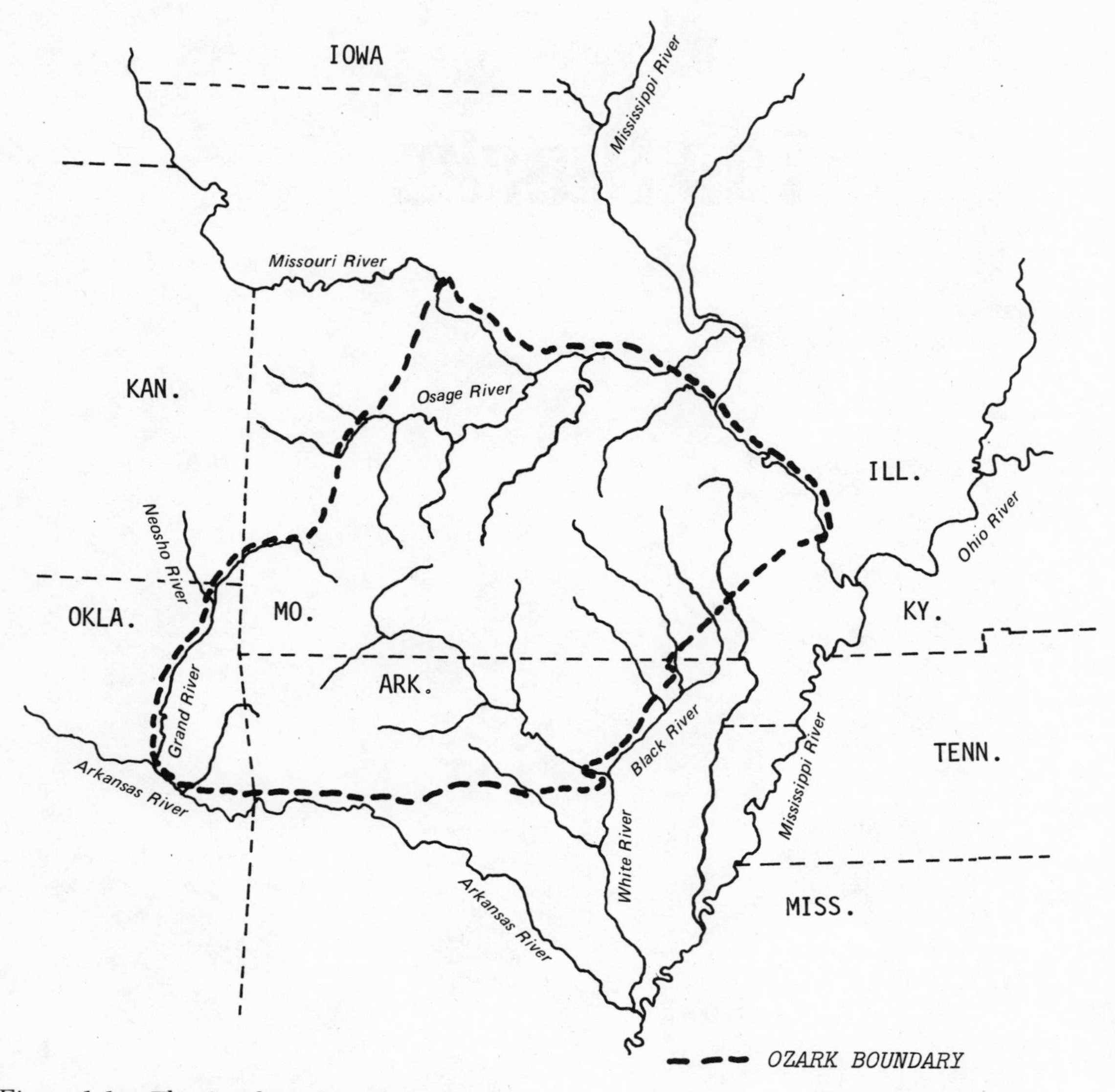

Figure 1-1. The Ozarks and bordering rivers.

1. The Ozarks: What and Where

As defined by geographers, a region is a portion of the earth's surface that has one or more elements of homogeneity distributed more or less throughout the area. The Ozarks is one of America's great regions, set apart physically by rugged terrain and sociologically by inhabitants who profess political conservatism, religious fundamentalism and sectarianism, and a strong belief in the values of rural living. This popular image of the Ozarks, though widely accepted, is poorly understood in geographic terms. In a word, the boundaries of the Ozarks are vague to most people and subject to interpretation and disagreement by the experts.

As delimited by geographers, the Ozarks are in four states: Missouri, Arkansas, Oklahoma, and Kansas (fig. 1-1). The total area may be estimated at 60,000 square miles, larger than Arkansas. Sometimes the Shawneetown Hills, which stretch across southern Illinois, are included in the Ozarks, but just as often they are linked to the limestone low-plateau country that extends through southern Indiana, central Kentucky, and into Tennessee.

The boundaries of the Ozarks are marked in a general way by major rivers (fig. 1-1). On the east is the Mississippi. Its significance as a boundary is enhanced because it forms the boundary between Illinois and Missouri. On the north the Ozarks extends just beyond the Missouri River to include a narrow strip of ravines and ridges that etch the north bluffs.

The Black River parallels the southeastern boundary of the Ozarks, collecting runoff from small Ozark streams as it finds its way across the alluvial flatlands to join the White River. The southern boundary follows along the low hills that parallel the north side of the fertile Arkansas River valley. The western boundary is not as well defined. In the southwest the Neosho River (sometimes Grand River) and its tributary, Spring River, form a visible boundary. The remainder of the western boundary, from a few miles north of Joplin to Howard County, follows the seam where Pennsylvanian-age rocks (formed 280–320 million years ago) overlap older Mississippian-age rocks. No striking changes in land-form features distinguish the Ozarks from territory to the west, but instead there is a gradual transition from forested hills to level, cultivated fields.

The unifying geographical criteria of the Ozark region include greater relief and steeper slopes than surrounding areas; surface rocks that are older than those exposed outside the Ozarks; the abundance of dolomite, as opposed to limestone (the two appear similar to the eye, but dolomite is formed by replacement of calcium in limestone by magnesium); the prevalence of the flinty, hard rock known as chert as nodules in limestone and dolomite; the abundance of karst features, such as springs, caves, and sinkholes that are produced by groundwater action on bedrock; the prevalence of average to poor soils except in the stream valleys; the extensive forests of oak, hickory, and pine; and the abundance of high-quality water resources, including rather swift-flowing streams and large man-made reservoirs. These are the physical traits most remembered by visitors, most widely publicized by the tourist-recreation industry, and most commonly associated with the region by those who have never visited it. It is perceived as a sparsely populated semiwilderness with superb scenic attractions. This is essentially correct.

The cultural traits that distinguish the Ozarks are more difficult to define, and for the most part they are more argumentative. First, the region is rural. This is the least argumentative and perhaps the most important cultural fact relating to the Ozarks. Rural suggests open country, farming, and contrasts with city life. To some it implies rudeness and lack of polish; to others it signifies idealized simplicity and peacefulness, and apartness from the world. All these things may be found to a greater or lesser degree in the Ozarks. Although it is true that urban centers—such as Springfield, Joplin, Fayetteville-Springdale, and the urban fringes of St. Louis—exert strong cultural influences on the Ozarks in many ways, the general character of day-to-day living in most of the region is rural.

Second, the Ozark heritage springs from the Upper South hill country. The first immigrants, mainly from Tennessee, Kentucky, and nearby parts of the southern Appalachians, occupied the choice lands and established self-sufficient farms. Most were descended from Scotch-Irish stock. Because for many years only a few outsiders entered the area, the economic activities, technologies, values, beliefs, and general way of life came to be patterned after that of the first immigrants. Even today most of the Ozark counties are more than 98 per cent white, native born. Most are Protestants. Settlement geographers recognize this process of cultural imprint as the principle of *first in time, first in importance*. Dr. Robert Flanders of the Ozark studies faculty at Southwest Missouri State University has characterized the Ozarks as a semiarrested frontier. This useful concept recognizes the persistence of traditional lifestyles, slowness to accept changes, and the presence of a distinctive cultural landscape in which much of the past has persisted. Upon the combined framework of rurality, the Upper South hill country heritage, and the semiarrested frontier may be hung most of the cultural baggage and popular imagery of the Ozarks: disdain for city life and education, suspicion of outsiders (especially representatives of federal and state agencies), conservative politics (whether Democrat or Republican), good-old-boyism, red-necks, clannishness, casual regard for time, reverence for outdoor activities (especially hunting and fishing), independence and closeness to nature, tall tales, fundamental religious beliefs, brush-arbor revivals, river baptisms, and characteristic speech habits. To say that the culture of the Ozarks is changing is a truism, for there is little in the world that doesn't change. However, the rate of change and the process of change from place to place within the Ozarks has been variable, so that much that was still is, much that was is gone, and the remainder, mainly imagery, never existed.

A third distinctive cultural element is the Ozarker's uncommon sense of place. They think of themselves as Ozarkers, and, half-jesting, they refer to nonresidents as outsiders. This is apparently a learned trait; outsiders soon begin to think of themselves in the same terms, either as acculturated Ozarkers or as dyed-in-the-wool outsiders. The word *Ozark*[1] appears everywhere and in various forms. Schools, churches, planning agencies, clubs, and businesses carry the name. The 1977 Springfield, Missouri, telephone directory carried no less than seventy-seven listings with *Ozark* in the title.

The consciousness of place and the liking for naming things is a primitive human trait. There are no names without people, and with people there are names. Man, the namer, has found rich resources in the Ozarks. There are countless ridges, hills, valleys, branches, hollows, coves, caves, springs, creeks, rivers, stores, hamlets,

1. The abbreviation of place-names was common with the French in America. The French post on the Arkansas, and the river, were shortened to *Aux-Arcs* or *Aux-arcs* (pronounced *Ozark*). The term means, literally, "to the Arkansas" or "to Arkansas Post."

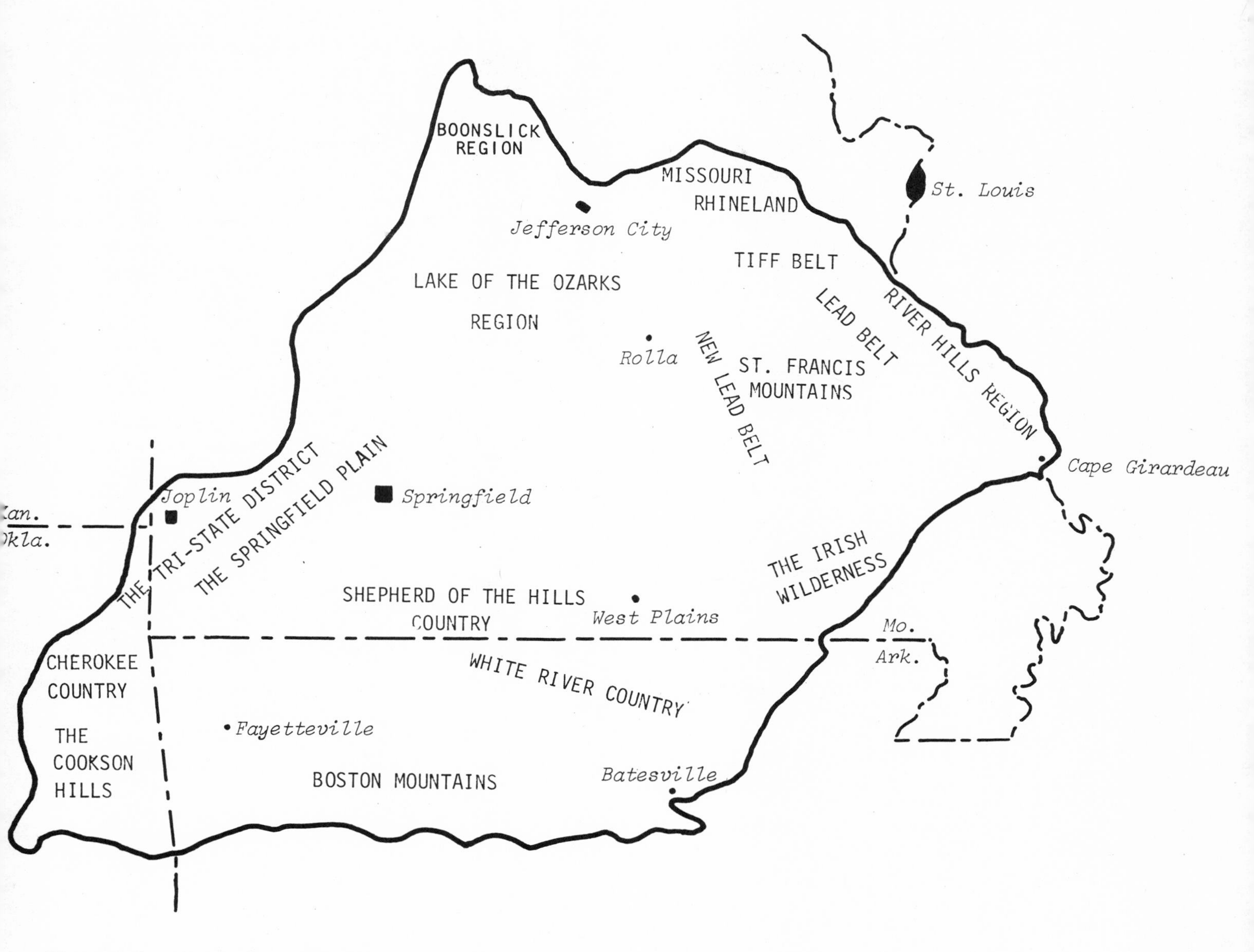

Figure 1-2. Vernacular regions of the Ozarks.

villages, towns, cities, mines, and mills that call for names. A variegated topography invites many names. On the Gladden 7½-minute Quadrangle (map), which covers a small portion of Shannon County, there are no less than sixty-two place-names for physical features. There are many vernacular regions with undefined boundaries within the Ozarks (fig. 1-2). Even within a given county there are small subregions that are recognized and named.

High density of place-names seems to coincide most often with a cultural back ground in agriculture. In most European countries—and in many countries outside Europe—the peasant held tenaciously to his land, cultivating its fields, building walls and bestowing names on them. In a hill district such as the Ozarks a field of corn might have been no larger than a lawn for a private home, and it was usually fenced and often named. Generations of the same family often lived in the same community, so that family history is intermingled with the landscape in an uncommon way. Life is integrated with the landscape in a natural way that is understood by everyone. Thus the Ozarker is a kind of homespun Lockian who thinks of the landscape as an object that penetrates the mind and alters the man.

The fourth cultural trait of the Ozarks is the relative stability of the social system as against the fluidity of social relations that is typical of the United States. Things are relatively uncomplicated. There are strong and stable kinship relations that extend back generations. Social activities focus on schools and churches, and these institutions are dependable and predictable. Ozarkers know who their friends are and who their enemies are and what to do about it. There are few ego problems or questions about belonging. The rigors of making a living in a region blessed with only modest resources have built character, or at least the idea is widely accepted, and a kind of kinship or bond forms from a shared experience in an Ozarks understood by all.

The cultural traits described herein are hardly unique to the Ozarks. They are traits found everywhere to a certain extent, but particularly in rural America. In the Ozarks these traits are accentuated, drawn together, and combined in unique and interesting ways. Isolation has played a part in this, as have physical and cultural barriers to the diffusion of new ideas and the immigration of new people. It is a culture worth studying and a region worth visiting. And most important, the people, in all their varying circumstances of life, are worth knowing.

Selected References

Fenneman, Nevin M. *Physiography of Eastern United States*. New York: McGraw-Hill Book Co., 1938.

Gastil, Raymond D. *Cultural Regions of the United States*. Seattle: University of Washington Press, 1975.

Odum, Howard W., and Moore, Harry Estill. *American Regionalism*. New York: Henry Holt and Co., 1938.

Sauer, Carl O. *The Geography of the Ozark Highland of Missouri*. The Geographic Society of Chicago Bulletin No. 7. Chicago: University of Chicago Press, 1920.

Stewart, George R. *Names on the Globe*. New York: Oxford University Press, 1975.

Thornbury, William D. *Regional Geomorphology of the United States*. New York: John Wiley and Sons, 1965.

2. Landforms and Geology

The Ozarks has the general shape of a parallelogram. The region is part of the Interior Highlands Province, which includes the tightly folded and strongly faulted rocks of the Arkansas Valley and Ouachita Mountains (fig. 2-1). Its major subdivisions are the Boston Mountains in the south, the St. Francis (St. Francois) Mountains in the east, the Springfield Plain in the west, and the Salem Plateau, which incorporates the remainder of the upland surface. The region and its parts are named rather carelessly; established use takes precedence over definitive meanings. Thus the region is variously called the Ozark Mountains, Ozark Plateau, Ozark Plateaus, Ozark Upland, Ozark Highland, and Ozark Hill Country. Because the region is neither very high nor mountainous and because *upland* has a very general meaning, I prefer to use it. The western tableland of the Ozarks is referred to as the Springfield Plain or the Springfield Plateau. Considering the general elevations, which are only slightly higher than the central Ozarks, and in view of its more gentle terrain, one name seems as suitable as the other.

The bedrock is domed upward elliptically, being highest along the central line running from a point near Ste. Genevieve, beside the Mississippi River, to the Missouri state line near the southwestern corner of Stone County. The highest elevations in the region are found in the Boston Mountains of Arkansas, where there are extensive uplands of more than 2,000 feet elevation in Madison, Newton, Washington, Franklin, Johnson, and Pope counties. A few summit areas in extreme western Newton County exceed 2,500 feet. For the most part the central Ozarks are lower than the southern and western rimlands, but elevations in the St. Francis Mountains generally exceed 1,600 feet and the highest elevation in Missouri (1,778 feet) is at the summit of Taum Sauk Mountain in Iron County. Elevations nearly as high are reached on the western rimlands in western Wright County, Missouri, where the summits near the hamlet of Cedar Gap reach 1,728 feet above sea level.

The variegated landforms and relief are the result of several factors: different resistance to weathering and erosion of any two adjoining rock masses, the structure (tilt) of the rock layers, the porosity of the rocks, and the work of streams. For some readers it may be helpful to visualize the Ozarks as a huge layer cake in which the center has been eaten out. In-facing cuestas (hills with steep scarp slopes and gentle back slopes) mark layers of resistant rock that are underlain by weaker rocks.

Gravel bar at Mill Spring on the Black River, Wayne County, Missouri, *circa* 1918. (Reproduced from C. L. Dake, "The Sand and Gravel Resources of Missouri," *Missouri Bureau of Geology and Mines*, 2d. Series, 15 (1918): 236.)

Rivers and Streams

The elevation of the country around the foot of the Ozark Upland varies from 400 to 800 feet above sea level, causing streams to flow outward radially. From a northeast-to-southwest line near the center of the dome, the drainage runs northward to the Osage, Gasconade, Meramec, and Missouri rivers and southward to the White, Eleven Point, Current, Black and St. Francis rivers. Small streams drain the eastern border to the Mississippi River; the north slope of the Boston Mountains is tributary to the White River by way of the King and Buffalo rivers; the south slope of the Boston Mountains drains to the Neosho and Arkansas rivers through the Illinois, Mulberry, Cadron, and Little Red rivers. All of the streams have cut valleys of substantial depth. Toward the heads of the streams that flow northward the valleys are shallow and rather wide because of the small size of the streams and the great distance they flow before reaching a large river. The same characteristic holds for the streams flowing southeastward from about the central part of Howell County, Missouri. The streams flowing from the western and southern parts of the Ozarks have cut deep, narrow gorges from their heads. Chert-gravel eroded from surrounding bedrock clogs most stream channels.

The streams of the Ozarks are distinctive in that even though they are deeply entrenched into the plateau surface they follow meandering courses. This may be due to establishment of the stream courses at a time when they drained a low-lying plain. The entrenchment occurred gradually as the region was uplifted over long periods of time. The belts of hills along major streams are characterized by bold limestone bluffs, particularly along the outside bend of meanders. Not infrequently the processes of weathering and erosion have resulted in cutoff meander loops and the isolation of hills in the center. These isolated hills are known as lost hills because they are detached from other ridges or uplands. Cote Sans Dessein, another type of lost hill in the alluvial valley of the Missouri River east of Jefferson City, was isolated by widening and eventual coalescence of the valleys of the Missouri and Maries rivers.

The valleys of the larger Ozark streams, notably the Missouri and Mississippi, have flat meadowlike floors over which the stream channels meander in winding courses. Meander scars, oxbow lakes, backwater swamps and marshes, and sandbars are typical floodplain landforms. Such lowland areas, referred to as bottoms or bottomland, were preferred sites of settlement by pioneers. The fevers (malaria) discouraged some from settling in the first bottoms, but second bottoms were nearly always settled early because of their fertile soils, good drainage, and elevation above flood stages. These sites were likewise the preferred locations for Indian settlements; today they provide rich hunting grounds for archaeologists.

The entrenched stream valleys and forested slopes provide exceptionally advantageous conditions for construction of dams and reservoirs. Dams of relatively small size may back up water for several miles, providing power for generation of electricity and freshwater-lake recreation. Because little land is in cultivation, the rate of siltation is very slow. Powersite Dam, constructed in Taney County, Missouri, in 1914, was the first of more than a dozen reservoirs to be constructed in the Ozarks.

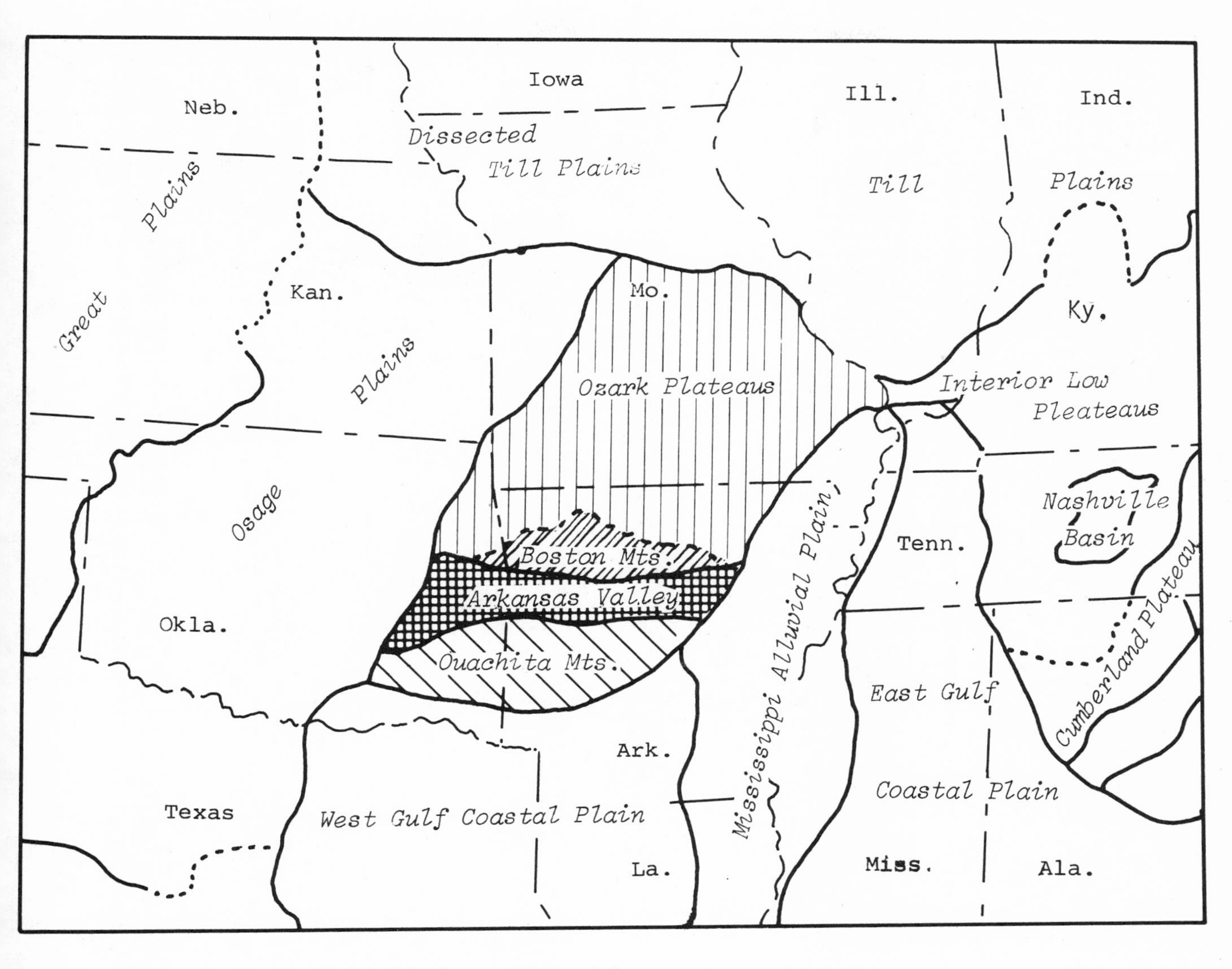

Figure 2-1. The Ozark upland and adjacent physical divisions.

Karst Features

The limestones and dolomites of the Ozarks are subject to solution by groundwater (fig. 2-2). Over millions of years the movement of rainwater through cracks and crevices (joints) in the rock has caused large amounts of the rock to dissolve, resulting in solution channels, caves, springs, and the development of sinkholes at the surface. When several large sinks are formed close together, the result is a solution valley. Some of these valleys are very large; for example, Limestone Valley in southern Newton County, Arkansas, cut into the plateau several hundred feet, is four or five miles long and a half-mile wide. Valleys that probably were formed in the same manner include nearby Hidden Valley and Walnut Valley, Wiley's Cove in Searcy County, and the Richwoods near Mountain View, Arkansas. Large collapsed cavern systems, such as Grand Gulf near Koshkonong, Missouri, are not uncommon, but cone-shaped sinks (dolines) are very common

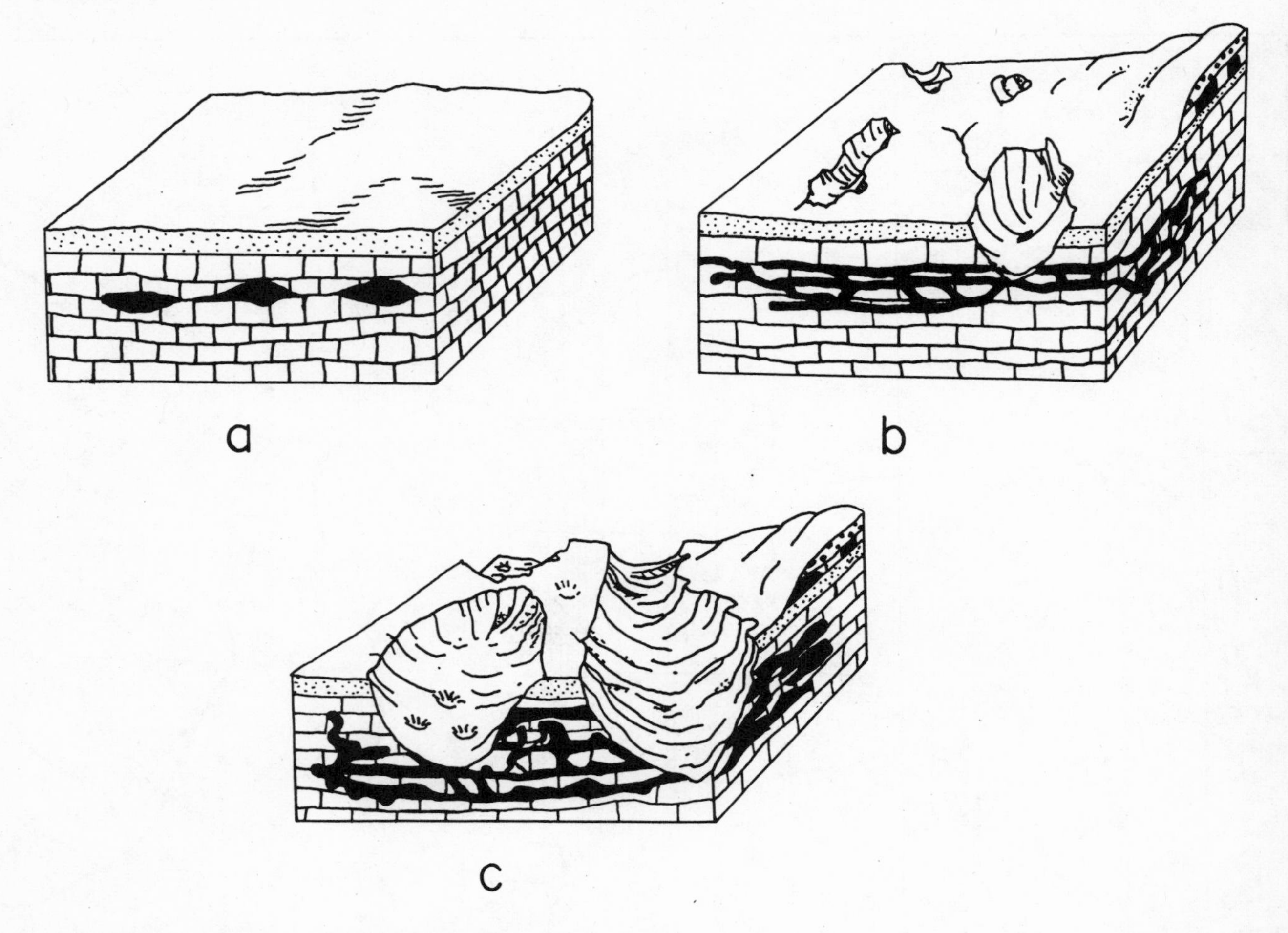

Figure 2-2. Sequence of karst development.

and many reach depths of 80 feet or more. Natural bridges are also fairly common. Because water moves freely through the limestone, many of the small surface streams are dry much of the year. Such streams, known as losing streams or losers, lose water through subsurface channels and have dry stream beds only a few miles downstream from points where water is flowing freely.

Upland areas, described as prairies by early settlers, are typically karst plains where the rolling surface is largely an expression of sinkhole development. Extensive karst plains are found in the vicinity of Springfield, Lebanon, Mountain Grove, Salem, West Plains and Perryville in Missouri and near Harrison, Mountain Home, and Springdale in Arkansas.

Local Relief

So far as ruggedness is concerned, the central part of the Ozarks is not extremely rugged. The most traveled highway, Interstate 44, traverses the region, following mainly upland divides where relief is very modest. Only in Phelps and Pulaski counties in the rugged land along Roubidoux Creek and the Little Piney and Big Piney rivers does the relief and scenery rise to the expectations

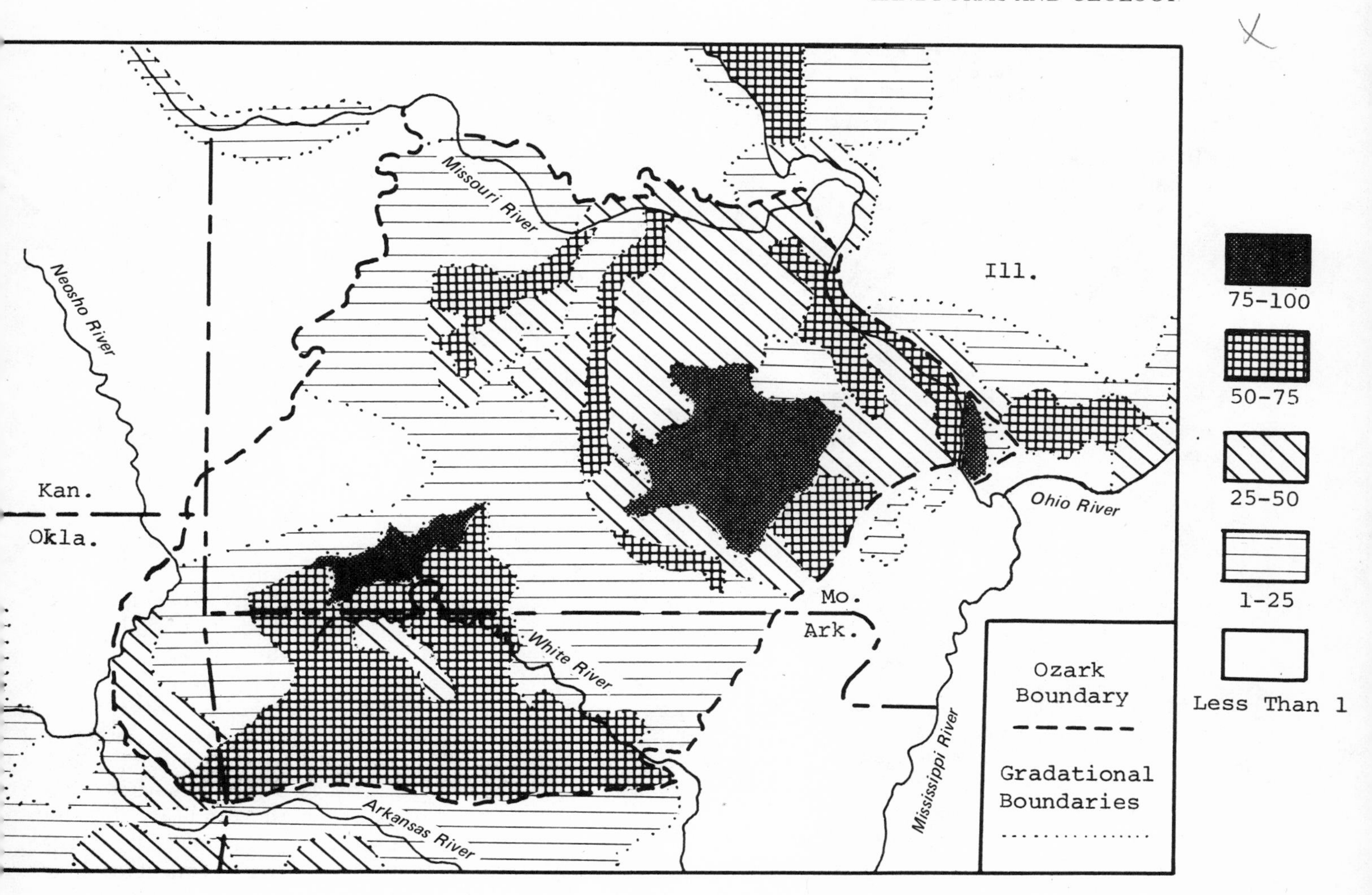

Figure 2-3. Percentage of land in slopes exceeding 14 per cent.

of most travelers. The greatest local relief (distance between valley bottoms and ridgetops) and steepest slopes are in the Boston Mountains, the St. Francis Mountains, and in the drainage basins of the White, Current, and Black rivers (fig. 2-3). Relief is especially pronounced where resistant strata form escarpments, the most striking of which is at the north front, or boundary, of the Boston Mountains, where sandstone beds stand as much as 800 to 900 feet above the limestone plains extending northward. Others are the Eureka Springs Escarpment, which outlines the headwaters of the White River and extends north of Springfield; the Avon Escarpment at the eastern border of the Farmington (Missouri) Basin; the Crystal Escarpment, which runs north to south from a point near Pacific, Missouri, through Ste. Genevieve County and Perry County; and the Burlington Escarpment, which parallels the Crystal Escarpment nearer the Mississippi River.

Geographic Regions

The Ozarks can be divided into geographic regions in such a way as to distinguish each area that has internal unity of geographic environment and contrasts with the surrounding areas. For this

Diamond Cave, Newton County, Arkansas. (Courtesy Arkansas History Commission.)

purpose the location of the area, surface features, drainage, soils, minerals, water supply, and vegetation are taken into account. The map of the geographic regions of the Ozarks (fig. 2-4) follows closely the work of Marbut[1] and Sauer.[2] In order to round out the entire Ozarks, the Springfield Plain has been extended into Oklahoma and Arkansas and the Boston Mountains have been included.

The Ozarks include only two regions worthy of being called mountains: the St. Francis Mountains in eastern Missouri and the Boston Mountains in northern Arkansas. There are three border regions: on the north the Missouri River Border, on the east the Mississippi River Border, and in western Missouri and extreme northern Arkansas the Springfield Plain. The Central Plateau, a less-dissected region in southern Missouri, is surrounded by belts of hills: the Courtois Hills on the east, the Osage-Gasconade Hills on the northeast, and the White River Hills on the south.

The Missouri River Border is a transitional area to the glacial plains of northern Missouri. Included is a narrow band of hills north of the Missouri River. In its course through this region, the river is confined in a valley scarcely two miles wide bordered by precipitous rock walls. The current is deflected from one side of the valley to the other and the stream bed is constantly shifting, particularly in the crossings from one side of the floodplain to the other. Navigation on the Missouri River, though safer than in former times, continues to be hazardous. Bottom farms are flooded frequently. Limestone bluffs, undercut by the river and faceted into pyramidal forms by tributary valleys, are bare of vegetation except for a few hardy cedars (juniper) that cling to precarious ledges.

Most of the region is rolling upland suitable for agriculture. The largest and best of the level tracts is the Tipton Upland (fig. 2-5). Soils are much above the average of the Ozarks. In stream valleys, first-bottom soils are fertile but subject to flooding and often are poorly drained; second-bottom alluvial soils on natural terraces are preferred because they are better drained and usually above the highest waters. Upland soils benefit from the presence of a wind-deposited silty loess. Near the Missouri River, where loess deposits are thickest, these soils are referred to as bluff soils.

The Mississippi River Border consists of a narrow strip along the Mississippi River. Most of the area is drained by small streams that drain directly to the Mississippi and away from the St. Francis

1. Curtis F. Marbut, "The Physical Features of Missouri," *Missouri Geological Survey*, vol. 10.

2. Carl O. Sauer, *The Geography of the Ozark Highland of Missouri*, Geographical Society of Chicago Bulletin no. 7 (Chicago: University of Chicago Press, 1920).

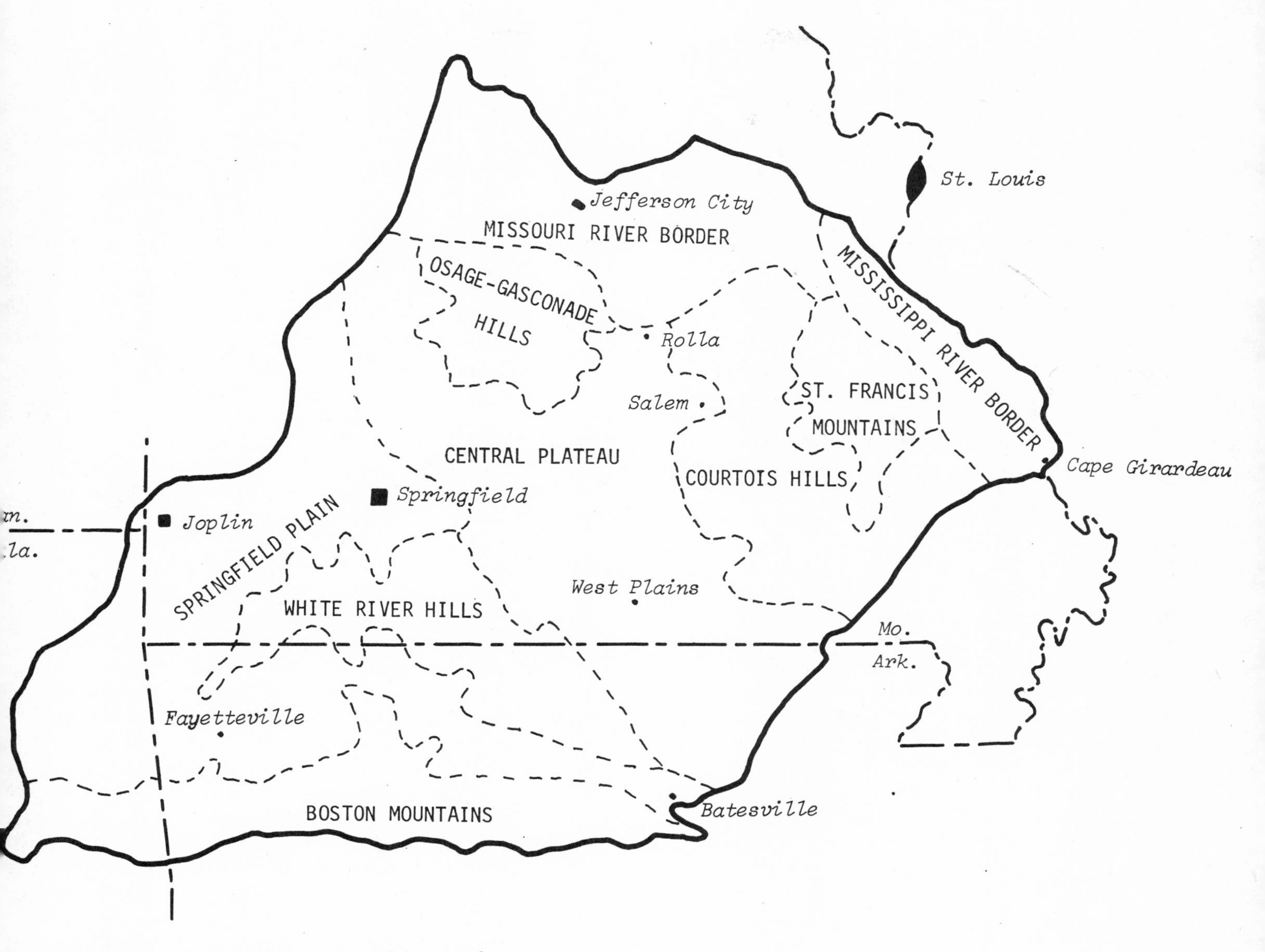

Figure 2-4. Geographic regions of the Ozarks.

Mountains. The general slope is eastward, and because elevations vary from 1,778 feet on Taum Sauk Mountain to 460 feet at Ste. Genevieve, the descent is rapid. Because the layers of limestone and sandstones are tilted steeply to the east, their eroded faces from west-facing escarpments. The most notable of these is Crystal Escarpment, where soft sandstones have been weathered and eroded, leaving the overlying limestones standing in bold relief.

Hilly belts extend back from the streams; an extensive hill belt in the drainage area of the River Aux Vases is known as the Becket Hills. The most extensive upland area is the Barrens in Perry County, where large sinkholes are more numerous than in any other section of the Ozarks. In

Perry and Cape Girardeau counties many of the sinks, clogged with loess, form natural ponds that have been used as a source of water for livestock since the first white settlers arrived.

The relief is greatest along the west-facing escarpments and where streams descend to the Mississippi River. In many locations the hills overlooking the Mississippi floodplain take on the appearances of bluffs. At Wittenburg, in Perry County, glaciers (Illinoisan age) blocked the main valley, diverting the river to its present narrow channel. Fountain Bluff, cut off from the Ozark Upland, forms a lost hill in the Mississippi Valley. Two miles downstream is Tower Rock, a small, steep-sided limestone island in the river channel.

At Cape Girardeau the Ozark Upland ends abruptly at the Ozark Escarpment, which extends in a southwesterly direction into Arkansas, marking the boundary between the Ozark Upland and the Gulf Coastal Plain Province. The remarkably straight alignment of the escarpment is thought to be the result of erosion by the Mississippi River when it occupied a westerly course at the foot of the Ozarks.

The Springfield Plain is a gently sloping surface that forms the western border of the Ozarks. It is bounded on the east by the Eureka Springs Escarpment and the rugged hills along the Pomme de Terre and Osage valleys. Relief is less and soils are better than in any other large district of the Ozarks. Near the escarpment, relief is as much as 500 feet, and isolated hills have been detached from the plain by weathering. These hills are variously known as balds, knobs, mounds, or mountains. Much of the upland originally was in prairie grass and resembled the plains region in eastern Kansas. Although the native bluestem grasses have been plowed under except in scattered locations, the names of the prairies remain to designate local vernacular regions. Among the larger and better-known uplands in Missouri are Kickapoo Prairie and Grand Prairie (Greene County), Sarcoxie Prairie (Jasper County), Diamond Grove Prairie (Newton County), Oliver's Prairie (Newton County), Washburn Prairie (Barry County), and White Rock Prairie (McDonald County). In Oklahoma, Jay Prairie in Delaware County is worthy of note. Several large upland prairies are found in the Arkansas portion of the Springfield Plain (fig. 2-5). The larger ones are Ham Flat, Pine Flat, Kings Prairie and Western Grove uplands in the eastern part of Boone County and the western part of Marion County; Harrison Prairie in Boone County; Berryville Prairie in Carroll County; and the extensive coalescing prairies of Washington and Benton counties.

Though isolated in pioneer days because of its distance from navigable streams, the Springfield Plain eventually was settled more heavily than the interior hill districts. Springfield, which has adopted the title Queen City of the Ozarks, is the largest city in the Ozark region with a population of 120,096 in the federal census of 1970. Washington and Benton counties in Arkansas also were settled heavily at an early date, and today the cities of Fayetteville, Springdale, Rogers, and Bentonville form the Ozarks' second-ranking urban area.

The St. Francis (St. Francois) *Mountains* lie in the eastern Ozarks, but they are geologically and physiographically the center of the region. Their landforms are unlike those in any other district. Sauer likens the knobs of igneous rocks to isolated remnants rising "like irregularly distributed mountain islands above the basins formed by the weak limestones and shales."[3] The knobs of granite and felsites are slowly being exhumed by weathering and erosion. The relief in the igneous rocks was etched in ancient times and is slowly being uncovered as the overlying sedimentary rocks are removed. Some of the mountains, such as Buford Mountain, Bono Mountain, Taum Sauk Mountain, Black Mountain, Mudlick Mountain and Profitt Mountain, are linear in shape. Others, such as Shepard Mountain and Pilot Knob, are cone shaped.

Deep gorges, called shut-ins, have been carved in the resistant igneous rocks. The area's relief is exceeded only by that of the Boston Mountains. The St. Francis Mountains include four major limestone basins: Fredericktown, Farmington, Mineral Point–Potosi, and Richwoods. Minor basins include Belleview (Bellevue) and Arcadia valleys in Iron County, and Patterson and Lodi in

3. Ibid., p. 67.

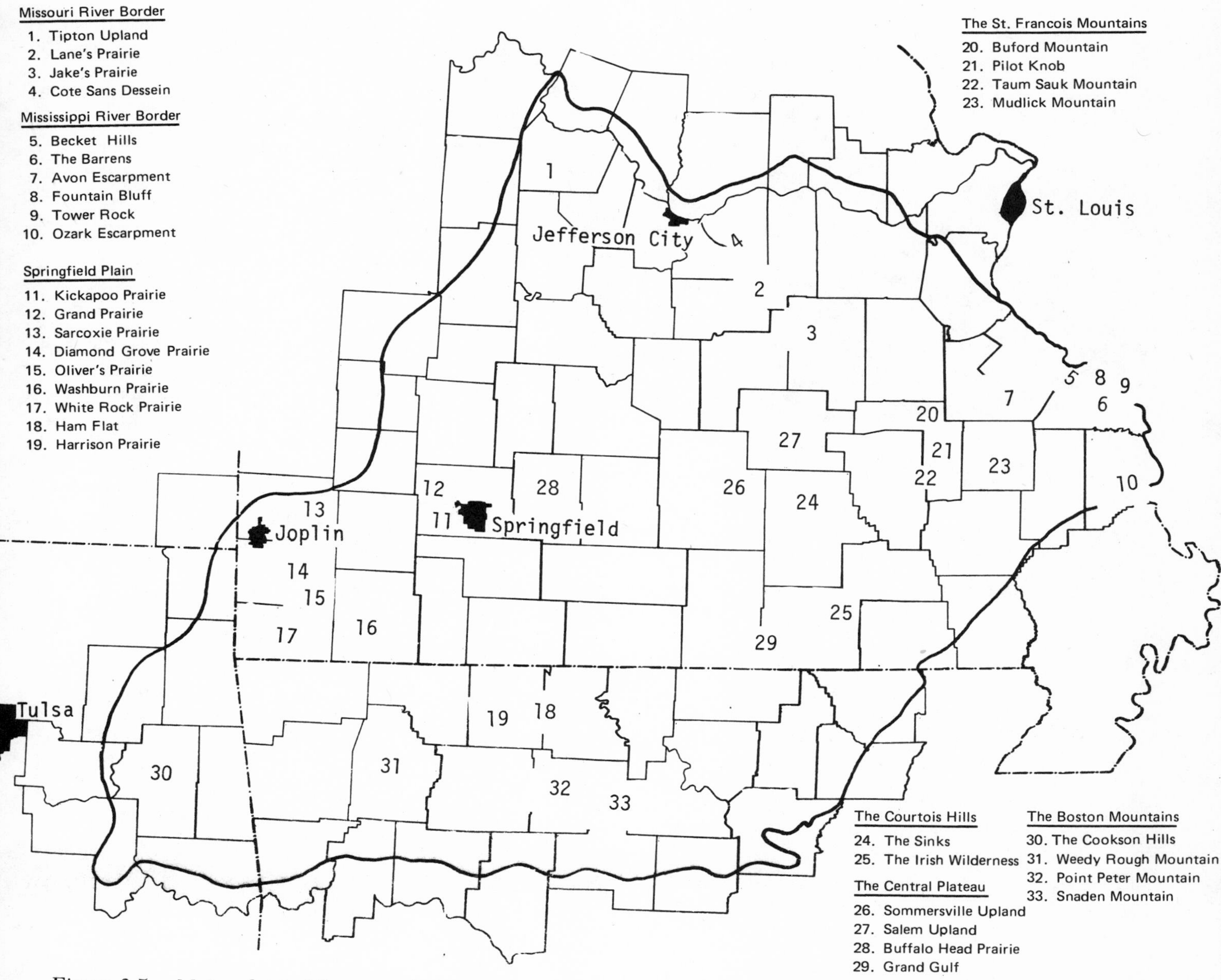

Figure 2-5. Major physical features of the Ozarks.

Taum Sauk Reservoir on Profitt Mountain near Lesterville, Missouri.

Wayne County. All of these basins were among the first permanent settlements in the Ozarks and became prosperous farming communities.

The Courtois Hills Region has the steepest average slopes and wildest terrain of any part of the Missouri Ozarks. Although it does not have the greatest relief, it is the most rugged district in Missouri, consisting of a maze of deep, confined valleys and sharp ridges. The ridges, ordinarily forested with oak, are chert covered to the extent that bedrock is exposed only infrequently. Chert (flint), a resistant rock imbedded in softer limestones and dolomites, accumulates at the surface in many sections of the Ozarks but is especially abundant in the Courtois Hills.

The region is named after Courtois Creek in Crawford County, one of the earliest valleys to be settled but only one of several streams in the district with steep valley walls and chert-clogged channels. "Down in the hills and hollers" applies to this region more than any other section. Tributaries of more than two dozen rivers and large creeks have cut the plateau surface into intricate detail. The Gladden 7½-minute Quadrangle covers approximately 36 square miles along the Current River and includes more than forty hollows. Similar landscapes are found throughout the Courtois Hills. Strikingly rugged terrain is typical of the Irish Wilderness in Oregon, Carter, and Ripley counties near Greer Spring on the Eleven Point River.

Greer Spring is only one of several spectacular springs in this region. Among the best known are Round Spring and Alley Spring near Eminence and Big Spring near Van Buren. Caves, sinkholes, and solution valleys are also quite characteristic of the region. The Sinks and the natural tunnel on Sinking Creek, a tributary of the Current River, are spectacular solution landforms.

Until recent years, when rich lead deposits were discovered in ancient reef deposits buried more than 900 feet beneath the surface, timber was the main source of income. Lead and zinc ores from the New Lead Belt, or Viburnum Trend, have brought new income into what was formerly one of the poorest districts in the Ozarks.

Agriculture possibilities are very limited. Population is mainly confined to the valleys, where soils, terrain, and excellent springs provided settlement niches. The best farming conditions are in the south, where the Castor, St. Francis, Black, and Current rivers have developed wide bottoms. Because it is the largest area of severely dissected country, the Courtois Hills ranks with the Boston Mountains of Arkansas as a region of isolation and limited agricultural possibilities. Many unsurfaced roads can be traveled only in a pickup truck, and even the best bituminous-surface roads wind along ridgetops and descend into valleys on steep grades.

The White River Hills lie at and beyond the margin of the Burlington limestone in northern Arkansas and southwest Missouri. The limestone is underlain by much weaker beds and has formed a high and persistent escarpment exceeded only by the Boston Mountain Front. Along the escarpment, long, narrow ridges have been eroded, and in a number of cases outliers from one to ten miles across have become detached from the main body of limestone. These limestone buttes are conspicuous, and if they are only sparsley forested, they are known as knobs, balds, or mountains. Usually, only the higher and more isolated hills, such as the Gainesville Monadnock group, are named. There are many prominent conical hills

Cedar glade in the White River Hills. Thin soils and exposed bedrock are typical of glade land.

Natural bridge between two sinkholes, Camden County, Missouri.

that have received such names as Bald Jesse, Naked Joe, and Griffiths Knob, all suggestive of their character.

The hills are nearly as rugged as the Osage-Gasconade Hills and the Courtois Hills, and the scenery is even more attractive. Forested slopes, bold limestone cliffs, and parklike cedar glades combine with lobate ridges and fertile bottomlands. The region has some of the largest caves in the Ozarks, and streams and springs abound. Several large lakes—Beaver, Table Rock, Taneycomo, Bull Shoals, and Norfolk—have been impounded along the White River. The result is a scene that combines splendor, variety, and charm.

The Osage–Gasconade Hills Region includes the ridges and steep tributary valleys along the Osage and Gasconade rivers and their larger tributaries. In no other place in the Ozarks are the large streams so deeply entrenched into the upland. The dam at Bagnell on the Osage River formed Lake of the Ozarks in spectacular meander loops. In Pulaski County the Gasconade River has created eight-mile Moccasin Bend, which brings the river back to within a thousand feet of the beginning of the loop.

The region is also known for its karst features, notably springs, caves, sinks, and natural bridges. Hahatonka Spring near Lake of the Ozarks and Stark Caverns near Eldon are two of the most publicized scenic attractions.

The Central Plateau is surrounded on three sides by rugged hill districts. The plateau and the Springfield Plain are the only parts of the Ozark Plateau that have not been dissected thoroughly. However, portions of the plateau, where streams cross the region, show extreme dissection.

Karst features are common throughout the region, including the part that extends into northern Arkansas. Sinkholes as much as 50 feet deep are found in the vicinity of Mountain View, Missouri. Until recently, iron ores were mined from sinkholes in the vicinity of West Plains and at other locations. Nearly every valley has abundant springs, and some, such as Blue Spring and Althea Spring on the North Fork River and Mammoth Spring in extreme northern Arkansas, are widely known. Near Koshonong, Missouri, is a large collapsed cavern, known as Grand Gulf, that is nearly 90 feet deep and more than 1,000 feet long (fig. 2-5).

The best agricultural land is on the uplands,

Boston Mountain cove south of Harrison, Arkansas.

Johnson's Shut-ins on the Black River near Lesterville, Missouri.

which are extensive in some areas. The larger upland tracts were named at an early date and always have been known as productive agricultural islands in the forested interior Ozarks. The larger tracts are the Salem, Licking, and Sommersville uplands; the Lebanon and West Plains prairies; and Buffalo Head Prairie in Dallas County, Missouri.

The Boston Mountains lie in northern Arkansas and northeast Oklahoma. The northern boundary, the Boston Mountain Front (or escarpment), marks a sharp change in topography, rocks, and soils from the country north of it. The boundary is a definite line, easily identified and traced on the ground. The southern boundary is not so sharp and easily recognized, since the change in the character of rocks, soils, and topography is more gradual. The southwestern section, in Oklahoma, is named the Cookson Hills in reference to the lower elevations found there.

Because the rock strata in the Ozark Dome slope downward in all directions from the St. Francis Mountains in eastern Missouri, the rocks on the margins are younger than the ancient crystalline rocks in the core. Thus the rocks of the Boston Mountains are among the youngest in the Ozarks, and the limestones and dolomites that cover most of the Ozarks are less important in both thickness and extent. From the same point of view, shales stand first in importance, sandstones second, and limestones third.

The striking feature of the Boston Mountains is a relatively smooth, but by no means flat, plateau surface, which, except in small areas, slopes gently southward. Maximum elevations are reached in the central section, where elevations above 2,000 feet obtain over much of Madison and Newton counties in Arkansas. The single highest elevation is 2,578 feet in extreme western Newton County, 806 feet higher than Taum Sauk Mountain in the St. Francis Mountains.

It is in the central section that the relief and wilderness character are most pronounced. South of Harrison the Boston Mountain Escarpment stands more than 1,000 feet above the Springfield Plain, and mountain outliers comprised of sandstone and shale have been detached from the main upland during millions of years of erosion. The most prominent of these isolated mountains, the Boat Mountain group, eight miles southeast of Harrison, stands in splendid isolation 1,000 feet above the Springfield Plain and about eight miles away from the front.

Granite boulders at Elephant Rocks State Park near Graniteville, Missouri.

Unconformable contact between Precambrian rhyolites and stratified Cambrian sedimentary rocks, Taum Sauk Power Station near Lesterville, Missouri.

Within the Boston Mountains are a few lowland basins, unimportant from the point of view of area but once important from the point of view of the prosperity of the few farmers who were so fortunate as to occupy them. The most important of these are the Richwoods of Stone County and the Limestone Valley of Newton County. Streams enter and leave these valleys through narrow gorges, so both outlets are narrow, deep, and wild canyons. The floor of Limestone Valley is about 700 feet above sea level and is smooth and nearly flat. The slopes rise steeply to the upland about 2,000 feet above sea level. The valleys were formed in part by solution of limestones. The term *cove* is applied to them and to many smaller lowlands of the same type.

The valleys were once more heavily settled; brush and scrub timber choke fields that formerly grew crops of corn and cotton. Agriculture has declined over the years because of isolation, poor roads, long distances to markets, and the small amount of level land and fertile soils.

Most of the highest summits in the Boston Mountains are named. In Oklahoma there are several prominent summits southeast of Tahlequah, including Sugar, Walkingstick, Welch, and Muskrat mountains and the Brushy Mountains. From west to east in Arkansas some of the better-known mountain summits are Hale, Anderson, Pine, Grassy, Locust, Meadow, Patrick, Weedy Rough, Moss, Owens, Ricketts, Horn, Point Peter, Greeshaw, Irons, Blue, and Snaden (fig. 2-5). In addition to the mountains, there are many high flats and ridges.

Geology and Mineral Resources

Ozark rocks are mainly sedimentary (formed by the settling into beds of masses of sediment) and igneous (formed by solidification of hot mixtures of minerals). The oldest rock formations are the igneous rocks that appear at the surface in the St. Francis Mountains in southeastern Missouri.[4] The igneous rocks are of two kinds, granites and porphyries. It may be imagined that ages ago the surface of much of the Ozarks consisted of lava, with molten rock below. The lava probably cooled quickly and formed rhyolite porphyries, a name derived from the texture, wherein larger crystals

4. Uranium half-life dating methods date these rocks at approximately 2.4 billion years old.

occur in a groundmass of finer crystals. Streams have cut into the resistant rhyolites, forming steep-walled shut-ins, such as Johnson's Shut-ins near Lesterville. Porphyries of varying colors form most of the symmetrical knobs or mountains of the St. Francis Mountains.

Beneath the insulating cover of porphyry, other molten material solidified slowly to form a coarse-grained granite, such as that occurring in quarries near Graniteville. Missouri granite is composed of pink feldspar and clear, glassy quartz mineral grains. Huge blocks have weathered into spheroid shapes at various locations, notably at Elephant Rocks State Park near Graniteville.

The sedimentary rocks are of two main groups. One is composed of limestone formed while the Ozarks were not only covered by water but were far from any land area. Nearly all the Ozarks are underlain by these limestones. The other group of rocks was formed when Missouri was either part of a continent or covered by a shallow sea near land; sandstones, shales, and certain limestones fall into this group. Rocks of this type are found mainly in the Boston Mountains.

The rocks of the earth's surface also may be classified according to age. Three of the four major time spans (eras)—Cenozoic, Mesozoic, Paleozoic, and Precambrian (Proterozoic and Azoic)—are represented in the Ozarks, along with eight or nine of the subdivisions of the ages (periods) (fig. 2-6). If all of these subdivisions were superimposed at any one place, they would form a column 3,500 feet high from the top of the granites and felsites. The thickness of the igneous rocks is unknown. The rocks do not underlie the whole region, but by upfolding of beds or through downcutting by streams they are brought to the surface at one place or another. The oldest rocks, which are exposed in the St. Francis Mountains in Iron, Reynolds, and Madison counties, form the center of the Ozark Dome and form the foundation for the rock beds that underlie large parts of Missouri, Kansas, Arkansas, Illinois, and Iowa.

For purposes of mapping, the rocks are divided into groups, each group usually including more than one kind of rock or more than one formation. On the geologic map (fig. 2-6) the Precambrian-age granites and felsites are shown in the darkest shade. They are found in southeastern and southern Missouri, the main outcrops in the St. Francis Mountains and smaller exposures in Shannon County, where the Current River has cut deeply into the overlying sedimentary rock layers. A long period later, an ocean invaded the valleys and rose high on the rounded igneous-rock hills. The gravel and boulders accumulated on the low surface and were cemented to form the sandstones and conglomerates of the Cambrian-age La Motte formation. Clay mud was washed far out into the quiet arms of the ancient sea and upon compaction became shale as we see it today. Gradually the land sank beneath the sea, and the calcium and magnesium that went into solution to the ocean became limestone and dolomite (calcium-magnesium limestone) in the clear-water portion of the ocean. The Bonne Terre dolomite, a gray and rather coarsely crystalline variety, was deposited in thick beds. It is comparatively free of flint and decomposes readily to a fertile and easily tilled red clay soil. Huge deposits of disseminated lead (with zinc, copper, and silver) have been found in this formation. The lead-zinc ores were mined for more than 250 years in the Old Lead Belt in St. Francois and Madison counties and currently are being mined in the New Lead Belt of western Iron and northern Reynolds counties.

Barite (barium sulfate, $BaSO_4$, locally called tiff) remains, after the weathering of portions of the Cambrian dolomites, as a concentrated ore deposit in the residual soil above the limestones. The Tiff District of northeastern Washington County is one of the major barite mining districts in the United States. Although most of the mining and washing of barite is now mechanized, the earlier hand mining of the tiff digger was publicized in writings about the district.

The second period of the Paleozoic Era, the Ordovician, began with the advances of seas over all of the Ozarks. Deposits of dolomite up to 500 feet thick were laid down; then the seas retreated from most of the state, and many narrow valleys were eroded in the emerging surface. The retreat of the seas probably was accompanied by a climatic change to very arid conditions. During this period, sand was deposited over large areas. The sandstone, called the St. Peter, is loose and friable, easily quarried, and widely used in the manufacture of glass.

After the St. Peter sandstone was deposited, the seas advanced again and nearly the entire

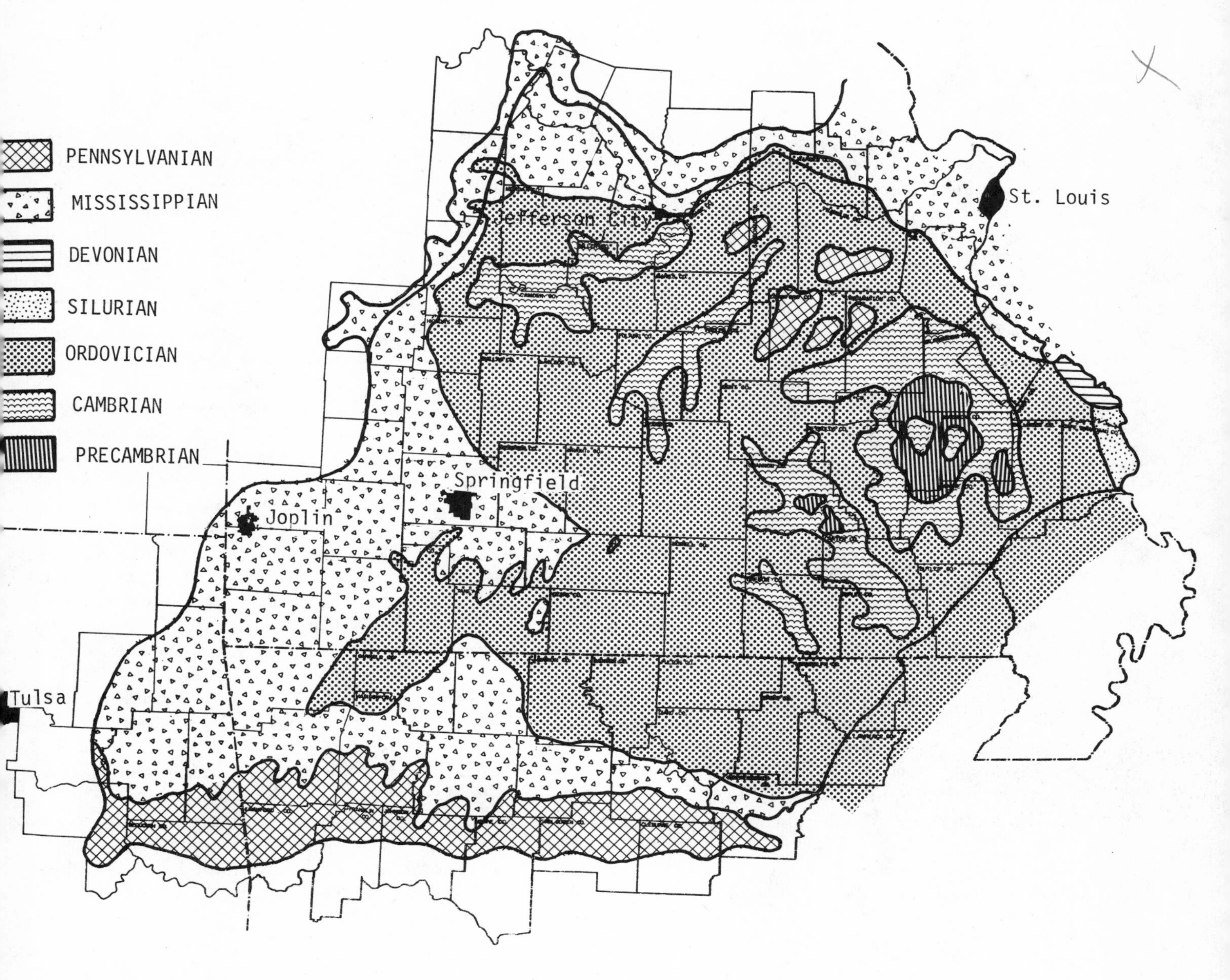

Figure 2-6. Geologic age of bedrock.

region was covered with dolomite (Gasconade formation), thin limestone (Kimmswick formation), shale and sandstone (Roubidoux formation), and, finally, dolomite (Jefferson City formation). The Jefferson City formation's dolomite rocks are the thickly bedded soft, white, noncrystalline "cotton rock" and the heavily bedded, slightly crystalline gray limestone called "spotted rock."

During Silurian time the seas covered only the extremities of the Ozarks, in the southeast, northeast, and northwest. Limestones and shales accumulated to thicknesses of less than 100 feet. In the early part of the Devonian Period, seas advanced over a small area near Grand Tower, Ste. Genevieve County, and in late Devonian time, a narrow bay extended westward about a hundred miles from the mouth of the Missouri River and along the northeastern Ozark border.

After erosion in late Devonian, seas of the Mississippian Period advanced from the east and south and covered the region. Thick deposits of limestone were laid down, notably the St. Louis, Keokuk, and Burlington formations. These rock layers now form a partial ring around the Ozark region from Perry County to the extreme southwest.

The end of Mississippian time was the final chapter of Ozark marine history. It was under the sea at various times thereafter, but for short periods only, and the later stratified rocks of the Ozarks are made up of land material. The first formation was a series of sand and clay beds, called the Cherokee shales. This probably was deposited around an Ozark island. Thick beds of Pennsylvanian-age sandstones and shales are found in the Boston Mountains.

In Pennsylvanian time, fireclays were deposited in ancient sinkholes along the northern Ozark border. In many localities during the same period, iron ores were concentrated in sinkholes. After the seas withdrew from the Ozarks late in Mississippian time, all of the region was land. So far as is known, no Triassic or Jurassic seas covered any part of the Ozarks, and not until late Cretaceous did the Gulf of Mexico extend as far north as the mouth of the Ohio River.

Geologic evidence indicates that the Ozarks were uplifted in Tertiary time (65 million years ago) after being eroded to a subdued surface known as a peneplain. Since the Tertiary uplift, the region probably has been uplifted more than once. The exact cause is uncertain, but gradual adjustments of a similar nature are believed to result from imbalances in the earth's crust.

The last major event in the geologic history of the Ozarks was the advance of glaciers, three in number. Only the northern and eastern margins of the region were effected. Along the Missouri River, which was the approximate southern boundary of the ice, and in a narrow belt down the Mississippi River is a deposit of a porous, brownish clay loam. This material, loess, probably was deposited in river valleys by meltwaters and later blown by winds onto nearby bluffs. It forms the basis of the most fertile body of upland soil in the region.

The Ozarks lie within the part of North America that is generally free of serious earthquakes, but on December 16, 1811, a quake of very high intensity occurred in the New Madrid region of southeast Missouri. Other severe quakes and minor shocks followed for several months. No deaths were known to have resulted because the area was only sparsely settled, but if a similar quake were to occur today, the loss of life and property would almost certainly be great. Fissures were opened in the ground, and craterlets and mounds of sand were formed during the movement. The largest surface manifestation of the New Madrid earthquake was the dropping of a basin that filled with water to form Reelfoot Lake in western Tennessee a short distance east of the Mississippi River. The lake is 60 to 70 miles long, 3 to 20 miles wide, and in some places 50 to 100 feet deep. The forest trees in the area were more or less completely submerged. Further deep adjustments in the earth's crust have continued to take place northward toward St. Louis, as is indicated by the slight shocks that occur occasionally. Minor regional shocks, discernable as far away as Springfield, occurred in 1967 and 1975.

Earthquakes are the tremors or vibrations that arise from fracturing of rocks with the earth. Other causes of quakes are of so little consequence that they need not be mentioned. Stresses develop near the earth's surface, or at some depth, until they exceed the strength of the rocks, which then fail or break. Movement may be vertical or horizontal or both, and the break is technically called a fault.

A Controversial Geological Problem

There are six interesting geologic features that outcrop in the Ozarks, and they are called cryptoexplosive (hidden explosive) structures. These isolated structures appear to occur linearly along the same latitude, approximately 37° 40′. Each is named after a nearby location: the Weaubleau structure in Hickory County, the Decaturville structure in southern Camden County, the Hazelgreen structure on the Pulaski-Laclede county line, the Crooked Creek structure in southern Crawford County, the St. Francois structure in St. Francois County, and the Avon structure in Ste. Genevieve County.

An interesting fact is that sometimes meteorites

enter the earth's atmosphere almost simultaneously from the same orbit and, if large enough, crash to the earth's surface and form large craters or upwarped shattered-rock structures (explosive structures). Since the meteorites could enter almost simultaneously from orbit, the large explosive structures could occur linearly.

Because some of the typical volcanic and meteorite-impact phenomena are not observed in the rocks of each of these six areas and because the six structures can be explained only by volcanic or meteor-impact phenomena, there is controversy about whether they were caused by igneous volcanic activity or the impact of meteorites.

Griesemer Quarry and underground storage in the Burlington limestone at Springfield, Missouri

Selected References

Beveridge, Thomas R. *Geologic Wonders and Curiosities of Missouri*, Missouri Division of Geology and Land Survey, Educational Series no. 4. Rolla, Mo.: 1978.

Branson, Edwin Bayer. *The Geology of Missouri*. *University of Missouri Studies*, nol. 19, no. 3, Columbia, Mo.: 1944.

Bretz, J. Harlan. *Geomorphic History of the Ozarks of Missouri. Missouri Geological Survey and Water Resources*, Second Series, vol. 41. Rolla, Mo.: 1965.

Collier, James E. "Geography of the Northern Ozark Border Region," *University of Missouri Studies*, Vol. 26, No. 1. Columbia, Mo.: 1953.

Cozzens, Arthur B. "The Natural Regions of the Ozark Province," Ph.D. dissertation, Washington University, 1937.

Dake, C. L. "The Sand and Gravel Resources of Missouri," *Missouri Bureau of Geology and Mines*, 2d. Series, vol. 15 (1918).

Fenneman, Nevin M. *Physiography of Eastern United States*. New York: McGraw-Hill Book Co., Inc., 1938.

Flint, Timothy. *A Condensed Geography and History of the Western States or Mississippi Valley*. Vol. 2. Cincinnati: William M. Farnsworth, Printer, 1828.

Fuller, Myron Leslie. *The New Madrid Earthquake*. U.S. Geological Survey Bulletin 494. 1912. Cape Girardeau, Mo.: Ramfre Press, 1958.

Gist, Noel P. *Missouri: Its Resources, People, and Institutions*. Columbia, Mo.: Curators of the University of Missouri, 1950.

Hayes, William C., et. al. *Guidebook to the Geology of the St. Francois Mountain Area*. Missouri Geological Survey and Water Resources Report of Investigations no. 26. Rolla, Mo.: 1961.

Huffman, George G. *Geology of the Flanks of the Ozark Uplift*. Oklahoma Geological Survey Bulletin 77. Norman, Okla.: 1958.

Marbut, Curtis F. "The Physical Features of Missouri," *Missouri Geological Survey*, vol. 10. Jefferson City, Mo.: 1896.

Maxfield, O. O. "Geography of the Boston Mountains." Ph.D. dissertation, Ohio Statae University, 1963.

Penick, James, Jr. *The New Madrid Earthquake of 1811–12*. Columbia, Mo.: University of Missouri Press, 1976.

Sauer, Carl O. *The Geography of the Ozark Highland of Missouri*. The Geographical Society of Chicago Bulletin no. 7. Chicago: University of Chicago Press, 1920.

Snyder, Frank G., et. al. *Cryptoexplosive Structures in Missouri*. Missouri Geological Survey and Water Resources Report of Investigations no. 30. Rolla, Mo.: 1965.

Thacker, Joseph L., and Satterfield, Ira R. *Guidebook to the Geology Along Interstate 55 in Missouri*. Missouri Department of Natural Resources, Division of Geology and Land Survey Report of Investigations no. 62. 1977.

Thornbury, William D. *Regional Geomorphology of the United States*. New York: John Wiley and Sons, Inc., 1965.

3. Weather and Climate

The first white settlers from Tennessee and Kentucky found few unfamiliar climate conditions in their new homeland. Since the Ozark region lies at about the same latitude as Kentucky and Tennessee, the temperatures are similar. Its more westward position in the continent of North America makes the Ozarks somewhat less humid and more subject to droughts.

Both the day-to-day fluctuations in temperature, precipitation, and humidity that determine weather conditions and the long-term averages and extremes of these elements that comprise the climate of the Ozarks are determined primarily by a midcontinent location in the middle latitudes. Certainly the altitudes and relief are not sufficient to affect, to any significant degree, the climate of the region.

The northern two-thirds of the Ozarks has a Humid Continental climate; in the Boston Mountains and a portion of southern Missouri the climate is Humid Subtropical. These climate boundaries are arbitrary and are convenient only for identifying broad climate types. In fact, the climate of the Ozarks is so variable that a person who has lived in the region only one year cannot make a true estimate of the kind of weather that might be expected during the next twelve months. A similar statement may be made concerning the seasons: the experience of one summer, or of one winter, will not give a correct idea of a general summer or of general winter conditions. The same may be said for any month of the year.

Winds and Storms

The winds are largely cyclonic and the weather is quite variable. The Ozarks are too far south for their temperatures to be affected for long periods by the strong winter high-pressure cells of the north-central states, but occasionally a strong high-pressure cell or two from high latitudes will bring prolonged and bitter cold temperatures. The extreme cold temperatures—reaching −10°F to −15°F—that occurred in January and February, 1977, were unusual for their severity and duration. Lesser lows and highs from the Great Plains region move across the Ozarks regularly.

The wind of maximum frequency is southerly or southeasterly. There is a slight increase in the frequency of northerly winds with increase in latitude, and northerly winds are more frequent throughout the region in the winter months. Summer winds are more noticeable during the day than at night; winter winds are as common at night as during the day. At Springfield the mean velocity is 10.1 miles per hour, being highest in

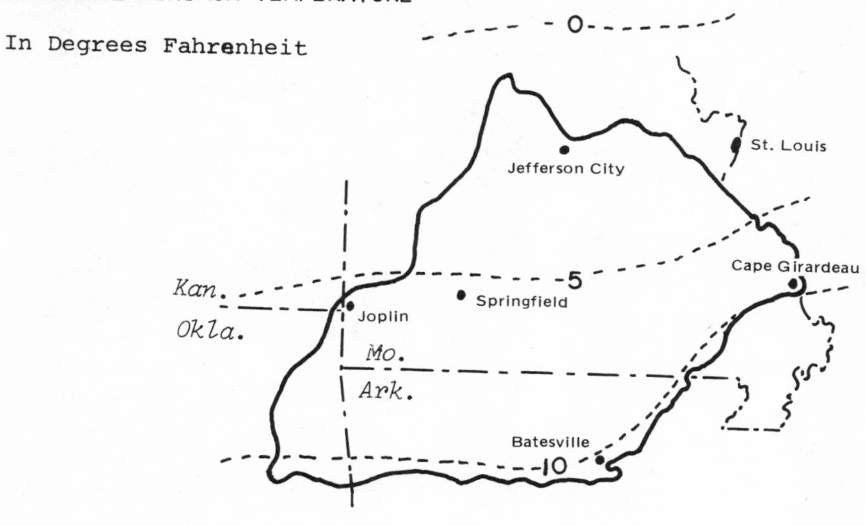

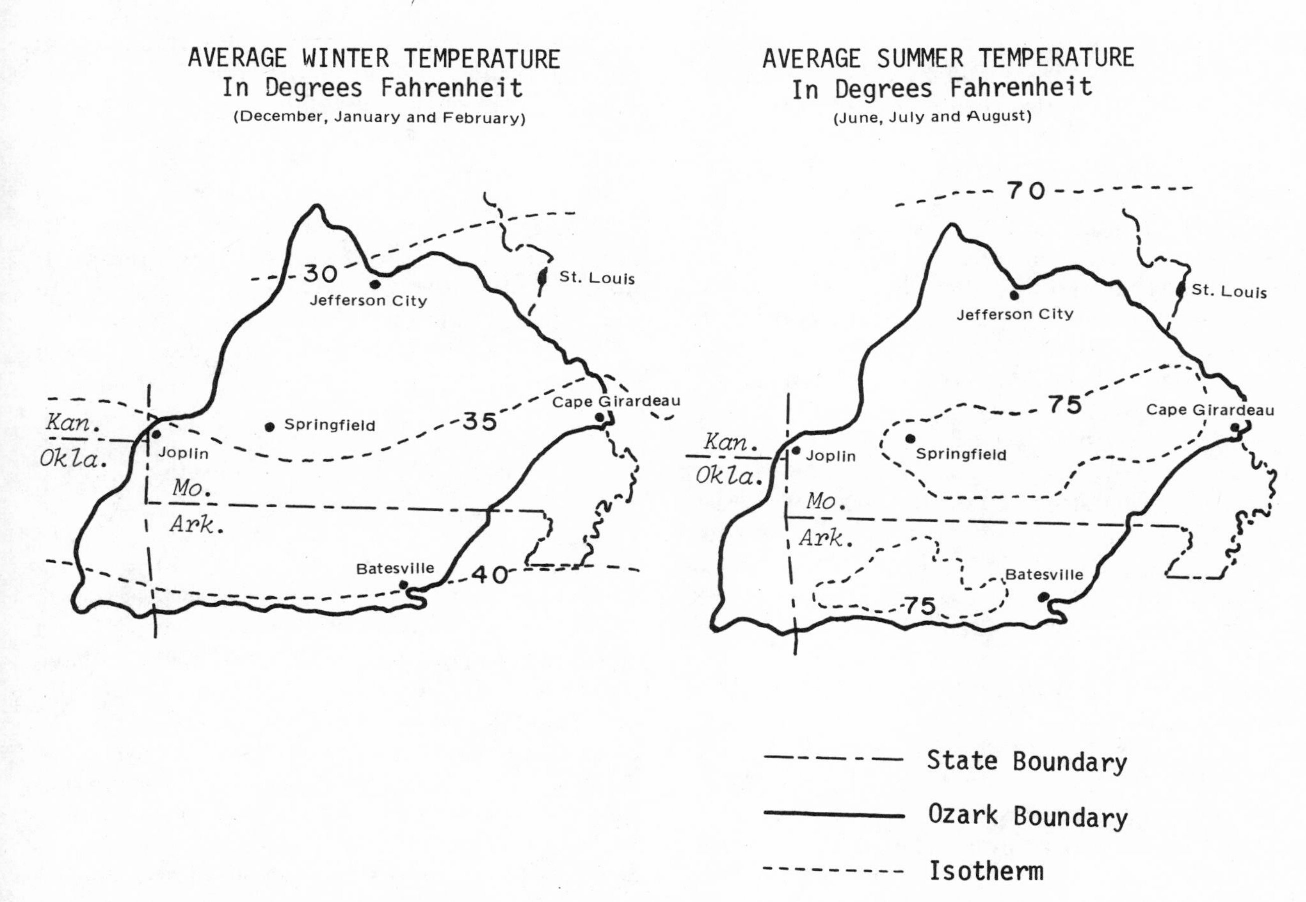

Figure 3-1. Temperature averages. Source: *Atlas of American Agriculture* (1936).

March (12.4 mph) and lowest in August (7.4 mph).

In midsummer a brisk wind from the southwest for a few days continuously is likely to become a hot wind, and much damage to growing crops may result. During late summer and early fall, for a period of several weeks, there is little wind, the sun seems as hot as in midsummer, and the sky takes on a hazy, purplish color, especially in the late afternoon; this is the renowned Indian Summer of the Ozarks, the time of storing away crops for winter, gathering nuts and apples, and greeting tourists, who come in large numbers to enjoy the Ozarks' finest season. In winter the winds often change direction quickly; cold, brisk winds may blow from the north for several days, sometimes accompanied by fine, dry snow. At other times during the winter the brisk wind of the day quiets down at the approach of sunset, and the night is calm.

Tornadoes are of annual occurrence in the region, although the likelihood of visitations for any one locality is very slight. Most of these storms invade the Ozarks from Oklahoma and Kansas, and the western border is most subject to them. Powerful twisters have struck in the vicinity of Springfield on at least five occasions: 1880, 1883, 1915, 1972, and 1975. The first destroyed the town of Marshfield and resulted in the death of at least a hundred persons. The storm of 1972 caused heavy damage in Republic and destroyed several airplanes and severely damaged buildings at Springfield Municipal Airport. Although tornadoes are most frequent in the period from April 1 to June 30, they occur in all months. The storm that hit Springfield's airport came in mid-December, 1972.

Tornado forecasting and storm warning systems have done much to reduce the number of deaths and injuries. The violent tornado that struck Neosho in April, 1975, at 5:00 P.M. caused severe property damage in residential areas and in a major shopping center, but because of advance warning, there were no casualties and the number of injuries was small.

The average annual temperature of the Ozark Upland is 55°F, which is the average for the city of Springfield. The coldest month of the year is January. This does not necessarily mean that the temperature during January is always lower than it is during the other winter months, but an average January has a few more cold days than either an average December or an average February. January is also the month in which the temperature contrasts among various parts of the Ozarks is greatest, amounting to a maximum of 12 degrees between the extreme north and south. In April there is only 4 degrees' difference between the north and south, and in the three summer months almost none (fig. 3-1).

Winter in the Ozarks usually sets in about the latter part of December and continues through January and February, with occasional cold outbursts in early March. Each of the winter months has twenty-five to thirty days when the temperature during the warmest part of the day is at 32°F or above and only one to three days when the temperature drops below zero. About three cold waves a season sweep over the region, the average length of each being about three days, but prolonged cold periods, such as those of January and February of 1977 and 1978, may occur. The mean daily range in temperature (day's maximum minus the day's minimum) throughout the year is 18.2 degrees; in winter 16.8 degrees, in spring 19.0 degrees, in summer 18.3 degrees, and in autumn 18.8 degrees.

Extreme temperatures of 100 degrees or above may be expected during an Ozarks summer. For the region as a whole, extremely high temperatures are likely to occur on one or two days in late June, three to five days during each of the months of July and August, and perhaps a day or two in early September.

Humidity and Precipitation

The average relative humidity at Springfield is 73 per cent; 77 during the winter months, 75 in summer, and 70 in spring. The average number of clear days per year is 150, partly cloudy 127, and cloudy 88. August, September, and October have the largest number of clear days; those with the most cloudy days are December and January, each with 11. May has an average of 12 rainy days, whereas October has only 7. In the eastern part of the Ozarks and on the south flank of the Boston Mountains, the humidity is slightly higher than at Springfield. On the whole the region is one of abundant sunshine. The maximum frequency of

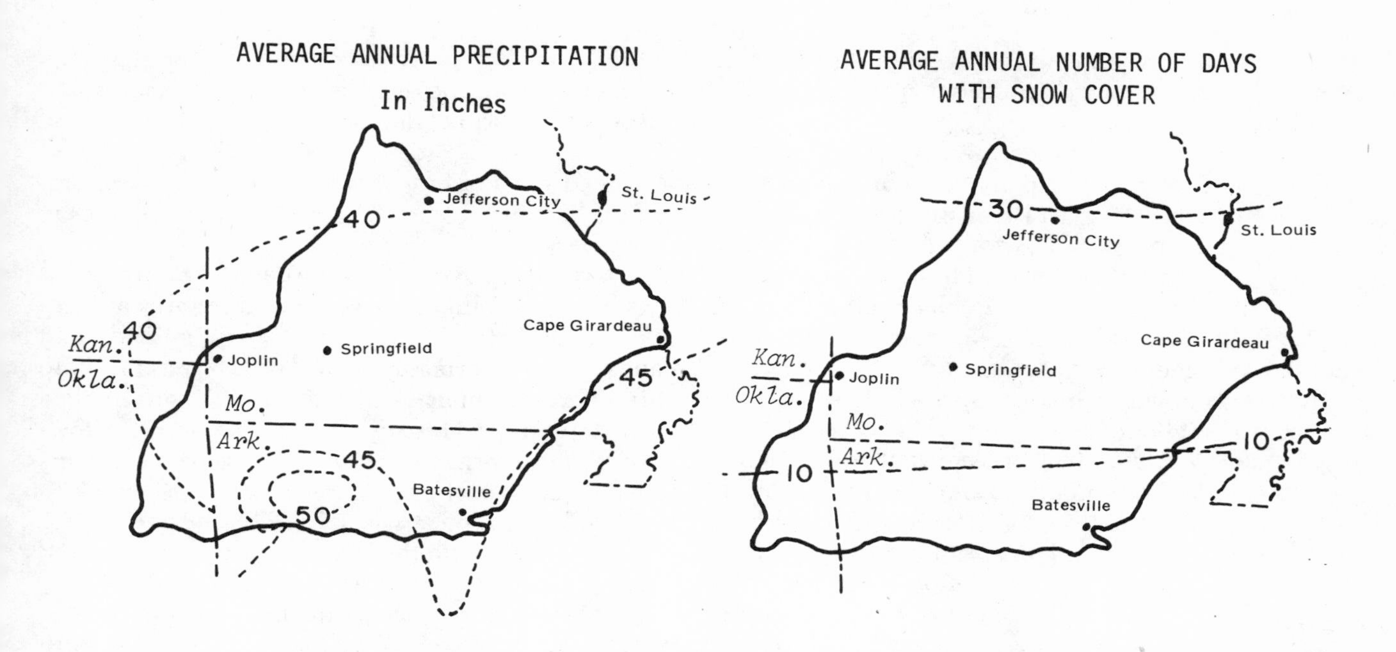

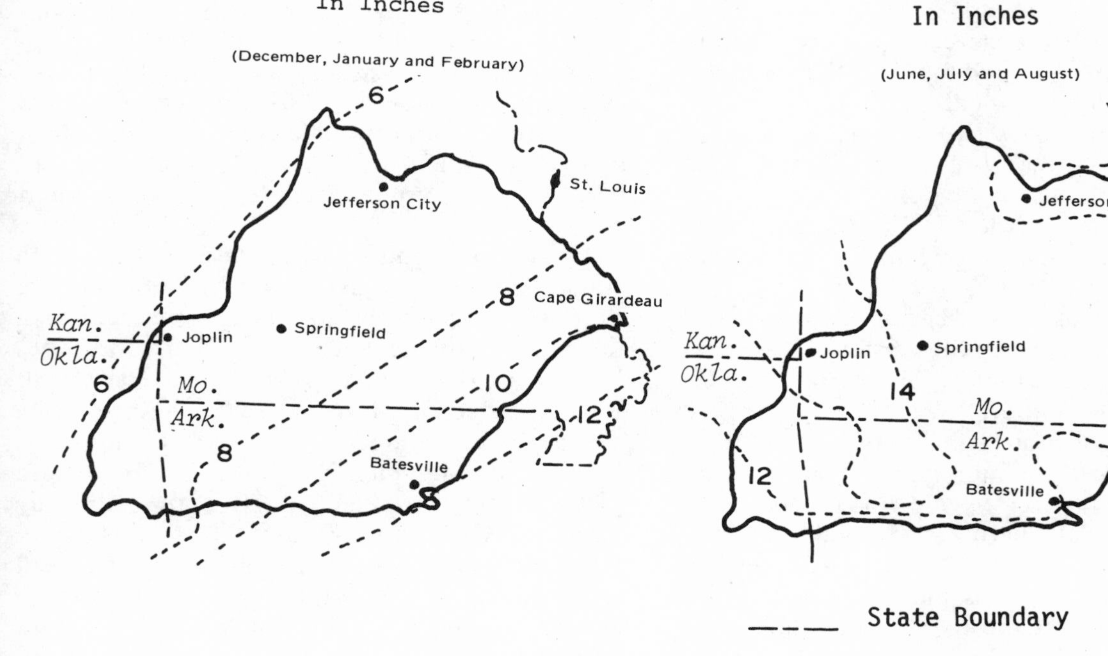

State Boundary

State Boundary

Isohyet

Days with snow cover

Figure 3-2. Precipitation averages. Source: *Atlas of American Agriculture* (1936).

rains in spring, and of sunny weather in late summer, is favorable for production of a variety of crops.

Precipitation is largely in the form of rain (fig. 3-2). The average totals range from 36 inches on the northern Missouri River Border to more than 50 inches near the Arkansas River. Annual amounts at representative stations: Jefferson City 36 inches, Springfield 41, Poplar Bluff 48, Eureka Springs 49, Fayetteville 45, Harrison 43, Marshall 50, Muskogee 42.

The average snowfall at Springfield is only 15.9 inches, or about 3.5 per cent of the total precipitation and less than half the snowfall at Chicago or New York. The amount of snow that falls is quite variable. Stations on the northern border have received no snow in January in some years, while very heavy snows of 20 or more inches are not infrequent. Snowfall can be heavy in the Boston Mountains, but averages are modest: Fayetteville 10 inches, Harrison 12, Muskogee 6, and Ozark 6. On the northern border, snow may remain on the ground a week or perhaps two, but in the Arkansas Ozarks it usually melts in a day or two. Nevertheless, because state and county highway crews are poorly equipped to handle heavy snow, roads are sometimes difficult to travel. Schools in the region usually allow two to five snow days in their schedules to make up for days when roads are impassable.

The latitudinal position of the Ozarks favors sleet storms and freezing rain. Freezing rain causes considerable damage to trees and wires and makes travel extremely hazardous for a day or two. In November, 1848, the western Ozarks experienced a big sleet that was extraordinarily destructive. In December, 1972, a heavy freezing rain in the same section brought down power lines and left farms and communities without electricity for several days. Dairymen were unable to milk until National Guard units brought in portable generators to supply power for the electric milking machines. Hail is most frequent in the western Ozarks, but the region as a whole normally experiences 15 to 20 damaging hailstorms in the period from May to September.

General Weather Variations

Ozarks weather is very changeable throughout the year, but more so during winter than any other season. The dry season usually sets in about the latter part of June or the first part of July and lasts forty to sixty days. During this period, widespread rains of more than one inch are not common, and the greater part of the rainfall comes in showers.

Droughts have done more damage than periods of excessive rain. They cover a larger area and are more prolonged, they affect both uplands and river bottomland, they cause permanent injury to field crops, and they affect farm and village alike by depleting water supplies as reservoirs are lowered and springs stop flowing. Severe droughts have occurred in 1881, 1911, 1913, 1914, 1935, 1936, 1955, 1956, 1975, and 1976. The one in 1975 persisted through the fall and winter months, and reservoir levels dropped to record lows. Many boat docks and marinas on Lake of the Ozarks, Table Rock Lake, and other Ozark lakes were stranded high and dry. Water levels on Beaver Lake dropped to expose the foundations, stone bridges, and amphitheater of Monte Ne, the popular resort constructed by the eccentric but nationally known Coin Harvey. People flocked to the site to take their first look at the well-known resort, which was inundated when Beaver Dam was completed in the early 1960's. Small communities and farms without reliable water supplies had to haul water as groundwater levels dropped and wells went dry.

Heavy downpours often are associated with squall lines, fronts, and isolated thunderstorms. Because of steep slopes, runoff is rapid, and flash floods are frequent. Such floods are of short duration but are destructive of property and farmland. It is recorded that in May, 1892, the Big Piney River rose 30 feet between 4:00 P.M. to midnight. During the same month, the Current River rose 27 feet in about the same length of time. On July 1, 1973, 19 inches of rain fell southwest of Springfield and sent torrents of water down small valleys that had been without even the semblance of a stream a few hours before. Chert washed from hillsides covered acres of bottomland along the Finley River, and roads in Stone County were closed for days by deposits of chert that in some places reached the second strand of wire on fences. Bridges were washed out, disrupting travel for several weeks. In 1961 an even more disastrous flash flood swept through Harrison,

Arkansas and destroyed four-fifths of the business district.

Temperature ranges are extreme at times. The highest temperature ever recorded in the Missouri Ozarks was 116°F at Marble Hill in 1901; the absolute high in the Arkansas Ozarks was 120°F at Ozark. Absolute minimum temperatures are by no means mild; both Fayetteville and Marshall in Arkansas have recorded −24°F. Springfield has recorded an absolute range of 135 degrees, with such anomalous temperatures as 74°F in January and 33°F in October and April.

Microclimate

Within the Ozarks, temperatures will vary widely with the orientation of slope, nature of surface materials, relief, and presence of water. South- and west-facing slopes receive the greatest amount of sunlight and are subject to higher rates of evaporation. Ferns, most mosses, and most wild flowers do not appear on south-facing slopes. Here also are the purest stands of oak and hickory. North-facing slopes generally have much more undergrowth. In winter, perhaps the most noticeable effect of temperature differences within a small area is the duration of snow and icicles on the north-facing slopes. The latter, often several feet long as they hang from cliffs, may not melt completely for many days after daytime temperatures have reached the 50's.

Air drainage creates the most readily observed temperature differences in summer. Nights are notable for the cool breeze that drains down the slopes, beginning an hour or two before sunset. The effects of daytime temperature variations are most easily felt in flying over the Ozarks in a light plane, which is easily affected by air currents.

Early-morning fog is common in the valleys in the hill and mountain districts because of the drainage of cool air into the valleys overnight. The fog usually dissipates by midmorning as temperatures climb in the valleys. Heavy fogs often hover over the large water bodies, such as Lake of the Ozarks, Beaver Lake, Pomme de Terre, Table Rock, and Bull Shoals. A bluish haze is characteristic in panoramic views in the hill districts, even in fair weather.

Hot summer temperatures are moderated by shade and cool spring water. Many of the early resorts were built close to large springs or caverns. At Welch's Cave and Spring on the Current River, Dr. C. H. Diehl constructed a rest home at the entrance to the cave in 1916 and benefited from the natural air conditioning. Pipes brought cool air from the cave to patients' rooms.[1]

The average length of the growing season for the Ozarks as a whole is nearly six months. The likelihood of unseasonable frost depends much more on topographic location than on latitude. As a rule, frosts occur in the valleys several weeks earlier in fall and later in spring than they do on the uplands, especially in the case of the larger valleys lying in the hill regions. The margins of the uplands have the best air drainage and are least subject to frosts.

On the whole the Ozarks has a humid climate reasonably free from severe drought in most years. It is well moderated, of the continental type, pleasant and healthful, and well suited to a large variety of crops.

Weather Lore

It is natural for agricultural people to be concerned about weather conditions. Before scientific forecasting was available, farmers had to depend upon their own observations, and there is no denying that some of them were extraordinarily skilled in making short-range predictions of rain and frost. For long-term forecasts, people depended on *The Farmer's Almanac*, folklore, and weather signs. Certain people were believed to be gifted with the ability to predict weather, and there are many Ozarkers who still take amateur weather predictions very seriously. Until recently the Springfield newspaper continued to publish a monthly forecast by a local weather prophet.

The most comprehensive list of Ozark weather signs was compiled by Vance Randolph, noted folklorist and authority on Ozark folk culture.[2] Many, if not most, of the weather signs and superstitions collected by Randolph were not unique to the Ozarks but were widely popular in rural

1. Margaret Ray Vickery, *Ozark Stories of the Upper Current River* (Salem, Mo.: The Salem News, n.d.)

2. Vance Randolph, *Ozark Magic and Folklore* (New York: Columbia University Press, 1964); see chapter 2, "Weather Signs," pp. 10–33.

America. A few of the signs have some basis in actual atmospheric changes or changes in organisms that are broadly predictive of weather trends. Many others have no apparent connection to weather.

A few of the popular Ozark weather signs serve to illustrate their general character. A strong wind in tall, dry grass is a sign of rain before nightfall. A cat's sneeze, a wolf's howl, the cock's crow, and livestock (of any type) turning their backs to the wind are sure signs of rain. It is believed that wild animals become more active before a storm. Other signs popular in the Ozarks and familiar to most readers include the groundhog, rainbow, fog, rings around the moon, early budding of trees, and the croaking of frogs.

Many of the weather superstitions have a rather humorous character. The dried blood of a murdered man will supposedly liquify when a big rain is approaching. One may assume that this forecast method is used only infrequently. The number of fogs in August is supposedly predictive of a like number of snows in winter. Every 100-degree day in July predicts a 20-below-zero day the following January. Long-range folk forecasters hold that the weather conditions for the first twelve days of January are predictive of the weather for the next twelve months. Thus, presumably, a dry January 4 produces a dry April and a snowy January 8 results in August snow flurries.

Selected References

Gist, Noel P. *Missouri: Its Resources, People, and Institutions*. Columbia, Mo.: Curators of the University of Missouri, 1950.

Local Climatological Data, Springfield, Missouri, Annual Summary With Comparative Data, 1967. Washington, D.C.: Environmental Science Services Administration, U.S. Department of Commerce, 1967.

Maxfield, O. O. "Geography of the Boston Mountains." Ph.D. dissertation, Ohio State University, 1963.

Randolph, Vance. *Ozark Magic and Folklore*. New York: Columbia University Press, 1964.

Sauer, Carl O. *The Geography of the Ozark Highland of Missouri*. The Geographic Society of Chicago Bulletin no. 7, Chicago: University of Chicago Press, 1920.

Trewartha, Glenn T. *An Introduction of Climate*. 4th ed. New York: McGraw-Hill Book Co., 1968.

Vickery, Margaret Ray. *Ozark Stories of the Upper Current River*. Salem, Mo.: The Salem News, n.d.

4.

Indians of the Ozarks

Cultural information about the Indians of the Ozarks has come largely from archaeological studies. Written history provides only a bare sketch of the Osage and Missouri Indians, who lived in and along the margins of the Ozarks. Some of the earliest descriptions of the Ozarks relate to the historic voyage of Marquette and Joliet down the Mississippi River in 1673. Much that can be learned through archaeology was left unwritten between 1673 and 1830, and thousands of years of unwritten Indian history preceded that period.

The Indians of the Ozarks were not seriously studied until they had been moved to reservations, and by that time their customs, habits, and possessions had changed considerably through contact with people of European background. Even while in the Ozarks the native inhabitants were undergoing cultural change as they were exposed to metal tools, trade items, and new religious beliefs.

The prehistory of the region is being carefully reconstructed from archaeological research conducted by several universities and the Smithsonian Institution, but large areas have barely been examined by trained specialists. Research in the region has been directed at establishing a general framework of cultural groups while salvaging archaeological sites. The thousands of known campsites, villages, burial grounds, inhabited caves, small mounds, and pictograph sites represent only a fraction of the archaeological resources in the area.

Time periods extending back into prehistory have been described for both Missouri and Arkansas.[1] The periods and their approximate duration are shown in Table 4.1.

The Ozarks were discovered by early hunting groups approximately fourteen thousand years ago, with the possibility of even earlier sites that have not been discovered and dated. Now extinct forms of mammals, such as the mastodon and mammoth, roamed the northern part of the Ozarks and perhaps furnished part of the diet for the first Indians to penetrate the region. The distribution of Paleo-Indian sites in Missouri suggests these early hunters were exploiting resources that were more abundant along the Missouri and Mississippi river valleys.

Climatic changes during the Dalton and Archaic periods provided a stimulus for social and technological changes, which are preserved in the archaeological record. Prehistoric Indians during

1. Carl H. Chapman, *The Archeology of Missouri*, vol. 1 (Columbia, Mo.: University of Missouri Press, 1975). See also Charles R. McGimsey, "Indians of Arkansas," *Arkansas Archaeological Survey Popular Series*, no. 1, 1969.

TABLE 4-1
Time Periods in Early Missouri and Arkansas History

Period	Duration	Characteristics
Historic Period	A.D. 1700–A.D. 1835	European Contact
Mississippian Period	A.D. 900–A.D. 1700	Village Farmer
Woodland Period	1000 B.C.–A.D. 900	Prairie-Forest Potter
Archaic Period	7000 B.C.–1000 B.C.	Forager
Dalton Period	8000 B.C.–7000 B.C.	Hunter-Forager
Paleo-Indian Period	12000 B.C.–8000 B.C.	Early Hunter

these periods were not totally reliant upon hunting for their food supply, since they had discovered how to gather and prepare various seeds, roots, and fruits. During this period, the size of the nomadic hunting and gathering groups increased, and seasonal villages were formed. Ground stone tools appear during the Archaic Period, along with greater diversity of chipped tools. The weapons and tools were fashioned from native chert, but the bow and arrow apparently were not known. The nature of the Indians' houses, if such existed, is unknown; they often frequented caves or natural rock shelters. Their open-air villages and campsites were situated on high terraces or hilltops near a constant water supply.

The use of pottery marked the beginning of a new period in the prehistory of the Ozarks. The early pottery was crude but functional, and it represented a striking change in the mode of habitation and conditions of life. Woodland pottery was made from clay that contained small amounts of sand, crushed bone, or crushed limestone, which the Indians had added to act as temper. Pottery made or traded for during the Mississippian period often contained small pieces of crushed mussel shell as temper.

The practice of constructing low mounds for burial of the dead also was inaugurated during the Woodland Period. Pipes and evidence of ceremonial smoking became more common in the region. The bow and arrow increased the effectiveness of the hunters, and the use of pottery expanded the Indians' ability to cook and store food. They became more sedentary and began to cultivate small gardens to supplement food which they hunted and gathered.

Hopewell villages and burial sites have been discovered along the eastern and northern margins of the Ozarks; they date from the middle and late portions of the Woodland Period. The center of the Hopewell Culture was situated in Ohio, where prehistoric burial sites consist of large circular mounds that contain elaborate trade goods. The Hopewell Culture maintained an extensive trade network that brought obsidian (volcanic glass) from the Yellowstone; mica, quartz crystals, aventurine, and chlorite from the southern Appalachians; marine shells from the Florida Gulf Coast; and galena (lead) from northwestern Illinois or from the Ozarks.[2] Research at Hopewell sites along the Missouri River has indicated that the sites were possibly colonies established along trade routes.[3] Evidence of Hopewell influence in the interior of the Ozarks indicates a very limited amount of trade and borrowing of technology between isolated Woodland groups and the Hopewell villages along the Missouri River. The decline of the Hopewell communities along the margins of the Ozarks was tied to the general deterioration of the major Hopewell centers east of the Mississippi River.

After the Hopewell Culture languished, the native inhabitants of the Ozarks maintained their

2. Gary A. Wright, "Ohio Hopewell Trade," *Missouri Archeological Society Newsletter*, no. 269, 1973.

3. J. Mett Shippee, "Archaeological Remains in the Area of Kansas City: The Woodland Period, Early, Middle, and Late," *Missouri Archaeological Society Research Series*, 1967.

self-sufficient social and subsistence institutions. Within a few generations, another outside culture was beginning to influence the Indians living in the Ozarks. The Mississippian Culture developed in what is now the southeastern United States and spread north through the Mississippi Valley. These people were agriculturalists and lived in permanent villages. Houses were permanent structures, rectangular or square in shape, with walls of daub and wattle and roofs of thatch. In the fertile Mississippi Valley, large, flat-topped earthern mounds were built for ceremonial purposes. These tiered pyramids had large buildings on top and a ramp or stairway leading to them. Pottery making developed fully, and elaborate effigies of animals and human beings were molded on their containers; extensive trade was conducted with Gulf Coast peoples for marine shells. Again the Ozarks was peripheral to this main stream of cultural change; while those groups situated along the margins of the Ozarks were significantly modified, the more isolated groups often were oblivious to the grand developments in the Mississippi Valley. There are no remains of massive ceremonial mounds like those at the Libroun Site in southeast Missouri, nor were the villages fortified. Several theories can be constructed to explain the lack of Mississippian influence within the Ozarks: difficulty of travel, sparse population, scarcity of suitable agricultural land, paucity of other resources, the native Ozark Indians' natural resistance to change, long-standing hostilities between the two groups, and a lack of interest among the Mississippian Culture peoples for contact with groups living in the Ozarks. Whatever the factor, or combination of factors, many portions of the Ozarks in Missouri and Arkansas remained isolated during the Mississippian Period and continued the traditions of the Woodland Period.

The Historic Period

The final period of Indian occupation in the Ozarks was marked by the appearance of groups that were present during the time of European contact. The larger native tribes include the Osages, Illinois, Caddos, and Quapaws. The Osages occupied most of the interior and western Ozarks, the Illinois lived along the Mississippi River Border, the Caddos hunted in the Arkansas and southwest Missouri portion of the Ozarks, and the Quapaws occupied only a small section of the southeastern hills. All of these tribes were dependent upon both hunting and agriculture for their food. Although their villages were permanent, much of their time was spent on extended hunts.

Pottery vessels from the Historic Period were well made and decorated. By 1700, trade was well established with the French; consequently, the Indian cultures began to change. The Indians found that some European goods were superior, and the old arts fell into disuse. The horse brought rapid change; it allowed the Osages to hunt on the plains west of the Ozarks.

The story of the Indians' displacement from their homelands in North America is one of the most tragic of epics. The government made treaties containing terms that were never met, and some of the documents never were considered seriously by the whites. Congress often was poorly informed of the Indians' circumstances. Some of the agents and military officers who administered the terms of the treaties were able and did good work, but nearly as often they were corrupt or inexperienced and incompetent. Often the leaders of the tribes were themselves corrupt, so that bribery and personal favors to prominent Indian families became an accepted way of doing business. By the time the Cherokees reached the Ozarks, intermarriage had become so common that many of their chiefs had more white ancestors than Indian. All of this caused an undue and unnecessary amount of suffering and hardship for the Indians in the inevitable transfer of lands and the melding of cultures.

So it was, then, that the Ozarks first became part of the western dumping grounds for tribes dispossessed in the East; then, as white settlers entered the region, these Indian peoples were again dispossessed and crowded into smaller and smaller land reserves farther west. They were immediately in conflict with the Indian peoples that inhabited these western lands.

Even before the Ozarks came into the possession of the United States in 1804 after the Louisiana Purchase of 1803, several groups of eastern Indians had moved into the region. Serena, a chieftain of the Kickapoos, led a small

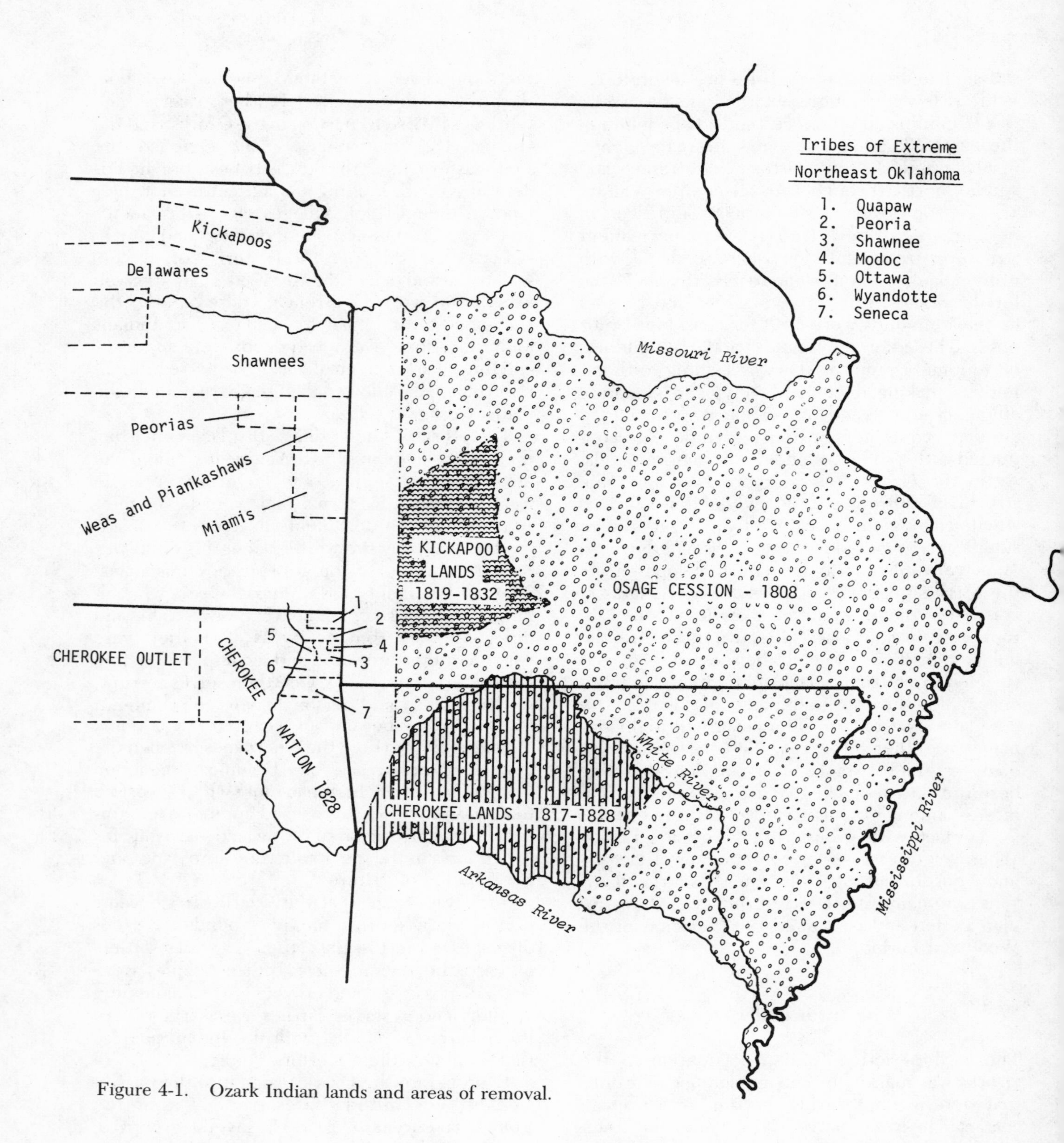

Figure 4-1. Ozark Indian lands and areas of removal.

group, probably fewer than four hundred souls, to land west of St. Louis. The Spaniards were receptive to Indian immigration, believing that the presence of a friendly Indian population would help them to retain possession of their land west of the Mississippi River. By 1784 they had settled Shawnees and Delawares on land grants in what is now southeast Missouri and northeast Arkansas. In 1785 some of the Cherokees who were dissatisfied with the Treaty of Hopewell immigrated to the vicinity of the St. Francis and White rivers in northeast Arkansas.

The Osage Indians gave up their claims to the major portion of the Ozark Plateau in their first treaty with the federal government in November, 1808. The document was drawn up at Fort Osage, situated on a bluff overlooking the Missouri River about twenty miles east of the present site of Kansas City. The Indians gave up all their land between the Missouri River and the Arkansas River lying east of a line running due south from Fort Osage to the Arkansas River (fig. 4-1).

The Osages largely ignored the terms of the treaty so far as hunting privileges were concerned. They always contended that they had given up only the land, not their right to hunt on it. They occasionally raided the early white settlements and took scalps and slaves from the Indians (Kickapoos, Cherokees, Piankashaws, Shawnees, Weas, Peorias, and Delawares) who had exchanged their lands east of the Mississippi for territory in the former terrain of the Osages.

The War of 1812 was a time of bitter conflict between American frontiersmen and Indian tribes that were led to believe they would profit from the defeat of the Americans. After the war, renewed emphasis was placed on Indian removal. Under the terms of the Treaty of Edwardsville and the Treaty of Fort Harrison, both of which were signed in 1819, the Indiana and Illinois Kickapoo tribes were granted land in southwest Missouri (fig. 4-1) in exchange for their land east of the Mississippi River and a stipend of money.

In 1821 and 1822 a band of twenty-one hundred Delawares, already twice removed form their homeland in the Middle Atlantic States, was located along the James River on land now encompassed by Christian, Stone, and Barry counties. Although the location was to be temporary, some of the Delawares and a few Shawnees from southeast Missouri joined the main body of Kickapoos in the James River country. Apparently the Kickapoos and Shawnees ranged widely in the Ozarks; it is reported that the Kickapoos had hunting camps as far east as Jefferson County and on the Current and Gasconade rivers.[4] Most of the counties in southwest Missouri and northwest Arkansas have accounts of Shawnee and Delaware villages within their boundaries. The sheer number of reports would lead one to think that many of them were seasonal hunting camps. Shawnee settlements noted by Ingenthron[5] included Shawnee Town, near present-day Yellville, Arkansas; Crook Creek Camp, near what is now Harrison, Arkansas; Garther Cove Camp, at the eastern foot of Garther Mountain; Long Creek Camp, near the present town of Alpena; and a camp on sShort Creek. The Delawares had a number of dwellings on Long Creek in what is now Carroll County, Arkansas, in addition to their main villages between the White and Osage rivers. A large village of about five hundred inhabitants was located within the present boundaries of Springfield.

By the 1820's the Ozarks had become a kind of refuge for fragments of the eastern Indian tribes that had been buffeted about for several years. Probably, to some of these people the rugged isolation of the Ozarks provided a welcome relief from the harassed and vagabond life they had been leading. In 1819 a group of about sixty Peorias was living at the mouth of Bull Creek. A few miles east, a village of Miamis was at the mouth of Swan Creek, and a band of Piankashaws had settled on Cowskin Creek near the present town of Ava, Missouri. Peorias and Piankashaws reportedly lived near the present site of Forsyth, Missouri, on the White River, and a small band of Wea Indians lived near the spot where Beaver Creeks flows into White River. By the mid-1820's about eight thousand Algonquians and six thousand Cherokees inhabited southwest Missouri and northwest Arkansas.

4. Louis Houck, *A History of Missouri*, 1, 208–19 (Chicago: R. R. Donnelly and Sons, Company, 1908), pp. 208–219.

5. Elmo Ingenthron, *Indians of the Ozark Plateau* (Point Lookout, Mo.: The School of the Ozarks Press, 1970), p. 115–16.

The first Cherokees to enter Arkansas fled to the swamps of the St. Francis River after participating in a massacre at Mussel Shoals on the Tennessee River in 1794. This band was augmented in later years by others who wished to escape the white man's encroachment on Cherokee territory in the East. In 1808 some of the Western Cherokees petitioned President Jefferson for land elsewhere, that they might move from the swamps. Nine years later, on July 8, 1817, the United States and the Cherokee Nation signed a treaty granting a large tract that included the Boston Mountains (fig. 4-1). A line extending northeastward from a point near the present city of Morrilton to the White River near Batesville was the eastern boundary. The western boundary, undecided until 1825, began at a point ten miles upstream from Fort Smith, extending northeastward parallel to the eastern boundary to the White River. The Arkansas and White rivers were the southern and northern boundaries, respectively. There is no record of the exact number of Cherokee Indians who made a new home in this grant. Between two and three thousand already were in Arkansas at the time the treaty was signed, and another three thousand probably had immigrated by 1819.[6]

Discontent among white settlers was directed toward the Cherokees living on the land awarded the Indians in 1817. When Schoolcraft and Drummond passed down the White River in 1818, they stopped and spent a night at the home of Mrs. John Lafferty, the widow of one of the first settlers above Batesville.[7] Schoolcraft found Mrs. Lafferty very much excited, as were all her neighbors on that side (the right bank) of the river. She and others had improved farms upon which they had lived for several years but which, under the treaty with the Cherokees, they were to be forced to relinquish. Mrs. Lafferty was making arrangements then to move across the river to another farm (it lay in what is now Izard County) that belonged to her husband. She died there in 1832.

As a result of agitation by white residents and others who wanted to extinguish Indian claims in Arkansas Territory, negotiations were entered into and the Cherokee Nation ceded to the United States all of the land obtained in 1817. In return the Western Cherokees received land in Indian Territory (now eastern Oklahoma). Most of the Cherokees in Arkansas moved there, joined by an almost steady stream from the Eastern Cherokee Nation during the next decade. Some of the Cherokees on Upper White River stayed longer. In the mid-1830's many of them still lived on their improved claims, having intermarried with the early white settlers; probably, a few descendants of these mixed marriages still live in the region.

The Cherokees who moved to Indian Territory were joined in 1838 and 1839 by the main body of Eastern Cherokees, who were driven from their homes and marched along the Trail of Tears across the Ozark Plateau. Because the Cherokee Nation remains an important aspect of Ozark cultural geography, its story will be elaborated later as one of the permanent immigrant groups.

Conditions were hard for the potpourri of Algonquian peoples in southwest Missouri. By the mid 1820's wildlife, a principal part of the Indians' livelihood, was becoming scarce; armed with the white man's weapons, the Indians were becoming quite destructive to it. Many of the tribes had become accustomed to a government dole and had become, essentially, wards of the state. Frequently, Indian life is depicted sentimentally as a kind of carefree existence in which a simple, untroubled people live in harmony with nature. This letter, written by William Anderson, principal chief of the Delawares, to General William Clark, tells of their pathetic condition:

> Last summer a number of our people died just for the want of something to live on. We have got a country where we do not find all as stated to us when we was asked to swap lands with you and we do not get as much as promised us at the treaty of St. Mary's neither. Father—we did not think that big man would tell us things that was not true. We have found a poor hilly stony country and the worst of all no game to be found on it to live on. Last summer our corn looked very well until a heavy rain came on for 3 or 4 days and raised the

6. Charles C. Royce, "The Cherokee Nation of Indians," *Fifth Annual Report of the Bureau of Ethnology* (Washington, D.C.: Government Printing Office, 1887), p. 218.

7. Henry Rowe Schoolcraft, *Journal of a Tour into the Interior of Missouri and Arkansas in 1818 and 1819*, in *Schoolcraft in the Ozarks*, ed. Hugh Park (Van Buren, Ark.: Press-Argus Printers, 1955), p. 152–53.

waters so high that we could just see the tops of our corn in some of the fields and it destroyed the greatest part of our corn, punkins, and beans and a great many more of my people coming on and we had to divide our stock with them. . . .[8]

In a span of seven years—between 1825 and 1832—treaties were negotiated with the several tribes in southwest Missouri for their removal from the newly created state into what is now Kansas. General Clark, who was respected by most of the Indians, was instrumental in working out treaties that cleared the Ozark region in Missouri and Arkansas for settlement by whites.

The final phase of Indian settlement in the Ozarks was carried out in what is now Oklahoma. Before the Civil War, bands of Senecas, Seneca-Shawnees, and Quapaws had been removed from Ohio to the northeast corner of Indian Territory between the Neosho River and the Missouri state line. In 1867, room was made in this area for several small bands of Indians from Kansas. Kaskaskias, Miamis, Peorias, Weas, and Piankashaws were settled on land vacated by readjustment of the Seneca-Shawnees. The Ottawas settled on a small reservation along the Neosho River, the Modocs were put on the border of Missouri, and the Wyandottes occupied 20,000 acres ceded by the Senecas (fig. 4-1).

The Cultural Landscape

Except for the Cherokees and the other small bands of eastern tribes that were settled in Oklahoma, the Indians had little impact on the landscape. The Osages, hereditary landlords of most of the Ozarks, were still living at a rather primitive cultural level when they were removed to lands farther west. They lived in a hunting-gathering-farming economy, with heavy emphasis on hunting. In April or May they planted their crops near the villages and, leaving them unfenced and sometimes unattended, took off on hunting excursions that sometimes lasted up to three months. In late summer they returned so that the women could harvest, dry, and store the crops of beans, corn, pumpkins, and squash. An autumn hunt lasted into early winter. Furs, wild game, nuts, and wild fruits were brought back to the villages. Winter was a time to feast—until food supplies were exhausted—and to make preparations for the spring hunt for beaver and bear. At other times the Osages participated in trading and periodic warring expeditions.

Their settlements consisted of round or oblong huts built of poles forming a bow or arch and meeting at the apex. Over this framework, buffalo hides, reeds, cattails, and other thatch materials were interwoven to provide a weatherproof shelter. The shelters built at hunting camps were much more crude. Schoolcraft described those he saw on Swan Creek in 1818 as "inverted bird's nests" made of slender poles and interwoven branches and thatch, apparently somewhat in the fashion of the modern-day brush arbor used in the Ozarks for outdoor church services in the summer months.[9]

On the whole, however, the Osages did not modify the physical landscape greatly. The cultural landscape they built was simple, consisting of a few huts and clearings that were quickly obliterated by the forces of weather and encroaching vegetation. The eastern tribes that settled temporarily in Missouri and Arkansas possessed many of the white man's tools and implements, but their residence was of such short duration that they left little imprint on the land other than depleting the population of wildlife.

The Cherokees, however, were one of the Five Civilized Tribes and were equipped not only with the white man's tools and implements but also with his culture, including religion; the desire to provide for education; improved and systematic planting, cultivation, and harvesting of crops; and construction of substantial dwellings and laying out of towns. The Cherokees were great builders by Indian standards, and they developed a cultural landscape much like that of the white settlers and their descendants. But there were differences in their occupation of the land, some of which may still be seen.

8. Ingenthron, *Indians of the Ozark Plateau*, p. 140.

9. Schoolcraft, *Journal of a Tour. . .*, in *Schoolcraft in the Ozarks*, ed. Park, p. 107.

Selected References

Chapman, Carl H. *The Archaeology of Missouri*. Vol. 1. Columbia, Mo.: University of Missouri Press, 1975.

——— and Chapman, Eleanor F. *Indians and Archaeology of Missouri*. Missouri Handbook no. 6. Columbia, Mo.: 1964.

Gibson, Arrel M. *The Kickapoos*. Norman: University of Oklahoma Press, 1963.

Houck, Louis. *A History of Missouri*. Vol. I. Chicago: R.R. Donnelly and Sons Co., 1908.

Ingenthron, Elmo. *Indians of the Ozark Plateau*. Point Lookout, Mo.: The School of the Ozarks Press, 1970.

Lightfoot, B. B. "The Cherokee Immigrants in Missouri 1837–1839," *Missouri Historical Review*, vol. 56, January 1962.

McGimsey, Charles R. "Indians of Arkansas," Arkansas Archaeological Survey Popular Series no. 1. 1969.

McReynold, Edwin C. *Oklahoma: A History of the Sooner State*. Norman: University of Oklahoma Press, 1954.

Royce, Charles C. "The Cherokee Nation of Indians," *Fifth Annual Report of the Bureau of American Ethnology*. Washington, D.C.: Government Printing Office, 1887.

Scholtz, James A. "A Summary of Prehistory in Northwest Arkansas," *Arkansas Archaeologist*, Vol. 10, No. 1–3, 1969.

Schoolcraft, Henry Rowe. *Journal of a Tour into the Interior of Missouri and Arkansas in 1818 and 1819*. In *Schoolcraft in the Ozarks*, edited by Hugh Park. Van Buren, Ark.: Press-Argus Printers, 1955.

Shippee, J. Mett. "Archaeological Remains in the Area of Kansas City: The Woodland Period, Early, Middle, and Late." *Missouri Archaeological Society Research Series*, 1967.

Thomas, Ronald A., and Davis, Hester A. "Excavations in Prall Shelter (3BE187) in Beaver Reservoir, Northwest Arkansas," *Arkansas Archaeologist*, vol. 7, no. 4, 1966.

Woodward, Grace Steele. *The Cherokees*. Norman: University of Oklahoma Press, 1963.

Wright, Gary A. "Ohio Hopewell Trade," *Missouri Archaeological Society Newsletter*, no. 269, 1973.

5.

Settlement: The First Phases

There were three phases in the settlement of the Ozarks[1] The first of these was the Old Ozarks Frontier, which progressed from the eastern border to the lead and iron mines in the eastern interior and finally overspread the whole region, though thinly, by 1850. The first white settlers were French Creoles who established small settlements on the banks of the Mississippi River. A few Americans arrived before the Louisiana Purchase of 1803, but most came later. By 1840 the residue of the Cherokee Nation had come over the Trail of Tears to the western Ozarks beyond the new states of Missouri and Arkansas. The exceptional characteristic of the Old Ozarks Frontier was that, except for the German border settlements close to the Missouri and Mississippi rivers, a few mining districts, and a few trade centers, it did not pass away.

The second settlement phase was part of the post–Civil War national development that historians refer to as the Reconstruction, or New South. It was a time of rapid railroad construction and the spread of the elements of modernity that always followed the rails. The New South Ozarks developed as corridors cutting through and eventually surrounding the Old Ozarks Frontier. The railroad brought commercial agriculture, corporate mining and lumbering, prosperity, energy, and money; the new Ozark immigrants were progressive, liberal, capitalistic, educated, and bourgeois in culture. This second-sequent occupancy, superimposed on the Old Ozarks Frontier and powered by the steam locomotive, influenced the back country for half a century or more, resulting in a variegated pattern of economic linkages, cultural landscapes, and ways of life.

The third phase of occupancy began with the events connected with World War I and has proceeded to the present. World War I "sent shock waves along the railroad corridors and into much of the region: the draft, high agricultural prices, borrowing to bring more marginal land into production, soldiers' pay sent home, new war-stimulated extractive industries."[2] Three more times (World War II, Korea, Vietnam) such shock waves washed over the Ozarks, each time reaching farther onto ridgetops and back into isolated valleys, now carried by the new power generated in the internal-combustion engine. In the 1930's the New Deal agencies discovered Ozarks "pov-

1. Robert Flanders, "Shannon County of the Ozarks," Developmental Grant Proposal, Southwest Missouri State University, Springfield, 1977, p. 10.

2. Ibid., p. 13–14.

erty," and through political propaganda the national stereotype of the Ozarks was born. Ozarkers received relief commodities and discovered such new foods as grapefruit and oranges, and, for the first time for many, they learned that they were poor by comparison. The federal government became the Ozarks' largest landholder, employer, builder, preserver, destroyer, political power, social servant, and dependent. The Works Progress Administration, Civilian Conservation Corps, and a host of social agencies provided work, training, education, and sustenance. The national parks and national forests were established during the same decade. The army bases at Fort Leonard Wood, Fort Chaffee, and Camp Crowder came later, as did the Corps of Engineers and its dozen reservoirs. Tourism, second-home development, skyrocketing land prices, and the population explosion of the 1960's and 1970's—all are part of cosmopolitan Ozarks history.[3]

All three archetypal national histories persist in the Ozarks. They are manifested in human attitudes, beliefs, and daily activities. They also may be discovered by the careful observer in the landscape of the region in relict buildings, abandoned farms, and traditional technologies.

Primary Phase—The French

The peculiar development of the Ozarks is due in large part to its location at the funnel opening of the Ohio-Mississippi river immigration route. The Ohio Valley served as a great collector of people who had moved westward progressively from the Tidewater to the Piedmont and through the Appalachian Mountains to the uplands of Kentucky and Tennessee and the fertile glaciated plains north of the Ohio River. The Ozarks served as a rugged bastion deflecting the main flow of population to the bordering river routes via the Mississippi, Missouri, and Arkansas. The population that moved along the river borders was of variegated origin, drawn from large sections of the East, yet for decades the Ozarks remained a backwater area along the mainstream of westward settlement and economic development.

3. Ibid., p. 14.

The present territory of the Ozarks was originally part of the French province of Louisiana, but before cession of the western bank of the Mississippi to Spain in 1762, it was almost unexplored and unoccupied. Nevertheless, the French were the first immigrant group to explore and settle in the region. They entered the Mississippi Valley from their settlements on the Great Lakes. In their quest for furs and minerals, the French systematically explored the rivers of the interior lowlands of the United States. The Mississippi was the main link between the major French settlements on the Great Lakes and in Lower Louisiana. The eastern Ozarks was stratigically located in the midsection of their vast domain, where the great east-west navigable rivers, the Ohio and Missouri, entered the Mississippi. It is not surprising that the French early established settlements along this strategic section of the Mississippi that linked the great interior rivers: the Upper Mississippi, the Wisconsin, the Illinois, the Missouri, the Ohio, and the Arkansas. Many expeditions followed the voyage of Marquette and Joliet in 1673, and by 1699 the French had established a permanent settlement at Kaskaskia, on the Illinois side of the Mississippi across from Ste. Genevieve, as a mission to the village of Kaskaskia Indians. Soon after that, Cahokia and Fort Chartres were constructed on the fertile Illinois bottoms (fig. 5-1). Reports of Scottish financier John Law's plans for the Mississippi Company focused France's attention on the Mississippi Valley in the years 1717–20. Even though the plans did not materialize, the French soon followed with trading and mining ventures.[4] Settlement was in the familiar sequence; missionary, followed in order by fur trader, soldier, and farmer. The French, familiar with frontier conditions in Canada, eked out a living by combining fur trading, boating, and a casual form of agriculture. Because of fertile soils and favorable growing conditions, a surplus of grain was available to ship to New Orleans in exchange for manufactured goods.

Probably through their contacts with the Indians, the French soon were apprised of mineral wealth in the hill country to the west. The lead

4. Duane Meyer, *The Heritage of Missouri: A History* (St. Louis: State Publishing Company, 1970), p. 33.

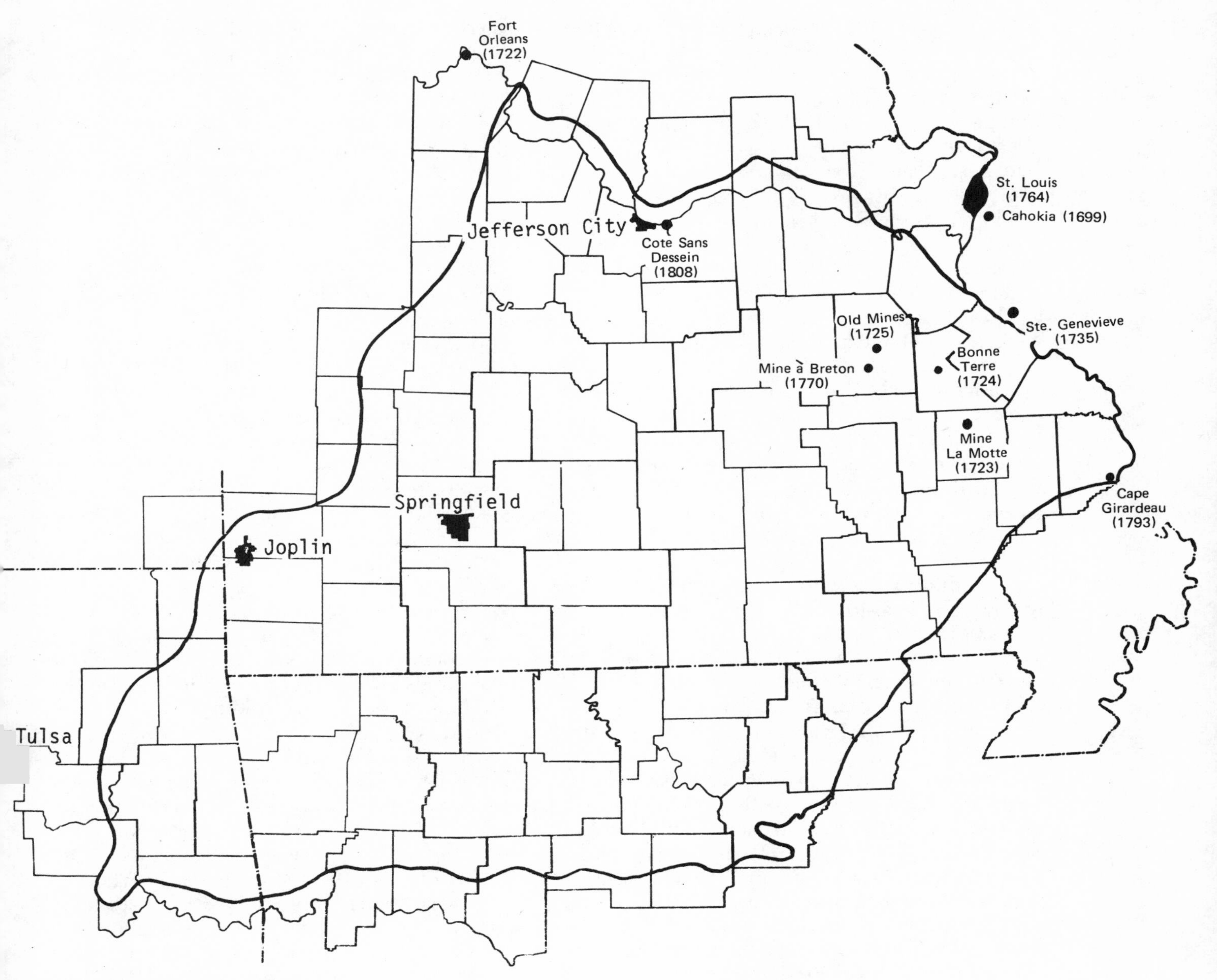

Figure 5-1. French settlements.

deposits on the Meramec were known as early as 1700, and in 1702, d'Iberville asked for patents to work the mines. Salt springs on Saline Creek below Ste. Genevieve were known even before Kaskaskia was settled. It was the salt springs and lead ore that attracted permanent settlement to the west bank of the Mississippi. In 1704, Governor Bienville reported that Frenchmen were settled west of the river. Thus the first official documentation of white settlement in the Ozarks was made three-quarters of a century before the American republic was born.

Stories of huge stores of silver and gold seized by the Spaniards in Peru and Mexico prodded the French to explore the interior Ozarks. The apparent abundance of lead, which often occurs with silver, inflamed the French with hope that they would find a bonanza. As might be expected, discoveries of silver soon were reported and investors were quick to underwrite prospecting and mining ventures. In 1717 the Company of the West gained control of Louisiana, and by 1719 it had established exploratory mining on the Meramec. Failing to find silver, the master smelter apparently salted the mine with a few ounces of the precious metal. Thus the legend of silver mines was established in the folklore of the region, never to be purged entirely.

The first large-scale effort to explore and exploit minerals was the expedition of Philippe Renault, who in 1720 entered the lead diggings in Washington and St. Francois counties "with two hundred artificers and miners provided with tools" and, reportedly, with slaves for working the mines. The expedition uncovered rich deposits of lead at the confluence of the Big and Meramec rivers, and the site was granted to Renault in 1723. It was the first land grant of record in Upper Louisiana.

Renault's explorations were exhaustive and several rich deposits of lead were discovered, but precious metals were not found. In 1723, Mine La Motte was established a few miles north of present Farmington. The mines at Fourche à Renault were opened in 1724–25, and work in the Old Mines north of Potosi started about 1725 (fig. 5-1).

As mining operations gradually expanded, the French established permanent residences on the west bank of the Mississippi River. The first settlement was established on the floodplain in the Big Field below the present site of Ste. Genevieve and across the river from Kaskaskia (fig. 5-1). The date of earliest settlement in old Ste. Genevieve is uncertain, but it was probably about 1735. After 1763, when the lands east of the river were deeded to Protestant England, many French families moved to Ste. Genevieve to be under a Catholic government. By 1769 the population of Ste. Genevieve and vicinity was estimated at about six hundred, exceeding that of the St. Louis area at the time. Additional immigration to the Mississippi's west bank was brought on by Indian raids and Clark's capture of Kaskaskia during the American Revolution.

The site of Ste. Genevieve was subject to flooding, and in 1785, *l'année des grandes eaux,* the town was virtually destroyed. Residents of the old town and many residents of the towns on the Illinois side moved to the new town founded at the bottom of a hill to the north. Then, in 1787, the new government of the United States established the Northwest Ordinance, which prohibited slavery in the Northwest Territory, and this prompted a number of wealthy slave owners to move to Ste. Genevieve. At the close of the eighteenth century, near the end of the French period, the French population lived primarily in Ste. Genevieve and New Bourbon, a town about a mile downriver, and in scattered temporary settlements at Mine à Breton (Potosi), Old Mines, Mine La Motte, and St. Michaels (Fredericktown).

Most of the Frenchmen were engaged in one or more of four occupations: salt making; mining, farming, trading. Salt was made by evaporating weak brine from springs on Saline Creek below Ste. Genevieve. The salt not only supplied the needs of the French settlements but was an important item of commerce. The digging and smelting of lead in the area now included in Washington and St. Francois counties was done in the fall after the crops were in and lasted until the onset of winter. This was the time when the pits were driest. The galena ore was dug entirely from residual clays with wooden shovels and was heaped on piles of burning logs to be melted down. At first the lead was molded into the shape of a collar and draped across a horse's neck for transportation to the Mississippi River; later, two-wheeled carts were used to transport lead to the wharf at Ste. Genevieve. Farming was done in the Big Field and upland Grand Park. Wheat and corn were staple crops in the Big Field, and in spite of the constant threat of flooding and a somewhat casual approach to cultivation, enough wheat was grown to supply local needs and ship surpluses to New Orleans. The bottomland Big Field was favored and was divided into lots, distributed among the heads of household. Grand Park was a communal pasture for livestock. Trade in furs, grain, and salt provided a livelihood for many of the settlers. In addition to the settlements at Ste. Genevieve, the French established small ones, consisting of only a few families, at Cape Girardeau and on the Meramec.

By 1700 the French had pursued the fur trade

into the Missouri Valley. Fort Orleans was built near Brunswick in 1722 to control nearby Indians. Since the fur traders frequently moved about, often living with the Indians, only a few permanent settlements were established. St. Charles and a small village at the mouth of La Charette Creek in Warren County were the only settlements on the Missouri at the time of the Lewis and Clark Expedition in 1804. The villages were a collection of poor cabins and huts. Unlike the French at Ste. Genevieve, the voyageurs of the Missouri River frequently intermarried with the Indians.

The founding of St. Louis was a milestone in the settlement of the Mississippi Valley. The first house in St. Louis was erected by Pierre Laclede Liguest of the firm of Maxent, Laclede and Company, merchants of New Orleans, who held a license for the fur trade on the Missouri River. After a winter at Fort Chartres, Laclede established his trading post at St. Louis in February, 1764. The location, near the mouths of the Missouri and Illinois rivers, was ideal for control of the fur trade of the Upper Mississippi Basin, and the site, on a natural landing on an outcrop of limestone on the first high ground south of the mouth of the Missouri, was free of flooding and malaria. St. Louis was strategically located to serve as an entrepôt for the products of the Ozark region.

The southern reaches of the Ozarks were explored by the French at an early date. In 1673, nearly a century before the founding of St. Louis, Marquette and Joliet, with only two canoes and five boatmen, reached the mouth of the Arkansas River. Almost ten years later, in 1682, La Salle visited the village of the Quapaws in Arcansa—the land of the downstream folk. In 1686, La Salle's faithful lieutenant, Henri de Tonty, on an expedition to look for his missing leader, established Arkansas Post some fifteen miles west of the Mississippi near the confluence of the White and Arkansas rivers. The main thrust of French interest, however, was concentrated on the branching Mississippi, Ohio, and Missouri river systems.

In 1765 an English garrison arrived at Fort Chartres, and the exodus of the French from the east bottomlands on the Mississippi began. In three years St. Louis was a thriving town of more than five hundred inhabitants, already rivaling Ste. Genevieve as the largest settlement in the Mississippi Valley north of New Orleans.

After Spain took formal possession in 1770, that portion of Louisiana north of the Arkansas River was known as the Illinois country and was ruled by a succession of Spanish lieutenant governors at St. Louis. The governors, however, identified themselves with the province; French remained the official language, even of official documents, and the transfer of allegiance brought no break in the continuity of the history of the district. The Spanish lieutenant governor was an absolute ruler, receiving orders only from New Orleans; he controlled the troops and militia, acted as chief justice under a code that did not recognize trial by jury, and was unrestrained by any popular assembly.

There was a steady and healthy growth in population, at first of Frenchmen from Canada, Kaskaskia, or New Orleans, reinforced after 1790 by Americans from Kentucky, until, at the time of the Louisiana Purchase, the population of the district was somewhat over six thousand. There were commandants, subordinate to the governor of St. Louis, at New Madrid, Ste. Genevieve, New Bourbon, St. Charles, and St. Andrews. The towns were strung out down the Mississippi from of the mouth of the Missouri. New Madrid and Cape Girardeau contained a large number of Kentuckians, but most of the newcomers settled on detached farms along the creeks between St. Louis and Ste. Genevieve and around St. Charles. The settlement, French in culture but governed by Spaniards, was made up largely of Americans.

The economy was mostly agricultural, and with few exceptions there was little distinction of rank or wealth. The richer men were merchants who sent the products of the colony to New Orleans or Montreal and sold manufactured goods to people. The younger men spent their winters with professional trappers on the Upper Missouri or Mississippi rivers, collecting furs, one of the staple exports. Furs, lead, salt, and wheat were carried downriver; in the long and tedious return voyage against the current, the boats were laden with the few articles of luxury required by the colonists, such as sugar, spices, and manufactured goods. Artisans were few and barely competent, so that

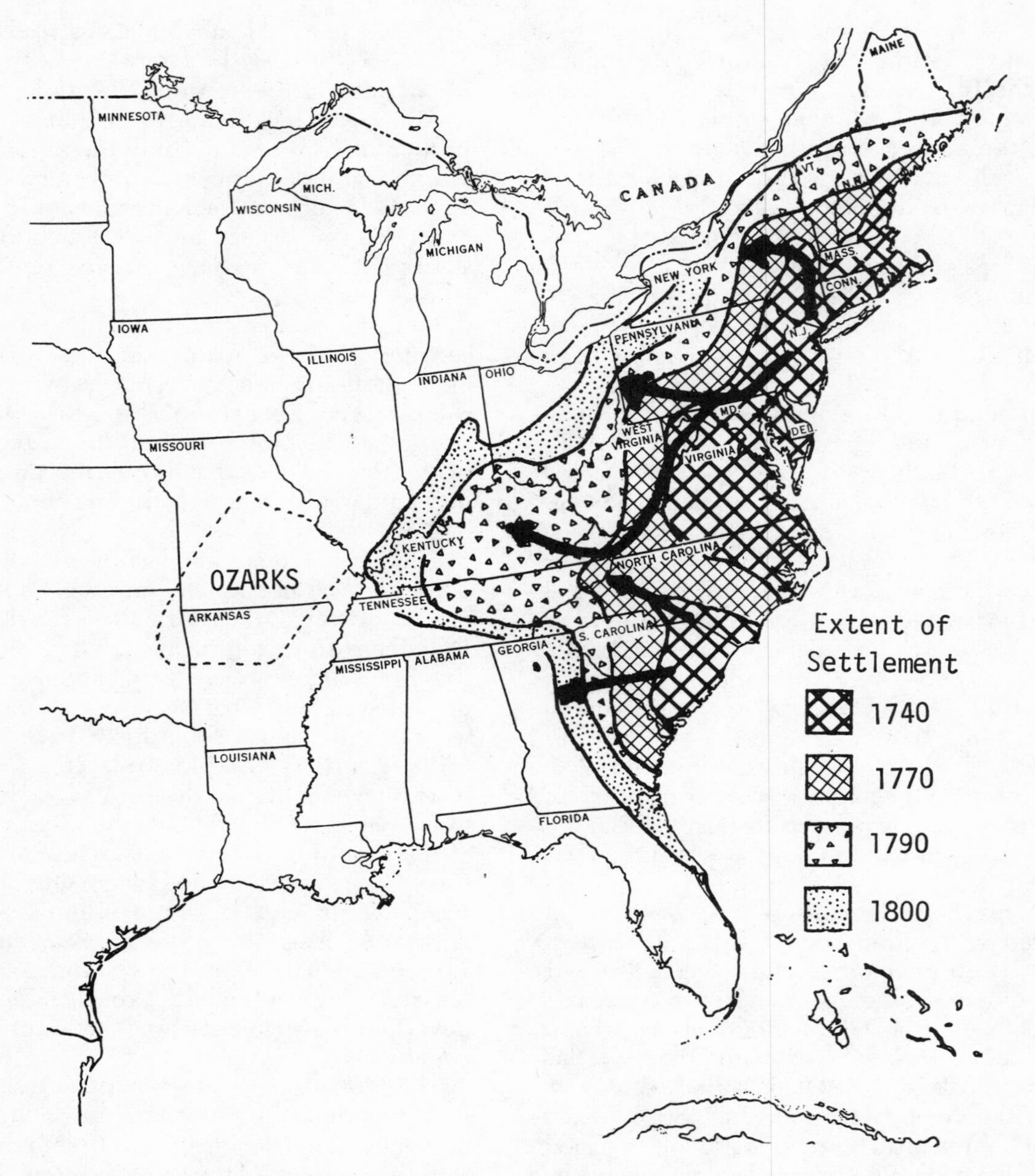

Figure 5-2. The settlement frontier and migration routes. Adapted from Gerlach, *Immigrants in the Ozarks*.

nearly all implements, except the rudest, were imported. Even the spinning wheel was a rarity among the French, and butter was a delicacy. The Americans were more enterprising, but they had only slight influence on their neighbors.

The intellectual life was not of a striking character. There was no provision for education, and illiteracy was prevalent. There were few books and those mainly in the libraries of the priests. Religion was Roman Catholic by law, but Protestant Americans were not molested as long as they worshiped quietly. There was no political life, no town meetings, no elections. Taxation was light; land was freely granted for nominal fees, and on the whole the Spanish governors were lenient and tolerant. There was rude abundance, a gentle, easygoing people, and a general absence of unrest.

The French controlled the great interior plains and low plateaus of the United States for nearly a century and a half, but they left almost no landscape imprint—and precious little to remember. As one geographer[5] has said, the French were like Kilroy; and, like the imaginary omnipresent World War II soldier who wrote "Kilroy was here" on trucks, buildings, and latrine walls around the world, the French presence in the Ozarks is known mainly through place-names and, except for the eighteenth-century houses at Ste. Genevieve and the few French families in Washington County, Missouri, little else.

Primary Phase—The Americans

The Louisiana Purchase was consequent to westward expansion of population and colonization in America. There were four main routes from the Atlantic to the Ohio, all following river valleys as lines of least resistance (fig. 5-2). The northern and easiest passage—via the Mohawk River valley, later followed by the Erie Canal and now by the New York Turnpike—was barred by the Iroquois Indians until about 1800. So the earlier pioneers crossed Pennsylvania to Pittsburgh or followed the Potomac or the Yadkin rivers into the Shenandoah Valley and crossed the ridges of the Appalachians through several passes, of which Cumberland Gap was the most popular. In any case the settlers planned to reach the Ohio, or the Tennessee, or the Cumberland. The wanderings of Daniel Boone in eastern Kentucky in 1769–71 mark the beginning of migration. He was followed by a constantly increasing stream of settlers from the back country of Virginia and the Carolinas. They were quite different from the planters of Tidewater plantations. In their veins was a liberal infusion of Scottish and Irish blood. They were restless, adventurous, enterprising, and brave to a fault, the ideal people to win the first struggle with the wilderness.

Mountaineer in coonskin cap and homespun jacket. (Courtesy Arkansas History Commission.)

Probably, the first American settlement in trans-Mississippi territory was Morgan's colony at New Madrid in 1788. Because Spain feared British attack on her far-flung empire, Spanish

5. John Fraser Hart, "The Middle West," *Annals of the Association of American Geographers*, 62: (June 1972): 258.

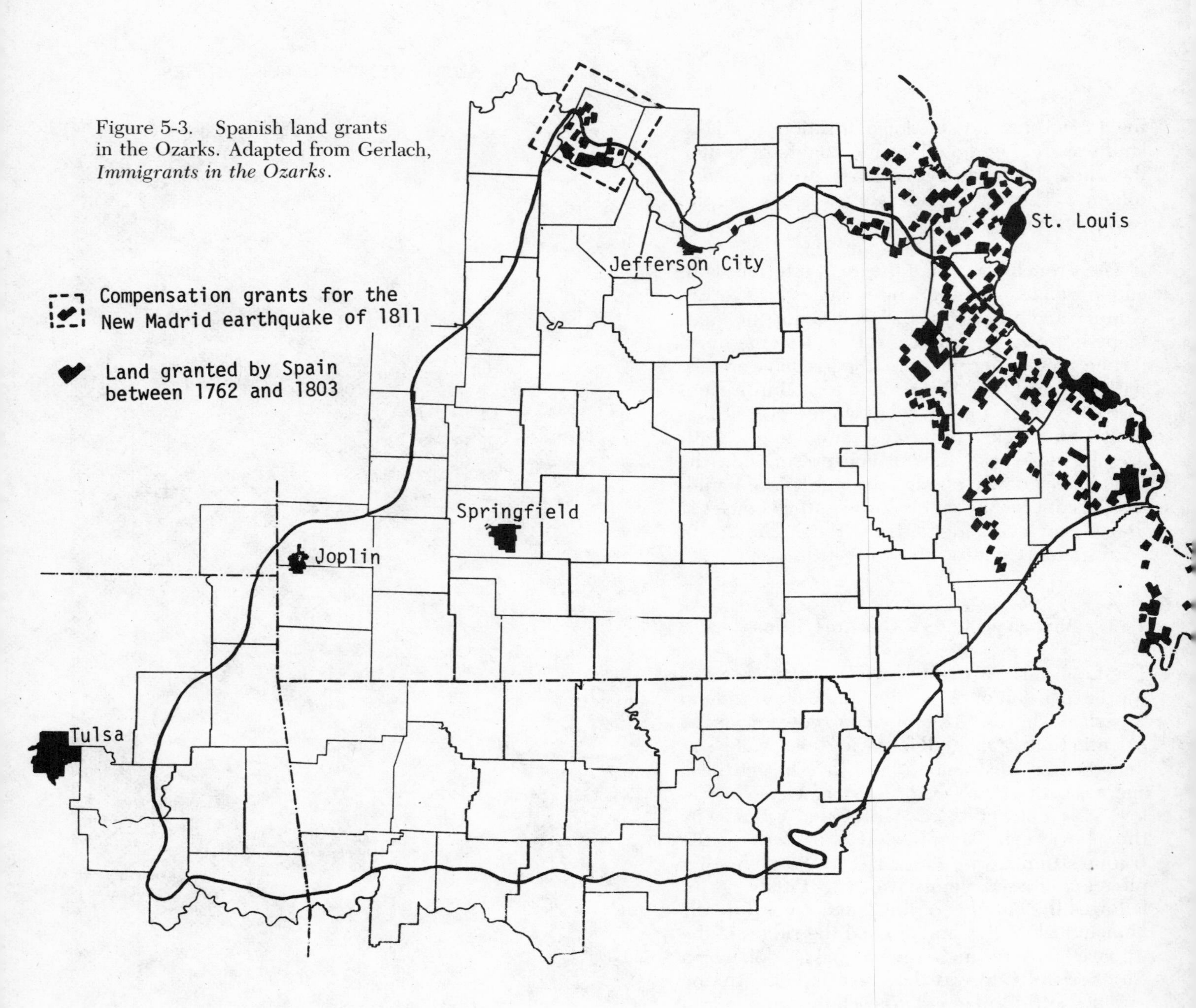

Figure 5-3. Spanish land grants in the Ozarks. Adapted from Gerlach, *Immigrants in the Ozarks*.

officials welcomed American immigrants and offered attractive land grants. The Americans, accustomed to loose government on the frontier, were willing to transfer their allegience to the Spanish king in return for large, gratuitous tracts. Because French traders boasted widely of the lead mines and fertile soils and because the prairie regions to the north were considered less suitable for agriculture, American settlers who moved down the Ohio River were quick to take up lands along the eastern Ozark border. Slave owners were attracted to the Missouri River bottoms, where soils and climate were suited to hemp and tobacco. The trans-Mississippi lands were cheaper, could be acquired in smaller tracts, and the titles were more secure than in Kentucky, where titles often were contested.

From 1796 to 1803 the Spaniards were overwhelmed with petitions for land grants. The Spanish grants, as they are still called, form a

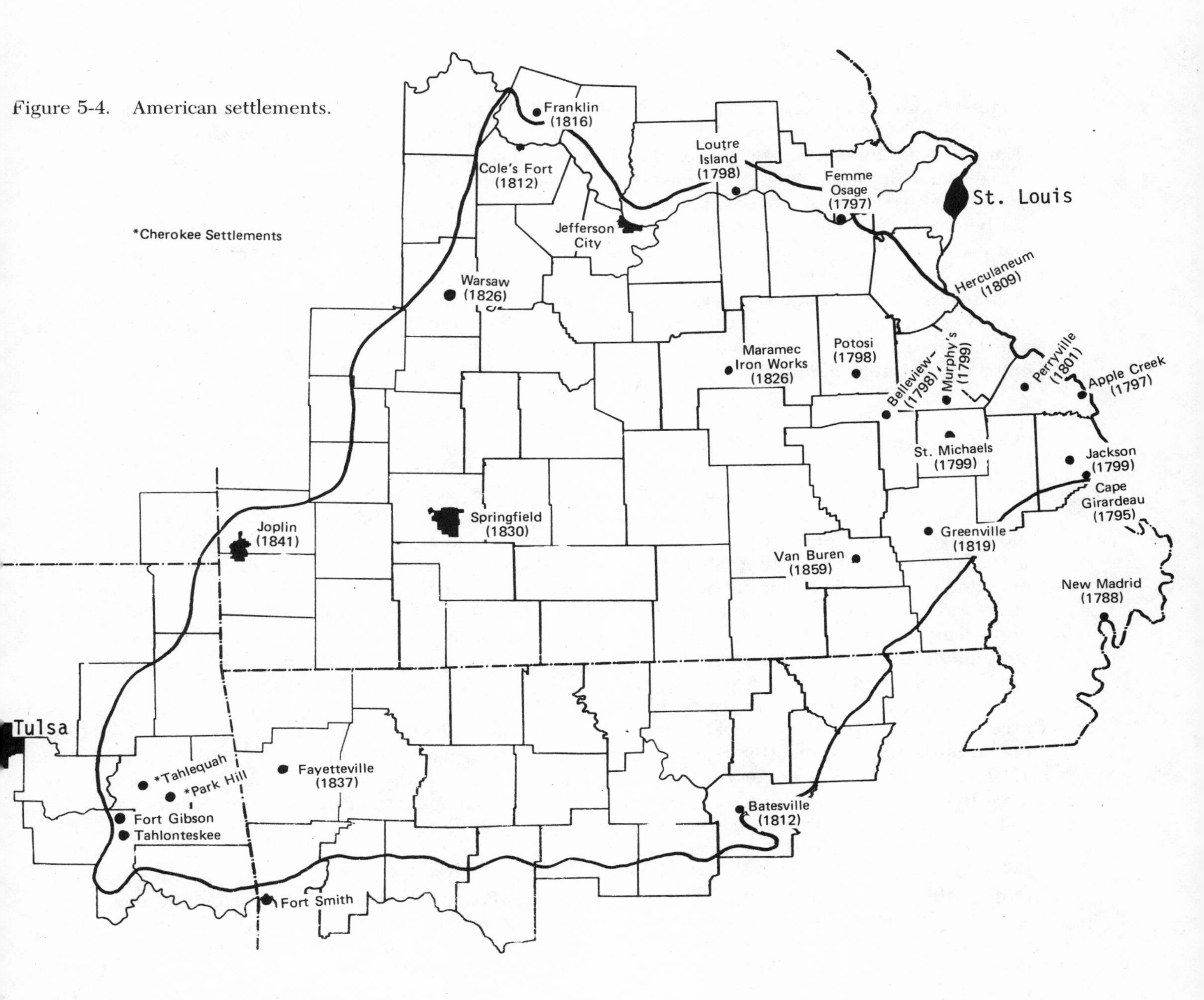

Figure 5-4. American settlements.

mosaic of irregular tracts, mostly in the Fredericktown soils, the Hagerstown loess, and alluvial soils (fig. 5-3). The better lands of the Mississippi and Missouri river borders and the St. Francois Mountains were the first to be settled. Large tracts were claimed in Arkansas, but there was far less settlement.

Many of the Spanish grants were fraudulent and were subjected to title investigations for many decades. The 1815 law that allowed settlers to relocate lands damaged or lost in the New Madrid earthquakes of 1811–12 introduced many contested titles in the Missouri Valley. Perhaps even more rapid settlement would have occurred if land titles had been more secure and the price of land ($1.25 per acre) had been lower.

The first immigrants were southerners, mainly of Scotch-Irish descent and of the yeoman farmer type, mainly poor, nonslaveholders. Most were from Tennessee, North Carolina, Virginia,

Pennsylvania, and Kentucky. Most probably were of the restless frontier type cut in the mold of Daniel Boone and Kit Carson. A wealthier group, slave owners from the South, occupied the better river bottoms, where slaves could be used to clear timber and plant fields of hemp, tobacco, and corn. A third type was the townsman, a man usually with some capital to invest in commerce or in manufacture of commodities needed on the frontier. Very often, members of this group became the leaders of communities and the organizers and initiators of things modern.

The Geography of Early American Settlement

The progression of settlement was, by and large, in the form of detached farms or small hamlets along rivers and creeks. Uplands usually were settled later because of their generally poorer soils and problems in obtaining water. Very soon there was an inhabited strip along the Mississippi and inland to the lead mines. Another strip of settlement followed the Missouri River.

One of the first American settlements was at Cape Girardeau, where farmers cleared land on a creek south of the present site of the city in 1795, on bottomland along nearby Hubble Creek in 1797, and on the Whitewater River in 1796 (fig. 5-4). By 1799 they began to occupy the upland soils, and these, derived from weathered limestones (Hagerstown soils), proved to be well suited to corn and wheat, the staple pioneer crops. Millsites were plentiful, soils were fertile, and the settlements were linked to the outside world via the Mississippi River. Settlement progressed rapidly, and by 1821 the county had a population of 7,852.

Cape Girardeau, the river port and first town to be established, had three hundred inhabitants by 1811, but its growth was eclipsed by the founding of Jackson in the midst of the fertile upland soil districts. Jackson is still the county seat, even though Cape Girardeau, after challenges to land titles were cleared, became the county's primary city.

Settlement throughout the eastern border progressed at about the same time as that in the Cape Girardeau district and in the same sequence; well-drained bottomlands were settled first, but fertile upland soils were entered nearby at the same time. In Perry County, Pennsylvanians entered the Bois Brule Bottoms of the Mississippi in 1787, and other Americans occupied the bottoms along Brazeau and Apple creeks in 1797. A large group of Kentuckians entered the upland prairie or barrens, of Perry County from 1801 to 1803.[6] Perryville, founded in 1822, became the primary settlement of the Barrens, and St. Mary's became the chief port for the district and for Mine La Motte.

Americans settled at Ste. Genevieve primarily to engage in business and commerce, particularly that connected with the lead mines to the west. However, larger numbers of Americans were attracted to the lead district in St. Francois and Washington counties. Moses Austin, an entrepreneur and metallurgist, secured a square league of land at Mine à Breton (Potosi) in 1798, and in 1799 a settlement was established. Families who accompanied Austin settled near the mines and on fertile farm lands in the Belleview Valley. Several new discoveries of lead were made in St. Francois County at Mine à Joe (Desloge), Mine à Lanye, Mine à Maneto, and Mine à la Plate. These mines, all on Big River, were the beginning of what was to become the fabulous Old Lead Belt, which produced lead and zinc ores until 1973. Many other mines were opened in Washington County. In 1819, Schoolcraft listed forty-five, of which twenty-five were in the vicinity of Potosi.

Only a few sections of the St. Francis region were suitable for agriculture, and these were discovered and settled by 1810. The reputation of the soils in the limestone basins was appreciated widely, and both the Belleview Valley and Murphy's (Farmington) were settled by 1798. The Arcadia Valley, St. Michaels (Fredericktown), and other pockets of alluvial and limestone soils were settled at about the same time. There were a few widely scattered farms farther north on the Meramec and on Plattin and Joachim creeks.

An examination of topographic maps shows that the better soils and mineral lands were claimed under Spanish grants before the Louisiana Purchase in the Missouri Ozark counties of Cape

6. Sauer, *Geography of the Ozark Highland*, pp. 105–106.

Girardeau, Perry, Ste. Genevieve, St. Francois, Washington, Madison, and Jefferson. These grants, usually rectangular in shape but only occasionally oriented in cardinal directions, are especially numerous near Jackson, Perryville, Ste. Genevieve, Farmington (Murphy's), Potosi (Mine à Breton), Fredericktown (St. Michaels), Greenville, and along the Joachim and Plattin valleys in Jefferson County (fig. 5-3).

Evidence that the Missouri River was on the main route to the west and was nearly as accessible as the Ozarks' Mississippi River Border is borne out by the fact that several American settlements had been established there before 1800. Kentuckians, notably Daniel Boone and his followers, settled in St. Charles County and southern Warren County only a few miles above the mouth of the Missouri. In 1797, Boone located on the bottoms of Femme Osage Creek in Warren County, and settlements soon followed on Tuque, La Charette, and Lost Creeks. Apparently the tributary valleys were preferred; they offered fertile soils, had good springs, and provided easy access to the Missouri River but were safe from its devastating floods. The Loutre Island settlement (1798) in Montgomery County was established in the Missouri floodplain but on a higher tract of alluvium that remained dry during floods.

The Boonslick country in Cooper and Howard counties was settled first in 1810, although Boone reportedly boiled salt at the springs as early as 1807. Its reputation spread quickly because of the timber, grass, good water, good bottomland, extensive areas of loess soils, and many salt springs. The earliest settlements were at Heath's Creek Salt Springs on the Lamine River in Cooper County and near New Franklin in Howard County. Although immigrants of diverse circumstances and origins came to the Boonslick country, the region was especially attractive to southern slaveowners.

Boonville (Cole's Fort) was established in 1812 on the south bank of the Missouri River where it makes a rectangular bend to the north. In 1816 the town of Franklin was laid out, near the present site of New Franklin, across the river from Boonville. Franklin profited from the land office established there, while Boonville was a harbor and trading town for the western Ozarks. Many other towns soon sprang up between Boonslick and the Loutre Island settlement. Bottomland could be purchased at one to five dollars an acre, and the influx of immigrants encouraged entrepreneurs to establish towns at strategic locations. Gasconade was founded at the mouth of the river of the same name as one of the proposal sites for the state capital. At the mouth of the Osage River, town promoters sold lots for Osage City; Newport occupied a similar position at the mouth of Boeuf Creek. The bustling examples of Pittsburgh, Cincinnati, and St. Louis inflamed nearly every settler with visions of wealth and business. A host of towns (Pinckney, Thorntonsburg, Missouriton, Roche au Pierce, and Columbia) were set up on the floodplain at landings.[7] Malaria and floods took their toll, and only the bluff towns, Boonville and Jefferson City, survived to prosper.

Settlements along the Ozarks' southern river route progressed much slower. In 1804, Thomas Jefferson dispatched William Dunbar and Dr. George Hunter, both natives of Natchez, Mississippi, to explore the Red and Ouachita rivers and look for some hot springs that—as reported by the Indians—lay in the mountains near the headwaters of the Ouachita. The journal of the Dunbar-Hunter trip reveals that the region through which the travelers passed was practically uninhabited. In 1806, Lieutenant James B. Wilkinson of the Zebulon M. Pike Expedition descended the Arkansas River from the Great Plains to the Mississippi in two canoes, but all he had to record concerned the topography, the forests, and the great herds of buffalo, deer, and other wild animals. Thomas Nuttall,[8] an Englishman trained in botany, geology, and geography, traveled down the Ohio and Mississippi rivers and ascended the Arkansas to a point a short distance beyond Fort Smith in 1819 and 1820. New Madrid was described as a dying French hamlet after the great earthquakes of 1811 and 1812, Arkansas Post was a settlement of thirty or forty houses scattered along almost three miles, and there were widely scattered settlements as far upriver as the garrison at Fort Smith. A spot where the Southwest Trail from St. Louis crossed the Arkansas was known as "Mr. Hogans, or the settlement of the Little

7. Ibid., p. 112.

8. Thomas Nuttall, *A Journal of Travels into the Arkansas Territory* (Ann Arbor: University Microfilms, 1966).

Rock." Cadron, a few miles from the highway west of Conway, was the third of the earliest settlements in the Arkansas Valley. By the time of Nuttall's visit Arkansas lands had caught the attention of speculators, notably William Russell of St. Louis, who had acquired large Spanish grants and became the dean of large-scale speculators.

Settlement of the Springfield Plain lagged behind that of the eastern and northern Ozark borders. Its few navigable streams, the Osage, White, and Neosho, were far from the main routes of commerce, dangerous and only seasonably navigable. The rugged hills of the interior discouraged overland travel, and the vast mineral wealth of the Joplin area was not discovered until later.

The earliest white settlement of record was at Delaware Town, southwest of Springfield, in Christian County, Missouri, where Wilson's Creek joins the James River. The settlers had followed a circuitous route from their homes on the Muskingum River in Ohio: down the Ohio, south on the Mississippi, then up the Arkansas, White, and James rivers. The region had an excellent reputation for game and was known in Tennessee as the Country of the Six Bulls (corrupted from *boils*, or springs), and it was from Tennessee that most of the early immigrants came.

The Osage River had become a navigation route by 1830, and Warsaw was transformed into a major jumping-off place for immigrants and, later, wagoneers and traders. In spring and fall, keelboats could reach Osceola, but Warsaw was the main port on the river and second in importance only to Springfield among the towns in southwest Missouri. Overland roads left the Missouri River at Boonville and Jefferson City.

Other overland routes from the Mississippi River crossed the interior Ozarks via upland divides. The most important was Ridge Road from St. Louis by way of Rolla, Lebanon, Marshfield, Springfield, Mount Vernon, Neosho, Bentonville, and Fayetteville, a route later followed closely by the Frisco (St. Louis–San Francisco) Railroad, U.S. Highway 66 and most recently by Interstate 44. A branch of this road, beginning at Ste. Genevieve and passing through Caledonia and Steelville, joined the main trail near St. James.

The pioneers were preponderantly from Tennessee, followed by Kentucky, because of easier access from these states. They were, by and large, of the same type as those who settled the Mississippi and Missouri river borders, albeit there were fewer slaveholders among them. They followed the same practices in selecting sites for homes; the first to enter the region chose bottomlands near springs and close to timber. The fertile upland prairies were settled next, and succeeding immigrants located on less choice tracts.

The settlement of Springfield was typical. John Polk Campbell, a Tennessean, visited the site in 1829, found good soils in the Kickapoo Prairie and in the small bottoms along Jordan Creek (a tributary of Wilson's Creek) and abundant good water issuing from springs along the creek bank. He returned the following year with his family and friends; several cabins were erected close by a sinkhole spring, or natural well, under the north-facing valley slope.

Isolation and poverty of resources in the interior Ozarks were the principal reasons for the slow progress of settlement there. As was noted earlier, settlement had penetrated nearly every fertile valley in the St. Francis Mountains to the margins of the Courtois Hills by 1810. This region of scanty resources served as a barrier that deflected immigration north and south. Only after the border regions of the Ozarks were well settled did immigrants begin to enter the interior.

The valleys were narrow and offered fewer possibilities for agriculture; therefore, settlement was slow in the Courtois and Osage-Gasconade hills and longest delayed in the wilderness on the Arkansas-Missouri border and the Boston Mountains. Many of those who came were unable or unwilling to meet the competition of life in more progressive regions. The central Ozarks offered few prizes to ambitious men, and, being cut off from the rest of the state, people developed slight interest in outside affairs. Only in recent years, as schools have improved and radio and television have become nearly universal, has interest grown in the history and culture of the region among the residents.

Settlements, undoubtedly temporary, were observed by Schoolcraft on the Upper Gasconade in 1818–19. Saltpeter caves were worked in the same area about the same time. In 1825, Samuel Massey opened the Maramec ore bank and in

1829 the Maramec Iron Works. By 1835 there were 50 families at the settlement. Later, several other furnaces were constructed in Crawford and Dent counties.

From 1817 to 1825, land bounties granted to soldiers of the Revolutionary War and the War of 1812 stimulated population growth in the Ozarks. Surveys of the pre-emption lands were begun in 1819, ushering in an era of speculation with the Pre-emption Act of 1820. However, because of the availability of superior lands in other districts, these laws had little influence on land purchases in the interior Ozarks.

Agricultural settlement went first to the larger and more accessible valleys and then to progressively smaller and more isolated streams. By 1825 there were settlements at Wayne County on the St. Francis River, in Ripley County on the Current River, in Oregon County on the Eleven Point River, and along the Osage, Gasconade, and Meramec rivers on the north slope of the Ozark Dome.

In Arkansas, settlement progressed in the established manner: from larger river valley to smaller tributaries and finally to upland prairies or, in the Boston Mountains, to benches and upland flats. Batesville was settled by Missourian John Reed about 1812. He built a house at the mouth of Poke (Polk) Bayou, where a fork of the Southwest Trail crossed the White River. A ferry was put into use there as early as 1818, and a land office was established about the same time. Major Jacob Wolf established a trading post at the mouth of the North Fork of the White River in 1810, and Jacob Mooney of McMinnville, Tennessee, established a community at Wildcat Shoals in Baxter County. Settlement spread up the White River and its tributaries so that by 1818, when Schoolcraft visited the White River country, settlements were well established at the mouths of Beaver and Swan creeks in Taney County, Missouri.

The Osage Indians relinquished most of their land north of the Arkansas River, including all but a small portion of the Boston Mountains, in the Treaty of Fort Clark on November 10, 1808. This area was then legally open to white settlers, but because of the abundance of land in more accessible areas, few took advantage of the opportunity to acquire tracts in the Boston Mountains. Between 1817 and 1828, Cherokee Indians were given lands in northern Arkansas in exchange for their property in the East. Since only a few whites were living in the Boston Mountains, this had little effect on settlement.

The first Americans in the Boston Mountains came by way of the Arkansas River and its larger tributaries: the White, Neosho, Illinois, and Little Red rivers. Eight families from North Carolina set up housekeeping on the south side of the Arkansas River at Crystal Hill in 1806. This settlement was so isolated that when Major Gibson of the U.S. Army stopped there in 1815, he learned that the people had not heard of the War of 1812. Kentuckians immigrated to the vicinity of Batesville about 1812. The Oil Trough (Trove) Bottoms on the White River below Batesville were regarded as prime land, and the fertility of the soils was said to rival that of the soils in the American Bottoms on the Mississippi River below St. Louis.

Data on the early residents of Newton County, Arkansas, show that the initial settlement of the county was fairly complete by 1860, having been made in the previous three decades following the Cherokee Treaty of 1828. Most of the best land was purchased in tracts of forty acres for $1.25 per acre. Very little land was claimed under military warrant, and little good land was left at the time the Homestead Act was passed in 1867. The leading states of birth of heads of families in the county were Tennessee with 126, North Carolina 48, Kentucky 21, and South Carolina 13.

The minimum price of $1.25 an acre for public lands was considered too high for uplands in the interior. The Graduation Act of 1854 stimulated land entries, however, and by 1858, 1,890,000 acres of Missouri Ozark land were sold, of which 1,140,304 brought 12.5 cents per acre and 227,940,000 acres brought 25 cents an acre. Much of the land was purchased by speculators, so the increase in population was not proportionate to the amount of land sold. Geographic factors were very important in the disposal of the public domain. The best lands were settled first, of course, and by 1867 only 1,800,000 of Missouri's 41,000,000 acres remained unclaimed.[9] All of the land granted to the University of Missouri under

9. John J. Jones, "The Morrill Lands of the University of Missouri," *Missouri Historical Review*, 51 (January 1957): 126.

John Ross, principal chief of the Cherokees at the time of removal to Oklahoma. (Courtesy Oklahoma Historical Society.)

the Morrill Act of 1862 lay in the Ozarks. What remained north of the Missouri River had by that time been picked over so much that only small tracts remained.

The region suffered heavily during the Civil War because the settlements were weak and isolated and the wild, broken hills afforded protection for lawless bands. Many of the counties on the Missouri-Arkansas boundary suffered substantial decreases in population during these troubled years.

The morphology of settlement in the interior districts was strongly shaped by kinship. The Chilton family of Shannon and Carter counties in the southern Courtois Hills of Missouri serve as an example. Thomas Boggs Chilton, the son of a Welsh immigrant, was born in Maryland in 1782 and eventually immigrated to eastern Tennessee, where he married. In 1816 he moved his family from Rhea County to New Madrid in southeast Missouri. Two years later the family moved to the mouth of Henpeck Creek on the Current River in what later became Carter County. Later, Thomas C. Chilton, a cousin, moved from Knox County, Tennessee, to a point on the Current River two miles below the Jacks Fork. A year later, in 1837, his brother, Truman Chilton, joined him, having immigrated from Boone County, Tennessee. From the same county in 1841 came Thomas T. Chilton, son of Truman Chilton, to settle near the original site of Eminence on the Jacks Fork. Many other Chiltons came to the southern Courtois Hills, mainly from counties on the Upper Tennessee River.[10]

With regard to site selection and the manner of locating fields and houses, the Chilton farmsteads, on slipoff slopes on Jacks Fork below the mouth of Storys Creek, on Current River below Blair Creek, and near the mouth of Big Shawnee Creek, are no different from those of contemporary and later immigrants. Very often an entire creek valley or hollow would be taken up by an extended family. Surname sequences in the manuscript census of Reynolds County affirm that kinship was important in the settlement process. The surnames of heads of households in one sequence reads: Satterfield, Martin, Parker, Parker, Asher, Satterfield, Parker, Bay, Satterfield, Robinnet, Asher. That this was commonplace is further indicated by examples from the Shannon County manuscript census: Crabtree, Crabtree, Lewis, Summers, Summers, Summers, Lewis, McDonald, Lewis.

The Cherokees

The history of the settlement of the Oklahoma Ozarks is largely the story of the removal of the

10. Harbert L. Clendenen. "Settlement Morphology of the Southern Courtois Hills, Missouri, 1820–1860" (Ph.D. diss., Louisiana State University, 1973, pp. 28–29).

Rose Cottage, home of Chief John Ross, at Park Hill near Tahlequah, Oklahoma. (Courtesy Oklahoma Historical Society.)

Five Civilized Tribes—Cherokees, Chickasaws, Choctaws, Creeks, Seminoles—from their ancestral homes in the southern Appalachian uplands. The vanguard of these tribes, six or seven thousand Choctaws and Chickasaws from northern Mississippi and West Tennessee moved up the Arkansas Valley in 1832 to settle south of the Arkansas in what is now Oklahoma. These Indians had been stricken with cholera and "had to be driven almost like sheep."

The real tragedy, however, involved the removal of the Eastern Cherokees, who occupied a large area in southeast Tennessee, Alabama, western North Carolina, and northwest Georgia. They numbered more than 16,500 by official count in 1835, many of them living as prosperous farmers in houses that often had two stories and were well furnished and in the happy possession not only of devoted missionaries but of a written language, with books and journals printed in it since 1828. In 1829 the Cherokees owned some 22,000 cattle, 1,300 slaves, 2,000 spinning wheels, 700 looms, 31 gristmills, 10 sawmills, 8 cotton gins, and 18 schools. They had never recognized as full members of their tribe the 3,000 Cherokees who went west to Arkansas in 1818,

The Trail of Tears, a painting by E. James. (Courtesy Oklahoma Historical Society.)

under the terms of Andrew Jackson's 1817 treaty. They had foreseen, rightly, that the early removal was but part of a deep-laid government plan to force all Indians from the country.

The discovery of gold near Dahlonega, Georgia, brought on a rapid series of events that led to Cherokee removal. The State of Georgia now declared, despite the Cherokee Treaty of 1817, that it had the right to seize all Cherokee lands and property. Since no Cherokee was accepted as a witness in court, this was the beginning of the end. A huge rift appeared in the Cherokees' ranks as they were driven from their homes by the force of armed mobs. One faction was in favor of selling the tribe's Georgia lands to the state and moving to Indian Territory, where the Arkansas Cherokees had preceded them by 1828. This was the compromise group led by John Ridge, the best orator in the tribe, and Elias Boudinot, the most learned and intelligent of the Cherokees. It was opposed by John Ross, who lived where Chattanooga stands today and who insisted that the Cherokees' lands, for which the United States was ready to pay five million dollars were worth at least twenty million. All this was in keeping with Ross's character; he was only a quarter Indian, the son of a Scottish trader and a half-blood woman.

Through an emissary who was not at all averse to bribery, about five hundred members of the tribe were induced to assemble, and on December 29, 1835, they signed a treaty in which they sold all their lands for the sum originally proposed and agreed to go west. The first group to leave consisted of about 600 comfortably fixed members of the Treaty party. Major Ridge, father of John Ridge and the most politically powerful of the treaty signers, departed March 3, 1837, with his family, eighteen slaves, and 466 other Cherokees, half of them children. They traveled by flatboat down the Tennessee River from Ross's Landing to the Mississippi and then traveled up the Arkansas River to Fort Smith, arriving there on March 27. Dr. John S. Young, who took charge of the movement, ordered about 150 bushels of cornmeal, 78 barrels of flour, and 12,000 pounds of bacon stowed on the boats to feed the travelers along the way.

The Cherokees arrived in time to see the bottomlands bright with redbud blossoms that ranged in color from pink to purple. Dogwood

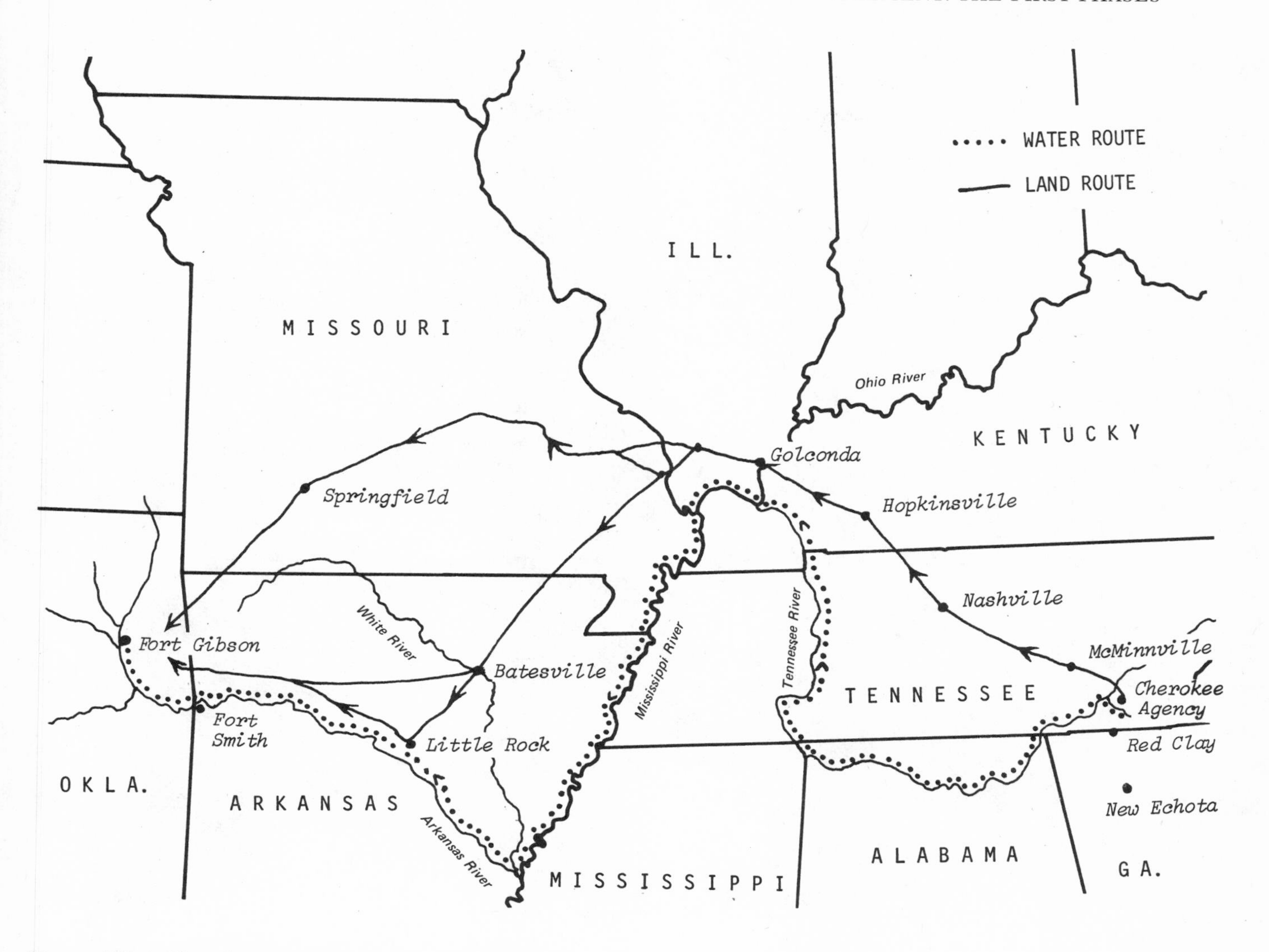

Figure 5-5. Cherokee migration routes, 1838–39.

bloomed in gleaming white among the oaks, which, in late bud, were just taking on a greenish hue. Ridge settled at the mouth of Honey Creek, which rises in Arkansas, flows for a brief stretch through the corner of Missouri, and turns in Oklahoma at Southwest City before it flows into the Neosho, or Grand River. Ridge put his slaves to work, bought stock and farming equipment, and soon had the beginnings of a splendid farm.

The movement of the Ridge party contrasts sharply with that of the main body of Cherokees, under the supervision of John Ross, over the Trail of Tears. When the latter refused to leave their homes, the U.S. Army was called in, and in the winter of 1837 and 1838 federal troops rounded up all but a few hundred, who had retreated into the inaccessible fastness of the Great Smokies, and put them into what would today be called concentration camps along the Tennessee River. By this time even John Ross realized that nothing further could be done and agreed to depart, if it could be done without further interference by the Army. The Cherokees were unable to leave until the end of the very hot, very dry summer of 1838.

Murrell Mansion at Park Hill near Tahlequah, Oklahoma, was built by George Murrell, white trader and supporter of John Ross. Many of the house's furnishings were imported from France. (Courtesy Oklahoma Historical Society.)

Now about fifteen hundred strong, they left in large groups in wagons, on horseback, or on foot, taking a winding route, by way of Nashville, cross western Kentucky and through Illinois to cross the Mississippi at Cape Girardeau (fig. 5-5). There they took several routes across northern Arkansas and southern Missouri to their destination in northeast Oklahoma. This was the Trail of Tears, witnessed by a few white travelers, who marveled at the Indians stoicism and discipline. The journey cost about four thousand lives in all and was not completed until March, 1839. Along the way the Cherokees buried several renowned old chiefs, innumerable infants, and Ross's own Cherokee wife, Quatie, who sickened aboard the steamboat that carried her husband and was buried at Little Rock.

When they arrived in Indian Territory, members of the Treaty party accepted the government of the Western Cherokees as their own. There was no written constitution and only a few written laws. Twice a year the Old Settlers met in council at Tahlonteskee, their capital, where, in a small council house, they elected their chiefs and other national officers. The coming of the Ross faction, later known as the Late Immigrants, created an integration problem. Under their persuasion the capital was moved to Tahlequah in 1839, and since they outnumbered the Old Settlers and the Treaty party by more than two to one, their leaders soon gained control of the government. On June 22, 1839, three parties of the Late Immigrants, bent on revenge on leaders of the Treaty party, murdered John Ridge, Elias Boudinot, and Major Ridge. This led to reprisals and counterreprisals, factional and family feuds, and bitter political struggles among the Cherokees for decades.[11]

The migration of the Cherokees to the Oklahoma Ozarks was part of the final chapter of the primary phase of immigration. The settlement of the Ozark Upland, which had begun with the eighteenth-century French settlements, was complete by 1850. Density maps (fig. 5-6) show that the population moved inward from the Ozarks' major rivers: the Mississippi, the Missouri, and the Arkansas. The areas in St. Francois and Washington counties in Missouri were settled early, as were the more favorable agricultural lands. The heaviest early settlement occurred in the more accessible places; this was particularly true of areas near the land offices at St. Louis, Frankfort, and Springfield in Missouri and around Batesville in Arkansas. It is probably not too much to say that settlement followed the surveyor's chain and compass. Some of the early surveyors became rich by purchasing the best lands for resale to speculators.[12] As new lands were surveyed and information concerning them became available, settlers were encouraged to spread outward from the heavily populated sections and into the remote interior.

11. Morris L. Wardell, *A Political History of the Cherokee Nation, 1838–1907* (Norman: University of Oklahoma Press, 1977).

12. Josiah H. Shinn, *Pioneers and Makers of Arkansas* (Baltimore: Genealogical Publishing Company, 1967), p. 107.

Fort Gibson military garrison in the Oklahoma Ozarks. Among its distinguished visitors and officers were Robert E. Lee, Jefferson Davis, Sam Houston, Zachary Taylor, George Catlin, and Washington Irving. (Courtesy Oklahoma Historical Society.)

Character of the Immigrants

It has been noted that most of the American immigrants were of Scotch-Irish stock. They were experienced frontiersmen; independent, resourceful, strong, familiar with frontier inconveniences, possessed of an amazing knowledge of ways to wrest a living from the forest, and accustomed to facing hardships of arduous travel or starvation or the dangers of Indian raids. The Scotch-Irish were known as Ulstermen, Presbyterian Irish, or, before 1812, when the first large groups of Irish Catholics began to arrive in America, simply the Irish. After large numbers of Irish Catholics arrived, it was necessary to distinguish between the two groups, so the immigrants from northern Ireland were known as the Scotch-Irish.

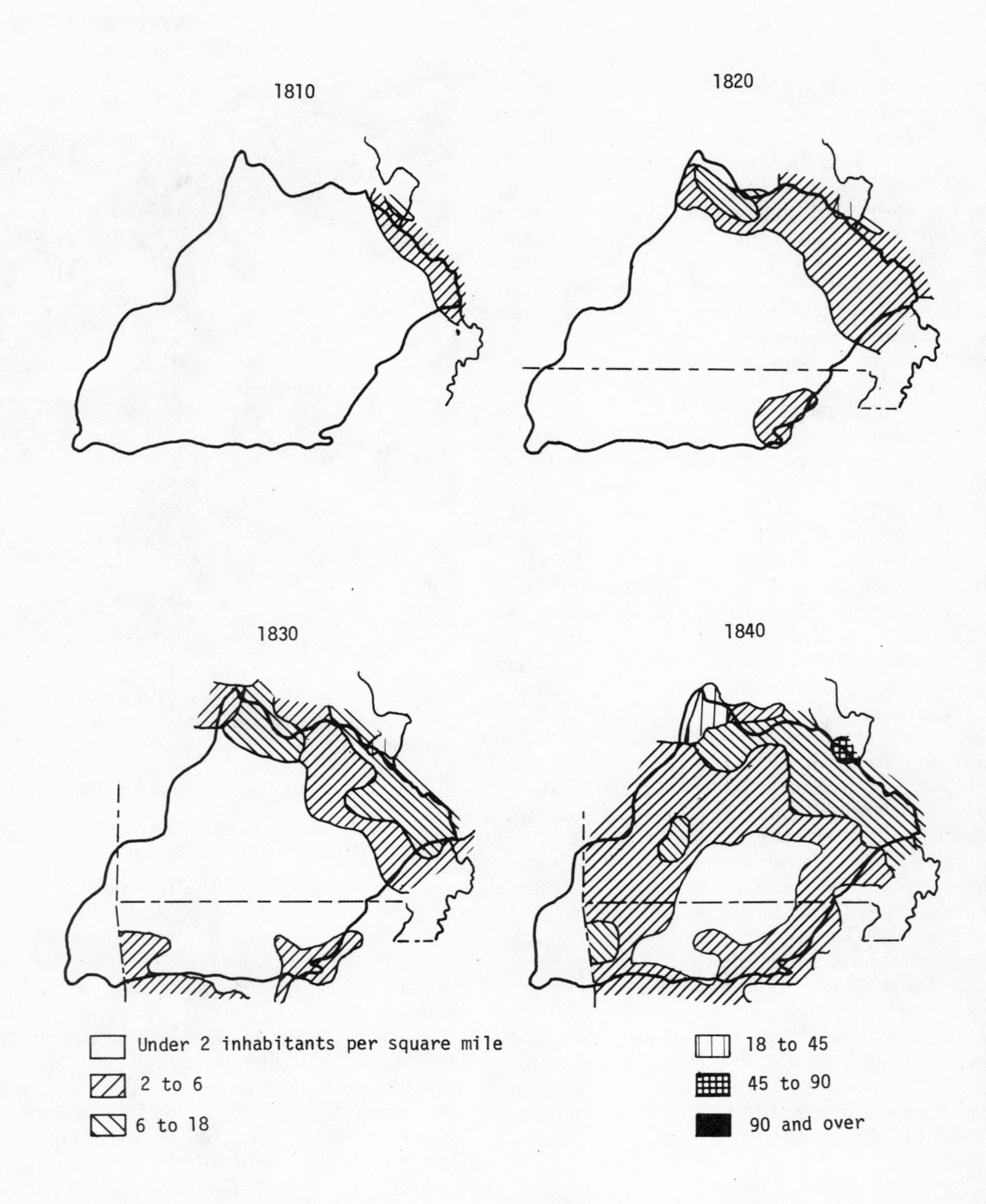

Figure 5-6. Ozark population density, 1810–40.

Better people to subdue a frontier could not have been recruited. They were descended from Lowland Scots who immigrated to Ulster Plantation in Northern Ireland in the early years of the seventeenth-century at a time when the first Virginia plantations were being established. The Scots who flocked into Ulster carried with them long experience in dealing with the predatory Celtic clansmen in north Scotland. The Lowlanders were accustomed to regarding the clansmen as raiders, pillagers, cattle thieves, and murderers. Hardened by perpetual contact with barbarism, the Lowland Scots had no scruples about making merciless reprisals. The people were hard; the law was hard.

At the time the Scots immigrated to Ulster, Ireland was a wilderness of forests, bogs, and peat barrens inhabited by Irish clansmen whom the Scots called the Irishes. The Scots settled in towns, around castles, and made use of a small amount of adjacent land; the Irishes stayed in the back country. The guerrilla war that ensued between these two hardy groups has continued to the present, with only brief times of relative peace between major conflicts. It was a proverb that the Irish could never be tamed while the leaves are on the trees, meaning that winter was the only season in which they could be pursued in the woods. The settlers were surrounded by a hostile population, with almost daily risks from raiders and in almost constant alarm of a general uprising. Long familiarity with the raiding Highland Scots enabled the Scotch-Irish to cope with the Irishes, who wandered with their cattle all the summer in the hill country and all the winter in the woods. The Scotch-Irish held their ground, throve, and spread, gradually giving Ulster a Scottish character.

A people accustomed to pacification of wild Irish clans and inured to the hardships of the Irish wilderness were natural-born frontiersmen, and so they were when they emigrated to North America. From Nova Scotia to the West Indies, the Scotch-Irish were among the frontier vanguard. They became the chief frontiersmen of Maine, New Hampshire, and Massachusetts; in the South they moved from the Tidewater settlements into the Piedmont; and from their main base in Pennsylvania and Maryland they crowded into the western counties of Pennsylvania along Braddock's Road and along the major river routes. They engulfed the Quaker settlements and crowded south down the Great Valley into western Virginia and eastern Tennessee. Following the trail cut by Daniel Boone via Cumberland Gap, the Scotch-Irish entered Middle Tennessee and the Bluegrass region of Kentucky. A flood of Scotch-Irish descended on the new states in Transappalachia as additional routes through the Appalachian Mountains were perfected.

The Scotch-Irish attained wide acclaim as Indian fighters; accusations that they were cruel to the Indians go back to the beginnings of Scotch-Irish settlement. The Scotch-Irish frontiersmen were descended from a people familiar with hostile neighbors, and they were accustomed to rendering cruel punishment in kind. When scalps were taken by Indians, the frontiersman would retaliate by taking Indian scalps; in Massachusetts a bounty of one hundred pounds sterling was placed on them. During the Indian Wars, the Transappalachian region became a no-man's-land beset by general guerrilla warfare. The Scotch-Irish, by historic tradition and temperament, were well suited to the conflict.

Much of the information concerning the Scotch-Irish immigrants to the Ozarks comes from family diaries and a few early histories. The detailed reports found in the manuscript census are an additional source. Morrow's study of the manuscript census of 1870 for Richwoods Township in Miller County, Missouri, provides an overview of the population at the end of the primary phase of settlement.[13] Demographically, the Ozark frontier had many similarities with today's Third World countries. There were 2,283 people in the township, most of them under forty years of age. In fact, only one person in eight (12.5 per cent) was over the age of forty, and 63 per cent of the population was twenty years old or younger. There were only two octogenerians in the entire township. Three-fourths of the population was literate; but among the people over thirty years of age the illiteracy rate increased to more than 30 per cent. The average household had 5.3 persons, but the households ranged in size from 1

13. Lynn Morrow, "A Preliminary Survey of Richwoods Township, Miller County, Missouri, 1870."

Ozark pioneer couple. (Courtesy Arkansas History Commission.)

person to 13. Three-fourths of the residents had migrated from Tennessee and Kentucky or from other parts of Missouri, but nineteen states provided immigrants. There were very few foreign immigrants: three from England, one from Ireland, and one from Russia. Most of the people were farmers. The occupation breakdown yields 199 farmers, 17 farm laborers, 15 domestic servants, 12 widow ladies, 11 housekeepers, 6 teachers, 3 blacksmiths, 3 physicians, 2 dry-goods merchants, 2 store workers, 2 sawyers, and 1 each of the following: shoemaker, harnessmaker, retired farmer, miller, and minister of the Gospel. There was relatively little wealth aside from the land; more than 30 per cent of the population listed between six hundred and one thousand dollars as the value of their real estate, and only seven residents had land holdings assessed at more than two thousand dollars. As for personal property, the largest number of people had between three and four hundred dollars' worth, so that the average settler was worth perhaps one thousand dollars to fifteen hundred dollars in terms of real and personal property.

At the close of the primary phase of immigration, then, the Ozarks was inhabited by a hardy breed of Scotch-Irish immigrants who were engaged mainly in subsistance farming. Among them were a few artificers, professional men, and preachers. They were poor but nearly self-sufficient and skilled at living under isolated conditions.

Negro Population

The Negro population of the Ozarks has never been large, but the largest numbers of Negroes entered the region during the primary phase of settlement. In fact, Negroes were brought to the Ozarks as slaves by the French in the eighteenth-century. It is reported that Philippe Renault purchased slaves in Santo Domingo in 1719 to provide laborers for the mines to be opened in the eastern Ozarks.[14] The French at Ste. Genevieve owned slaves to do the rugged work connected with tilling fields and digging lead in the mining districts. In 1819, Nuttall expressed surprise that a small French settlement in the Arkansas Valley was not self-sufficient in foodstuffs, since the residents owned slaves.

The American settlers brought their slaves with them, so the Negro population of the Ozarks, in nearly every section, was contemporary with the first white settlements. The wealthier planters, who possessed slaves also could afford the most fertile and most accessible lands; for this reason, slaves were not numerous in the interior sections of the Ozarks. The largest numbers were found in the border districts, the Missouri Valley, the mineral area in St. Francois and Washington counties, and the Arkansas Valley. By 1860, when the Negro population reached its zenith, Negroes accounted for slightly more than 10 per cent of the population in these counties. Only a few interior areas were fertile enough or sufficiently well settled to attract slave owners. The most notable areas were in Greene County, Missouri, and in Washington and Benton counties in Arkansas. Then, too, the Cherokees who settled the Oklahoma Ozarks owned several hundred slaves.

It is difficult to determine slaveholders' feelings toward their bondsmen. Wills and other documents, however, indicate that the Negroes were considered as property.[15] From a physical standpoint, slaves probably received reasonably good treatment. The family of George Washington Carver, the noted botanist, were slaves on a farm close to Diamond, Missouri. Apparently, they were treated relatively well by the owners.

Most hiring contracts stipulated that the slave be properly maintained. Samuel Massey, superintendent of the Maramec Iron Works near present-day St. James, Missouri, regularly leased or owned fifteen to twenty-five slaves from 1828 until the Civil War. They were assigned the heaviest and dirtiest work connected with digging and hauling the ore. Most of the hired Negroes at the ironworks belonged to masters living in counties bordering the Missouri River. The standard price was $100 per year and maintenance for good unskilled hands, $120 and up for skilled hands, and $25 to $50 for women and girls who worked as domestic servants in the boardinghouse.[16] The contracts protected both sides with legal provisions. If a slave ran away or died, the ironworks paid only for the time actually worked. The owner could collect damages if a slave was injured or died because of neglect or cruelty.

In some cases, probably rare, slaves were treated almost like members of the family. Jacob Mooney, one of the first settlers in Baxter County, Arkansas, brought in several Lungeons, presumably the mixed Negro and Cherokee people known as Melungeons in the southern Appalachians. Mooney was ostracized for living with these "foreigners." It is reported that he permitted his men to marry Quapaw women who lived in the area.[17] His actions were never forgiven; after he and his men had died and the cemetery was fenced, Mooney's grave and the graves of the mixed bloods who lived with him were left outside.

The New South phase in Ozarks history was a time of declining Negro population. Slavery had been abolished; possessing no land or property, and faced with little opportunity for employment, many of the Negroes moved to cities in the North. The conditions that obtained for them in the Ozarks were the same as throughout the South, except there were fewer social ties to cause them

14. Henry Rowe Schoolcraft, *A View of the Lead Mines of Missouri* . . . (New York: C. Wiley and Co., 1819), p. 15.

15. Phillip V. Scarpino, "Slavery in Callaway County, Missouri: 1845–1855, Part II," *Missouri Historical Review*, 71 (April 1977): 267.

16. James D. Norris, *Frontier Iron: The Story of the Maramec Iron Works: 1826–1876* (Madison: State Historical Society of Wisconsin, 1964), p. 39.

17. Mary Ann Messick, *History of Baxter County, 1873–1973* (Mountain Home, Ark.: Mountain Home Chamber of Commerce, 1973), p. 7.

to remain in their home areas. In the rural areas the decline in Negro population occurred mainly as slow attrition; as young Negroes moved away, and as their grandparents died, many Ozark counties became pure white.

There were troubled times for Negroes after the Civil War. Lynchings occurred in Springfield in 1859, 1871, and 1906, all for alleged rapes, The 1906 lynching of three young Negroes took place in the public square and received publicity throughout the Ozarks. The *Springfield Republican* carried seven-column headlines on its front page:

> THREE NEGROES LYNCHED BY MAD MOB—INFURIATED MOB OF WHITES TAKE AN ALLEGED MURDERER AND THE ASSAILANTS OF A BOLIVAR GIRL FROM THE COUNTY JAIL AND STRING THEM UP TO THE ELECTRIC LIGHT TOWER IN THE PUBLIC SQUARE—JAIL DOORS ARE BATTERED DOWN WITH HEAVY TIMBERS AND THE PLEADING BLACKS ARE HALF CARRIED, HALF DRAGGED TO THE SCENE OF EXECUTION—WHEN LIFE IS EXTINCT THE MOB IN ITS THIRST FOR VENGEANCE APPLIES THE TORCH—HOWLING, SURGING MASS OF HUMANITY CROWDS THE PUBLIC SQUARE AND APPLAUDS THE LYNCHERS[18]

After this ghastly event there was a great deal of anti-Negro sympathy in the rural counties, which undoubtedly contributed to Negro migration.

Between 1860 and 1930 the Negro population in the Ozarks declined from an estimated 62,000 persons to 31,000. In 1930 six Ozarks counties had no Negroes, and in most of the remaining interior sections, there were no more than 10 in each county. It was possible for young whites to grow to manhood without seeing a Negro, and octogenarians may have seen black people on only one or two occasions. Until recently there was considerable discrimination toward Negroes in eating establishments, movie theaters, and other public and private gatherings. A few towns sported signs at their city limits: "Nigger, don't let the sun set on your heels here." There were few racial problems, however, because there was really no reason for a Negro to stop off in such towns.

18. *Springfield Republican*, April 15, 1906.

The current distribution of black population in the Ozarks is not unlike the pattern established during primary immigration; the border counties have the largest numbers, and there are very few blacks in the interior rural counties. Only five counties—Cole and Boone in Missouri, Faulkner and Conway in Arkansas and Muskogee in Oklahoma—had more than 2,500 blacks in 1970. All of these counties are on the border. The largest black populations in the interior counties are found in Greene County (Springfield) and Pulaski County, which includes the soldiers at Fort Leonard Wood. The total black population of the Ozarks in 1970 was estimated at 26,758, of whom 19,938 or 75 per cent, were in the border counties.

Selected References

Bench, Cecil C. "Population Distribution in Early Missouri." Master's thesis, Clark University, 1971.

Britton, Wiley, *Pioneer Life in Southwest Missouri*. Kansas City, Mo.: Smith-Grieves Co., 1929.

Campbell, Rex R., and Baker, Thomas E. *Negroes in Missouri—1970: An Analysis of the Racial Characteristics of the Missouri Population Using the 1970 Census of Population*. Jefferson City: Missouri Commission on Human Rights, 1972.

Clandenen, Harbert L. "Settlement Morphology of the Southern Courtois Hills, Missouri, 1820–1860." Ph.D. dissertation, Louisiana State University, 1973.

Collins, Charles D. "Settlement Geography of Stone County Missouri, 1800–1860, With Emphasis on Rural Aspects." Master's thesis, University of Arkansas-Fayetteville, 1971.

Doran, Michael F. "Negro Slaves of the Five Civilized Tribes." *Annals of the Association of American Geography* 68 (September 1978): 335–50.

Duffner, Robert William. "Slavery in Missouri River Counties, 1820–1865." Ph.D. dissertation, University of Missouri-Columbia, 1974.

Flanders, Robert. "Shannon County of the Ozarks," Developmental Grant Proposal, Southwest Missouri State University, Springfield, 1977.

Fletcher, John Gould. *Arkansas*. Chapel Hill: University of North Carolina Press, 1947.

Ford, Henry J. *The Scotch-Irish in America*. New York: Arno Press, 1969.

Gerlach, Russel L. *Immigrants in the Ozarks: A Study in Ethnic Geography*. Columbia, Mo.: University of Missouri Press, 1976.

Hart, John Fraser. "The Middle West." *Annals of the Association of American Geographers*, vol. 62, June 1972.

Haswell, A. W., ed. *The Ozark Region: Its History and Its People*. Vol. 1. Springfield, Mo.: Interstate Historical Society, 1917.

Henderson, John R. "The Cultural Landscape of French Settlement in the American Bottom." Master's thesis, Illinois State University, 1966.

Hewes, Leslie. "The Oklahoma Ozarks as the Land of the Cherokees," *Geographical Review* 32 (1942): 269–81.

Houck, Louis. *A History of Missouri*. Vols. 1, 2, and 3. Chicago: R. R. Donnelly and Sons Company, 1908.

Jones, John J. "The Morrill Lands of the University of Missouri," *Missouri Historical Review* 51 (January 1957): 126–38.

Lightfoot, B. B. "The Cherokee Immigrants in Missouri, 1837–1839," *Missouri Historical Review* 56 (January 1962): 156–67.

Messick, Mary Ann. *History of Baxter County, 1873–1973*. Mountain Home, Ark.: Mountain Home Chamber of Commerce, 1973.

Meyer, Duane. *The Heritage of Missouri: A History*. St. Louis: State Publishing Co., 1970.

Morrow, Lynn. "A Preliminary Survey of Richwoods Township, Miller County, Missouri, 1870." Paper for Historical Geography of the Ozarks, Department of Geography and Geology, Southwest Missouri State University, Springfield, 1977.

Norris, James D. *Frontier Iron: The Story of the Maramec Iron Works, 1826–1876*. Madison: State Historical Society of Wisconsin, 1964.

Nuttall, Thomas. *A Journal of Travels Into the Arkansas Territory*. Ann Arbor: University Microfilms, 1966.

Reid, John P. *A Law of Blood: The Primitive Law of the Cherokee Nation*. New York: New York University Press, 1970.

Ronnebaum, Chelidonia. "Population and Settlement in Missouri, 1804–1820." Master's thesis, University of Missouri-Columbia, 1936.

Sauer, Carl O. *The Geography of the Ozark Highland of Missouri*. The Geographic Society of Chicago Bulletin no. 7, Chicago: University of Chicago Press, 1920.

Scarpino, Phillip V. "Slavery in Callaway County, Missouri: 1845–1855, Part II," *Missouri Historical Review* 71 (April 1977): 266–83.

Schoolcraft, Henry Rowe. *A View of the Lead Mines of Missouri Including Some Observations on the Mineralogy, Geology, Geography, Antiquities, Soil, Climate, Population, and Productions of Missouri and Arkansas, and Other Sections of the Western Country.*. New York: C. Wiley and Co., 1819.

Shinn, Josiah H. *Pioneers and Makers of Arkansas*. Baltimore: Genealogical Publishing Co., 1967.

Shoemaker, Floyd C. *Missouri Day by Day*. Vols. 1 and 2. Columbia, Mo.: State Historical Society of Missouri, 1942.

Springfield Republican, April 15, 1906.

Walz, Robert B. "Migration Into Arkansas, 1834–1880." Ph.D. dissertation, University of Texas, 1958.

Wardell, Morris L. *A Political History of the Cherokee Nation, 1838–1907*. Norman: University of Oklahoma Press, 1977.

Wilkins, Thurman. *Cherokee Tragedy*. London: Macmillan Co., 1970.

Woodward, Grace Steele. *The Cherokees*. Norman: University of Oklahoma Press, 1963.

6.

Settlement: The Later Stages

As has been noted, the earliest settlements in Missouri were along the Mississippi, Missouri, and Arkansas rivers, and until the latter half of the nineteenth century these rivers and their tributaries were the main avenues for immigration. The American population of the Ozarks was largely from the states lying immediately to the east, from the Upper South and Lower Middle West; it has been noted that many were of Scotch-Irish decent. The rank of states according to origin of immigrants to Missouri in 1860: Kentucky (99,814), Tennessee (73,954), Virginia (53,957), Ohio (35,389), Indiana (30,463), and Illinois (30,138). The mountain man from Middle and East Tennessee was especially attracted to the Ozarks, where land was cheaper. Manuscript census records show that the settlers in Shannon, Dent, and Carter counties between 1820 and 1860 originated in Tennessee (284), Illinois (171), Kentucky (63), Arkansas (54), Indiana (48), Alabama (38), Virginia (11), and North Carolina (4). Records for Newton County, Arkansas in the Boston Mountains show a preponderance of settlers from Tennessee. The leading states of origin in 1850 were Tennessee (126), North Carolina (48), Kentucky (21), South Carolina (13), Alabama (9), Virginia (9), and Missouri (8).

After the Civil War and with resumption of peaceful conditions, a new era of railroad construction began, and this stimulated immigration (figs. 6-1 and 6-2). The railroads provided improved connections with the states north of the Ohio River, and by 1890 the Lower Middle West had replaced the Upper South as the leading source of immigrants to Missouri. Illinois (135,585) was the top supplier, followed by Kentucky (99,985), Ohio (84,907), Indiana (70,563), and Tennessee (67,591).

The background of many immigrants to the Ozarks in the post–Civil War era differed from that of the pioneer people. They were the carriers of the New South culture: government officials; entrepreneurs; veterans of the Civil War; capitalists interested in mining, lumbering, railroad building and town founding; land speculators; resort builders; and venturers of assorted types who would take hold of almost any project that promised rewards. Compared with the primary immigrants from the southern uplands, the newcomers were urbane, educated, and progressive. Some lingered only a while before seeking more promising opportunities elsewhere; most found a permanent place in Ozark society. Whether they stayed briefly or

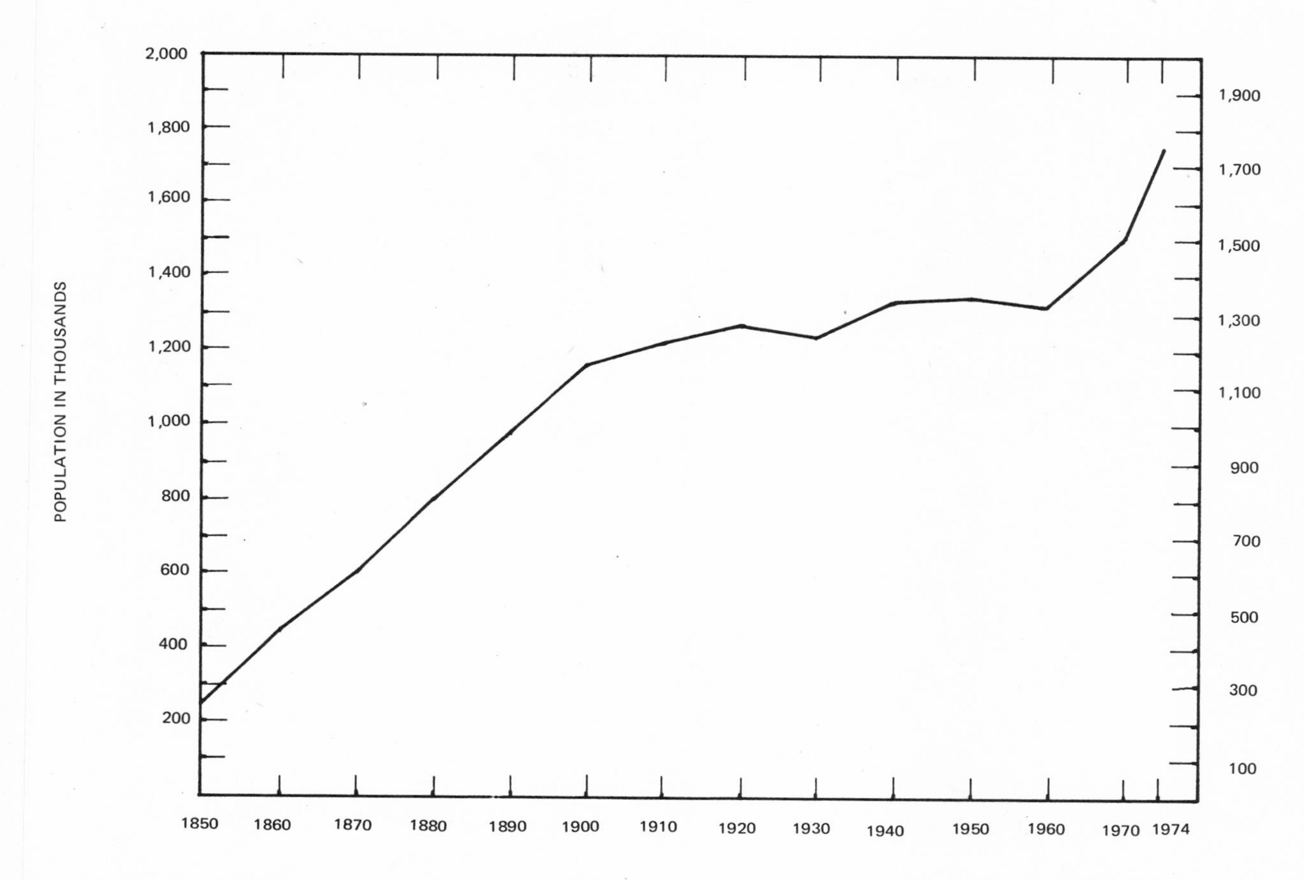

Figure 6-1. Population trends in the Ozarks. The graph includes all of parts of 93 counties in Missouri, Arkansas, Oklahoma, and Kansas. The population of border counties was apportioned on the basis of the percentage of the county within the Ozarks.

permanently, however, all of them helped to shape the culture of the Ozarks in the areas where they settled.

Foreign Blood

Among the post–Civil War immigrants were foreign people, most of them fresh from Ellis Island, who carried their own European customs and traditions. In fact, there were some foreign groups among the first settlers, and the story of foreign immigration to the Ozarks goes back a generation before the Civil War, when large numbers of Germans settled in the hills bordering the Missouri and Mississippi rivers. Gerlach[1] has studied the immigrant groups most recently and most exhaustively. He found that the culture of the several immigrant groups has persisted to the present, depending on their numbers and the strength of their traditions. The geographic patterns of language, religion, education, and land use were shaped, in part, by the foreign imprint.

Germans were the only major non-English-speaking people in the Ozarks. The Polish and Bohemian settlements of Franklin and Gasconade

1. Russel L. Gerlach, *Immigrants in the Ozarks: A Study in Ethnic Geography* (Columbia: The University of Missouri Press, 1976).

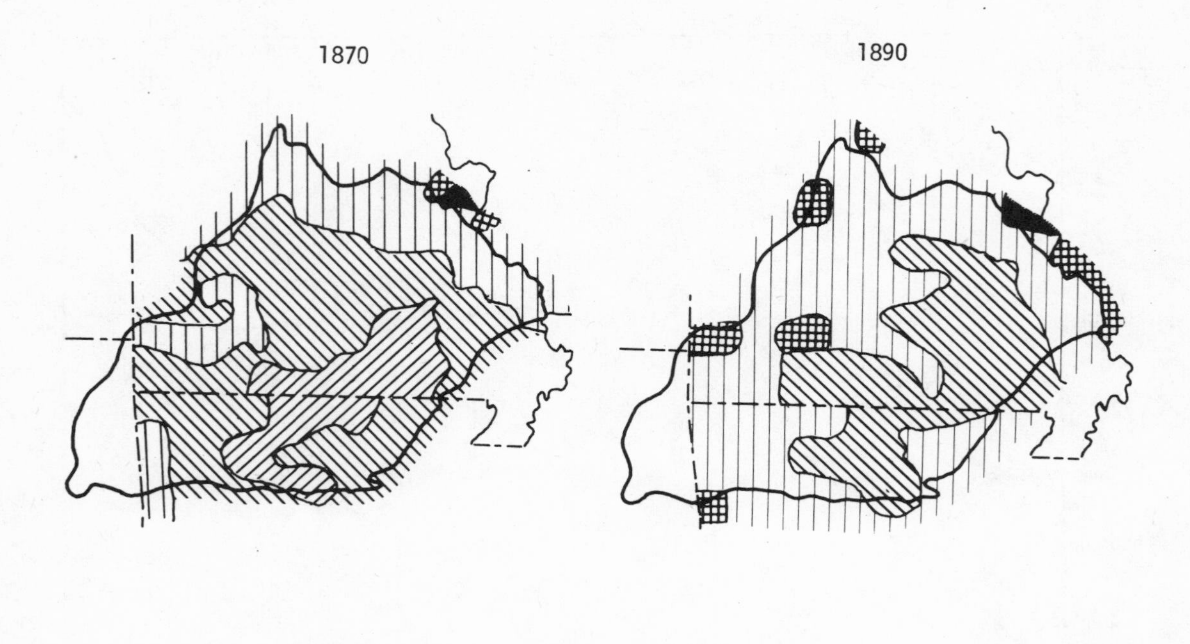

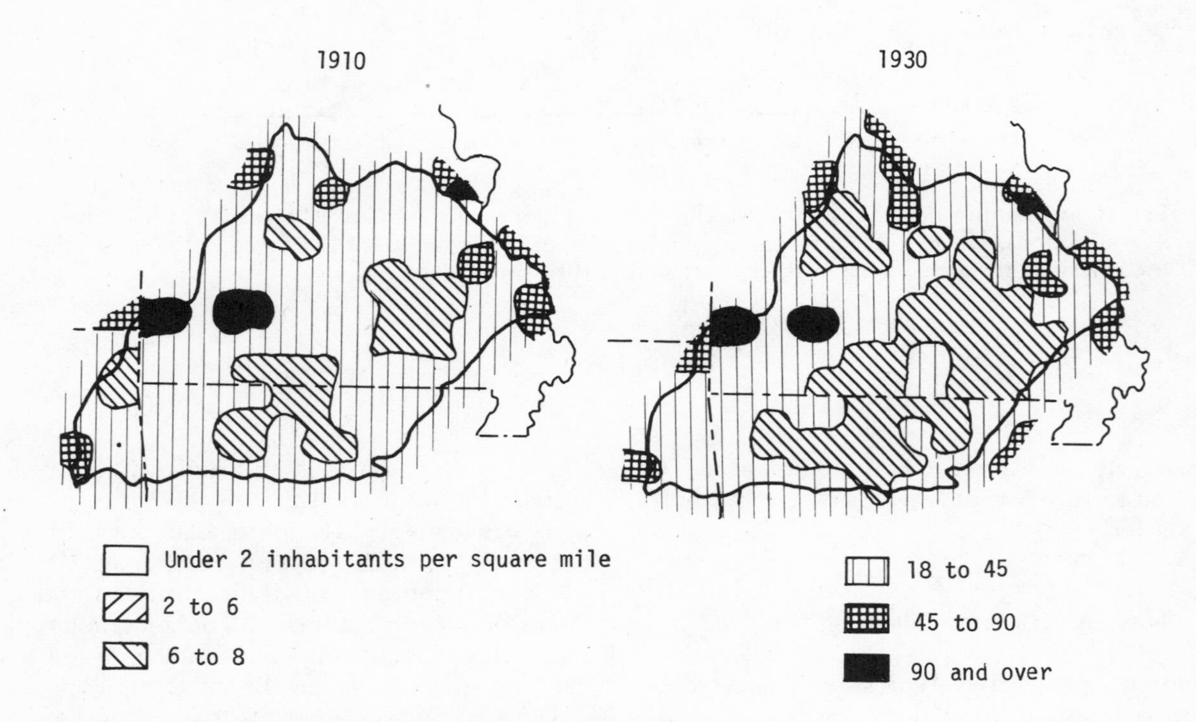

Figure 6-2. Density of population in the Ozarks, 1870–1930.

counties and the Italians at Tontitown and Rosati were nearly negligible by comparison. The larger part of the Germans located in the Missouri and Mississippi River border regions in compact settlements.

The earliest Germans were the so-called Whitewater Dutch, who settled in Bollinger County. These colonists from North Carolina, not being in contact with other German groups, gradually dropped their use of the German language.

Between 1830 and 1850, large numbers of Germans immigrated to the northern and eastern Ozarks. They were primarily of four types: educated men of the *Jungdeutschland* movement, who had been suppressed by a reactionary government; romanticists, who wished to escape a convention-ridden society; religious separatists, who sought to escape the repression of an established church; and the common man, who sought to improve his economic situation.

A book by Gottfried Duden, *Riese nach den Westlichen Staaten*, was circulated widely in Germany, and because of its glowing description of the region along the Missouri River, large numbers of Germans were influenced to move to the Lower Missouri Valley. By the end of 1832, there were at least thirty-three German families established on the Missouri and twenty in the old Boone settlement on Femme Osage Creek. Dutzow was founded in 1834 in Warren County by the Emigration Society of Giessen. Washington was settled by an emigration society from Berlin, and in 1838 the largest colony was located at Hermann. Hermann was settled by an emigration society in Philadelphia. On the Mississippi River Border, Germans settled in Cape Girardeau County in 1833, and in 1835 or 1836 a Swiss colony was established at Dutchtown.

Catholic Germans settled at Westphalia in Osage County in 1833. Several other Catholic settlements grew up near by at Taos in Cole County and at Richfountain, Loose Creek, Lustown, and Frankenstein in Cole County. Other German Catholics settled at New Offenburg and Zell in St. Genevieve County. In a short time the county had a German-speaking majority. In 1839, Protestant separatists settled at Wittenburg, Altenburg, and Frohna; it was this group that nurtured the Lutheran Church–Missouri Synod.

Bollinger Mill and covered bridge on the Whitewater River, Cape Girardeau County, Missouri. Surrounding farms are operated by descendants of Germans who immigrated in the 1790's.

Besides the frontier location, the geographic bases of German settlement were the region's accessibility from Europe by way of New Orleans and the Mississippi River, the low cost of land, and the similarity of soil, climate, and vegetation to conditions in the homeland. The Germans were successful farmers, especially with the loess soils on the uplands; these lands were cheaper, and many of the immigrants had worked similar soils in Germany. Gradually the German settlements expanded from poor to better land. The immigrants were clannish, so they settled amid the older German communities. As they accumulated wealth, they bought out their American neighbors; many of the latter are reported to have sold out because they did not want to live among the Germans. Furthermore, the Americans had become great buyers and sellers of all kinds of property, and land, which could be obtained free or at little cost farther west, was but another commodity to be bartered or sold.

By 1859 the German settlements of Washington and Hermann had become important

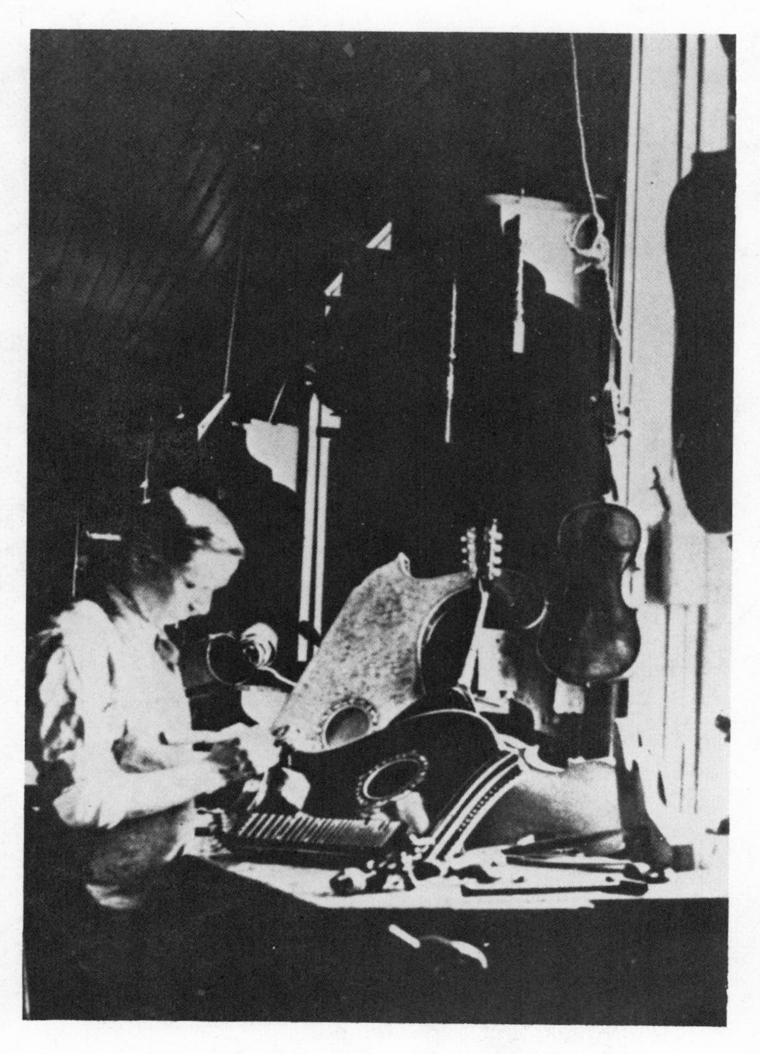

George Hesse working on a zither about 1912. (Courtesy Missouri State Historical Society.)

towns; Jefferson City was half-German, Boonville one-fourth. The Census of 1870 showed that people of German birth or parentage accounted for more than 20 per cent of the population in Osage, Franklin, and St. Louis counties. These counties, along with the city of St. Louis, made up the so-called Missouri Rhineland. German-born made up 10 per cent of the population in Cole, Jefferson, Ste. Genevieve, Perry, and Cape Girardeau counties.

The German settlement of the eastern and northern borders of the Ozarks was part of a larger settlement picture as Germans located along the interior waterways of the United States.[2] Many counties bordering the Ohio River and the Upper Mississippi River and their tributaries received large numbers of German immigrants, and Milwaukee, Cincinnati, and St. Louis became important centers for German culture. By 1900, South St. Louis had become widely known as a German community. Even now the city is known for its fine German restaurants and for the traditional music and customs that have been preserved to some degree. The 1976 St. Louis telephone directory lists thirty-three pages of names beginning *Sch*, an indication of the importance of the Germans' in the population of St. Louis.

The pattern of ethnic settlements in the Ozarks is related to physical conditions and transportation routes (fig. 6-3). The influence of navigable rivers and railroads on the location of settlements is apparent. Relatively few Germans settled in the less accessible Arkansas and Oklahoma Ozarks.

The larger of the scattered German settlements in Missouri include Freistatt in Lawrence County, Lockwood in Dade County, and the settlements in Greene and Christian counties. The larger towns along the railroads in southwest Missouri, notably Springfield, Monett, and Pierce City, attracted many Germans. The railroads, particularly the Frisco, had acquired large federal land grants and were anxious to attract settlers. They are reported to have sent executives directly to Germany as recruiters in an effort to dispose of land and to promote growth and prosperity for their lines. Likewise, the Scottish-owned Missouri Land and Livestock Company, which owned more than 350,000 acres in southwest Missouri, advertised extensively in Europe.[3]

Although the railroads did not succeed in attracting the variety or number of foreign-born people to the Ozarks that they did in the Upper

2. Hildegard B. Johnson, "The Location of German Settlements in the Middle West," *Annals of the Association of American Geographers*, 41 (1941): 1–41.

3. Larry A. McFarlane. "The Missouri Land and Livestock Company, Limited, of Scotland: Foreign Investment on the Missouri Farming Frontier, 1882–1908," (Ph.D. diss., University of Missouri-Columbia, 1963), pp. 198–235.

Figure 6-3. Foreign settlements.

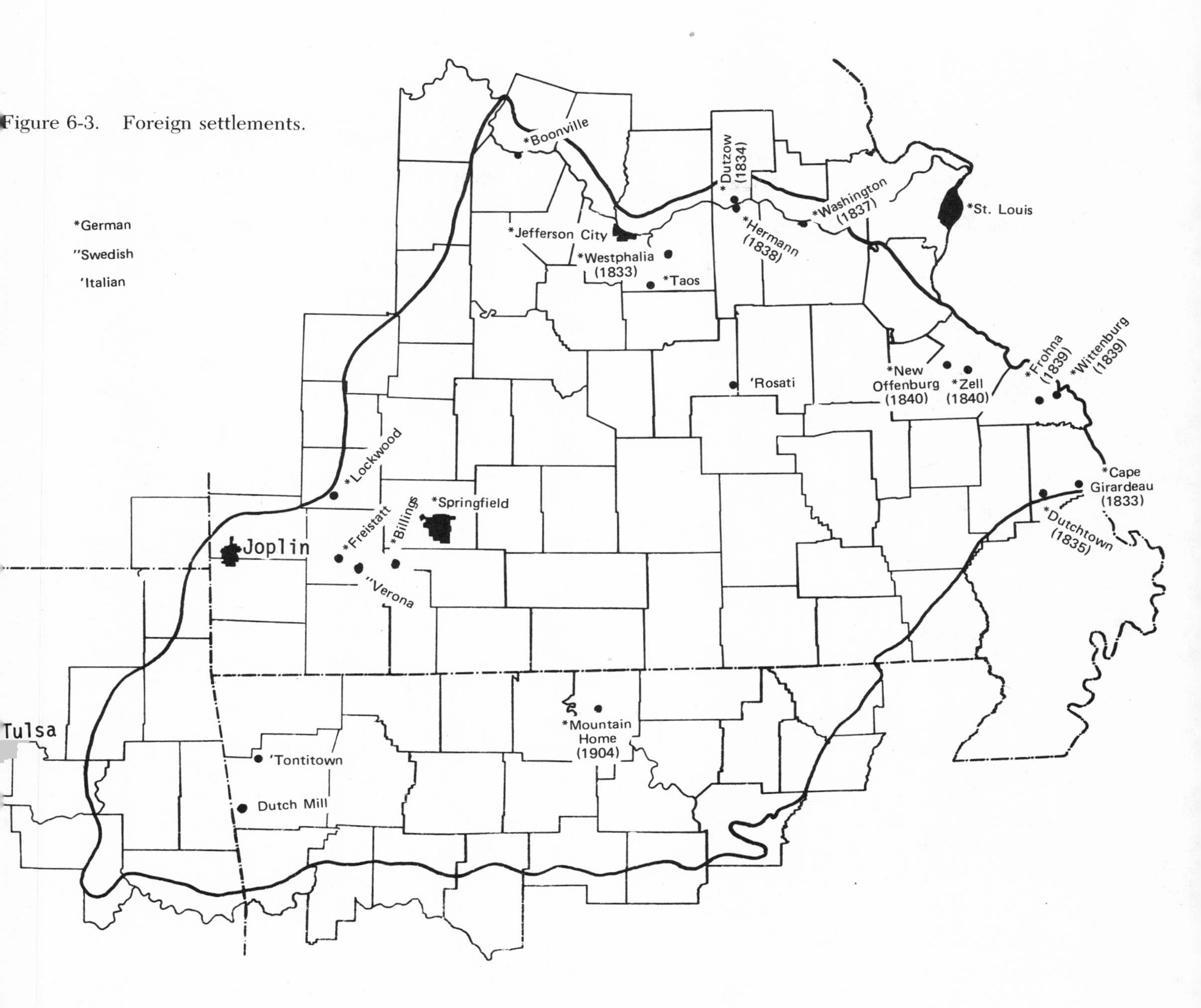

Middle West and Great Plains, there were, nevertheless, a number of different groups. French Waldenses settled south of Monett, German Catholics were attracted mainly to the larger towns, a Swedish colony was set up at Verona, a small colony of Polish settlers located at Pulaskifield in Barry County, and Moravian settlements were founded in Laclede, Dade, and Ripley counties and in scattered locations in southeast Missouri.

The Italian colonies at Tontitown in Washington County, Arkansas, and at Rosati in Phelps County, Missouri, were established in 1900 after an earlier attempt to settle in the cotton country of the Mississippi bottoms in Arkansas. These immigrants were more successful in the Ozarks, where they established vineyards and orchards. In southeast Missouri a small Hungarian group settled near Poplar Bluff, and there were small settlements of Poles, Yugoslavs, and Germans in nearby counties.

Until Oklahoma attained statehood in 1907, the

conditions of tribal land tenure were not conducive to the settlement of foreign-born groups. For agricultural people interested in establishing homes, clear title to land was essential, and because Oklahoma land titles were always in doubt, many immigrants were discouraged from settling in Indian Territory. The Arkansas Ozarks attracted somewhat more Germans, but because of the remoteness, far from other German groups, their number was small and the imprint of their culture was never very strong. In the 1830's a small German settlement was established at Dutchtown, in Washington County, Arkansas. It flourished for a time, but most of these families moved because of the unsettled times during the Civil War.

After the war, when railroads were built into northwest Arkansas, the larger towns—Fayetteville, Rogers, Bentonville—attracted some German immigrants. One of the most distinctive groups were the German-speaking Swiss who settled near Altus, Arkansas, on the extreme southern flank of the Boston Mountains. They arrived, in the 1880's and immediately planted their vines and religion in Ozark soil. Both the vineyards and the Roman Catholic church have thrived; today there are several large vineyards and commercial wineries in the vicinity of Altus. The largest of these, Wiederkehr Wine Cellars, produces wines of national reputation. Overlooking Altus from the Boston Mountain foothills is the massive stone church built by parishioners.

Character of the Second-Phase Immigrants

The carriers of the New South culture in the Ozarks were a mixed lot. The New South image consisted not only of the works of individuals but also the widespread influences of institutions, notably state and national government, schools, and churches, and the pervasive effects, sometimes dominance, of the new corporate immigrants: the lumber companies, the mining companies, and the railroads. The role of corporations and institutions in shaping the Ozarks scene is discussed elsewhere; three examples of individuals from the New South will serve to illustrate representative types.

Jonathan Fairbanks, graduate of the New Ipswich Academy in Massachusetts, moved to Springfield, Missouri, in 1866 after holding teaching positions in Massachusetts and Ohio and venturing into an ill-fated partnership to manufacture steam engines. He was encouraged to go to Missouri and enter into partnership with John C. Wilbur, an old friend from Ohio. The two operated a sawmill and planing business, with mills at Strafford and Carthage and a retail outlet in Springfield. Fairbanks immediately became active in civic affairs, serving as city councilman, mayor, and board member of the newly founded (1867) public schools. In 1873, because of the financial panic, Fairbanks' business failed and he was forced to sell his home and real estate holdings. Disheartened, he planned to leave Springfield and return to Ohio, but a school board member, who had recognized Fairbanks' educational training and aptitude, persuaded him to serve as superintendent of the Springfield schools.

Fairbanks filled that post continuously (except for 1877) until 1912. He proved to be a capable teacher with outstanding administrative ability, a man adept and sensitive in dealing with the Negro population, particularly when the expansion of Drury College required condemnation of the colored school. During his tenure the faculty in the Springfield schools increased from a "handful of teachers" with county certificates to a "corps of over one hundred," most of whom were graduates of state normal schools.

Fairbanks' experience in politics was useful in dealing with financial matters. Under his direction nineteen schools were constructed, and Springfield High School, the pride of the city, was considered one of the best in Missouri. He has been referred to as Mr. Springfield Public Schools, an appropriate recognition of his contribution to the development of one of the significant institutions of the New South Ozarks.[4]

Another New South immigrant from the North, Dr. Charles Bunyan Parsons, was to play an important role in the development of lead mining in the eastern Ozarks of Missouri. His work and

4. Peggy Stepp, "Jonathan Fairbanks: 'Mr. Springfield Public Schools' " (Master's seminar paper, Department of History, Southwest Missouri State University, 1972).

ingenuity were instrumental in devising methods to extract ore. He was a dentist, but after practicing in Michigan, he served as a captain in the Union Army, resigning in 1863 because of bad health. In 1867, persuaded by his doctors that he must get into some calling where he could be outdoors more than his dental practice would allow, he assumed responsibilities as resident manager of the St. Joseph Lead Company's Ozark operations.

The company, incorporated in New York in 1864, had acquired, from Anthony La Grave, 946 acres of land around the present town of Bonne Terre. When Dr. Parsons arrived in 1867, the works consisted of a small crushing mill, three small furnaces, and a few hand-operated jigs. Ore was gathered by hand from so-called openings, which were no more than shallow pits, and from a few inclined drifts leading to bedrock.

Dr. Parsons had read a magazine article about a new invention, the diamond drill, that would cut deep and bring up samples of the rock through which it had passed. He brought such a drill to the Ozark lead district, where its use proved to be the first step toward progressive modernization. Over the years, large areas of good ore were discovered as diamond drills continued to reveal the character of the rock and the minerals imbedded therein.

The discovery of new ore bodies and the increase in production led to improved smelting processes and new means of separating ore from waste rock. Skilled metallurgists from Germany were employed, and the St. Joseph Lead Company extended its holdings in the vicinity of Bonne Terre, Leadwood, and Doe Run. During the 1890's, many mining companies were organized in St. Francois County; they merged with the larger companies and later became part of the St. Joseph operations. Among the new ones were Desloge Consolidated Lead Company, Flat River Lead Company, National Lead Company, Doe Run Lead Company, Central Lead Company, Federal Lead Company, and Theodore Lead Company. Between 1867 and 1910, under Dr. Parsons' management, St. Joseph Lead Company grew from an uncertain operation producing a little more than seventeen thousand dollars worth of salable goods annually to an entity that distributed nearly two million dollars in dividends, invested a like amount in improvements, and was responsible for creating a thriving community of five thousand persons.

A third example will serve to round out the characterization of the New South immigrants. Powell Clayton, born in Pennsylvania, went to Kansas in his youth and there acquired considerable knowledge of the violent political movements that attended the birth of that divided state. As an officer in a Kansas regiment, he served in Arkansas in 1862–63 and showed himself to have much courage and resourcefulness as a commander; his defense of Pine Bluff, by means of cotton-bale barricades, against a violent Confederate attack in 1863 was well known. In 1865, like many other Northern men, he married a Southern woman and, with cotton selling at record prices, soon became a wealthy planter.

His entry into politics came with Reconstruction. He was an able speaker, capable of coherent and forceful argument, and was especially adept at backing his opponent into an utenable or ridiculous position. It was for this reason that the Arkansas Republicans, led by such men as Logan H. Roots, builder of a large carpetbag fortune, and other shrewdly unscrupulous men chose him as candidate for governor. He was elected in 1868 at the age of thirty-five, and four years later, at thirty-nine, he was elected to the U.S. Senate.

In 1871, Clayton persuaded the legislature to pass an act establishing a state university. True to its traditions, Fayetteville, a booming New South Ozarks town, voted bonds to build the University of Arkansas, which enrolled its first students in 1872. Apart from the state university, the Clayton administration set up public school systems throughout Arkansas. Institutes for the blind and deaf were established, and other institutions offering education for a nominal fee sprang up. A flourishing small college serving many of the brightest boys of the Ozark region was established at Quitman in Van Buren County.

After completing his Senate term in 1877, Clayton moved from Little Rock to the new-rising watering place of Eureka Springs, a stagecoach journey of some eighty-four miles through the wildest and remotest part of the Ozarks. He arrived at Eureka Springs with visions of grandeur: the area should be developed as a nationally known health resort. In short order he had persuaded several men of considerable wealth to associate themselves with his effort. He was the prime mover in encouraging the Frisco to build the Missouri and Arkansas Railroad from Seligman to Beaver. The Eureka Springs Railway, financed largely by Logan Roots and other close associates of Powell Clayton, was constructed from Beaver to Eureka Springs. The locomotive used on the first run in September, 1883, was appropriately, the *Powell Clayton*. The goal of Clayton's efforts in securing a railroad for Eureka Springs was to support his heavy investments in real estate. His most notable was the widely known Crescent Hotel, a massive resort structure equipped with a grand ballroom overlooking the spring basins below. This elegant hotel, still in operation but somewhat the worse for wear, is a salient reminder of the New South era in Ozark history.

Sequent Occupancy: The Third Phase

The beginning of the cosmopolitan phase of Ozark immigration is contemporary with the automobile age and has continued through the spate of technological advances and governmental and institutional changes of the past half-century. These Ozark immigrants are even more difficult to characterize than those of the New South era. They are mainly of three types: returnees, escapists, and opportunity seekers. The returnee is a familiar type. In this group are people who once lived in the Ozarks, moved away, but, for one reason or another, returned. Some came back in the 1930's when Depression hard times hit the automobile plants in Detroit, the steel mills in Chicago, and the packinghouses in Kansas City. The returnees came to weather the Depression among friends and family, where familiar patterns of subsistence living could be supplemented by cash income from "working out" in a "green mill" or canning factory, or by "catching on" with a harvest crew headed north across the plains, or, perhaps, by picking peaches "on the western slope," or working in whatever manner a dollar could be made.

More recently, returnees are coming back to the Ozarks, usually in their later years (but not always), to retire or to prepare to retire. Many, if not most, have met with some success in the outside world. They are returning not of necessity but of free choice; they are seeking out familiar surroundings, old friends, and they hope to find—and sometimes do—the stable social relations and slower pace of life that they have remembered. Some have good reason to return; they have inherited property, a family business or a farm. Others, depending on their circumstances, settle in a comfortable house overlooking a golf course at Bella Vista, or they may purchase a five-acre farmette and contemporary bungalow overlooking one of the large lakes, or they may live in a mobile home on a country road conveniently close to friends or relatives.

A second cosmopolitan immigrant type is the escapist. The civil-rights movement of the 1950's and 1960's, followed by the environmental movement of the 1960's and 1970's, focused the nation's attention on the ills of city life: traffic congestion, crowds, racial strife, crime, routine and colorless jobs, and the problems of air and water pollution. The city's glitter and mystique are no longer in; the good life is to be found someplace else. The backflow of population from large metropolitan centers to medium-size cities has grown steadily, spurred by newspaper headlines calling attention to the fact that people are fleeing major cities. The 1975 urban population estimates showed only six of the nation's twenty largest cities with more people than they had in 1970. St. Louis, on the Ozarks border, declined 15.6 per cent (97,000 people) between 1970 and 1975. City life is out, and rural life is in. The popular image of the Ozarks is that of lonely roads, forested hills, unpolluted streams, friendly people, and an easygoing lifestyle. Presumably the Ozarks has all the good things not found in the city. When they retire, most people stay in the houses they have worked to pay for, close to friends and familiar social contacts, but for those who choose to relocate, the Ozarks offers the amenities of escape from the diseconomies of city life.

The retirement escapee grew up during the Great Depression, was drafted into military service or worked in booming defense industries during World War II, prospered during the 1950's and 1960's, and has earned retirement benefits from military service, government employment, or private-industry pension plans. Nearly all qualify for Social Security benefits. Many grew up with kerosene lamps, horse-drawn farm implements and all the privations of pre-REA rural life. They are nostalgic about things old, but they want none of it as a steady diet. They have tasted the good life, found it to their liking, and so long as the electricity flows, country life is fine.

The back-to-the-land people make up a second category of escapists. They are the product of the environmental movement, well versed in the excesses of big business, the evils of population growth, the inevitability of the total depletion of nonrenewable natural resources, and they are determined to find a simple and more self-sufficient lifestyle in the Ozarks. The back-to-the-land people may be of any age or background, but most are under thirty and have no previous experience with rural living. They learn gardening, preserving and canning food, felling trees, and splitting kindling, with determination bordering on fanaticism. Usually they settle in old farmhouses, but occasionally they build a house and farmstead from scratch. Organic gardening is their main source of home-produced food; sometimes chickens are raised, but usually there is little livestock. They come as individuals, married couples, and sometimes in communal groups. Very few achieve anything close to self-sufficiency. Food stamps and off-farm employment help make ends meet.

Many of the back-to-the-land people have useful talents; probably a majority have some college background. At their worst they become hypocrites to their own ethos by advertising and selling "five-acre tracts that can be subdivided and sold as one acre lots to other 'organic farmers.' " At their best they become responsible citizens active in community affairs. Those who stay for more than a year or two either find permanent employment or accept the hard work and the level of living provided by subsistence agriculture.

The third type of cosmopolitan immigrant, the opportunity seeker, is even more difficult to characterize. The opportunity seekers are people looking for a place to work and a place to live. They are neither returning nor escaping. As a matter of fact, almost any other place that afforded the same opportunity to work, to use their skills, to establish successful businesses, and to provide a living for themselves and their families would have served as well. They are educators, construction workers, doctors, motel owners, restaurant managers, computer programmers, factory workers, and insurance salesmen. The opportunity seekers serve the escapists and the returnees and are themselves part of the growth syndrome; growth promotes growth. They settle close to where they work, which means they usually settle in or near one of the growing towns in the area. In terms of actual numbers, they are probably the most numerous. Opportunity seekers, more than any other group, account for the fact that Springfield's population increased from 120,096 to 131,557 between 1970 and 1975.

The Geography of Population

Beginning in the mid-1960's there have been unexpected population shifts in several regions of the United States. The Ozarks, along with the forested land in Wisconsin, northern Michigan, and Minnesota and the recreation-retirement states of the South and Southwest, have experienced rapid increases in population. Between April, 1970, and July, 1973, while the nation's population was growing 3.2 per cent, the Ozark-Ouachita region grew 9.4 per cent (fig. 6-1). It appears that many people are moving out of the central cities, most of them to the suburbs, but many have chosen to effect a major move to sparsely populated regions. Nine of the ten largest cities in the United States have decreased in population since 1970. The biggest rates of nonmetropolitan growth have occurred in retirement counties, such as those in the Ozark-Ouachita and Upper Great Lakes regions, in counties adjacent to metropolitan areas, and in counties with state colleges. Sixty-four of the ninety three Ozark counties had positive rates of migration in the 1960's; that is, more people were moving into these counties than out. The greatest rates of in-migration in the 1960's occurred in the lake districts and in the counties with larger towns. Lake counties that experienced rapid rates of growth in the 1960's included Camden (46 per cent), Taney (26 per cent), and Stone (16 per cent), in Missouri; Delaware (30 per cent) and

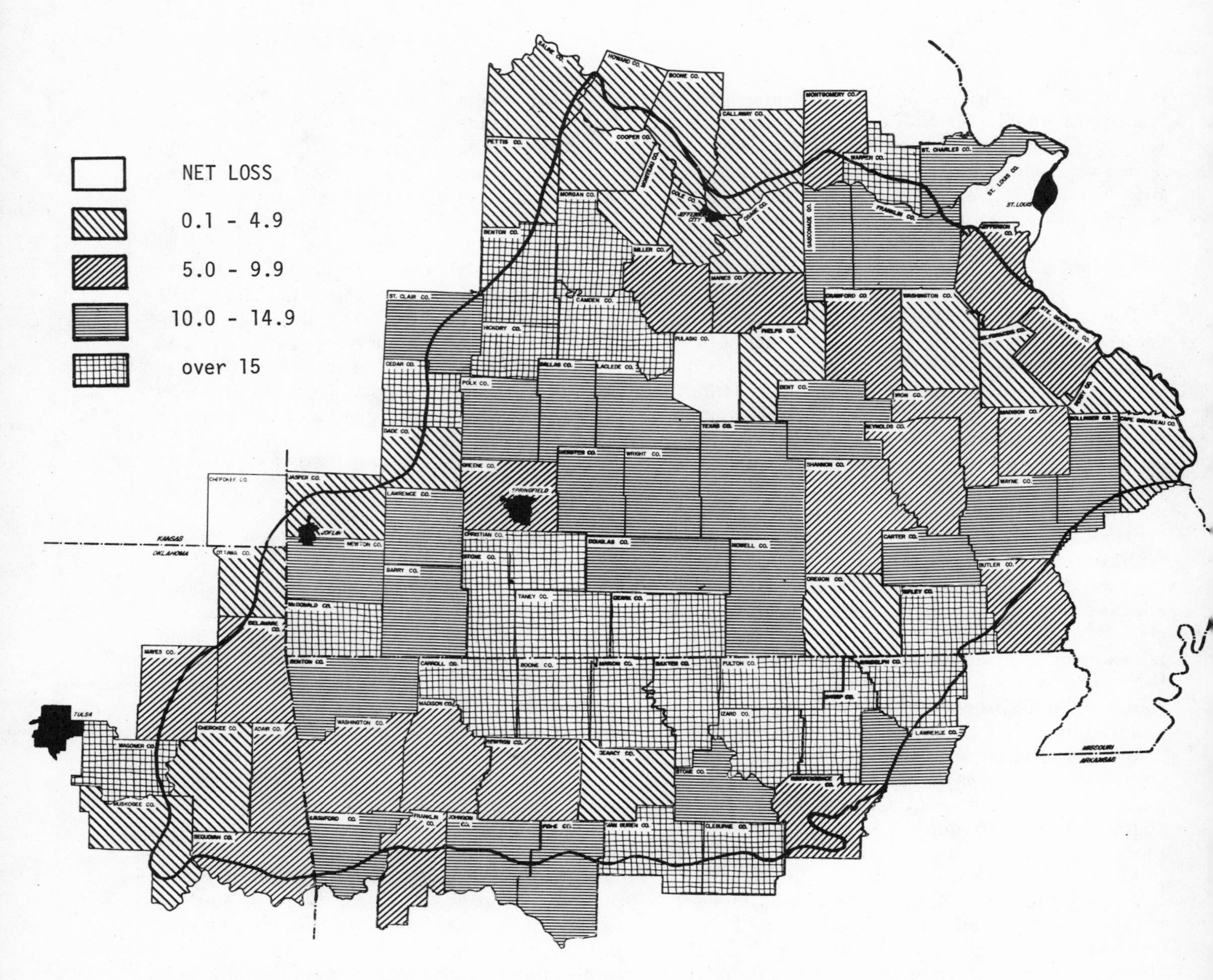

Figure 6-4. Per cent net migration, 1970–1974.

Cherokee (21 per cent) in Oklahoma; and Baxter (52 per cent), Marion (16 per cent), and Independence (8 per cent) in Arkansas. Missouri counties with growth centers include Greene and Christian (Springfield), Phelps (Rolla), Cape Girardeau, and Newton (Joplin and Neosho). In northwest Arkansas, Benton and Washington counties had large population increases (32 per cent and 25 per cent) resulting from the growth of Fayetteville, Springdale, Rogers and Bentonville.

Even more striking population changes are indicated by 1974 U.S. Bureau of the Census estimates (fig. 6-1). In the four-year period from 1970 to 1974 the population of the Ozarks increased to

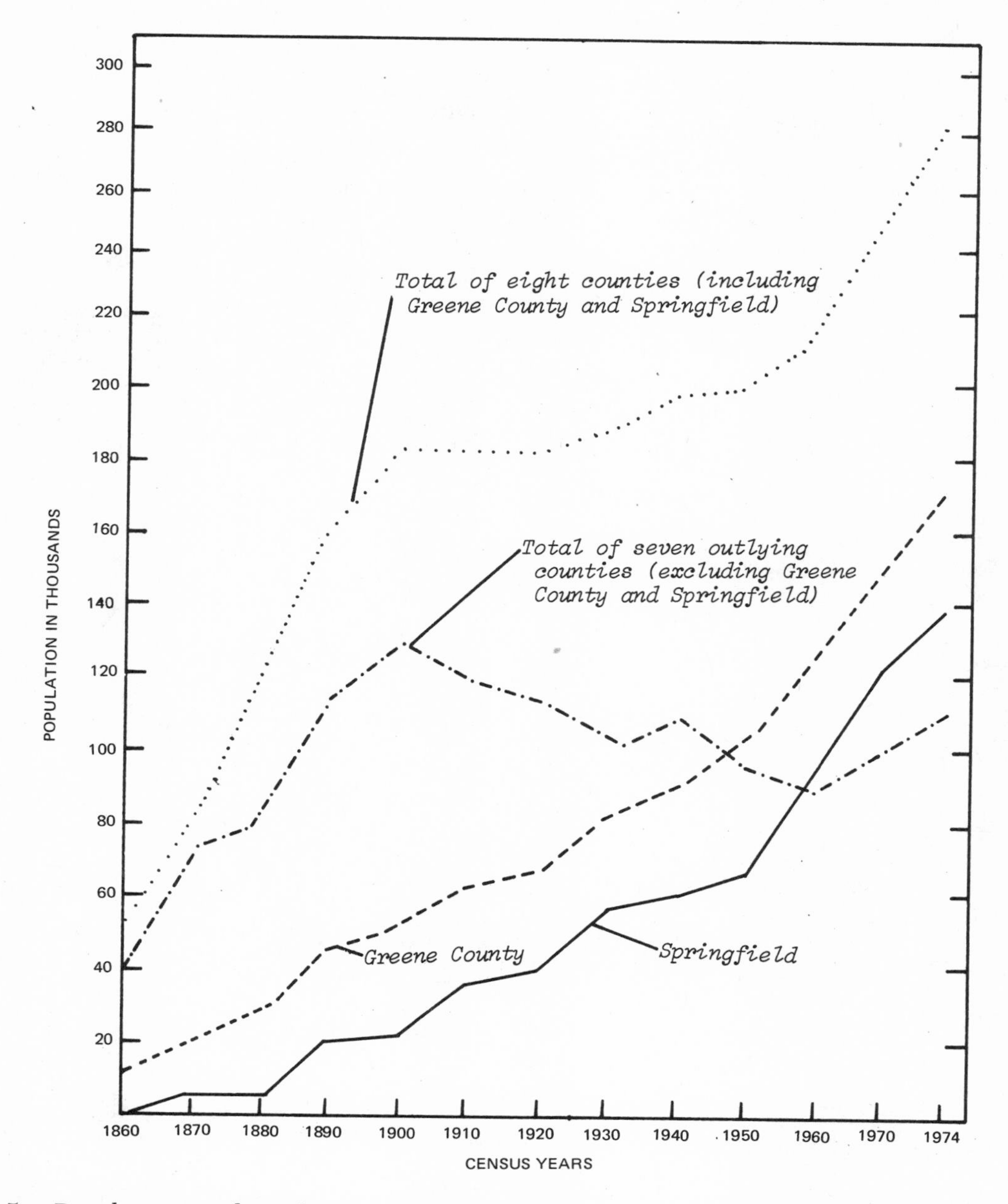

Figure 6-5. Population trends in the Springfield vicinity. Source: *U.S. Census of Population, 1860–1970; U.S. Bureau of Census Estimates for 1974.*

1,750,952 from an estimated 1,594,362. The total increase of 156,590 amounted to a 9.82 per cent, or an average rate of 2.45 per cent each year. This rate of increase would permit doubling of the size of the population in approximately twenty-five years. Seventy-nine per cent of the increase was due to net migration; the remainder was due to excess of births over deaths (fig. 6-4). During this period, only one county wholly within the Ozarks (Pulaski County, Missouri) experienced a decline

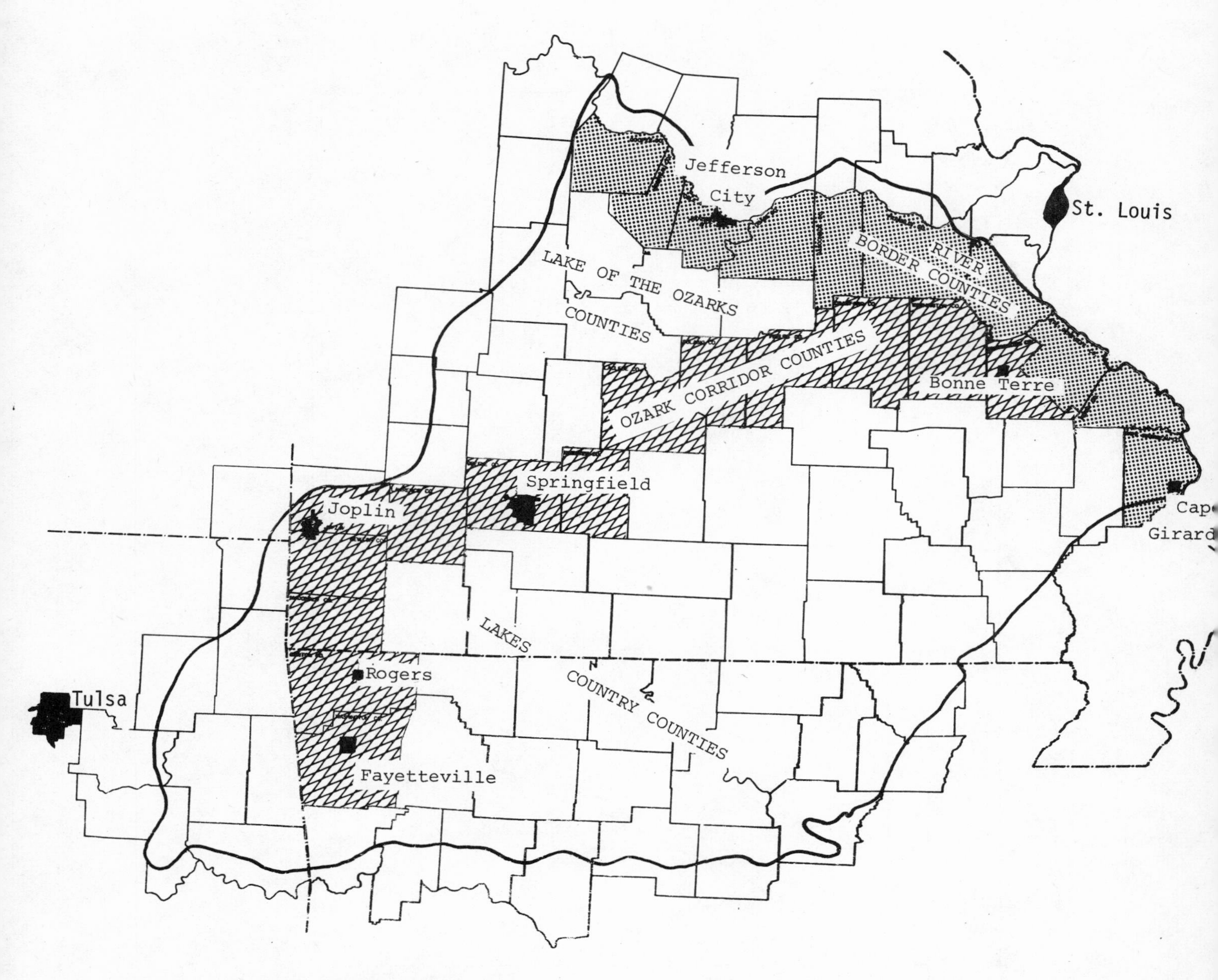

Figure 6-6. Population growth regions.

in population. In this instance the decrease was due to a reduction in the number of military personnel and their dependents at Fort Leonard Wood.

There have been three important trends in population distribution since 1910. The first is farm-to-city migration. This movement appears to be slowing, and, as was noted earlier, in some areas it has been reversed. Detailed study of the census reports shows that in the Springfield vicinity the movement continued strong for many years. Graphs (fig. 6-5) provide visual comparisons of the population trends of Springfield, Greene County, and seven outlying counties and the composite growth of the eight counties. The composite population has increased each decade since 1860, except from 1910 to 1920, when there was a small decrease in population. Greene County has shown a steady increase as a result of and parallel to the growth of Springfield, but the growth has been at the expense of the outlying counties. The seven outlying counties had marked increases in population during the settlement phase before 1900, but since that time, until recently, these counties have declined in population. The Springfield vicinity is a microcosm of the Ozark region: growth in the region as a whole, but major redistribution of the population, resulting in a less dispersed farm population and increasing importance for growth centers.

The second major trend is the buildup of population near major lakes and reservoirs (fig. 6-6). This is most striking in the vicinity of Lake of the Ozarks, Table Rock Reservoir, Lake Taneycomo. Bull Shoals Reservoir, Lake Norfolk, Greers Ferry Reservoir, Beaver Lake, and Lake of the Cherokees (Grand Lake). Population in the three-county area surrounding Lake of the Ozarks (Camden, Miller, Morgan) increased 6,700, or 14.8 per cent, in the period 1970–74. The seven-county area on the Missouri-Arkansas boundary (Barry, Stone, Taney, Boone, Carroll, Marion, Baxter) increased 20,900, or 17.8 per cent, during the same time span. Taney County's increase of 34.5 per cent gave it the fastest growth rate of Missouri's counties, while Baxter County's increase of 35.4 per cent was the fastest rate in the Ozarks and in the state of Arkansas.

Geographically, the population is strung out along the lake shores where roads penetrate the upland between inlets. Of necessity, because the lake shores are usually steep, the dwellings occupy the uplands. A large number of these homes are occupied by retired people, some area residents who have moved from farms, but most are from outside the region.

The third trend is toward redistribution of population along lines of transportation, and this occurs on two geographical scales: the major transportation corridor, such as Interstate 44, which attracts industry and commerce to towns located along it; the state highway or farm-to-market road, which provides easier access to nonfarm jobs. The net result of the latter situation has been to depopulate large areas that have poor roads and to concentrate population along the improved roads. In the hill districts there are places in which several contiguous sections of 640 acres have no habitation at all. These empty areas of the Ozarks are restricted to very rugged areas where the federal government has established national forests.

Two major corridors of counties (fig. 6-6) contain more than 56 per cent of the Ozarks' population. The river-border counties have a combined population of 371,389, or 21 per cent of the Ozark total. The fourteen counties in the Ozark Corridor have a combined population of 634,476, or 36 per cent of the total. Population in these two transportation corridors increased by 67,222 from 1970 to 1974, accounting for 43 per cent of the total increase in the 93-county Ozark region.

Case Studies of Population Relocation

To understand better the details and consequences of rural population shifts, let us examine two areas in detail. Maps of the two locations, quite unlike in physical conditions, afford insights into significant population redistributions.[5] The map of Buck Prairie Township in Lawrence County, Missouri, in 1879 shows that farmsteads were scattered and were much less oriented toward roads than in 1968 (figs. 6-7 and 6-8). Apparently the controlling factor in location of farmsteads was the property boundary of the farm. The 1968 map of the township shows a much denser pattern of settlement, but many farms have been abandoned. More farmsteads were oriented toward roads, probably a long-term process that occurred as farms were abandoned and new farmsteads were built. Gradually, those farmsteads at some distance from the improved roads were abandoned to avoid the trouble and expense of maintaining private lanes.

Even more marked changes have occurred in the settlement pattern in Linn Township in Christian County over the past half-century. A map compiled from the Christian County Plat Book of 1912 shows that of 131 houses in Linn Township,

5. Milton D. Rafferty, "Population and Settlement Changes in Two Ozark Localities," *Rural Sociology* 38 (Spring 1973): 46–56.

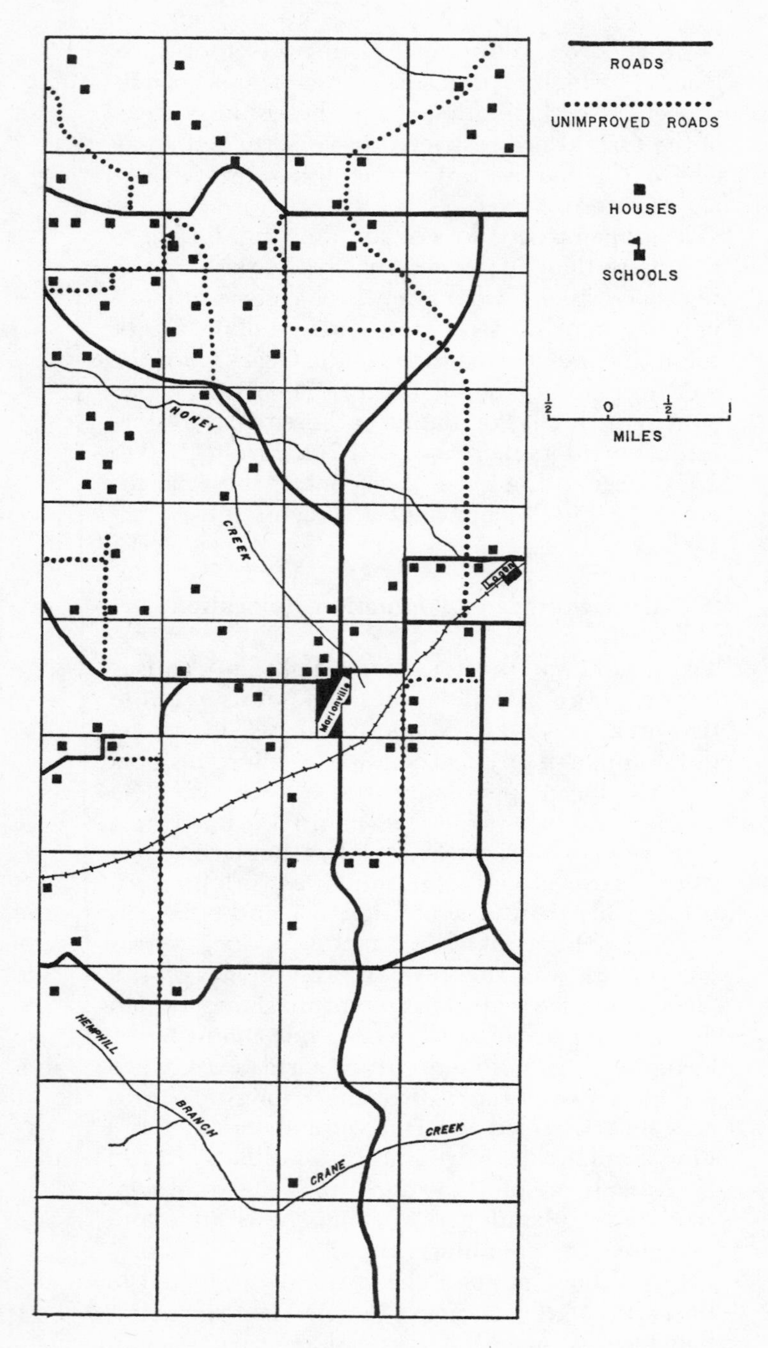

Figure 6-7. Settlement in Buck Prairie Township, Lawrence County, Missouri, 1879.

89 were located in stream valleys and only 42 were on ridgetops (fig. 6-9). In 1968 the situation was nearly reversed (fig. 6-10). Of 99 occupied houses, only 21 were in valleys and 78 were on ridges. Most of those in valleys were on the better-quality county roads.

At first appraisal, it appears that the population of Linn Township has moved uphill to gain easier access to the better public roads that follow the ridgetops. However, interviews with residents indicate that the population inversion that has occurred since 1912 is complicated and is the result of several factors. The valley farms were abandoned because agriculture is a numerically declining way of life. As farm families left the township, no alternate economic activity was available to attract people to the isolated valleys, where roads are often poor and subject to flooding during rainy periods.

The decrease in valley occupancy has not contributed significantly to the increase in ridgetop settlement; that is, the people who abandoned valley farms usually did not resettle on the ridges near the roads but instead left Linn Township. Settlement along the roads on the ridgetops represents a different type of people from the farmers who live in the valleys. Although ridgetop farms did exist in 1911, settlement was not dense except on Logan's Ridge.

The houses on the ridges in 1911 can be credited mainly to the growth and decline of the logging industry. With the completion of a railroad spur to Chadwick in 1882, the forests were rapidly exploited. By 1920, most of the better-quality timber had been cut and large timber tracts were sold off in small acreages. Many of the former sawmill workers stayed on, eking out a living from part-time logging employment and production from the small acreages they had acquired. The former logging trails, which followed the cleared ridgetops, attracted settlement in the form of shacks or small houses. Improved well-drilling technology undoubtedly was important for the increase in ridgetop settlement, since early ridgetop homes had to use sometimes unreliable water supplies from cisterns.

Additional small-subsistence ridgetop farms were established when it was discovered that strawberries and tomatoes could be grown profitably. In recent years the improved roads and spectacular scenery have resulted in the construction of weekend homes on the ridgetops; however, these are found only occasionally in the remote areas.

The shift of settlement from valleys to ridges probably was a slow process that proceeded with the ebb and flow of population in the township. Subsistence and part-time farming, coupled with a low cost of living, account for most of the increase in ridgetop houses since 1911. From 1910 to 1920, when the township gained substantially in population, the increase in settlement was on the ridges, probably due mainly to settlement on the cutover lands. Population declined during the next decade, the larger losses occurring in the valleys. From 1930 to 1940 the population grew slightly, and again the growth evidently was greatest on ridgetops. At least three new houses were built on Logan's Ridge during the 1930's. Since 1940 the township has lost population; traditionally, most of the people left the valleys.

When one observes that the 1970 population of Linn Township is 361 less than the maximum of 635 in 1920, the decline in total number of houses between 1911 and 1968 seems incongruously small. How does one explain that in 1911 there were 128 occupied houses and in 1968 there were 99, a decline of only 29 houses, while simultaneously the total population declined by more than 350? The explanation may lie in the normal demographic ebb and flow; that is, even if the number of houses had declined only moderately, the family cycle within each house could easily account for the reduction in population. The average number of people per house in 1911 was approximately five; in 1968 there were approximately three and one-half people per house. This does not seem unreasonable when one considers that a large share of the emigrants were young people in the age group that would have children at home.

Interviews with knowledgeable, longtime residents of Linn Township provide insight into the character of the present-day people, their occupations, their attitudes, and possible explanations for the persistence of ridge settlement. The male residents of the township were divided among three employment categories. According to a retired farmer who served as an informant, there were 32 nonfarmers, 45 part-time farmers, and 9

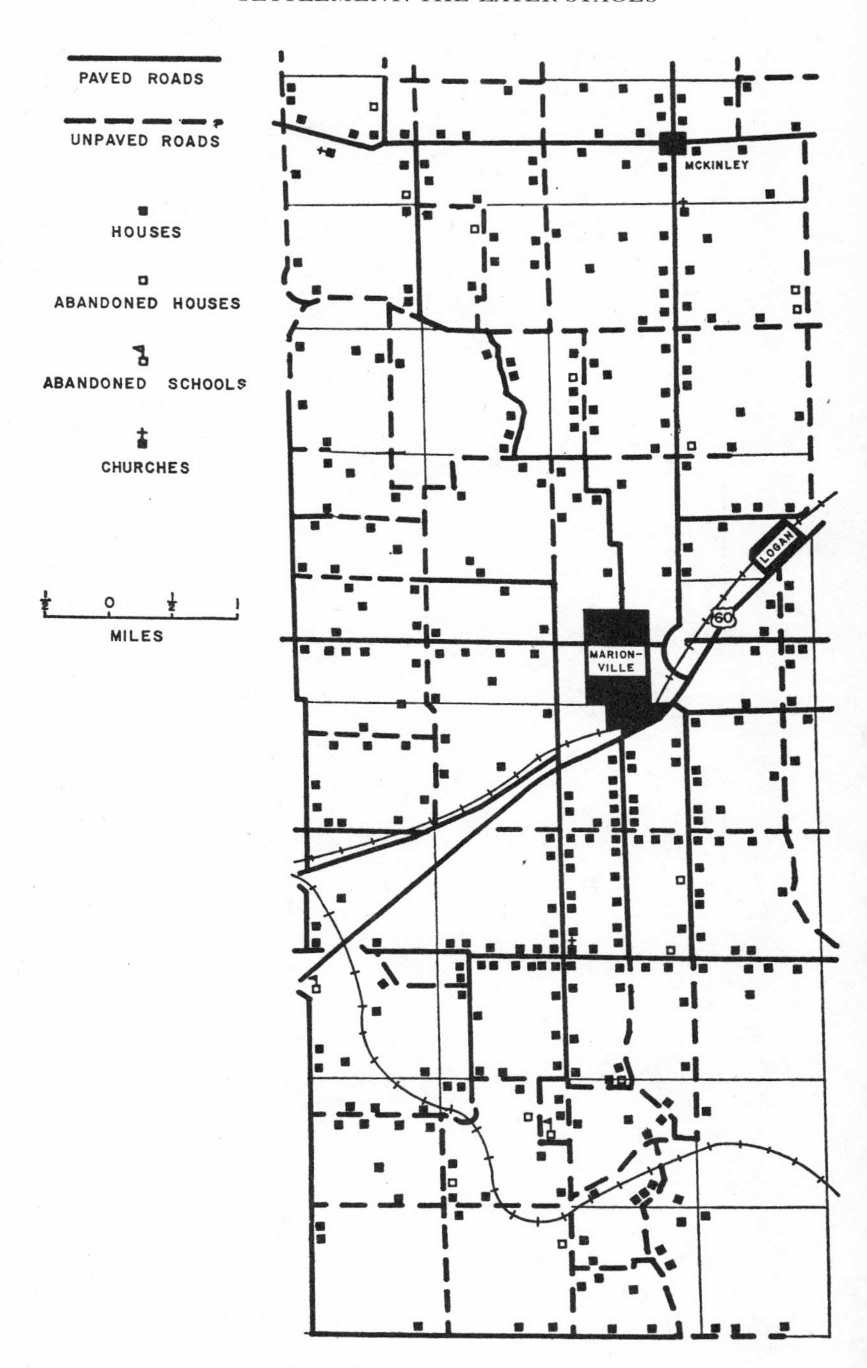

Figure 6-8. Settlement in Buck Prairie Township, Lawrence County, Missouri, 1969.

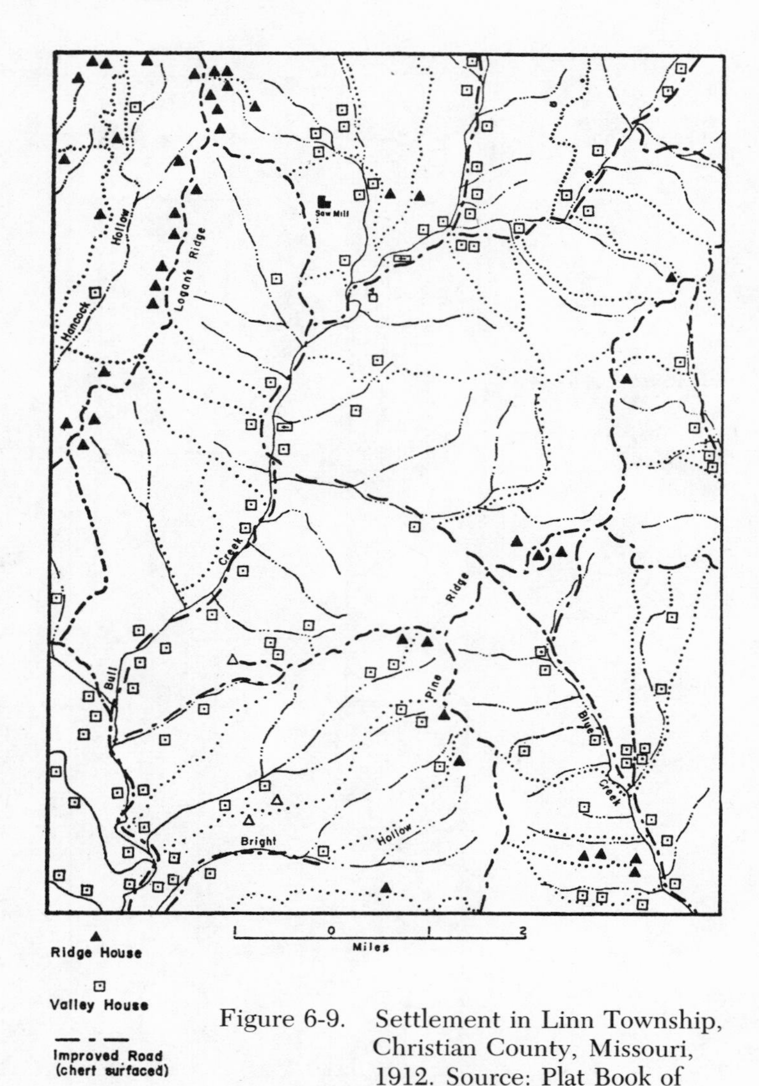

Figure 6-9. Settlement in Linn Township, Christian County, Missouri, 1912. Source: Plat Book of Christian County.

full-time farmers. Part-time farming is the largest category, accounting for 52 per cent of the employed males. Those classed as part-time farmers usually raise a garden and keep a few cattle from time to time but are supported mainly by Social Security, welfare, or regular or periodic off-farm employment of one or more members of the family.

Many farmers in the marginal lands of Ozark and Appalachian highlands have always looked to off-farm employment, either permanently or seasonally, to bolster family incomes. In the largest group are those who have chosen off-farm employment as a means to better living. A second group is comprised of former full-time farmers who choose to continue living on their farms after retirement. A third group includes those who either have returned to the area after a long absence or have chosen to locate there because of low-cost land and low-cost retirement living. One resident of Logan's Ridge established residence in the 1930's to weather the Depression, returned to his home in Detroit to work in the 1940's, and finally settled in the Ozarks in the late 1950's to spend his retirement years.

Most of the people have strong family and social ties in the community. All are white, and most are descended from old-stock Americans who migrated to Missouri before 1900. In conversation, one detects their preference for their nearly classless, individual-oriented, slow-paced life to the only visible alternatives. Similar attitudes have been noted in other sections of the Ozarks.

Although the population has declined since 1940, the rate of decline seems to be decreasing. The township population decrease between 1960 and 1970 was from 286 to 274, a loss of only 12. Since 1965, six new homes have been built and at least three mobile homes have been permanently located. All of these residences are on ridgetops close to all-weather roads and are occupied by people who are employed in Springfield or another nearby town.

The population redistributions that have occurred in Linn Township are strikingly different from those that have been described for an area of similar topography and relief in the interior Ozarks. Kersten[6] found that ridgetop settlement in Dent County declined markedly after the forests were depleted and that settlement was more permanent in the valleys. A more recent study of settlement patterns in the interior Ozarks revealed that long-distance commuting could become important in stabilizing out-migration. Residents of Reynolds County traveled one hundred fifty miles to St. Louis to work during the week and returned to their families and strong community ties on weekends.[7] Such long-distance commuting has been shown to be important in holding population in the coal fields of Pennsylvania. The persistence and moderate growth of ridge settlement in the rough hill country southeast of Springfield probably is due to the greater opportunity for residents to combine part-time farming with off-farm employment. This requires both reliable roads and nonfarm employment opportunities, conditions that do not always prevail in the interior Ozarks.

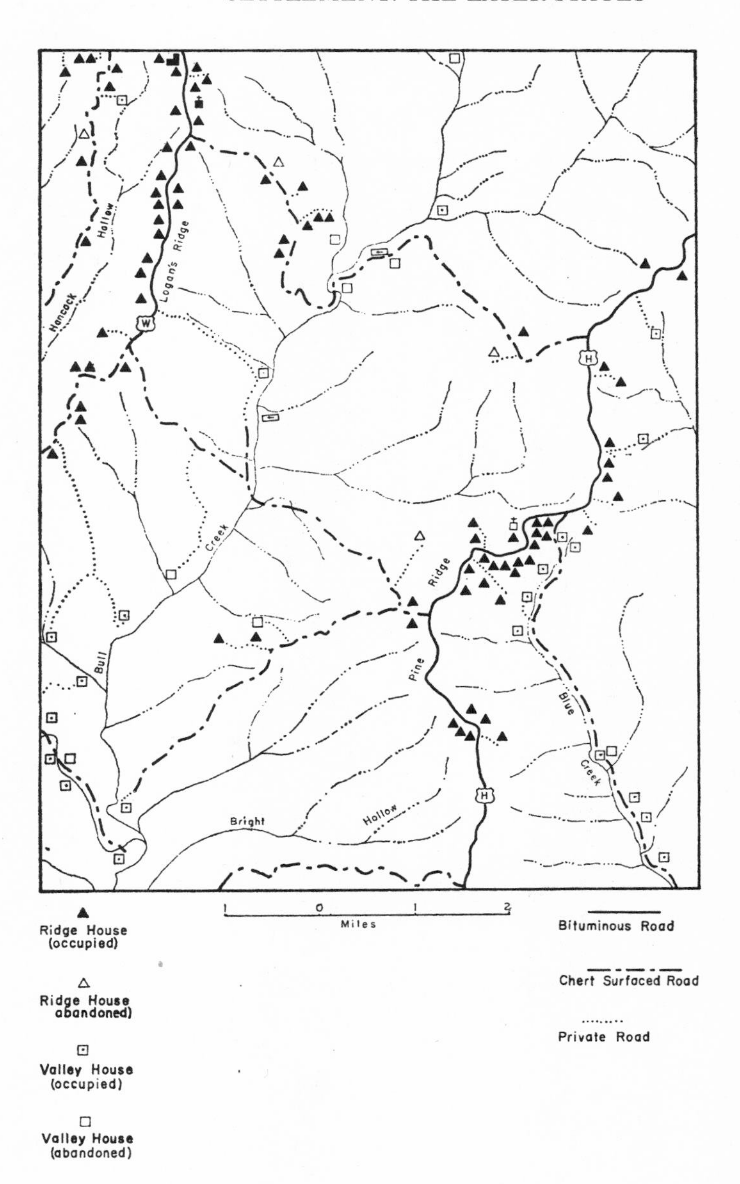

Figure 6-10. Settlement in Linn Township, Christian County, Missouri, 1968. Sources: general highway map of Christian County and field observations.

6. Earl W. Kersten, Jr., "Changing Economy and Landscape in a Missouri Ozarks Area," *Annals of the Association of American Geographers* 48 (December 1958): 398–418.

7. Milton D. Rafferty, "Logan Creek: A Missouri Ozark Valley Revisited," *Journal of Geography* 72 (October 1973): 7–17.

Selected References

Fletcher, John Gould. *Arkansas*. Chapel Hill: The University of North Carolina, 1947.

Gerlach, Russel L. *Immigrants in the Ozarks: A Study in Ethnic Geography*. Columbia: University of Missouri Press, 1976.

Gist, Noel P. *Missouri: Its Resources, People, and Institutions*. Columbia: Curators of the University of Missouri, 1950.

"The History of St. Joe," *St. Joe Headframe*, Special Edition. Bonne Terre, Mo.: St. Joe Minerals Corp., 1970.

Hull, Clifton H. *Shortline Railroads of Arkansas*. Norman: University of Oklahoma Press, 1969.

Johnson, Hildegard B. "The Location of German Settlements in the Middle West," *Annals of the Association of American Geographers* 41 (March 1941): 1–41.

Kersten, Earl W., Jr. "Changing Economy and Landscape in a Missouri Ozarks Area," *Annals of the Association of American Geographers* 48 (December 1958): 398–418.

McCune, Paul B. "Housing and Population Study of Linn Township, Christian County, Missouri, 1977." Term paper, Department of Geography and Geology, Southwest Missouri State University, 1977.

McFarlane, Larry A. "The Missouri Land and Livestock Company, Limited, of Scotland: Foreign Investment on the Missouri Farming Frontier, 1882–1908." Ph.D. dissertation, University of Missouri-Columbia, 1963.

Maxfield, O. O. "Geography of the Boston Mountains." Ph.D. dissertation, Ohio State University, 1963.

Paullin, Charles O. *Atlas of the Historical Geography of the United States*. Washington, D.C.: Carnegie Institute of Washington, 1932.

Rafferty, Milton D., Gerlach, Russel L., and Hrebec, Dennis. *Atlas of Missouri*. Springfield, Mo.: Aux-Arc Research Associates, 1970.

———. "Population and Settlement Changes in Two Ozark Localities," *Rural Sociology* 38 (Spring 1973): 46–56.

——— and Hrebec, Dennis. "Logan Creek: A Missouri Ozark Valley Revisited," *Journal of Geography* 72 (October 1973): 7–17.

Sauer, Carl O. *The Geography of the Ozark Highland of Missouri*. The Geographic Society of Chicago, Bulletin no. 7. Chicago: University of Chicago Press, 1920.

Stepp, Peggy. "Jonathan Fairbanks: 'Mr. Springfield Public Schools.'" Master's seminar paper, Department of History, Southwest Missouri State University, 1972.

Tadros, Helmi R. "Return Migration to Selected Communities in the Ozarks: A Predominantly Rural, Economically Depressed Region." Ph.D. dissertation, University of Missouri-Columbia, 1968.

U.S. Bureau of the Census. *U.S. Census of Population, 1970* and earlier dates. Washington, D.C.: Government Printing Office.

Walz, Robert B. "Migration Into Arkansas, 1834–1880." Ph.D. dissertation, University of Texas, 1958.

7.

The Civil War and Its Consequences

Because physical conditions were not suited to the development of large plantations of cotton, hemp, or tobacco—nor was there adequate transportation to support these commercial enterprises—most residents of the Ozarks were not slaveholders, and as we have seen, there was only a small number of slaves in the entire Ozark Plateau. Most of the slaves were brought to the counties bordering the Mississippi, Missouri, and Arkansas rivers. Nevertheless, there were slaveholders and slaves in several interior counties, and both Missouri and Arkansas had become addicted to the evil habit. Even the Cherokees, who had moved to what is today the Oklahoma Ozarks and who themselves were unfairly treated by the whites, were slaveholders. Principal Chief, John Ross, could speak eloquently in defense of Cherokee rights and at the same time use slaves to work his property at Park Hill. Missouri Senator Thomas Hart Benton was a slave owner throughout his life, but he recognized slavery as an evil and would not be a part of the extension of the practice. Others who owned no slaves at all defended slavery with their votes and sympathies, and in many cases they were later called upon to defend it with their lives.

Although there were few slaves and little sympathy for slavery in the Ozarks, there was no way to avoid being drawn into the conflict. In the 1850's, remoteness and isolation buffered Ozark people from the struggle over the issue of slavery in Bleeding Kansas, and there was little of the abolitionist activity that flared in states east of the Mississippi River. There were dedicated efforts in both Missouri and Arkansas to steer a neutral course before the South fired on Fort Sumter on April 12, 1861, and these efforts continued even after the conflict had begun. There were men, such as Sterling Price, former governor of Missouri, who were willing to compromise to the end. Price was to play a major role in the war as a Confederate general.

There was strong Union sympathy in the Ozarks. The influx of great numbers of Germans and a new wave of people from the Northern states in the years immediately preceding the war resulted in a large population that was hostile to slavery. St. Louis was a strong Union city because of its large number of Germans and Irish. Springfield, Rolla, Poplar Bluff, Cape Girardeau, and other larger towns in the Missouri Ozarks were known to have strong Union sentiments. Fayetteville and Batesville and the upland Ozark counties in Arkansas, if not pro-Union, were antisecession. When the vote was taken in the Arkansas convention to consider secession, only five of the seventy delegates had the temerity to vote no. Isaac Murphy, a tough old frontiersman from

Stand Watie, prominent Cherokee, member of the Ridge faction (Treaty Party), and Confederate general. (Courtesy Oklahoma Historical Society.)

the Missouri border, and four others from the Ozark Upland were the only dissidents. Murphy was appointed provisional governor of Arkansas after Little Rock was captured by the Union Army in 1863.

Among the Five Civilized Tribes in Indian Territory, secession was largely a matter of latitude. Wedged in a corner between strong proslavery populations in southwest Arkansas and northern Texas, the Choctaws had little chance to assert any choice in the matter. The Creeks, Chickasaws, and Seminoles were in a similar position but with less direct pressure from Southern interests. The Cherokees were strongly divided on the issue. Their principal chief, John Ross, wanted neither a Union nor Confederate alliance; he sought neutrality and peace. Yet the tribe allied itself with the South, and the warriers fought for the Confederacy or the Union—or shifted their allegiance from one side to the other, trying to anticipate the final outcome.

The defeat of Union forces at Wilson's Creek near Springfield on August 10, 1861 brought to the Cherokee Nation a surge of Confederate sentiment so strong that John Ross was no longer able to maintain his neutral position. Surrounded by armed Cherokees who were eager to fight for the Confederacy, he felt obliged to sign a treaty of alliance with the South. The Battle of Pea Ridge (Arkansas), fought between March 6 and March 8, 1862, caused a sharp reversal of Cherokee opinion. Cherokee recruitment into Union service became very brisk, and many of the soldiers who enlisted were veterans of Confederate regiments. Nevertheless, Ross would not repudiate the Confederate alliance.

The Conflict

Although the rugged terrain of the Ozarks would seem to dictate a marginal role in military affairs, the region's geography was such that some of the more important battles of the western campaign were fought within its borders. Among the responsible geographic factors for this was, first, the fact that the rugged interior prevented movement of large armies through the region between the core population areas in the Missouri and Arkansas river valleys. Thus the armies were forced to go around the western end of the Ozarks, where it was easier to move men and equipment and where the troops could be sustained in part by foraging and by raiding farms and settlements. Second, a trained cadre of officers was quickly recruited from the garrisons stationed in Indian Territory (today's Oklahoma and Kansas). Although many of the officers, both Northern and Southern, had been classmates at West Point or had fought as comrades in the Mexican War, those with the most recent battle experience came from the frontier. Third, Missouri was truly a border state, in both geography and sentiment, and both the Confederates and the Federals expected military victories to win the state. Fourth, both the Arkansas and Missouri rivers were considered to be strategic routes to the West. Fifth, the allegiance of the Indians who lived west of the Missouri and Arkansas borders was coveted by both sides. Sixth, the rugged Ozark interior was well suited to guerrilla warfare, not only by raiding parties from Federal and Confederate military units, but also by quasi-military groups, such as William Quantrill's Confederate Raiders and Jim Lane's Kansas marauders.

More often than not, both Confederate and Union troops were ill clad and poorly equipped. Many units had no uniforms and were armed with squirrel rifles. At first the number of volunteers exceeded the supply of weapons. Sterling Price recruited many new troops in Missouri after his victories at Wilson's Creek and Lexington, but two-thirds of his men were unarmed, and reports of an approaching Union force scared many away. Beans, cornmeal, and coffee were the staples for both armies. Garden vegetables, fruit, and meat animals were taken from farmers, at times leaving the civilian population with little or nothing to eat. Civilians who were fortunate enough to be paid for confiscated supplies with Union vouchers sometimes were able to receive payment, but those given the Confederates' Missouri scrip received nothing. Short-term enlistments of ninety days and a strong propensity for soldiers to desert after a major battle made it difficult for generals to know the strength of their own forces, let alone those of the enemy.

In proportion to her population, Missouri provided more men than any other state in the nation; 109,000 were Union soldiers, and 30,000 were in the Confederate Army. Together, these troops made up 60 per cent of the men eligible for military service. Arkansas supplied an estimated 46,000 Confederate soldiers, and another 6,000 served in the Union Army—an astounding number for a state that had a white population of only 325,000 in 1860. Truly, there were few pacifists or shirkers among the frontiersmen.

Nevertheless, neither the Confederate nor the Federal governments considered the military activities west of the Mississippi of vital significance. After the Battle of Wilson's Creek, the officer corps of the opposing forces considered the conflict west of the Mississippi a sideshow. The residents of the Ozarks would not have agreed; for them the war continued in a nearly unbroken chain of skirmishes and raids interspersed with major battles.

The war came quickly to the Ozarks (fig. 7-1). The Federal government established garrisons at St. Louis, Rolla, Boonville, Hermann, and Jefferson City in the summer of 1861. In Arkansas the Confederate Army captured the Federal arsenal at Fort Smith and gained control of the Arkansas Valley. A force under the direction of fiery Union General Nathaniel Lyon drove the Confederate forces of Missouri Governor Jackson and Colonel Marmaduke from Boonville, thereby gaining control of the Missouri River valley.

The first major conflict occurred at Carthage, Missouri, on July 5, 1861, when Federal troops, mainly Germans from St. Louis under the command of Colonel Franz Sigel, encountered the Confederate forces of Governor Jackson and General Sterling Price. After a short battle, Sigel's force of one thousand men retreated in the face of a Confederate force of four thousand.

By the middle of July, General Lyon had moved his soldiers to Springfield to join Sigel's. Upon arriving he found that his four thousand men were outnumbered by more than ten thousand Confederate soldiers and state militiamen in southwest Missouri under General Benjamin McCulloch. Lyon decided to make a surprise attack, believing he would either win or weaken the enemy forces so that they could not follow his retreat. Lyon's troops moved into position around the Confederates camped on Wilson's Creek about twelve miles southwest of Springfield, and at dawn on August 10, 1861, the Federal forces struck.

The battle raged for six hours. Casualties reached 2,330: 1,235 Union soldiers, including General Lyon, and 1,095 Confederates. The Federal troops limped back to Springfield, then retreated toward the railhead at Rolla. Technically, the Confederates were the winners, but because they had suffered severe losses, they could not take advantage of the situation. There was a renewed spirit among Southern sympathizers, however, for they believed that Old Pap Price and his Missouri troops had upheld the fighting ability that Missourians had traditionally assigned to themselves.

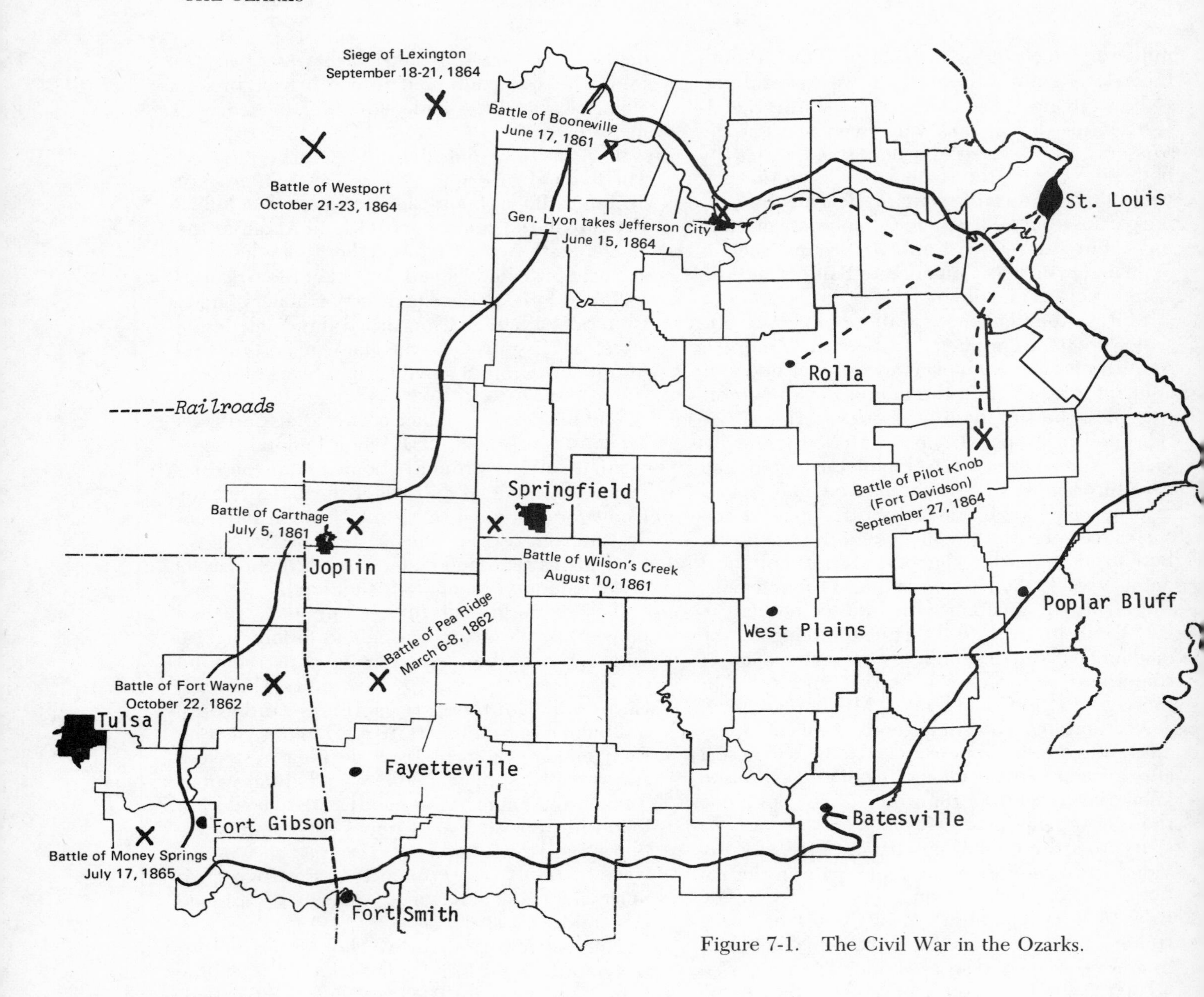

Figure 7-1. The Civil War in the Ozarks.

After occupying Springfield, Price's state militia advanced to Lexington, where, after a three-day siege, his forces captured a Union Irish brigade of three thousand men and substantial quantities of military supplies. Fearing that he might be cut off from the main Confederate force in Arkansas, Price retreated into southwest Missouri, where, after a while, he recaptured Springfield and held it during the winter of 1861–62. This was the last time Confederate forces controlled any part of Missouri for a protracted period of time.

General Lyon's Charge at Battle of Wilson's Creek, an engraving by F. O. C. Darley and H. B. Hall. (Courtesy Missouri State Historical Society.)

Placed in command of Federal forces at Rolla, Brigadier General Samuel R. Curtis marched an army of 10,000 men to Springfield in February, 1862, forcing Price to retreat into northwest Arkansas. Although Price was highly regarded by his troops, Jefferson Davis, president of the Confederate States of America, called him, simply, "the vainest man I ever met." After their retreat into Arkansas in 1862, Price's Missouri militia was combined with General Ben McCulloch's Confederate army; under the command of Mississippi-born General Earl Van Dorn, a West Point graduate, the combined forces reached 24,000 men. Another 1,000 Indians from the Five Civlized Tribes were added before the engagement with 10,500 Union troops, under the command of General Curtis, around Elk Horn Tavern at Pea Ridge, Arkansas. The battle lasted three days (March 6–8, 1862). After heavy losses on both sides and despite General Price's reluctance to halt the fighting, the Southern army withdrew.

It was a great victory for the Union. The Confederate thrust through the western Ozarks toward the Missouri heartland was blunted at Wilson's Creek, but at Pea Ridge, Confederate hopes to bring Missouri under their control were smashed. Four months later, on July 3, 1862, Colonel William Weer led a force of six thousand Union whites and Indians against the Confederate Cherokees under Colonel Stand Watie and a larger force of white Confederate soldiers under Colonel J. J. Clarkson. The battle, fought at Locust Grove in Indian Territory (Oklahoma), resulted in a rout of the Confederate forces. Men

Last Hour of the Battle of Pea Ridge. (Courtesy Missouri State Historical Society.)

who escaped went south to Tahlequah, where their story of Clarkson's defeat gave a powerful impulse to Union recruiting of Cherokees. Weer's Union troops advanced to Tahlequah, where Cherokee Chief John Ross was arrested and removed to Fort Scott (Kansas). From there he was sent to Washington and finally was permitted to remain in Philadelphia for the duration of the war.

In December, 1862, the last major Southern advance into the western Ozarks was mounted by General Thomas Hindman, the newly appointed commander of Confederate forces in Arkansas. On December 7, 1862, Hindman's forces met a Union army under General James G. Blunt at Prairie Grove, Arkansas, a conflict that had far-reaching consequences for the entire Southwest. After fighting all day, the two armies were still locked in a desperate struggle when darkness ended the fighting. Both commanders claimed victory, but after nightfall the Confederate infantry began a withdrawal toward Van Buren.

After 1862 the Confederates could not mount a major military campaign in the Ozarks, except for General Price's foray into Missouri in 1864. Most of the engagements, and there were many—135 in Missouri alone in 1863—consisted of Confederate recruiting operations or hit-and-run bushwhacking raids by Confederate guerrillas. Union garrisons at Springfield, Fayetteville, Fort Gibson, and Batesville were fortified outposts in a vast region open to raiding parties. In particular, the Arkansas cavalry and the Missouri cavalry, under the command of daredevils J. S. Marmaduke and Jo Shelby, were intensely active. They fairly rode around Curtis' army of occupation at Batesville, cutting off his line of communications through Missouri for ten days on one occasion, capturing wagons and supplies, and intercepting his telegraphic correspondence with his superiors in Missouri.

The official records of the War of the Rebellion list 573 battles, skirmishes, actions, burnings, and encounters in Missouri between 1861 and 1865. No part of the Ozarks region escaped the depredations of both sides, and nearly every county lists some event connected with the war as part of its history. Actions and skirmishes took place not only near the garrison towns, such as Batesville, Fort Gibson, Springfield, Boonville, and Cape Girardeau, but in quite remote locations, including Mountain Grove, West Plains, Doniphan, Warsaw, Eminence, Salem, Linn Creek, Humansville, and Hartville. However, the great battleground of the Ozarks was in southwest Missouri and northwest Arkansas. Springfield fell to the Confederates twice, and skirmishes were fought near Neosho, on nine different occasions: March, 1862; May, 1862; August, 1862; September, 1862; March, 1863; October, 1863; November, 1863; June, 1864; and November, 1864.

The Confederates' last major military effort was Price's raid in the fall of 1864. Aware that many Union troops had been moved to the eastern battlefields, Price moved his men north from the western Confederate heartland south of the Arkansas River. In his five-week foray into Missouri, Price aided the Confederacy by forcing Union commanders to recall some six thousand men from the Georgia campaign.

Price's army of twelve thousand men entered Missouri in Ripley County with the intention of raiding St. Louis. On September 27, 1864, at the Pilot Knob railhead, Price encountered a force of one thousand two hundred federal troops under General Thomas Ewing. Firing from behind earthworks at Fort Davidson, the Union troops inflicted more than one thousand casualties. Union losses were very light, and after nightfall the Union garrison slipped through the Confederate lines toward St. Louis after blowing up the powder magazine at the fort.

After losing some of his best cavalrymen at Fort Davidson, Price abandoned the plan to attack St. Louis. He marched north, then swung west toward Jefferson City. Concluding that it was too well defended, he continued west. Major skirmishes were fought at Glasgow and at Lexington, and there were many raids by Jo Shelby's cavalry units and the cruel guerrilla groups led by Quantrill, Bloody Bill Anderson, and George Todd.

As the Union defensive units grew and became organized, Price's situation became precarious. The daring raid became a retreat. As Price's forces moved westward from Lexington, the final crucial battle of the campaign was fought at Westport, October 21–23, in what is today part of Kansas City. It was a decisive victory for the Union forces, and when Price ordered his troops to move south, they abandoned supplies and wagons in their haste to regain refuge in Arkansas. The 1,434-mile raid ended in defeat.

The war brought out the best in some men, but it also revealed the worst in others. Men who might otherwise have led normal lives were prompted to pillage and rob. Many people were driven from their homes by foraging troops and raiding bushwhackers. Margaret Gilmore Kelso was a little girl during the war, but she recalled that many families from Arkansas moved into her neighborhood on Clear Creek in Greene County, Missouri. These people had lost everything they had:

> We called them refugees. Father gave them work, let them have corn and wheat for bread, cows to milk and a team to plow with. They were all honest and industrious, hard working people. Some of them stayed on after the war was over. Some of them went back to Arkansas and rebuilt their homes on their own land.[1]

Margaret's father was a staunch Union man and member of the "Home Guard." The family was frequently raided by the "Secesh." She describes one such occurrence:

> I remember one time when father was away, there was a forage train of I don't know how many wagons. They took all the corn we had in the crib and all the hay

1. Margaret Gilmore Kelso, "Memoirs" (manuscript, n.d.), p. 12.

we had. They also went to the smoke house and filled one wagon box full of meat. The foragemaster paid mother with Confederate money. It was perfectly worthless, he knew, but he put up a good show of being honest.[2]

Many of the raiders at the Gilmore farm apparently were local people who did not belong to either army. They carried out raiding parties when they knew the women would be alone. Mrs. Kelso recalled that "they had their lookouts and their get-together signals, and we could hear their whistles and horns when they were planning a raid. They usually disguised themselves and dressed in Union uniforms." On one occasion when young Margaret Gilmore and her brother were sent to warn a neighbor about a party of bushwhackers, she watched from a hiding place as the band turn into a relative's farm:

At the corner, they took another road and went to Aunt Lucinda Gilmore's home and robbed her. She was alone. Uncle John had not been dead very long, and she kept his clothes in a little side room. They were taking his clothing, his hat, and his gun. She clung to his gun and begged them to let her keep her husband's things. They knocked her down and kicked her, breaking her ribs, and beat her over the head with the butt of the gun. When Aunt Lucinda heard the bushwhackers had been to our place, she came over to see us. I can see her yet, as she sat there in the chimney corner, crying and telling us how they had abused her, and how bruised and battered she was. How black her face was! It was as black as flesh can be. She died a few days after she visited me, from the terrible beating they gave her.[3]

Reconstruction and Redrawing the Political Map

The Civil War had several important effects on the land and people of the Ozarks, and these lasted for several years. The broad national issues, such as slavery and the right of states to disregard federal laws, had been settled by the war. The western frontier states, including the Ozarks, participated in Reconstruction. Railroad building soon reached a furious pace, and economic development took the form of new farms, new manufacturing plants, new commercial and banking enterprises, and mineral and timber exploitation. Immigration to the Ozarks increased rapidly, and this time more of the immigrants came from the North. Many leaders in the economic resurgence were former Union officers who had served in the Ozark campaigns.

On the whole, however, the political destiny of the Ozarks was shaped by forces outside the region. The core political areas of both Missouri and Arkansas lie in the valleys of the two great rivers that flow through the two states. During the entire span of white occupation of the Ozarks, the region has contributed relatively few elected state officials. On the other hand, the Missouri and Arkansas valleys are in the mainstream of state politics. The three major contributors of state and national political leaders are Greene County, Missouri, which includes the Ozarks' largest city, Springfield; Washington County, Arkansas, which includes Fayetteville, site of the state university; and Tahlequah, Oklahoma, the capital of the Cherokee Nation. Jefferson City and Little Rock lie on Ozark borders but are politically aligned with the core areas of Missouri and Arkansas, respectively.

To say that Ozarkers were apolitical after the Civil War would be an overstatement, but no doubt isolation and lack of a developed economy were factors in the relatively lesser role Ozarks people played in the rapidly changing political situations of Missouri and Arkansas. In both states a loyalty oath was required of voters; the individual was compelled to swear he had never given aid or sympathy to the Confederate movement. This effectively disenfranchised at least a third of the otherwise eligible voters. Radical Republican governments were installed in both Arkansas and Missouri, but the Oklahoma Ozarks was returned to the Cherokee Nation under the supervision of the federal government. The Democrats regained control of the legislature and governorship in Missouri by 1870 and in Arkansas by 1874. Both states have been firmly in the Democratic column ever since, except for the terms of Republican Governor Winthrop Rockefeller in Arkansas and Republican Governors Herbert S. Hadley, Robert S. Hyde, Sam A. Baker, Henry S. Caulfield, and

2. Ibid., p. 9.
3. Ibid., p. 10.

Christopher S. Bond in Missouri. By 1876, Democrats had recaptured most of the elected offices in the county governments.

The transition period brought on by the Civil War was not yet over. At the county level, Democratic ambitions were crippled by economic and social changes; the Civil War had left the Ozarks ravaged and ruined. The Panic of 1873 brought on a depression, and the grasshopper plague of 1874 destroyed most of the crops. Most of the counties were heavily in debt as they borrowed to finance railroads, build new courthouses to replace those destroyed in the war, and to undertake other types of public improvements. The Democrats, being in power when the debts were made, were blamed for the high taxes required to pay them off. Taney County, Missouri, owed $44,000 in 1874, an extremely larged debt for that time, and it was not liquidated until the 1930's.[4]

The great amount of social unrest in the western Ozarks was another factor in the defeat of the Democrats and the rise of Republicanism in the mid-1880's. Crime and violence, which had become common during the war, continued. A certain class of citizens had grown accustomed to a shiftless way of life and held little regard for laws and the property of their neighbors. The region was still not fully settled, and isolation was a magnet for transient outlaws. Bands of marauders, led by such men as Jesse James and Cole Younger, robbed and plundered for two decades after the Civil War, and the Republicans used outlawry as an issue to weaken the Democratic party.

To combat lawlessness and oppose further increases in county debts, vigilance committees were organized. They were not of the same ilk as the Ku Klux Klan, but their central purpose—establishing order—was not altogether out of line with the Klan's goals. It was a time when law and order at any cost was gaining popularity and growing in strength throughout the South.

Vigilance committees were not new to the Ozarks. In the 1840's an organization known as the Slickers was formed in Benton County, Missouri, to "slick," with hickory switches, all suspected lawbreakers. Another group, known as the Enforcers, was active in Greene County, Missouri. During the war, nearly every county had a home guard, which took on the job of guarding bridges and railroads and providing some measure of civil control. No doubt the largest and most influential of the vigilance committees was the group of Taney County, Missouri, residents who watched the proceedings of county government and assisted law-enforcement officials in the pursuit, capture, and conviction of criminals. They were known as the Bald Knobbers because their meetings were sometimes held on isolated, treeless hills. A second group of Bald Knobbers was organized in Christian County in the 1880's when the railroad and sawmill town of Chadwick developed a lawless character.

After a few men allegedly were murdered by the Bald Knobbers and others severely intimidated, another group of citizens organized for the purpose of combating the activities of the Bald Knobbers. Known as the Anti–Bald Knobbers, they were mostly Confederate Democrats. The Bald Knobbers membership originally was composed of Unionists, Confederates, Democrats, and Republicans, but as time passed, some degree of polarization toward Republicanism developed.

In his account of Taney County politics, Elmo Ingenthron describes how the transfer of allegiance from the Democratic party to the Republican party occurred:

> The Bald Knobbers won the election of 1886, and the Republican Party which they dominated has won the majority of county offices in the elections ever since. For several years following the political victories of the mid-1880s, the two principal political parties in the country were the Bald Knobber-Republican and the Anti-Bald Knobber-Democrats.[5]

The Bald Knobber organization was discredited both locally and in the national press after its members raided an innocent family in Christian County and killed two men. More than a dozen Bald Knobbers were arrested, and on May 10, 1889, three of them were hanged at Ozark, Missouri.

4. Elmo Ingenthron, *The Land of Taney* (Point Lookout, Mo.: The School of the Ozarks Press, 1974), p. 227.

5. Ibid., p. 231.

Contemporary Politics

The political map of the Ozarks has not changed much since the 1880's. Southwest Missouri has the reputation of being solid Republican country, and the main strength of Republicans in Arkansas always has been in the northwestern counties. Residents of the eastern interior Ozarks, which experienced less bloodshed and civil strife, are strongly Democratic, albeit equally as conservative in their ideology as the rural Republicans. The northern and eastern Ozarks border counties, where there is a large German population, usually vote Republican in state and national elections. The counties of the eastern Mineral Area lean toward the Democratic ticket.

Over the years, in both political parties, a system of earning political clout has been practiced in Ozark counties much it has in many of the rural counties of the United States. This system can be described as good-old-boy politics. Birthright in one of the pioneer families is helpful in being elected to a local political office. However, performance of certain ritualistic activities usually is expected before one is selected to run for sheriff, judge of the county court, county clerk, or other office. Those who are successful in gaining the approval of the dominant party usually have performed various chores and possess various attributes that make them qualify as good old boys. For instance, this would include being on hand to assist with preparations for political picnics or gatherings; helping to get out the vote on election day by driving old folks to the polls in one's personal car; being a good hand at most things one undertakes; having a strong liking for manly sports, such as hunting and fishing; being good at telling an off-color joke in proper surroundings; being good at social conversation with women, but not to the extent of being a ladies' man; having a good sense of humor; and being willing to help out with family emergencies, such as serious illness or death, that strike one's neighbors. In the counties that vote solid Republican or Democrat, election to an office is fairly well assured when a good old boy gains the approval of leaders in the dominant party. Successful tenure in a county office is sometimes the steppingstone to state or national political offices.

There are signs, particularly in the counties that have experienced considerable growth, that the old system is dying out. In counties with large populations, such as Greene, Cole, Jasper, Jefferson, Cape Girardeau, and St. Francois in Missouri and Benton, Washington and Independence in Arkansas, the elected county officials may be responsible for budgets running into millions of dollars. Increasingly, voters are coming to recognize that officeholders should possess more qualifications than being a good old boy. Moreover, as more new people move into the region, one's birthright in a long-line Ozark family is of less importance in gaining political office.

The Question of Guns and Lawlessness

There is always a certain propensity for rowdiness and lawlessness in frontier areas, mining towns, and lumber camps. The Ozarks has had its share of violence and crime, and the historical geography of the region may have been a factor. Two large mining districts developed in the region, and the western border remained Indian country into the twentieth century. Indian Territory was recognized as a refuge for gangs of outlaws, such as the notorious band led by Tom Starr, a Cherokee descended from a family among those who signed the treaty of removal. Before the emergence of effective interstate law enforcement, which was facilitated by the creation of the Federal Bureau of Investigation, state boundaries were effective protection for lawbreakers. Four states meet in the rugged hills of the southwestern Ozarks: Kansas, Missouri, Oklahoma, and Arkansas. Thus the Ozarks, particularly the southwest, possessed many of the things that attracted the likes of the James gang, the Daltons, the Younger brothers, the Starrs, and, in the twentieth century, Dillinger, Bonnie and Clyde, and Alvin Karpis. This section, more than any other, became the robbers' roost of the Ozark region.

Some elements of frontier attitudes toward crime and the use of firearms persist. People living in rural areas of the United States almost always own guns and know how to use them. Most adolescent boys—and a large number of girls—can shoot rifles and shotguns. After all, hunting is an important form of recreation. Often, schools are dismissed during deer season so that teachers and students alike may take up positions in the forest.

There is a more subtle, deeper reason why rural people cling to their guns. They are in exposed positions, often out of sight of neighbors; sometimes, county law officers are an hour or more away by automobile. When a rural resident of the Lake of the Ozarks area was taken from his home one night and murdered during the late 1970's, television reporters who interviewed residents while the men accused of the crime were still at large learned that many were armed and prepared to defend themselves. The home-guard concept of individual protection is still strong in the Ozarks.

Selected References

Belser, Thomas A. "Military Operations in Missouri and Arkansas, 1861–1865." Parts 1 and 2. Ph.D. dissertation, Vanderbilt University, 1958.

Edwards, John H. *Noted Guerrillas: or the Warfare of the Border*. St. Louis: Bryan, Brand and Co., 1877.

Ellenburg, Martha A. "Reconstruction in Arkansas." Ph.D. dissertation, University of Missouri-Columbia, 1967.

Fletcher, John Gould. *Arkansas*. Chapel Hill: The University of North Carolina Press, 1947.

Ingenthron, Elmo. *The Land of Taney*. Point Lookout, Mo.: The School of the Ozarks Press, 1974.

Kelso, Margaret Gilmore. "Memoirs." Manuscript, n.d. In the possession of Robert K. Gilmore, Springfield, Mo.

Long, E. B. *The Civil War Day By Day: An Almanac, 1861–1865*. New York: Doubleday and Co., 1971.

McReynolds, Edwin C. *Oklahoma: A History of the Sooner State*. Norman: University of Oklahoma Press, 1964.

Meyer, Duane. *The Heritage of Missouri: A History*. St. Louis: State Publishing Company, Inc., 1963.

Missouri State Highway Commission and the Writers' Program of the Works Progress Administration. *Missouri: A Guide to the "Show Me" State*. American Guide Series. New York: Duell, Sloan and Pearce, 1941.

Upton, Lucille Morris. *Bald Knobbers*. Caldwell, Idaho: The Caxton Printers, 1939.

War of the Rebellion: A Compilation of the Official Records of the Union and Confederate Armies. 70 volumes in 128 parts, atlas. Washington, D.C.: Government Printing Office, 1880–1901.

Riverfront at Cape Girardeau. (Courtesy Missouri State Historical Society.)

8. Transportation and Communication

Although rivers are less important for commercial transportation in the Ozarks today, in the days of first white settlement the Mississippi, Missouri, and Arkansas rivers and their tributaries were the arteries that carried the Indian canoes, flatbottoms, and keelboats bringing raw products, as well as needed supplies, to trade centers and settlements. The first steamboat on the Mississippi River, the *Zebulon M. Pike*, traveled from Louisville, Kentucky, to St. Louis in 1817, pushing upstream at the impressive rate of three miles per hour. Two years later a specially designed shallow-draft steamer, the *Independence*, moved up the Missouri River to Franklin. In spite of navigation problems and the danger of explosion, the steamboat was a great improvement over keelboats and flatboats, which had to be pulled, poled, or paddled. Steamboats were faster, larger, and could carry heavier and bulkier cargoes. They could provide passengers with room, board, fashionable furnishings, and entertainment. Very soon regular packet service was established at several of the Mississippi and Missouri river towns that served as ports for the northern and eastern Ozarks. The usual ports of call were Cape Girardeau, Ste. Genevieve, St. Louis, St. Charles, Washington, Hermann, Jefferson City, Boonville, and Glasgow.

Although steamboat navigation on the Arkansas River was not as well developed as that on the Mississippi and Missouri, riverboats were important for the early settlement and commerce of the Arkansas River valley and southern Ozarks. Some of the Cherokees who moved to their new lands in Indian Territory during the 1830's traveled by way of the Arkansas River. Nevertheless, in the early 1840's only two or three steamboats a month reached Little Rock via a channel frequently described as "four feet deep and falling."

Only a few of the largest streams that drained from the interior of the Ozark Upland could be navigated. Shallow-draft steamboats landed at Warsaw regularly during the fall and spring months and could reach Osceola when conditions were especially favorable. Similar boats were used on the Current River to serve Doniphan during high water.

Massey and James, owners of the Maramec Iron Works, were persistent in their efforts to improve navigation on the Meramec and Gasconade rivers. Except during periodic rises, the Meramec was too shallow and had too many fallen trees in the channel to permit even a keelboat to pass the full 172 miles from the Mississippi to the ironworks. Nevertheless, heavy items, such as large forge hammers and anvils, were transported part of the way up the Meramec. In 1835 and 1836, Massey and James petitioned the Missouri

General Assembly for state aid in opening the Gasconade River to steamboats. They proposed to clear the Gasconade of all logs and snags obstructing navigation, to construct wing dams to channel the water, and to keep the river clear for a two-year period in return for a charter to collect tolls on the tonnage of all steamboats. The assembly turned down the offer, but Massey and James removed the snags and logs without state aid. The *Iowa*, *Howard*, *Dart*, and *Chastain* attempted to ascend the river, but low water turned them back. In 1849, flatboats were used successfully to transport iron blooms from Paydown to the Missouri River, where they were loaded on steamboats. Overland drayage from Meramec to Hermann averaged between two and four dollars per ton more.

The White River was the only stream flowing from the interior Ozarks large enough to become an important artery of commerce for steamboats. Most of the navigation was done during high water. The exact date W. M. Wolf brought the first steamboat up to Wolf House in Baxter County, Arkansas, is not known, but it was probably in the late 1830's or early 1840's. Before the steamboats came—and during the dry seasons—keelboats were poled upriver and floated back, carrying up to fifty bales of cotton.

Beginning at the south and running north there were landings at Chastain, Norfolk, Bomer's, Shipp's, Buford, Buffalo, Buffalo City, Mooney's Landing, Wildcat Shoals, and at McBee's Landing two miles up and across the river from Cotter. McBee's Landing was in Marion County and served as a shipping point for Flippin and Yellville. The steamboat *Ray* reached the mouth of the James River in 1859, the farthest point ever reached on the White River by a steamboat.

The shallow-draft boats were designed to run the rocky shoals and chutes of the White River. Most of them weighed fifty to two hundred tons and could carry seventy-five to five hundred bales of cotton. Several held mail contracts, including the *Jesse Lazear* and the *Monongahela Belle*, which carried mail from Batesville to Buffalo and Buffalo City. Steamboats provided the fastest and easiest mode of travel. The trip from Batesville to McBee's Landing, a distance of one hundred miles, took twenty-four hours, the return trip twelve hours. The boats were powered by wood-fired (preferably pine knots) steam boilers. Woodyards were located at all landings and at some points in between.

Showboats that played regularly to crowds at the Mississippi, Missouri, and Arkansas river towns sometimes traveled up the White River. Their arrival was always a time of great excitement, and throngs of people gathered at the landings. The first black men many of the children saw were deckhands on the boats.

The federal government spent considerable sums of money in the late 1800's to keep the river channels open. In 1870 the U.S. Army Corps of Engineers survey boat *City of Forsyth* made an extensive study of the White and Black rivers. It reported 2,019 snags and two wrecks hazardous to navigation.

In 1900, steamboats started bringing a new cargo upriver: supplies, equipment, and materials for railroad building. Ironically, the steamboats helped to construct the very thing that would drive them out of business. The railroad bridge at Cotter, Arkansas, was constructed so that it could swing aside to allow passage of steamboats. The turntable was used only once: in 1913 when the steamer *Huff* came up the White for a load of staves. Its coming created quite a stir along the river because by that time trains provided a faster, more economical, reliable, efficient service. The last steamboat to operate regularly on the Upper White River, the *Ozark Queen*, made her final trip on the regular run from McBee's Landing to Batesville in June, 1903.

For a time, boats operated on the White and Black rivers in the freshwater-mussel industry, just as they did on the Cumberland, Tennessee, and other rivers in the uplands east of the Mississippi. Dr. J. H. Meyers of Black Rock on Black River is credited with starting the "pearling boom." In 1897 he found a fourteen-grain, fine-luster, pinkish-colored pearl that generated a stampede of pearl hunters into the rivers. When some of the pearls brought five dollars to fifty dollars each, and there were rumors that others had brought more, the news traveled fast. One writer described the search on the White River as follows:

> I have seen as many as 500 men, women, and children of all sizes and colors on one bar, indiscriminately

mingled, wading in as far as they could reach bottom, some opening, others gathering shells. The wealthiest bankers, lawyers, merchants, doctors, etc., their wives and children, wading in with the poorest darkies, all laughing, singing, working day after day, the summer through.[1]

Large spherical pearls of desired color and luster were in demand for jewelry, but most of the shells were used to make buttons. Most of the button factories were downstream in Arkansas, but portable button extractors were built on a number of flatboats to operate on the Upper White River. It took about forty bushels of mussel shells to make a bushel of buttons, so blank buttons were sawed out at upstream locations and shipped to the factories for drilling and finishing.

Twenty-nine species of mussels inhabited the White River, but the most common types were *Actinonaurs carinata*, *Lampsilis ventricosa*, and *Pleurobema cordatum coccineum*. The industry was seasonal and did not interfere with farm activities. It lasted about thirty-five years: from 1900 to the mid-1930's. The mussel boats were among the last steam-powered boats to use the White River for commerce.

Downriver flatboat commerce continued well past the turn of the century on the White. Flatboats built at river landings kept moving cotton, crossties, grain, and cedar logs to markets in Arkansas and other downriver ports. Several rafts of crossties and cedar logs often were linked together with poles to form a snakeraft. These unwieldy craft were hazards for steamboats, and it was no easy task to halt the forward movement of a raft composed of as many as 1,500 logs or ties.

Nearly every permanently flowing stream in the Ozarks was used at one time or another to float crossties. Normally the ties were cut in winter and stacked alongside a stream to await the spring rise. Then they were floated downstream to shipping points on railroads. Most of the time, they were floated in the form of rafts, but sometimes they were simply pushed into the current to float downstream.

Interestingly enough, the popular sports of canoeing and float fishing on Ozark streams are protected by laws governing the use of streams for navigation during the logging era. In a landmark case, *Elder v. Delcour*,[2] the Missouri Supreme Court declared that all Missouri streams are open to canoeing and fishing because they are navigable waters by warrant of their use to float crossties.

Today the Mississippi River and its connecting systems of waterways comprise an expanding 22,000-mile navigation network. The Mississippi has an improved 9-foot channel throughout its course in Missouri; below St. Louis there are no locks or dams. The river is open to navigation from St. Louis to New Orleans twelve months a year and from early March to mid-December on the upper portion. Navigation to Chicago via the Illinois River is open the full year. The Missouri River has a 7.5-foot channel and is normally open to navigation from late March to the end of November. The Arkansas River and its northern tributaries, the Grand and Verdigris rivers, are navigable to the Port of Catoosa, a few miles east of Tulsa. This remarkable series of dams and locks, patterned after those on the Tennessee River, was the special project of Oklahoma Senator Robert S. Kerr, who worked untiringly year after year to secure the necessary votes in Congress to finance the project.

About ten common-carrier barge lines serve the Ozarks border. St. Louis is the largest river port, with two public docks and thirty-seven private docks. The other major Mississippi port serving the Ozarks is Cape Girardeau, which has twelve private docks and a shipyard. On the Arkansas-Verdigris the main ports are Catoosa (Tulsa), Muskogee, Fort Smith, and Little Rock.

When the element of speed is removed from transportation needs, commodites and products can be moved much less expensively by water. The coal and steel industries in particular have profited from cheap water transportation. Petroleum products and agricultural chemicals move upstream, while wheat, corn, and soybeans from the hinterlands move downstream toward foreign markets. Unfortunately, the Ozark region is not a market for large cargoes of bulky commodities, nor are the products produced in the region the

1. *The Independence County Chronicle* 9, no. 4: 29.

2. Hugh P. Williamson, "Restrictions and Rights of the Missouri Sportsman" (Missouri Department of Conservation Publication, n.d.).

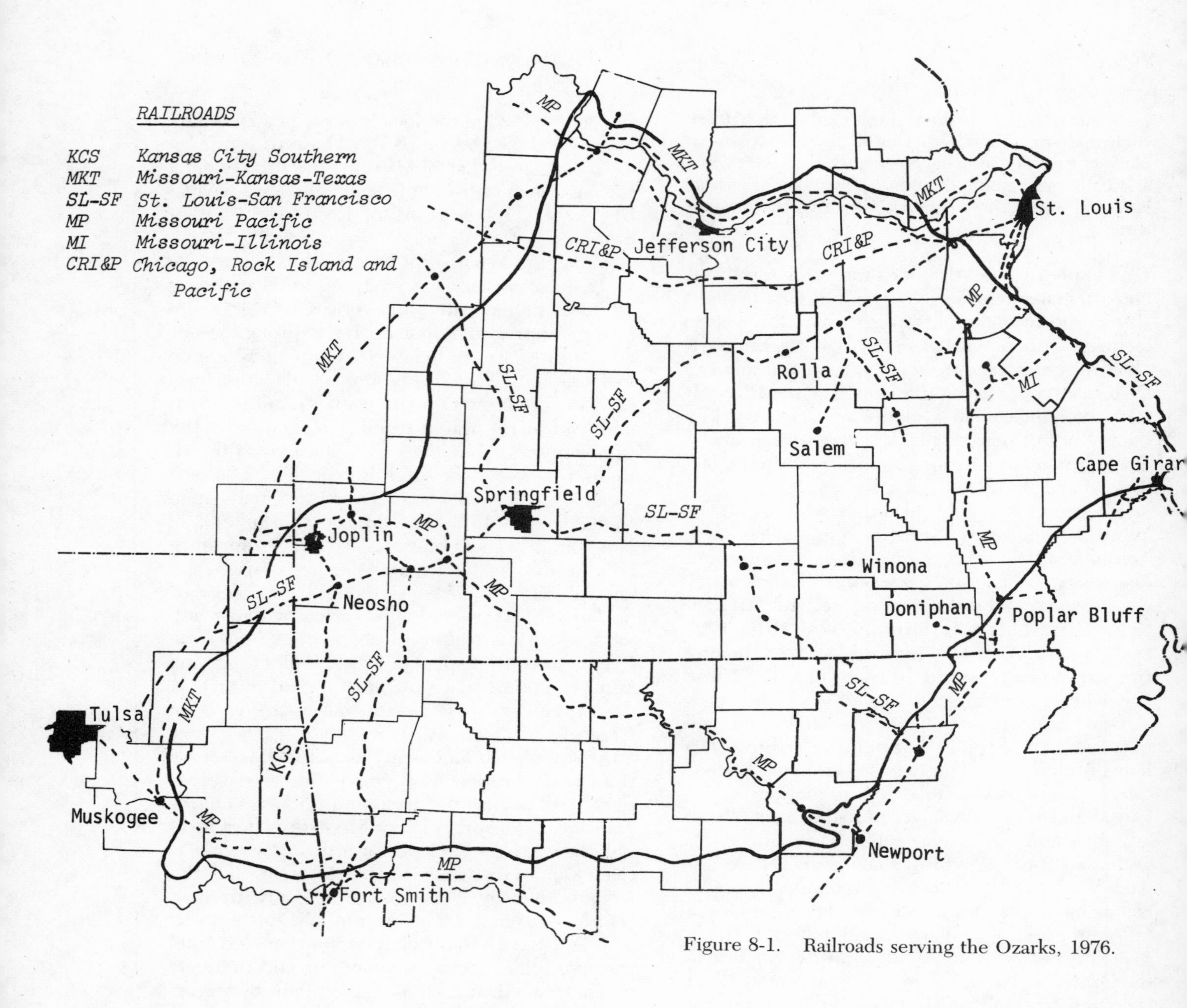

Figure 8-1. Railroads serving the Ozarks, 1976.

type that require water transportation. Such transportation, once essential for Ozark commerce, is now part of the past and it is not likely to regain its former significance.

Railroads

Much of the economic and cultural geography of the Ozarks is closely related to the development of a railroad network (fig. 8-1). Railroads were constructed to tap mineral and timber resources and to supply and haul products from farms. During the period just before the Civil War, the people of the United States were railroad minded; they thought and acted in terms of railroads. Politics, legislation, newspapers, public meetings, industry, and invention were made to serve this new means of transportation.

On February 13, 1859, the Hannibal and St.

Joseph Railroad was completed, the first across Missouri; unfinished lines of other railroads radiated from St. Louis. By February 1, 1861, the Pacific Railroad of Missouri was operating to Sedalia. It had been projected from St. Louis to Kansas City in the hope that the federal government would select St. Louis as the eastern terminus of the contemplated transcontinental railroad. The Southwest Branch of the Pacific Railroad of Missouri, running from the main line at Pacific, was extended to Rolla on January 1, 1861, and plans were made to extend it southwestward by way of Springfield to reach the rich mineral resources of Jasper County and to open that area to settlement. The St. Louis and Iron Mountain, planned from St. Louis to southeast Missouri to serve the lead and iron industries of St. Francois, Iron, and Madison counties, was finished as far as Pilot Knob on April 2, 1858. From Mineral Point, on the main line, an extension was laid to Potosi.

In these early years, railroads were passing from the hands of the practical mechanics and inventors into the hands of businessmen. The mechanics knew how to build steam locomotives that could chug along rails of wood or scrap iron. They had proved that the newfangled steam cars could move freight and passengers faster and cheaper than stagecoaches or canal barges. Railroads could also reach into the arid lands of the West, where steamboats were not practical.

Railroad building, however, required huge outlays of capital. Tracklaying alone cost twenty thousand dollars to fifty thousand dollars per mile, and millions were needed for rolling stock, yards, and stations. National, state, and local aid had been offered generously to private undertakings. The United States granted more than three million acres of land, and Missouri authorized an issue of state bonds, backed by first mortgages, upon the several railroads to the aggregate sum of twenty-four million dollars. Municipal, county, and township governments likewise indebted themselves. The national financial crises of 1861 caused suspension of interest payments by all railroads operating in the Ozarks. The question of foreclosure was dropped until the Civil War was over, but in the years immediately after the war, all of the railroads went bankrupt.

When the West found it didn't have the capital and talent to build transcontinental railroads, eastern financiers, among them Commodore Vanderbilt, Daniel Drew, Jim Fisk and Jay Gould, launched profitable and checkered careers. The process was simple. First, select a name, such as the Kansas City, Clinton and Springfield; the St. Louis, Salem and Little Rock; or the Arkansas and Oklahoma Railroad. Second, print a bond issue and map of the proposed route. Next, persuade the state legislature to issue a charter, in appreciation for which a portion of the bond issue is distributed to legislators or other influential citizens. Now, procure a land grant of alternate sections along the route. Next, collect subsidies and bribes from counties and towns that might or might not get the railroad. Look over mining lands in your sections and establish town companies and real-estate brokerages. Sell settlers land and supplies and haul out their products at inflated prices. It was a grand plan and it worked.

Many Ozark towns—Monett, Chadwick, Purdy, and Rogers, to name a few—were born as railheads and were named for railroad men. Other towns subscribed funds to construct a railroad but were bypassed when tracks were laid. Springfield and Lebanon, Missouri, are in the latter category.

Even less fortunate have been those Ozark towns and counties which raised funds but never got a railroad. At one time, Dallas County, Missouri, owed bondholders more than the value of all property, real and personal, in the county. In 1869 the county court subscribed $235,000 in bonds to the Laclede and Fort Scott Railroad Company, which was to build a line from Lebanon through Buffalo, the county seat, to Fort Scott, Kansas. The road was never built. In 1879 the county offered to pay the debt, which by then amounted to $244,755, for twenty cents on the dollar, but the creditors refused. The case eventually reached the Missouri Supreme Court, which supported the bondholders, but Dallas County judges were successful in avoiding process servers for decades. In 1899 the bondholders offered to settle the debt, which by then totaled $1,407,000, for $250,000, but Dallas County refused. Finally, in 1920, bondholders agreed to accept $300,000 in new bonds, which were retired on July 1, 1940, seventy-one years after the initial bonds were issued. Laclede County, where roadbed was built but tracks were never laid,

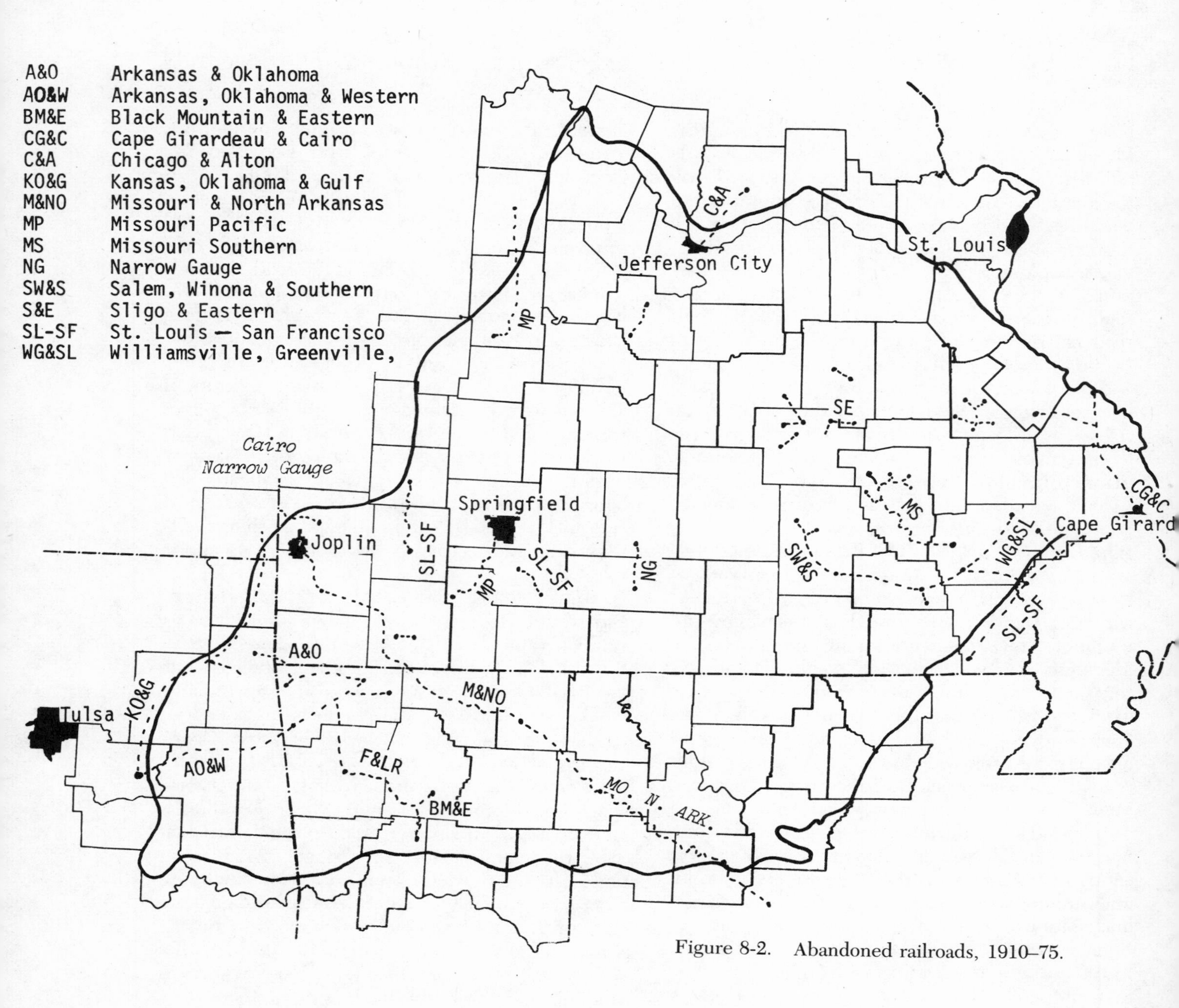

Figure 8-2. Abandoned railroads, 1910–75.

issued $100,000 worth of bonds for the Laclede and Fort Scott Railroad; they were retired in 1894.

St. Clair County, Missouri, has the distinction of being in rebellion against the federal government for some 30 years. In 1870 the county issued bonds to the Tebo and Neosho Railroad, which was to run from Clinton through Osceola, the county seat, to Memphis. The promoters sold the bonds to innocent purchasers, made surveys, then were never seen again. The bondholders soon demanded payment, but after meeting the first year's interest, St. Clair Countians refused to pay for merchandise not received. The bondholders secured a judgment in federal court in 1875, the county court being ordered to pay the claims. The court refused and the federal court issued a write of mandamus, which was ignored. The county court was cited for contempt. Federal marshals went to St. Clair County repeatedly to arrest the county judges, but they could never be found.

Hiding out became the county court's first order of business. It is reported that for many years candidates campaigned and were elected principally upon their commitment and ability to evade pursuit. Court sessions were held in isolated cabins, and strangers in Osceola were watched carefully, lest they be U.S. marshals in disguise. Eventually, the debt was liquidated by compromise and by the death of most of the interested parties.

About the turn of the century, it was recognized that not all of the railroad lines that had been built could be operated at a profit. The sheer complexity of management and transfer of goods worked toward consolidation of the many short lines. Since 1910 there has been substantial reduction of mileage in the Ozarks (fig. 8-2). The abandoned railroads tend to be of three types: lines that ran parallel to others and competed for traffic (the Kansas City, Clinton and Springfield is an example; it was abandoned after it was purchased by the Frisco, which already had a line between Springfield and Kansas City); short spur lines that were designed to serve a major town (such as the Missouri Pacific line from Crane to Springfield); and short lines built by mining and lumber companies to exploit raw materials. There are many abandoned Ozarks lines that were constructed to serve mines or sawmill towns.

Recounting the complete history of railroad construction and abandonment in the Ozarks would be a useful project that would require a volume or more. Nevertheless, a brief look at most of the lines abandoned between 1910 and 1975 will serve to illustrate the essential patterns of railroad development and decline.

There were two occasions when railroad abandonment was very rapid: from the 1930's through the early 1940's and from the late 1950's to 1975. These periods correspond to the Great Depression and the two decades following the Korean conflict. Before the 1930's most of the rail mileage, constructed by several dozen companies, had been consolidated into five major lines: the St. Louis–San Francisco (Frisco); the Chicago, Rock Island & Pacific; the Missouri Pacific; the Kansas City Southern; and the Missouri-Kansas-Texas (Katy).

The longest line abandoned in southern Missouri was the Kansas City, Clinton and Springfield, which ran from Raymore (north of Harrisonville) through Harrisonville, Clinton, Lowry City, and Fair Play to Ash Grove. It obtained track rights in Springfield in 1886 and was populated known as the Leaky Roof, a reference to the condition of its boxcars. The Kansas City, Clinton and Springfield paralleled another line between Springfield and Kansas City, and when both eventually came under control of the Frisco, the former was abandoned. The first stretch, from Lowry City to Harlan Junction, was abandoned in 1926. With the exception of a few miles of track from Ash Grove to Phoenix in Greene County, the rest of the line was abandoned between 1930 and 1935. The large limestone quarry at Phoenix kept the last section in use until 1943, when both closed.

The Frisco abandoned three spur lines in the Tri-State District in 1934—from Galena, Kansas, to the Hero Mine spur; from Prosperity Junction to Joplin; and from Webb City to Rex Branch Junction—because of curtailed production in the lead-zinc mines. In 1939 and 1940 the Missouri Pacific abandoned four lines in the Tri-State District: the run from Asbury to Carthage Junction; the Water Works spur, from Joplin to Grand Falls; the line from Webb City to Joplin; and the Webb City–Granby line. Generally depressed economic conditoins and mine closings were responsible for the abandonment.

In 1939, Frisco abandoned 41 miles of track connecting Bentonville, Arkansas, with Grove, Oklahoma, via Southwest City, Missouri. The line was constructed between 1899 and 1900 by the Arkansas and Oklahoma Railroad Company and was acquired by the Frisco in the early 1900's. Two other lines operated by Frisco have been abandoned in southwest Missouri.

The first ran from Ozark to Chadwick and was built in 1883 by the Springfield and Southern Railway Company; in 1885 it was added to the Frisco system. It was used primarily to transport railroad ties and lumber from the sawmills at Chadwick and Sparta. After all the timber had been cut, there was little for the Chadwick Flyer to haul, so in 1934 the line was abandoned. It is reported that business was so poor in the 1930's that the trainmen stopped to pick blackberries and shoot quail.

The other abandoned Frisco line ran from South Greenfield in Dade County to Mount Vernon in Lawrence County. It was constructed by the Greenfield and Northern Railroad Company in 1891 and was extended from Mount Vernon to Aurora in 1892. The connecting line from South Greenfield to Mount Vernon was abandoned in 1950.

Missouri Pacific's abandoned lines in the northern Ozarks include the Warsaw Branch, connecting Warsaw with the main line at Sedalia (abandoned 1946); the line from Booneville through Tipton to Versailles, which was built by the Boonville, St. Louis and Southern Railway Company (abandoned 1936); the ten miles of track from Bagnell Dam to Eldon (abandoned 1953), plus the remaining 34 miles from Eldon to Jefferson City, which was abandoned in 1963.

In southwest Missouri the Missouri Pacific abandoned the spur line connecting Springfield with Crane on the White River line. The spur, first owned by the St. Louis, Iron Mountain and Southern, ran through Battlefield and Clever to Crane. It was abandoned in 1970.

In the southwest quarter of Missouri are three abandoned lines classified as small roads by the Missouri Public Service Commission. The longest of these was the electric trolley line of the Joplin-Pittsburg Railway Company, which abandoned its trackage in 1954. It had been providing passenger service in the Tri-State District and the coal fields of southeast Kansas. The other two roads were the Cassville and Exeter and the narrow-guage Kansas City, Ozarks and Southern, built from Ava to connect with the Springfield-Memphis line of the Frisco at Mansfield. The Cassville and Exeter was laid in 1896, the other line in 1910. Both suffered from accidents and financial difficulties.

The Ava-to-Mansfield trackage was abandoned in 1935 after its primary source of revenue, railroad ties, dwindled. The Cassville and Exeter was not abandoned until 1956, but there were many years preceding its abandonment when it was not operational. Two years before it was abandoned, a Missouri Public Service Commission report had this to say about its condition:

It is also of interest to note that the Cassville and Exeter Railway Company, with a total of 4.7 miles of track is back in operation. This is one of the nation's shortest inter-city railroads. In one of our previous reports we pointed out that the line had been forced to quit operating because of washouts on its tracks and mechanical failure of its motive power. However, some of the businessmen in Cassville and Exeter became interested in the line, perhaps out of sentiment.

In the eastern Ozarks, the St. Louis, Salem and Little Rock was built in 1873 from Frisco's main line, passing through Cuba to Salem. No more track was laid toward Little Rock because of high construction costs and the Panic of 1873. Several branches from this line served the iron industry; tracks were laid to one or more of the sink-fill mines or were simply extended into a tract of timber that was to be used for charcoal to fuel the furnaces. One of the first branch lines was the seven-mile spur built in 1877 by the Cherry Valley Railroad Company to serve the Cherry Valley mines. Other spurs were constructed from Howe to Plank Mines, Bangert to Condray, and Bangert to DeCamp in Phelps County. Still another ran from Goltra in Crawford County to the Sligo Iron Furnace in Dent County. The spur from Bangert to DeCamp was built in three sections to satisfy demands for timber by the Sligo Iron Furnace. The first section, from Bangert to Winkler, was constructed in 1877 by the Dent and Phelps Railroad Company. Frisco gained control of it and extended it to Smiths in 1900 and to DeCamp in 1905.

The Sligo Furnace Railroad Company laid track from Goltra to the furnace in 1880; this line became part of the Frisco system sometime before 1910. The branch was extended to Dillard by the Sligo and Eastern Railroad but was abandoned in 1930, a decade after the furnace shut down. The iron mines and furnaces in Phelps, Crawford, and Dent counties (Steelville Iron District) were unable to compete with the large eastern iron and steel mills, and all branches of the line from Cuba to Salem had been abandoned by 1934.

Southeast of the sink-fill iron district in Reynolds County, the most extensive logging railroad in Missouri was built between 1886 and 1910. This line, commonly known as the Missouri

Southern Railroad, commenced at Leeper in Wayne County, where it joined the St. Louis and Iron Mountain Railroad. The first twelve miles of track, narrow gauge, was laid from Leeper to Penn in 1886 by the Mill Spring, Current River and Barnesville Railroad Company. The next year, the Mill Spring, Current River and Barnesville changed its name to Missouri Southern, apparently contrary to Missouri statutes governing corporations.

By 1896 the railroad had reached Barnesville (now Ellington) in central Reynolds County. In 1907 it was expanded to standard gauge, and by 1910 the end of the line was Bunker in northwest Reynolds County. Spurs had been built to Reynolds County lumber camps at Phelps, Guber, Farris, and Lyons. Later the line's longest spur was built from Hobart through Himont to Brushey in Shannon County. By 1920, nearly all of the timber had been cut and all the spurs in Reynolds County were taken up, leaving only the main line from Leeper to Bunker and the spur into Shannon County. Abandonment of the spur was authorized in 1940, and in 1941 the main line was abandoned. Thus in a span of little more than half a century the Hydra-like Missouri Southern lived out its life cycle, sprawling across Wayne, Reynolds, and Shannon counties, its many heads being lumber camps where men with axes and saws chewed into virgin pine and oak-hickory forests.

St. Francois is another Ozark county with many miles of abandoned trackage; the railroads came to haul the lead being mined there. The Mississippi River and Bonne Terre Railroad constructed branch lines in St. Francois County in the mid-1890s while building its main line northeast from Bonne Terre to the St. Joseph Lead Company's smelter at Herculaneum on the Mississippi River. The line made connections there with a railroad running south out of St. Louis. Twenty-two miles of track—from Bonne Terre to Howe in Jefferson County—was abandoned five years before the closing of the last mine in the Old Lead Belt in 1973. The Mississippi River and Bonne Terre Railroad (now the Missouri-Illinois Railroad Company) abandoned ten miles of track—from Turpin to Derby—in 1941. The other spurs were abandoned before 1930.

One of the longest stretches of track abandoned by the Missouri Pacific ceased operations in 1973 when the Interstate Commerce Commission authorized the abandonment of the line from Bismarck in western St. Francois County to Whitewater in Cape Girardeau County. Another relatively recent abandonment in the Old Lead Belt was trackage belonging to the St. Francois County Railroad Company. This small company operated between Hurryville, Farmington, and DeLassus, making a run of about ten miles in central St. Francois County, until its abandonment in 1957.

Some of the most ambitious railroad ventures attempted in the Ozarks were those that penetrated the rugged country in northern Arkansas. Here the hill folk were "introduced to the cold, hard facts of the financial world: you may build a railroad through the Ozarks, but is is a very different story when you try to operate trains over it *at a profit*."[3]

One of these ambitious ventures was the Missouri and North Arkansas, which was extended in segments until it connected Joplin, Missouri, with Helena, Arkansas, on the Mississippi River. From Joplin to Seligman by way of Neosho, the route was relatively easy, but southward it traversed the wild White River Hills, climbed the Boston Mountain Front at Leslie, and then followed the Little Red River southeast through the Boston Mountains. Branch lines were built to Eureka Springs and Berryville, and the Williams Cooperage Company's extensive tramway was connected at Leslie.

The railroad began in 1883 as a short line to serve the resort town of Eureka Springs and was officially complete for 368 miles between Joplin and Helena in 1909. It never prospered, although for a time large quantities of crossties and lumber were shipped by various firms, such as Doniphan Lumber Company and H. D. Williams Cooperage Company. Agricultural surpluses were always limited, but towns like Berryville, Harrison, Pindall, Marshall, Leslie, Edgemont, and Heber Springs were points of shipment for cotton, grain, and lumber products. Several large lumber mills were established along the line: Great Western

3. Clifton E. Hull, *Shortline Railroads of Arkansas* (Norman: University of Oklahoma Press, 1969), p. 53.

Mill Company, Geyhauser and Galhousen, Pekin Stave Manufacturing Company, and H. D. Williams Cooperage Company in Leslie; C. H. Smith Tie Company, Western Tie and Timber Company, W. R. Lee Wagon Hub Mill, Humphries and Bucklow Lumber Company, Gerwich and Waller Lumber Company, Goblebe Lumber Company, and National Cooperage and Woodworking Company in Shirley. In the 1920's the Missouri and North Arkansas was crippled by a violent strike from which it never recovered. Segments of the line gradually were abandoned until, in 1962, the shops and offices in Harrison were closed and the rails were taken up to be sold as scrap.

In northwest Arkansas, several rail lines were built to connect with the Frisco system that had been extended to Fayetteville in 1882. The Arkansas and Oklahoma Railroad, connecting Bentonville, Arkansas, and Grove, Oklahoma, has been mentioned. The Monte Ne Railroad was built to transport vacationers to Coin Harvey's resort at Monte Ne a few miles east of Rogers. The resort, consisting of cottages and a hotel overlooking a lake, was built between 1900 and 1905. Special trains were run by the Frisco from Springfield, Joplin, and Fort Smith to Lowell on the Frisco line south of Rogers. Visitors were transported from Lowell to Monte Ne by the Monte Ne Railroad Company. Although large crowds were attracted to the resort, the railroad—and eventually the resort—were financial failures.

The Rogers Southwestern (later the Arkansas, Oklahoma & Western), linked Rogers on the Frisco with Siloam Springs on the Kansas City, Pittsburg and Gulf (Kansas City Southern). Construction of the line, which passed through the small communities of Hazelwood, Hoover, and Springtown, began in 1904. The Arkansas, Oklahoma & Western took over the Monte Ne Railroad franchise for a time and plans were made to extend it eastward, but in 1914 the entire system was thrown into receivership and abandoned.

In 1886 a group of financiers interested in the timber of Washington and Madison counties were granted a charter to build a railroad up the West Fork of White River to St. Paul. The company was incorporated as the Fayetteville and Little Rock Railroad, and in 1897 the line was extended to Pettigrew. In 1915 the Black Mountain & Eastern Railroad was formed to extend railroad service across the Black Mountains from Combs in the White River valley to Cass on the Mulberry River. Winding through the Black Mountains, a train had to travel about twenty miles to make the twelve miles from Combs to Cass. The difficulties encountered in building the line and running trains loaded with lumber were many:

> To span the deep gulches reaching up the sides of the rugged mountain slopes, several wood trestles were constructed. Of the timber-bent type, they were more than 125 feet high. The bents were formed on the ground, then tilted to vertical position and secured. There is a report that the grade was so steep at the end of the road that a locomotive couldn't negotiate it with a train of logs, so the individual cars were snaked, one at a time, up the track by ox team to the crest of the grade.[4]

The mountains having been logged out, the line to Cass was abandoned in 1926. In 1937 the last train from Pettigrew made its run to Fayetteville, leaving behind a string of nearly abandoned old lumber boom towns.

It is doubtful that railroad abandonment has run its full course in the Ozarks. Only two lines of importance have been built during the past half-century: the Frisco spur, extended from the Salem branch to serve the new lead mines in western Iron and Reynolds counties in Missouri, and the Missouri Pacific spur from the Pea Ridge iron mine to the main line in Washington County, Missouri. Pre-1981 potential rail abandonments have been projected in a report from the Division of Budget and Planning in Missouri.[5] Among those with high probability of abandonment are the Frisco lines connecting Kansas City and Springfield, Pierce City and Carthage, Willow Springs and Winona; the Chicago, Rock Island & Pacific from St. Louis to Kansas City by way of Versailles; the Missouri-Illinois line connecting Ste. Genevieve, Bonne Terre, and Bismarck in Ste. Genevieve and St. Francois counties; and the

4. Ibid., p. 354.

5. David Moser et al., *Missouri's Transportation System: Condition, Capacity, and Impediments to Efficiency* (Jefferson City: Missouri State Office of Administration, Division of Budget and Planning, 1976), p. 170.

Missouri Pacific lines connecting Doniphan and Neelyville, and Jackson with the town of Charleston in the Mississippi lowlands.

Passenger service in the Ozarks is very limited. Amtrak serves only two border cities: Jefferson City and Poplar Bluff. Freight consists mainly of farm and food products, lumber and wood products, stone and refractory products, and metallic ores. Grain and feed are shipped into the Ozarks to support the dairy and poultry industries; coal and petroleum products also are hauled in by rail to power thermal electric plants and to supply bulk gasoline and propane depots. Much of the freight moves as through traffic between major cities outside the Ozarks. Several of the railroads serving the Ozarks get a substantial part of their revenue from so-called piggy-back service (trailer transport) and the shipment of new automobiles.

Logging train on the St. Paul Branch of the Frisco. (Courtesy Arkansas History Commission.)

Early Roads

The first roads in the Ozarks were the trails followed by the Indians in their hunting, warfare, and trading. Later, roads were hacked through the country between Ste. Genevieve and the lead mines. Between 1776 and 1799 the Kings Highway was laid out by the Spanish to link the Mississippi trading posts at New Madrid, Cape Girardeau, and Ste. Genevieve with St. Louis. Perhaps the best-known route across the Ozarks was the Osage trail that led to St. Louis. This route, which followed the upland, was used by immigrants to the western Ozarks. It was known by various names: Springfield Road, Ridge Road, and, later, when a telegraph line was strung alongside it, Old Wire Road. Other early Ozarks roads included the Old Iron Road, which linked the Maramec Iron Works with the Missouri River port at Hermann, and the Plank Road, over which iron was hauled from Pilot Knob to Ste. Genevieve.

By 1816 a trail had been marked to the Boonslick country. It paralleled the Missouri River and connected a number of settlements that had been established along the north bank of the Missouri between Boonslick and St. Charles. A similar trail paralleled the Arkansas River.

Many of the Ozarks' early roads were built as post roads to ensure the delivery of mail and maintain communications with St. Louis, where a central post office was established in 1805. As early as 1810, post roads had been established from Ste. Genevieve to Mine à Breton and from St. Louis to St. Charles. Another ran from Kaskaskia, Illinois, to Ste. Genevieve, thence, by way of the old Kings Highway, to Cape Girardeau and New Madrid. Later, post roads were established from Ste. Genevieve through Potosi to Union in Franklin County and from Potosi to Belleview and Murphy's (Farmington).

By 1819, Missouri could boast at least fifteen routes over which the mails were delivered once a week or once every two weeks. A list of post routes established in Missouri in 1819 was published by the *Missouri Gazette* for May 5 of that year. At that time there were no regularly scheduled routes in the Ozarks. In 1836 the journey to Little Rock still entailed weeks of discomfort on board a steamboat or an even more hazardous drive along a primitive wilderness road. The most important of these roads, the Military Road, or Southwest Trail, ran from St. Louis through the lead-mining district in southeast Missouri to Little Rock and on to the Red River. It was joined at

Ozark stage coach, 1905. (Courtesy Arkansas History Commission.)

County road between Linn Creek and Lebanon, Missouri, *circa* 1907. (Reproduced from Ernest R. Buckley, "Public Roads, Their Improvement and Maintenance," *Missouri Bureau of Geology and Mines*, 2d. Series, 5 (1907): 99.)

Batesville by a trace through the swamps from Memphis. The trees were "razed close to the ground," a statement which does not imply that all stumps were rooted out; there were no bridges and only a few ferries. Travel along Military Road from St. Louis to Little Rock must have been an adventure for even the hardiest souls:

> Along the Missouri border particularly, it was infested with gangs of desperadoes, living in abandoned cabins off the main route or moving about the country in order to lure any travellers who carried money, towards a woodland ambush in some secluded spot. Taverns were few; and the traveller, if he did not wish to camp out at night—a procedure which was always under risks as to the weather and was sometimes perilous besides because of wild animals, particularly panthers—had to endure an unvarying diet of fried pork, corn dodgers, and bad coffee (sometimes made of parched corn or acorns) sweetened with molasses, or "long sweetening." He had to also endure a table service so scanty that knives and forks were given knicknames; and usually he had to sleep in a single room with several other tenants, oftentimes in the same bed with another guest.[6]

6. John Gould Fletcher, *Arkansas* (Chapel Hill: The University of North Carolina Press, 1947), p. 80–81.

During the 1840's and 1850's, the rapidly expanding settlements demanded more mail facilities, and many post roads were laid out in the Ozarks. In 1850, George R. Smith, the founder of Sedalia, had a contract with the U.S. government for operating passenger and mail coaches over 483 miles of the Missouri Stage Lines.

The first mail-carrying stagecoach between Independence and Sante Fe began its first trip to the Far Southwest on July 1, 1850, over the Santa Fe Trail, marked by Pedro Vial in 1792–93 and by William Becknell in 1821–22. The establishment of the Butterfield Overland Mail in 1858 was the culmination of more than a decade of struggle toward regular communication with the Pacific Coast. The demand for rapid communication between East and West led to the development of the Pony Express, and on April 3, 1860, the first westbound rider left St. Joseph, the end-of-trail connection with the East, for Sacramento, California.

Toll roads became something of a mania about midcentury and 49 companies were chartered in

Crossing the Meramec River at Sand Ford below Meramec Caverns. (Courtesy Missouri State Historical Society.)

Missouri to construct plank roads. All but one were planned to connect some point in the state with the Missouri or Mississippi rivers. Because of limited state and federal support for road construction, toll roads continued to be built to connect larger interior towns with the closest town fortunate enough to have a railroad. Some of these connecting roads persisted until the 1930's.

The first wagon roads were made by felling timber so that the axle of a wagon would clear the stumps; improvement was left to travel. The soil was quickly worn away, exposing the underlying chert, which formed a natural macadam. There was little concern for bridges before the automobile became common. There were no bridges in Lawrence County, Missouri, in 1875, nor were they considered essential, "the streams being shallow and the fords solid." Dade County acquired its first bridge in 1892, but only after 20 years of agitation and assurances that the old ford on Sac River would be left intact, "thus giving the traveler an opportunity to water his horses." Wooden bridges were built at key places to cross the larger streams, such as the White, Current, Osage, and Meramec rivers. These were replaced by high steel-trestle bridges as they washed out.

Maintenance of secondary roads was usually under the direction of a township or special road-district overseer who was paid for his services. Theoretically, each male citizen was obligated to

Wagon and team on a dirt road, *circa* 1907. Split-log road drag is on the wagon. (Reproduced from Ernest R. Buckley, "Public Roads, Their Improvement and Maintenance," *Missouri Bureau of Geology and Mines*, 2d. Series, 5 (1907): 87.)

spend two days a year assisting the supervisor in working the roads, or one day a year with a team of horses or mules. The result was that very little was accomplished other than making temporary repairs to the almost impassable parts of the road. The most commonly used implement for improvement consisted of two logs or sawed oak timbers hooked up in tandem. This device, known as a split-log drag, was used to smooth ruts.

During the bicycle rage in the latter part of the nineteenth century, tours were organized to explore the Ozarks. Intrepid visitors were forewarned of poor roads in the interior counties by the *Road and Handbook of the Missouri Division of the League of American Wheelmen*, published in 1895. The information for Shannon County, Missouri, locates the county and describes the extent and condition of roads:

Shannon. In southern part, near boundary, south of Dent. Roads scarce. The County Surveyor kindly reports: Eminence northeast to Centerville, 40 miles, rough, hilly, dirt road. Eminence west to Houston, 40 miles, rough, hilly, dirt road, no bridges, via Alley, 5 miles; Somerville [*sic*] 18 miles. Riverside south to Somerville [*sic*], 20 miles. Eminence east to Russel, 13 miles. Low Wossie [*sic*] to Birchtree, via Winona, dirt road, 18 miles. Eminence southwest to West Plains, dirt road, 50 miles; via Birch Tree, 15 miles. Eminence to Van Buren, southeast, dirt road, 25 miles. Eminence north to Salem, 40 miles; via Roundspring, 11 miles. Birchtree east to Van Buren, 30 miles. Birchtree west to Mountain View, 13 miles. Eminence northwest to Riverside, 25 miles, and north to Salem, 18 miles more; via Jadwin, 7 miles.

Hotels: Eminence, J. A. Jadwin and J. M. Boyd. Birchtree, Cook, DePriest and Mahan. Winona, Lewis R. Pettitt, each $1 per day.[7]

Rural free delivery was introduced in Missouri on October 15, 1896, when three experimental routes were started at Cairo in Randolph County. It is a matter of speculation just why Cairo, a small village of two hundred inhabitants in northern Missouri, was one of the forty-four communities selected as centers for experimental routes. It is probable that Cairo received this distinction through the efforts of Uriel S. Hall of Randolph County, who was then a member of the House Committee on Post Office and Post Roads. Rural free delivery was immediately popular and was extended to six other Missouri communities in 1899. By 1901, forty-seven more communities, thirty-five north of the Missouri River and twelve south, had been added.

The development of rural free delivery was coincident with the development of automobiles. The good-roads movement received impetus from the Post Office Department requirement that new mail routes should be established only on roads that were passable in all seasons of the year. After the introduction of parcel post in 1912, rural free delivery naturally entered upon a period of expansion that further coincided with the growing popularity of the automobile. During the next two decades, the nation's and the Ozarks' first highway system became a reality.

Interest in roads had become strong by 1920. In 1917 the Missouri State Highway Commission was created by the legislature, and in 1921 the

7. M. J. Gilbert, *Road and Handbook of the Missouri Division of the League of American Wheelmen* (St. Louis: League of American Wheelmen, 1895), p. 216–17.

First commercial bus service to Doniphan, Missouri. (Courtesy Missouri State Historical Society.)

legislature passed the Centennial Road Act, which was designed to provide a network of roads connecting county seats. The commission immediately began to build a system of primary highways, supported by a sixty million dollar bond issue. In 1927, Missouri voted an additional seventy-five million dollar worth of bonds for construction of farm-to-market roads, which provided a network of graveled but well-engineered highways through sections not reached by primary roads. Road legislation was passed soon after this in Arkansas and in the new state of Oklahoma.

The first bituminous-surface highways were constructed in the late 1920's, and the first stretch of bituminous-surface road in the Ozarks was laid a few miles west of Springfield in 1927 (table 8-1). Bituminous surfacing of county roads began about 1950. In southwest Missouri the Greene County Court is credited with working out a system of priorities so that bituminous surfacing could begin; the same system is now used by many Ozark counties. Landowners whose property fronts on the road are charged a fee (per linear foot) for bituminous surfacing; after construction, all costs of repair and maintenance are borne by the county.

Bituminous surfacing of county roads has progressed very rapidly. By 1970 approximately eight hundred of the one thousand two hundred miles of county roads in Greene County had been surfaced. In some of the rural Ozark counties where special road districts still exist, progress has been much slower, but improvement of non-bituminous-surface roads has progressed steadily. U.S. Census of Agriculture statistics show that in only ten years, 1940 to 1950, the percentage of farms located on dirt or unimproved roads declined from 51 to 39.

In much of the Ozarks the care of roads lacking bituminous surfacing is made simple by the residual chert underlying the soil. After the overlying soil is bladed aside, the chert quickly becomes packed, forming a surface that permits all-weather travel. However, such surfaces are usually rough, and the sharp chert causes tires to wear badly. In more remote areas, roads receive little care, and where there are no ditches alongside them, the roads serve as drains for hillsides that are gullied, in many cases exposing outcrops of bedrock that make the road nearly impassable.

In the Ozarks, small streams are crossed most commonly by water gaps, the gravel deposits in stream bottoms having been scooped out and replaced with concrete slabs. Gravel fords are found throughout the area but are most prevalent in the White River Hills, the Osage-Gasconade Hills, the Courtois Hills, and the Boston Mountains. The upper reaches of the larger streams are crossed by concrete low-water bridges. These structures are normally dry, but after heavy rains the streams rise over them. Each year in the Ozarks several drownings occur when vehicles are swept from these picturesque crossings during times of high water. The following is a short notice from the Springfield newspaper:

TRUCK WASHES OFF LOW WATER BRIDGE

BRANSON (Special)—The body of a Greene County man was recovered from the waters of Bull Creek at 11 a.m. today, 25 hours after his pickup truck was found to have washed off a low water bridge. The truck was found about 500 feet below the bridge at 10 a.m. Sunday. It was believed to have been washed off late Saturday night or early Sunday morning by flood waters after torrential rains in the area.

TABLE 8-1
Dates of Construction of Highways in the Vicinity of Springfield, Missouri

Highway	Original Construction	Reconstruction
160 West	1927–34	
160 South	1934–45	1967–68
13 North	1936–38	1960
65 North	1925–32	1968
65 South	1922–32	1961–65
60 West	1931–35	1942–66
60 East	1934–35	1967–69
66 West	1926–28	1962
66 East	1923–25	1952
I-44 West	1962–64	
I-44 East	1958–68	

New federal highways have been constructed with less attention to the advantages of landforms. Streams are crossed by concrete bridges well above any water rise ever recorded. These roads cross valleys by long, easy grades made possible by cutting and filling. Vertical cuts of as much as 80 feet in bedded limestone, alternating with valley fills of almost equal height, make the new U.S. Highway 65 north of Branson one of the most easily traveled and picturesque drives in all of the Ozarks.

The overall pattern of roads in the Ozarks is a blend of a radial network, which is decended from the earliest trails through the country, and a rectangular road pattern, which derives from the federal land survey. To a remarkable degree, the main highways follow the earliest routes of travel. For example, Ridge Road, connecting St. Louis and Springfield, followed the crest of the Osage-White River divide, whence it derived its name. Through the years it has retained its position as the foremost route to and from Springfield, first as a wagon road, then as U.S. Highway 66, and most recently as Interstate 44. This route,

Low-water bridge on the James River, 1975. This type of bridge is common in the Ozarks.

Steel-trestle bridge on the Finley River at Riverdale, Christian County, Missouri, 1975.

more than any other, is the great transportation corridor of the Ozarks.

The main roads tend to follow the crests of ridges, but this is particularly true in the rougher regions. The ridge roads are never flooded and, although they may be very sinuous, they maintain a remarkable evenness of grade. In the breaks along escarpments, stream divides are sometimes so narrow that the roads occupy the entire crest. At other places the surface broadens out so that the farms and settlements are located next to the roads.

Farm-to-market roads vary greatly in geographic pattern. In the Springfield Plain and a few other level areas, the rectangular pattern is prevalent, with important breaks in the grid occurring where rougher land is encountered along the major streams. In southwest Missouri, where sinkholes are sometimes large, the rectangular pattern is little effected; roads frequently cross large sinkholes, some of which temporarily hold water, and this may block the road for days or weeks at a time.

In the hilly districts the rectangular road pattern is replaced by a sparse pattern of roads that alternately follow the crests of ridges or stream valleys, the former case being the more common. Private roads frequently branch off to farmsteads located at considerable distances from public roads. Most of these side roads are wretched trails, better traveled in a truck than in an automobile, and they frequently terminate at a small abandoned house surrounded by an assortment of sheds in varying states of dilapidation.

Newspapers

As soon as towns were founded, newspapers were established. Newspaper reading was the great American pastime. Like those of today, early newspapers reflected the attitudes of the period, the politics, the habits, and the hopes of the settlers. George W. Featherstonehaugh, a noted English traveler, described in his dry, humorous style the penchant for newspaper reading in Little Rock in the late 1830's:

> Americans of a certain class, to whatever distant point they go, carry the passion for newspaper reading with them, as if it were the grand end of education. . . . How could a town of 8000 inhabitants in England support a newspaper printed in the place? Where would its useful or instructive matter come from? Why, from those quarters which have already supplied it to those alone who want it. If such a town had a newspaper it could not be supported, and therefore it remains without one. But in Little Rock, with a population of 600 people, there are no less than three cheap newspapers, which are not read but devoured by everybody.[8]

The number of newspapers is surprising, even when one realizes that many of them lasted only a few years or sometimes only long enough to print a few issues. Nearly every county had a dozen or more at one time or another. For example, newspapers of record in Webster County, Missouri, included the *Marshfield Mail, The Sentinel, The Radical*, the *Marshfield Democrat*, the *Marshfield Chronicle*, the *Webster County News*, the *Webster County Record*, the *Fordland Journal, The Enterprise, The Flashlight, The Herald*, the *Seymour Citizen*, the *Fordland Times*, the *Rogersville Star*, the *Rogersville Reporter*, the *Rogersville Record*, the *Marshfield Herald*, and the *Niangua Tribune*.

In general the early newspapers were different from their modern counterparts in several respects. The front page, unlike those of today's large dailies, was filled with advertisements. Poetry was popular, and many peoms were published to commemorate notable events, to comment on politics, and to express the poets' sentiment or convictions. Because of the lack of rapid communication, news published in Ozark papers often was very stale. Surprisingly, the early newspapers carried much national and international news and a few vague accounts of local happenings. This was partly because editors were prone to reprint in their entirety editorials or stories from other newspapers.

Gradually, as better transportation became available, a few dailies extended their circulation in the Ozarks. The *Springfield Leader and Press*, the *St. Louis Post-Dispatch*, the *St. Louis Globe Democrat*, the *Kansas City Star*, the *Tulsa World-Tribune*, the *Arkansas Democrat*, and the *Arkansas Gazette* (Little Rock) are important dailies of the present time.

Local newspapers, many of them weeklies, continue to be popular (fig. 8-3). Usually there are only two, or at most three, in a given county. Often the most widely read newspaper is printed in the county seat, where revenues can be obtained by printing public notices. Frequently, local papers are consolidations of several small newspapers that were printed in the county and the old names are carried on the front page, or they may have their own mastheads and news printed on one of the interior pages. One such consolidation is the *Crawford Mirror*, which represents a merger of the *Crawford Mirror*, the *Steelville Ledger*, and the *Cuba News and Review*. In economic parlance, the local newspapers, by consolidating, are responding to the necessities of economies of scale: larger circulation reduces costs. The Ozark farmer understands the problem well, but he would more likely phrase it: "Get big, or get out."

The local newspapers carry mainly area news and state and national news that has a direct bearing on area economy and life. Because of the many columns of rural neighborhood news, the hometown weeklies circulate outside the Ozarks among people who want to keep up with Ozarks happenings.

The character of the news reported in one of the local papers is represented by a few stories from the Marshall, Arkansas, *Mountain Wave* from 1972 to 1976. There was a report of a mortgage burning by a church; several reports of local elections; store remodelings; openings of new businesses; Marshall's first radio station; improvements in physical facilities at several schools; a report on the new teen-age craze, Foosball; reports on innumerable athletic events; a feature article on the back-to-the-land people who have settled in Searcy County; several pictures of deer, wild turkeys, and fish taken by area sportsmen; several reports on the annual strawberry festival; countless accounts of visiting relatives and friends; the events of a canoe race, including a picture of Wrong-way Molder, who paddled upstream; several reports of high school alumni banquets; a story on Searcy County mat-

8. George W. Featherstonehaugh, *Excursion Through the Slave States* (London: 1844).

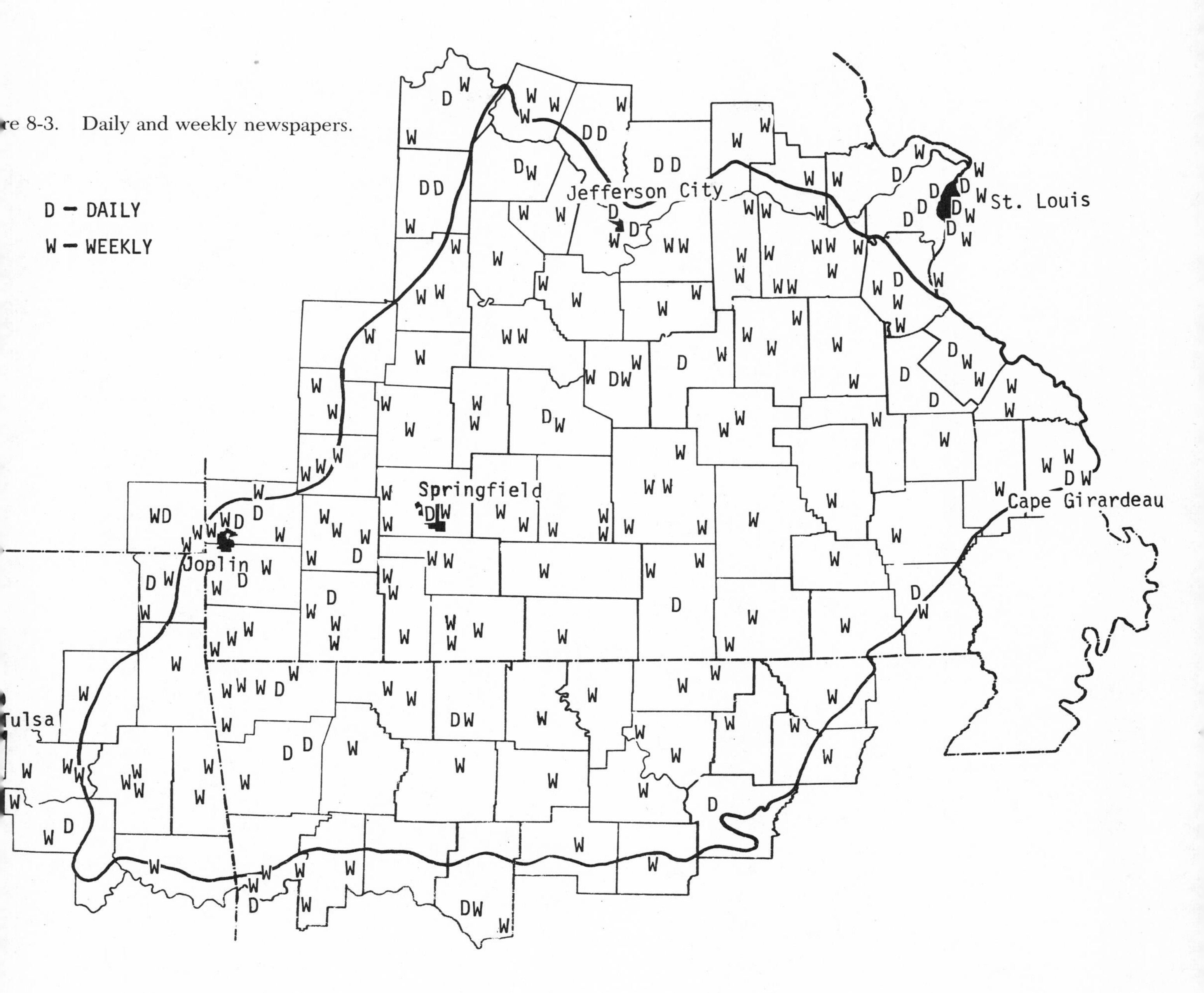

re 8-3. Daily and weekly newspapers.

riarchs; a report on a citizen who experienced a revelation from God; stories on oversize pumpkins, cucumbers, and tomatoes that were grown by area residents; a story on ribbon-cutting ceremonies for a new road to Snowball, Arkansas; reports on serious car accidents; and, of course, pictures of area beauty-pageant winners.[9]

9. Maurice Tudor, *Pictorial Crackerbarrel: Some of the Better-Told Tales of Searcy Countians and News Scenes as They Appeared in the Marshall Mountain Wave Newspaper, 1972–1976* (Marshall, Ark.: Marshall Wave, 1976).

The Telephone

The telephone, a novel instrument that gained an immediate following because of its practical utility and its entertainment value, spread rapidly through the Ozarks in the 1890's. At first, communities called telephone meetings and organized neighborhood telephone companies. Members were assessed a small fee of five to twenty dollars and were required to donate a number of days' work and a given number of poles. Construction costs were reduced by attach-

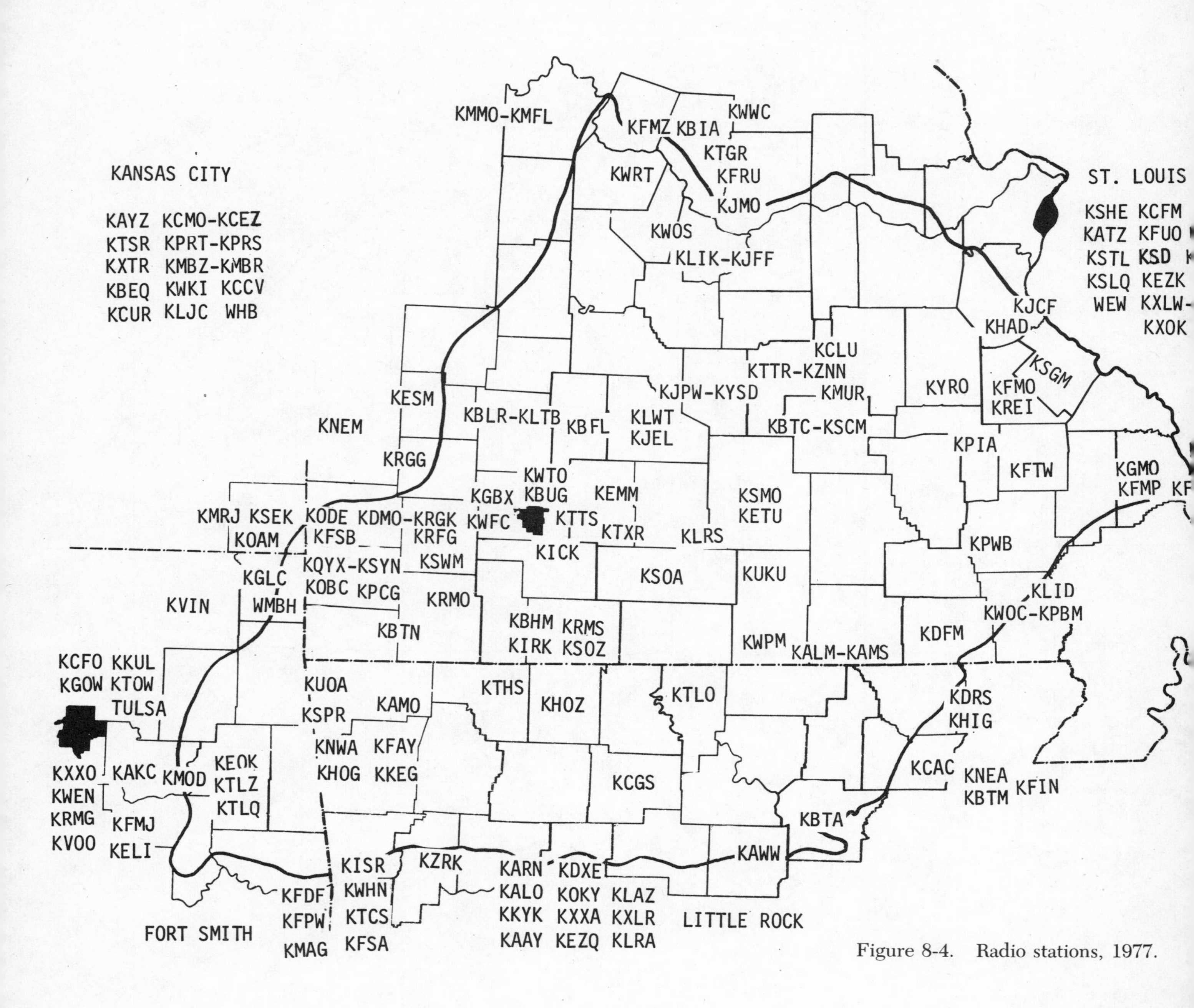

Figure 8-4. Radio stations, 1977.

ing the wire to trees along the way. Sometimes at annual and special meetings there were disputes over rules, dues, and maintenance. It is reported that final decisions at the Cuba, Missouri, telephone cooperative sometimes were made only "after a fist fight."[10]

10. James Ira Breuer, *Crawford County and Cuba, Missouri* (Cape Girardeau, Mo.: The Ramfre Press, 1972), p. 122.

After the small neighborhood lines were established, people began to express a desire to talk to people on other community lines. To accomplish this, connecting lines were built and switches installed, often in someone's home. The "exchange" in Cuba, Missouri, was moved to six different locations. In time, larger telephone companies were formed and more elaborate switching equipment was installed. For a time during the Depression years of the 1930's, many of the lines were abandoned because people felt they could no longer afford the luxury of a telephone. During the 1940's, improvement and consolidation of services continued, but party lines of three to six families were the rule and persons being called were signaled by a system of short or long rings. Most people on the community lines knew their neighbors' rings and would ring up a neighbor by turning the crank to produce the proper sequence of shorts and longs. To call on a different community line or to make a long-distance call, one had to go through the central switchboard operator.

Many regional telephone companies continue to operate in the Ozarks, but all of them are connected with the Bell System, most are equipped to handle direct long-distance dialing, and most have computerized billing.

Radio and Television

The first radio station to broadcast on a regular basis in the Ozarks was WEW at St. Louis University. Formerly known as 9YK, the station went on the air in April, 1921, on an experimental basis, broadcasting weather reports. By 1940 there were radio stations in nearly all the larger towns on the Ozarks border and a few stations in interior Ozark towns. Arkansas stations included KLRA, KARK, KGHI, Little Rock; KFPW, Fort Smith; KBTM, Jonesboro; and KUOA, Siloam Springs. KWTO in Springfield, one of the pioneer Ozark radio stations, gained national attention in the 1950's by broadcasting country music and Red Foley's "Ozark Jubilee." In the 1960's and 1970's, radio stations have become common throughout the Ozarks, so much so that most communities of five or six thousand residents can boast one (fig. 8-4).

After World War II television broadcasts began from the larger border towns: St. Louis, Kansas City, Memphis, Little Rock, Tulsa. Reception was poor at first, and television sets were an oddity. Stores that marketed them could be assured of a large crowd of viewers simply by placing a set in the store window and tuning it to the station with the least fuzzy picture. During the past generation television has become ubiquitous in Ozark homes, and a number of stations serve the region (fig. 8-5). Local live color broadcasts were inaugerated by KY-3 TV in Springfield in 1966. Tall towers for improved broadcast coverage have been constructed by most of the major stations serving the Ozarks.

Electricity, Petroleum, and Natural Gas

The Ozarks is well served by electrical power. The entrenched channels of Ozark streams provide nearly ideal conditions for development of dams and reservoirs to generate hydroelectric power. Large lakes can be created at relatively low cost, and because of their forested slopes the lakes are not subject to heavy siltation by eroded soils. Large reserves of coal, combined with reliable water supplies, both in the Ozarks and along the Mississippi, Missouri, and Arkansas rivers, make development of thermal electric power less costly than in many other parts of the United States. The electric-power grid blankets the region. Trunk lines supply the major urban centers, while smaller lines, many of them built by rural electric cooperatives under the Rural Electrification Administration, serve small towns and farms.

The Ozarks is strategically located near the oil and natural-gas fields of the Southern Great Plains and the Gulf Coast. Trunk pipelines carrying oil and natural gas from the Great Plains traverse central and northern Missouri on their way to the industrial states in the Northeast. Feeder pipelines from these trunks branch out to serve towns and cities along the way. Similarly, the main natural-gas and oil pipelines from the Gulf Coast fields pass up the Mississippi Valley to the Northeast. Nevertheless, the Ozark region is conspicuous by the absence of gas pipelines. Only the eastern, western, and northern borders are served by natural gas.

The availability of natural gas is extremely important for the development of certain types of industries. It is likely that reliable supplies of fuel will continue to be important in locating manufacturing plants, and in all probability the most reliable fuel supplies will be where large supply lines and storage facilities exist. Plans are under way to use salt-dome structures in Texas and Louisiana as large-scale underground storage reservoirs for

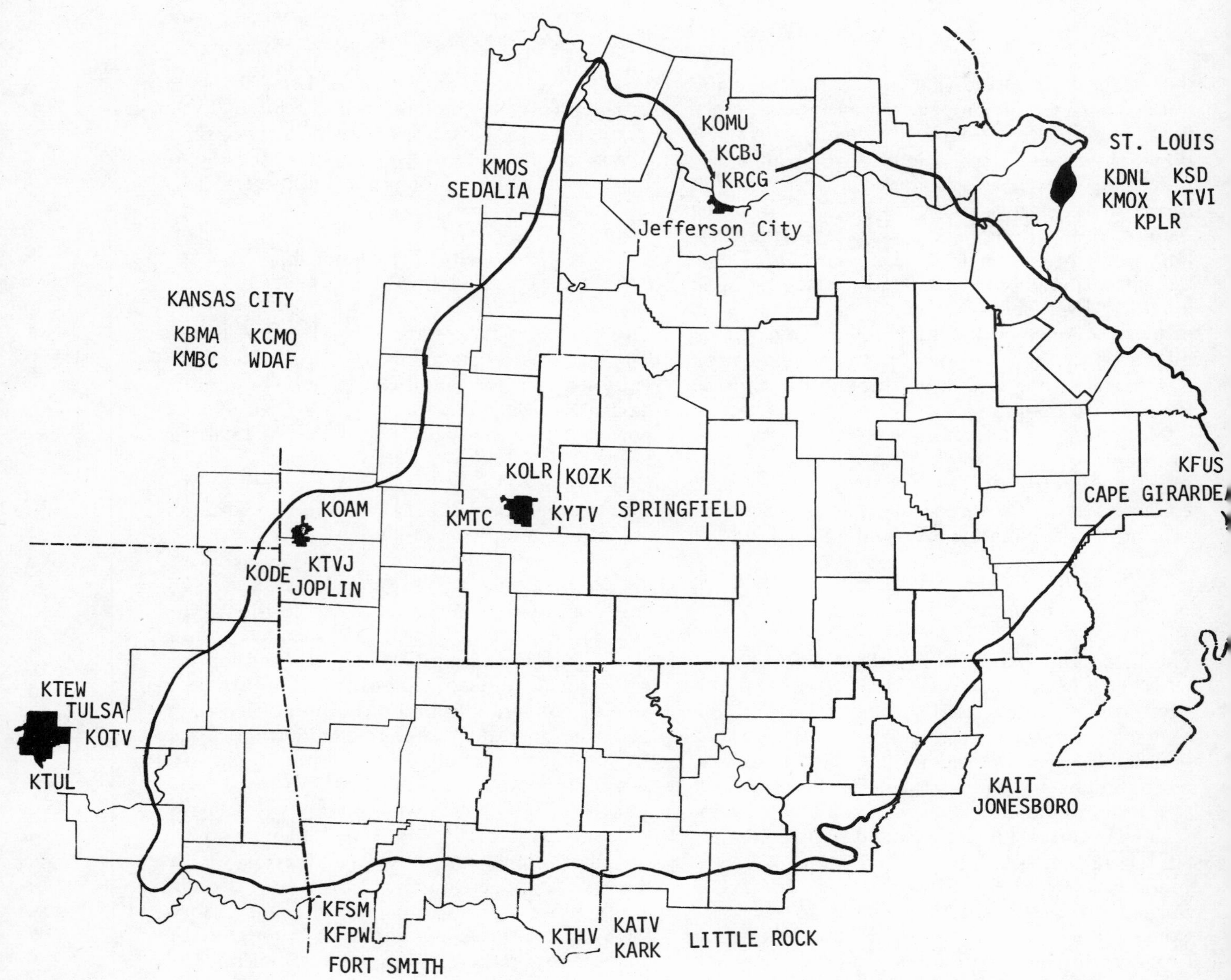

Figure 8-5. Television stations, 1977.

imported crude oil. Existing refineries and pipelines probably will process and distribute the products. From the standpoint of energy availability, there is little likelihood that large manufacturing plants will locate in the energy-poor interior Ozarks. The border areas, however, have better prospects.

The question of whether there will be a continuing supply of energy is a worldwide problem; it is no less a problem in the Ozarks than anyplace else. The Ozarks economy and lifestyle, except in a few remote locations, have become geared to cheap and abundant fuel, particularly gasoline, which permits long-distance commuting to off-farm employment. Higher gasoline prices undoubtedly will influence the development of manufacturing, second-home and retirement-home development, rural real estate values, and the tourist-recreation industry. Unfortunately, no comprehensive plans for the impending energy crisis were being developed at the local level in late 1978, partly because the recently formulated national energy policy has been slow in development.

Selected References

Breuer, James Ira. *Crawford County and Cuba, Missouri*. Cape Girardeau, Mo.: The Ramfre Press, 1972.

Buckley, Ernest R. "Public Roads, Their Improvement and Maintenance," *Missouri Bureau of Geology and Mines*, 2d. Series, Vol. 5 (1907).

Christian County Centennial, Inc. *Christian County: Its First Hundred Years*. Ozark, Mo.: 1959.

Donnelly, Phil M. "Rural Free Delivery Service in Missouri," *Missouri Historical Review* 35 (October 1940): 72–80.

Eaton, Clement, ed. *The Leaven of Democracy*. New York: George Braziller, 1963.

Featherstonehaugh, George W. *Excursion Through the Slave States*. London: 1844.

Fitzsimmons, Margaret Louise. "Missouri Railroads During the Civil War and Reconstruction," *Missouri Historical Review* 35 (January 1941): 188–206.

Fletcher, John Gould. *Arkansas*. Chapel Hill: The University of North Caroline Press, 1947.

George, Floyd Watters. *History of Webster County*. Marshfield, Mo.: Historical Committee of the Webster County Centennial, 1955.

Gilbert, M. J. *Road and Handbook of the Missouri Division of the League of American Wheelmen*. St. Louis: League of American Wheelmen, 1895.

Gist, Noel P. *Missouri: Its Resources, People, and Institutions*. Columbia, Mo.: Curators of the University of Missouri, 1950.

Handley, Lawrence R. "A Geography of the Missouri and North Arkansas Railroad." Master's thesis, University of Arkansas-Fayetteville, 1973.

Hull, Clifton E. *Shortline Railroads of Arkansas*. Norman: University of Oklahoma Press, 1969.

The Independence County Chronicle, vol. 9, no. 4.

Ingenthron, Elmo. *The Land of Taney*. Point Lookout, Mo.: The School of the Ozarks Press, 1974.

Interstate Commerce Commission Financial Dockets. Nos. 14102, 20496, 12695, 10897, 21832, 22767, 12204, 12977, 12788, 26350, 19844. Washington, D. C., U.S. Department of Commerce.

Messick, Mary Ann. *History of Baxter County, 1873–1973*. Mountain Home, Ark.: Mountain Home Chamber of Commerce, 1973.

Meyer, Duane. *The Heritage of Missouri: A History*. St. Louis: The State Publishing Company, Inc., 1963.

Miner, H. Craig. *The St. Louis–San Francisco Transcontinental Railroad*. Lawrence: University Press of Kansas, 1972.

Missouri State Highway Commission and the Writers' Program of the Works Progress Administration. *Missouri: A Guide to the "Show Me" State*. The American Guide Series. New York: Duell, Sloan, and Pearce, 1941.

Moser, David, et al. *Missouri's Transportation System: Condition, Capacity, and Impediments to Efficiency*. Jefferson City, Mo.: Office of Administration, Division of Budget and Planning, 1976.

Rafferty, Milton D. "Persistence Versus Change in Land Use and Landscape in the Springfield, Missouri, Vicinity of the Ozarks." Ph.D. dissertation, University of Nebraska, 1970.

———. "Trends in Ozark Roads and Bridges," *Ozark Mountaineer*, April 1974, pp. 21–27.

Sauer, Carl O. *The Geography of the Ozark Highland of Missouri*. The Geographic Society of Chicago Bulletin no. 7. Chicago: University of Chicago Press, 1920.

Williamson, Hugh P. "Restrictions and Rights of the Missouri Sportsman." Missouri Department of Conservation publication. N.d.

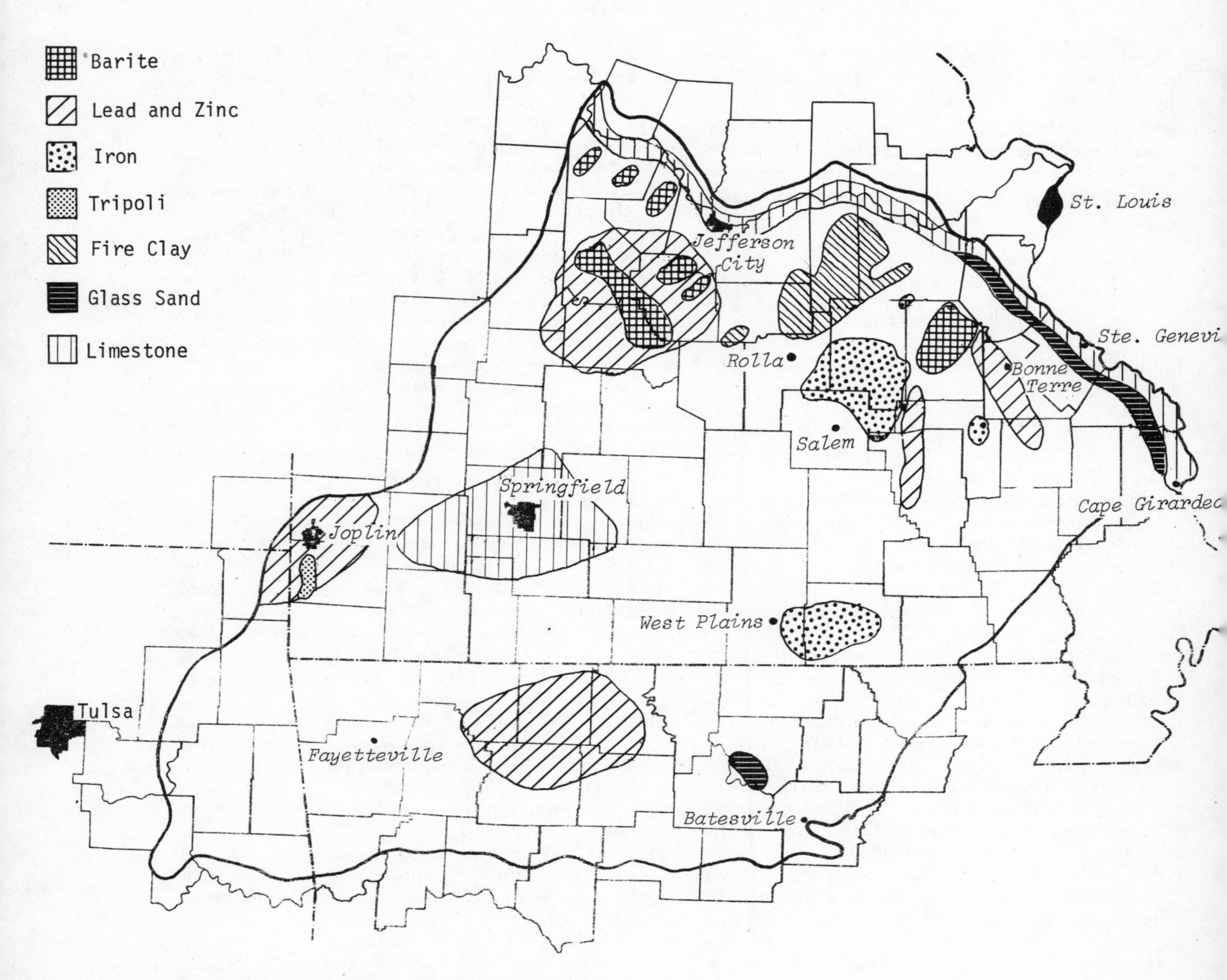

Figure 9-1. Mineral districts of the Ozarks.

9.

Mining: Its Geography and History

The Ozarks is one of the major mining districts of the United States. In addition to major deposits of lead, zinc, iron ore, and barite, the region produces fireclay, limestone, granite, and tripoli. The locations of major deposits of the various minerals are shown in figure 9-1.

Lead and zinc ores usually are found in close association. Historically, there have been four main lead-zinc belts in the Ozarks: the Mineral Area (also known as the Old Lead Belt) in St. Francois and Washington counties; the Tri-State Mining District of Missouri, Kansas, and Oklahoma; the Central Lead-Zinc District, which consisted of smaller and more scattered mines in Camden, Maries, Morgan and Miller counties; and the North Arkansas Lead-Zinc District, primarily in Marion, Benton, and Newton counties.

By far the most important mining districts were the Tri-State and the Mineral Area. The Tri-State Lead-Zinc District extended over an area of approximately 1,188 square miles, embracing Jasper and Newton counties in Missouri, Cherokee County in Kansas, and Ottawa County in Oklahoma. It has been known by a variety of names: the Southwest District of Missouri; the Joplin District; the Missouri, Kansas, Joplin District; and the Missouri, Kansas, Oklahoma District. *Tri-State Mining District* has become the commonly used name, although *Joplin District* is not a misnomer, since all mining camps in the three-state area came to be subsidiary to Joplin. In the Mineral Area, no one town assumed the dominance of Joplin in banking, merchandising, transportation, ore smelting, and the manufacture and supply of mining equipment. This district included the lead-zinc ores of Washington, St. Francois, and Madison counties; the barite ore of Washington County; and the iron deposits of Iron County. Various names have been applied to the Mineral Area and its parts. The lead mining areas were known as the Lead Belt, the Flat River District, and later, after the lead discoveries of the 1960's in western Iron and Reynolds counties, the old lead-zinc mining area was known as the Old Lead Belt. The name *Tiff Belt* is applied to the Washington County barite mines, while the iron mines of northeast Iron County were once known as the Iron Mountain District.

Smaller deposits of lead and zinc once were mined around the Mineral Area and over extensive areas in southwest Missouri and northern Arkansas. Shallow lead mines were worked in Crawford and Jefferson counties in the eastern Ozarks, and sizable lead-zinc deposits were mined near Aurora and at the Pearson Creek mines (Springfield) in southwest Missouri. Small lead deposits were worked from time to time in many Ozark counties, but the deposits were too small and remote for smelting operations to be of lasting importance.

Early Development Of The Lead Belt

Ever since the French entered Upper Louisiana, the eastern Ozarks has been recognized as a mining region of a diversified nature. Whether the first tales of mineral wealth were complete figments of the imagination or whether the French actually discovered minerals, we do not know, but by 1700 indisputable accounts of mineral discoveries began to trickle out. While traveling along the Meramec River in October, 1700, Father Gravier reported: "On the 10th day after proceeding a league, we discovered the river Miaramigoua [Meramec], where the very rich lead mine is situated twelve or thirteen leagues from its mouth. The ore from this mine yields three-fourths metal."[1] The implication that the mine already was in use by 1700 is obvious.

From that moment on, the area was known as a mining region. In 1817 the ill-fated Company of the West sent an expedition to explore the Ozarks and work the mines—in particular for silver, and in 1719, Sieur de Lochon "raised quite a quantity of ore" from a spot on the Meramec River. Some silver, perhaps salted, was obtained, along with forty pounds of lead.[2] As a result, constantly recurring rumors of silver mines became a part of the tradition of the area.

Discoveries and mining ventures followed apace. In 1712 a patent was granted to Anthony Crozat for various privileges in Louisiana, including proprietorship of all mines and minerals, and by 1719, organized mining got under way, for Renault had arrived with two hundred artificers and miners, plus a number of slaves. By 1720 he had begun operation on the Meramec, and in 1723, according to some, his agent, La Motte, discovered the famous Mine La Motte near present-day Fredericktown.[3] In the same year, the site at the junction of the Big and Meramec rivers was granted to Renault. It constitutes the earliest land grant in Upper Louisiana of which there is any record. The mines at Fourche à Renault were opened in 1724–25, and the Old Mines tract was opened in 1725–26.

The discoveries and mining ventures in Upper Louisiana soon were reflected in maps of the region, thereby implanting even more firmly the idea that here was a great metalliferous region. Homan's map[4] of 1720 designated the eastern Ozarks as *Regio Metallorium*, and in 1753, Du Pratz[5] indicates *Mine de Plomb*, *Mine de Meramec d'Argent* and *Mine de la Mothe d'Argent* as definite aspects of the landscape. Many other old maps are mentioned by Houck[6] and other writers. All of them indicate the presence of minerals in the St. Francis region.

At the same time, and subsequently, other changes were taking place. The first temporary mining camps were succeeded by the establishment of Ste. Genevieve about 1735, to be followed by St. Michaels (Fredericktown) in 1798, and Mine La Motte in 1763. Mine à Breton (Burton) was discovered in 1763 and settled in 1775.

At first the French carried out mining as an adjunct to agriculture or other activities. The habitation at the mines was seasonal; workers journeyed there after the crops were harvested in September or October and stayed until the mines became too wet to work or the weather too cold in December or January. Most of the mining was done around Mine La Motte, Mine à Breton, and Old Mines. The men of Ste. Genevieve and New Bourbon engaged in mining or dealt in lead as tradesmen; Ste. Genevieve was known as the lead entrepôt of the St. Francis region.

Aside from the appearance of permanent settlements, the actual mining of lead produced little change in the landscape other than that resulting from the appearance of new diggings, more furnaces, a larger area of land stripped of trees for

1. Louis Houck, *A History of Missouri*, vol. 1 (Chicago: R. R. Donnelly and Son, 1908).

2. Pierre François Xavier de Charlevoix, *Letters to the Duchess of Lesdiquières. . .* (London: R. Goadby, 1763).

3. Henry Rowe Schoolcraft, *A View of the Lead Mines of Missouri. . .*, in *Schoolcraft in the Ozarks*, ed. Hugh Park (Van Buren, Ark.: Press-Argns Printers, 1955), p. 154.

4. Houck, *A History of Missouri*, 1:276.

5. Le Page du Pratz, *Histoire de la Louisiane. . .* (Paris: De Bure, l'Ainé, La Beuve Delaguette, et Lambert, 1858), vol. 1, map opposite p. 138.

6. Houck, *A History of Missouri*, vol. 1.

fuel, and better-marked trails. The principal landscape features were the digging and the furnaces. The diggings were similar to the more recent gopher diggings for tiff (barite); they were nothing more than shallow holes with earth piled up about their edges, resembling a prairie-dog colony. Such individual diggings may be found today, many within a few feet of each other, each having been abandoned when it became too deep for easy operation or when the lead gave out. Wrote visitor John Bradbury:

> The workmen employed have no other implements than a pick axe and a wooden shovel and when at work appear as if employed in making tan pits rather than in mining. When they come to the rock, or to such depth that it is no longer convenient to throw the dirt out of the hole, they quit, and perhaps commence a new digging, as they term it, within a few feet of that which they previously abandoned.[7]

Prospecting was carried out rather haphazardly, but it was well known that most of the ore (galena) came from the Bonne Terre dolomite and the residual clays above it. The dark red Fredericktown soils, which form from weathered Bonne Terre clays, were prospected systematically. Bradbury explains the process:

> When the diggings become less productive than usual, they make trials on different parts of their lands, to discover where the ore is more abundant, that the diggers may be induced to remain with them. These trials consist in nothing more than digging a hole in some part of the woods, to the depth of three or four feet, and judging by the quantity of ore what degree of success may be expected.
>
> A little before I visited Richwoods Mines, the property of Monsieur Lebaume . . . he had made forty trials, by simply digging holes, not more than four feet deep, in places remote from each other on his land.[8]

The impact of American immigration to the mining districts at the turn of the eighthteenth century was revealed not only by the settlement of new villages but also by the effects on the older French settlements. The French element and the French atmosphere of Mine à Breton, Old Mines, and Mine La Motte were almost overwhelmed by the Americans. In 1798, Moses Austin was granted a square league of land at Mine à Breton, and in 1799 the first family settled there. Austin's settlement formed a nucleus for the Americans who came to that section, and by 1804 there were twenty-six families. When more Americans were attracted to the mines, the settlement of Mine à Breton became the town of Potosi. The increase in prospecting that resulted from American immigration led to the discovery of a number of mines. The Mine à Joe (Desloge), Mine à Lanye, Mine à Maneto, and Mine a la Plate (all on Big River) were opened between 1795 and 1801 and became the foundation of St. Francois County. Because the miners were an unruly class, county governments were organized in Washington and St. Francois counties at an early date to provide for sheriffs, courts, and jails.

Many other mines were opened in the Mineral Area, and Moses Austin—who introduced reverberatory smelters at Potosi and Herculaneum and was engaged in nearly all phases of the lead trade, including banking—complained that even more Americans would have been attracted to the area had it not been for the fact that as soon as a good-paying mine was discovered one of the French residents would produce an old French or Spanish land grant of uncertain origin in order to claim title to the property. In spite of the sometimes uncertain titles to land, prospecting and development of mine property proceeded so that at the outbreak of the Civil War most of the shallow lead ores were known.

Large-Scale Mining in the Old Lead Belt

The modern era of mining in the Lead Belt dawned as outside capital was attracted. The development of most of the lead-producing companies corresponds closely with that of the St. Joseph Lead Company, now the St. Joe Mineral Corporation. It was organized under the New York "Act to authorize the formation of corporations for manufacturing, mining, mechanical and chemical purposes" on March 25, 1864, with a capital stock of one million dollars, all of which

7. John Bradbury, *Travels in the Interior of America* (London: Sherwood, Neely, and Jones, 1817), p. 251.

8. Bradbury, *Travels in the Interior of America*, p. 251–53.

was issued to Lyman W. Gilbert of New York in payment for a 946-acre tract of mining land in St. Francois County (now Bonne Terre), Missouri.[9] The land had been owned by Anthony La Grave of St. Louis, who for many years had been interested in mining in that neighborhood and had produced considerable quantities of lead by using the crude smelting processes of that and earlier times. His tract and some adjoining lands were known as the La Grave Mines. La Grave acquired them through U.S. grants and through Spanish grants confirmed by the United States in 1834.

The St. Joseph Lead Company, a small eastern firm that represented one of the New South elements that were to bring irrevocable change to the Ozarks, had a most troubled beginning. The annual report of the trustees on June 13, 1865, summed up the year's business by stating that there had been "many serious and unlooked for drawbacks to rapid and successful operations during the year," such as "an immense drouth in July preventing the washing of mineral"; then, in early autumn, "a raid by the Confederate General Price's army, breaking up the company's operations and preventing the return of workmen for nearly two months"; then, "an usually severe winter"; and lastly, "the heavy floods of the spring, which destroyed railroads and highways, and prevented transportation for several weeks."

Shortly after assuming the company presidency on September 25, 1865, J. Wyman Jones appointed a new resident superintendent and employed a number of Cornish miners. These experienced hard-rock miners proved their worth in uncovering sheets of galena and blasting them into blocks that could be carried to a rude mill, where they were broken into smaller pieces with a hammer. The ore was then run through a set of Cornish rolls to pulverize it before it went to the hand-operated jigs. A jig consisted of a long pole lying across a large log or wooden horse with a sieve suspended from one end, filled with crushed ore and supplied with water, and a man astride the other end. This teeter-totter arrangement was operated in sharp up-and-down movements so that the heavy lead particles would settle to the bottom.

The smelters of that time were old-fashioned stone ovens, sloping to the front with a large firebox for wood beneath on one side, called reverberatory furnaces. The cleaned mineral was thrown into them. Through the combined action of heat and air, and by means of continuous stirring, after several hours metallic lead commenced running down the inclined hearth of the furnace into an iron pot. From there it was ladled into iron molds. A single furnace manned by six men could turn out thirty-two pigs of seventy-two pounds each in twenty-four hours.

In 1867, Dr. C. B. Parsons was employed as superintendent and in 1869 the St. Joseph Lead Company acquired its first diamond drill. Parsons proved to be a capable manager, and under his leadership the company prospered and eventually became the chief producing company in the Lead Belt. The diamond drill, which revolutionized exploration for lead and is used even today, consists of a rotating hollow pipe equipped with diamond cutting edges that cut out a core of rock several hundred feet long. Thus by boring a sufficient number of holes it may be determined whether mineral ores are of sufficient quality and quantity to warrant sinking a production shaft. From 1869 on, mining below the surface continued and the miners went wherever the lodes led them. Vast cathedral-like drifts were hewn out, and tracks were laid for transporting ore to the foot of the hoisting shafts. In the early days mules were used to haul ore underground, and most of the handling was done with pick and shovel. Steam engines powered the hoists and mill machinery. When electrical power became available, the number of men required to mine and process the ore was reduced.

Rapid expansion of operations followed the discovery of ore deposits with the diamond drill. By 1874 the company had sunk five shafts and had expanded the mill, machinery, and furnaces; houses and shops had been built; horses, mules, tramways, drills, and pumps had been added; and about one thousand acres of new land had been purchased. Because the company depended on wood for fuel, it was necessary to own a large quantity of timberlands to prevent higher costs. In 1879, Gus Sitz, a skilled German metallurgist, was employed, and the process of roasting ores before smelting them was introduced. In 1880 the

9. J. Wyman Jones, *A History of the St. Joseph Lead Company* (New York: St. Joseph Lead Company, 1892), p. 5.

St. Joseph Lead Company concentrator and smelter at Bonne Terre, Missouri, *circa* 1900. (Courtesy Missouri State Historical Society.)

mill was expanded and a narrow-gauge railroad was laid to Summit on the Iron Mountain Railroad. The Summit Railway was built and owned by the St. Joseph Lead Company and the Desloge Consolidated Lead Company. Before 1880 these companies had hauled supplies and pig lead to and from three different points on the Iron Mountain Railroad. During spring and fall the roads became impassible because of heavy, sticky mud. In fact, the shipping stations were changed from time to time with the hope of finding routes with shallower ruts.

Industrial growth and expansion was continuous. A modern mill was built after the old one burned in 1883, increasing the efficiency of extraction processes. Additional land was purchased from time to time, and in 1886 the property of the Desloge Consolidated Lead Company, consisting of 3,218 acres of land and a complete lead plant, was purchased. Between 1887 and 1890, St. Joseph constructed the Mississippi River and Bonne Terre Railway to Riverside on the Mississippi River just above Crystal City. The line was then extended southward through the mineral-rich Flat River country to intersect the Iron Mountain north of Farmington.

Construction of the new railroad opened the way for removing the smelting furnaces to the

Desloge Consolidated Lead Company concentrating plant and smelter, St. Francois County, Missouri, 1907. (Reproduced from Ernest R. Buckley, "Geology at the Disseminated Lead Deposts of Washington and St. Francois Counties," *Missouri Bureau of Geology and Mines*, 2d. Series, 9 (1908): 796.)

Mississippi River, where water and sand were abundant and where coke, coal, and fluxes could be obtained at much lower prices. The company acquired Herculaneum, a former smelting town but entirely abandoned by that time, as the site for its new smelter. In addition to a complete and modern smelter, which was completed in 1892, the St. Joseph Lead Company constructed houses, a store, and a laboratory in the style of company towns of that era. The smelter at Herculaneum, subsequently improved and enlarged several times, continues to serve as the smelter for St. Joe Mineral Corporation mines in the New Lead Belt. The selective-flotation process was adopted in 1911, and in later years new ore-milling techniques permitted production increases despite exhaustion of the richer lead reserves.[10]

At the turn of the century the St. Joseph Lead Company employed approximately eight hundred workers, and owned about thirteen thousand acres of land, and operated twelve farms under the management of William Hobbs.[11] In the span of thirty years, the Lead Belt had progressed from very shallow and widely timbered shafts, from which ores were hoisted by bucket and windlass, to modern steam cable hoists that brought ore to the surface from depths of four to five hundred feet. By that time the industry had become firmly based upon the great disseminated galena deposits in the lower half of the Bonne Terre dolomite. The formation, of late Cambrian age, has a thickness of nearly four hundred feet. Mineralization is believed to have been accomplished by solutions that entered the Bonne Terre dolomite through fracture zones and then spread laterally along selective permeable horizons within the formations. The resulting ore bodies are horizontal and vary from a few inches to several feet thick.

The steadily growing St. Joseph Lead Company eventually absorbed most of its competitors. In 1886 the Penn Diggings shaft was sunk, and its lead made it possible not only to pay for the new mill but also to finance the new railroad. Other land acquisitions in the vicinity of present Leadwood—such as McKee Diggings, the T. W. Hunt tract, the Hoffman tract, and the Jake Day tract—all proved to contain rich deposits of lead. Shortly after the Hunt tract was purchased, and operations were under way in a good ore body by 1900, houses were built for employees and the town of Huntington was born. The Hoffman tract was purchased and a shaft sunk in 1901. Again carpenters were brought in and employee houses were built, along with a company store. The settlement was named Owl Creek when the post office was established in 1901, but in 1902 the name was changed to Leadwood.

The St. Joseph venture in St. Francois County attracted considerable attention throughout the area. Just north of the company's property in Bonne Terre was a tract originally granted to Jean Baptiste Pratte, designated as U.S. Survey No.

10. Charles C. Roome, "Selected Aspects of the Southeast Missouri Mining Region" (Masters thesis, University of Missouri-Columbia, 1962), p. 52.

11. Jones, *A History of the St. Joseph Lead Company*, p. 39.

3099. The land was purchased by the Desloge family of Potosi, and mining operations began in 1874 under the name of the Missouri Lead and Smelting Company. The corporate name was changed to Desloge Consolidated Lead Company in 1876.[12] The firm operated three shafts and a large mill until a disastrous fire destroyed the mill in 1886. Rather than rebuild, Desloge sold out to St. Joseph. In the same year, J. Wyman Jones and other St. Joseph trustees formed the Doe Run Lead Company, which was subsequently absorbed by St. Joseph.

During the early 1890's, many new mining companies were formed in St. Francois County. They merged with larger companies and later became a part of St. Joseph operations. Among the newly formed companies were Desloge Consolidated Lead Company, Flat River Lead Company, National Lead Company, Doe Run Lead Company, Central Lead Company, Federal Lead Company, and Theodore Lead Company.

As deep mines and large mills were developed, the landscape imprint of mining became substantial. Shaft houses, concentrators, new and different furnaces, large sediment basins, and huge chat piles could be seen from a given vantage point. Three railroads eventually purchased the smaller roads that had been built into the district: the Missouri Pacific, the Missouri-Illinois, and the St. Louis–San Francisco. Improved highways linked the several towns of the Lead Belt with St. Louis and other cities and towns along the Mississippi border. The core of the Lead Belt, centering around the towns of Bonne Terre, Flat River, Leadville, Elvins, and Desloge, became an urbanized district of nearly a dozen small towns with a total population of more than thirty thousand persons. Flat River, Elvins, River Mines, Leadington, Cantwell, Esther, Desloge, Bonne Terre, and Leadwood blend almost indiscernibly. Fredericktown, near the site of the Doe Run mines, and Mine La Motte are nearby in northern Madison County.

By 1960 the St. Joseph Lead Company controlled 90 per cent of the area's lead production. Several nonpaying shafts had been abandoned and operations focused on a few that were producing richer ores. These included the Federal Mine at Flat River and mines at Leadwood, Bonne Terre, and Indian Creek (Washington County). In September, 1961, the huge Bonne Terre Mine was closed because of declining production resulting from leaner ores. In 1973 the last of the producing operations in the Lead Belt, the Federal Mine and its mill at Flat River, had been closed. By this time the development of Indian Creek Mine in Washington County and the even more important Viburnum Mine in western Iron County had become focal points of investment and mining development.

12. "The History of St. Joe," *St. Joe Headframe*, Special Edition, fall 1970, p. 7.

The Tiff Belt

Barite, or tiff, is a relatively soft, white to gray mineral. The properties of softness, chemical inertness, and weight make it valuable for many purposes. About 90 per cent is used in oil-drilling operations to hold gas pressure; the remaining 10 per cent is used as filler in paint, ink, paper, textiles, and asbestos products.

The Tiff District covers about seventy-five square miles in northeast Washington County, Missouri. Early on this region became a French pocket and remains so today. The story of the French in the area around Old Mines, Fertile, Cannon Mines, Belle Fontaine, Shibboleth, Mineral Point, and Potosi has been one of both exploitation and retention of old ways of living. It would be difficult to determine the extent to which the Creoles of Missouri were exploited. Friction arose from misunderstandings between two groups of people and from the fact that American settlers considered the French to be lazy, weak willed, and generally inferior.

Almost immediately after the Louisiana Purchase was consummated a few progressive Americans began to accumulate land in the vicinity of Old Mines. It has been noted that Moses Austin laid claim to a large tract of land on which he founded the town of Potosi. Another man, John Smith T, located at Shibboleth, one of the central Creole settlements. He was a colorful and well-educated individual who had legally affixed the letter *T* to his name to distinguish himself from other John Smiths and to show that he was from

Tennessee. By various deceptions and by a persistence in locating floating Spanish claims, he gained control of a large amount of land that was being lived on and worked by Creole families. Thus he became wealthy but gained the ill will of many people in the area. When Henry Schoolcraft came to visit in 1817, he referred to Shibboleth as "the feudal seat of John Smith T."[13] These men, and those who came after them as large landowners, gained control of productive lead deposits. They also controlled the region's commerce and sometimes operated large farms.

Living by their old traditions and with their old language and religion, the French Creoles mined lead and sold it to the landowners, who kept royalties for themselves. The Creoles earned barely enough to purchase necessities from the stores, which belonged to the landowners. This mode of life was semi-feudal: the Creoles living rent free on the land but impoverished and working for the landowners.

Until the 1850's, lead was the main product of the area. It was known, however, to have vast deposits of barium sulfate, also called barite, barytes, heavy spar, or tiff. The first records of tiff buying and selling are dated 1857.[14] As the mining of tiff replaced lead mining as the major industry of the area, the established relationship between landowner and tenant-miner persisted. Today the large frame houses and huge barns built by American landowners stand in sharp contrast to the small log cabins (some constructed as late as the 1950's) and shacks of the French families.

Shortly after 1900, when it was discovered that barite could be used as drilling mud to maintain pressure in oil and gas wells, mining companies began buying as much land as they could obtain. Nevertheless, until the 1930's no mechanized mining had been introduced because the cheap-labor force was large. Remaining as they did, illiterate and culturally isolated, the Creoles had virtually no outside assistance toward improving their standards. The retention of old traditions and ways of life were striking to Professor Joseph Carriere when he visited Old Mines in the 1930's:

> The reader will understand readily my emotion when, in Old Mines, Missouri, I came into contact with an isolated group, practically unknown to the outside world, among whom the language and some of the traditions and customs of the old French administration district of Illinois have survived until the present generation. . . . Scattered all along the countryside I found six hundred French-speaking families living in this community.[15]

In early days the Creoles and many American farmers found it possible to supplement their income with small-scale barite mining. Many of the French who lived in the vicinity of Old Mines eked out a living digging tiff after the mines closed. The common method of obtaining it is to dig the barite-bearing clay from surface excavations. The material is then placed in a device known as a log washer, which separates the clay and barite by knocking and rolling the material about. The barite freed from the clay is collected, the clay is allowed to collect in a tailings pond. In recent years the independent operator has been forced out of business by a few larger and more efficient operators.

The mechanization of mining, which began fifty years ago, has greatly increased the number of people who look to the city for employment. Today all mining is done with diesel shovels that work in open pits to a depth of twenty or thirty feet in the ore zone, which lies at the contact of the Eminence and Potosi formations. The barite is dug from the clay residuum and some upper levels of bedrock. The shovels load tiff-bearing earth into heavy-duty ore trucks, which haul it to the washer. At the washer, cleaned tiff is loaded into a truck to be taken to a mill and ground into powder. Waste rock and gravel are used to build dikes that provide a place to put silty waste mud pumped from the washer. Dams are built near some washers to form lakes for water supply; other plants pump water directly from creeks. Viewed from the air, the Tiff District, with its

13. Henry Rowe Schoolcraft, *Scenes and Adventures in the Semi-Alpine Region of the Ozark Mountains* (Philadelphia: Lippincott, Grambo and Co., 1853), p. 253.

14. David F. McMahon, "Tradition and Change in an Ozark Mining Community," (Masters thesis, St. Louis University, 1958), p. 23.

15. Joseph M. Carriere, *Tales from the French Folklore of Missouri* (Evanston, Ill.: Northwestern University Studies, 1937), p. 2.

shallow pits—some of them overgrown with scrub timber and used as community dumps—its sediment ponds, and its many hauling trails, appears blasted, forlorn, and desolate.

Since 1925, when drilling mud had come into its own, annual production of barite in Missouri has only rarely dipped below one hundred thousand tons and has exceeded three thousand fairly often since 1950. Nearly all of it comes from the Washington County Tiff Belt. In 1969 there were ten companies with sizable operations in the Tiff Belt (plus two small operations in Benton County in the Central Mining District).[16] There are twenty-five to thirty washing plants in Washington County. Total employment in all facets of the barite industry is estimated at about six hundred.

The Iron Mountain District

Ironworking in the Ozarks began with Ashebran's furnace, built near Ironton in 1815 or 1816. From then until now, iron has exerted a strong influence on Ozark geography and history.

Unlike most other products of the frontier, wrought iron could bear the cost of transportation to St. Louis, Cincinnati, and Pittsburgh by virtue of its high value. For this reason, it became one of the principal commodities shipped to the cities in exchange for manufactured goods. Farmers disposed of their produce in the ironworks settlements, and during off seasons they obtained employment as woodcutters, charcoal burners, and teamsters. Thus the ironworks furthered the settlement of lands within trading distance. From the late 1830's until the start of the railroad era in the 1860's, many roads were built or improved, primarily to connect the ironworks with their markets. Sections of the Old Iron Road between Maramec Spring Ironworks (in Phelps County) and Hermann correspond to present-day Missouri Highway 19. Likewise, sections of Missouri Highway 32 follow the Old Plank Road, built in 1853, from Ironton to Ste. Genevieve. The Iron Mountain Railroad ran from St. Louis through Iron Mountain, Missouri, and was designed, at least in part, to facilitate the development of ironworking in that area. Correspondingly, the Southwest Branch of the Pacific Railroad, now the Frisco, served the Maramec and Moselle ironworks.

The early ironworks of the Ozarks were in remote hilly districts. Because of the cost of hauling, it was necessary to choose furnace sites that afforded iron ore, limestone for flux, water power, and timber for charcoal making within a radius of a few miles. Therefore, the ironworks were located near ore and fuel, with little regard for the advantages or disadvantages of marketing the product. In the parlance of modern-day economic geographers, these early charcoal iron furnaces were raw material oriented instead of market oriented.

Ashebran's ironworks, which was small and primitive, was located near the entrance to Stout's Shut-in in Iron County, for the power for the air blast and hammer were provided by waterwheel. Springfield Furnace, on Furnace Creek about six miles south of Potosi, was founded in 1823. Like most of the early ironworks, it was operated as a plantation, a nearly self-contained community. Ore at the Ashebran and Springfield furnaces consisted of hematites mined from the igneous rocks in the St. Francis Mountains.

Capitalists became interested in Iron Mountain in 1836, mining began in 1844, and the first furnace was put on blast in 1846. Reports of nearly pure ore that could be used in blacksmiths' forges without treatment led to the wildest kind of enthusiasm. Plans were drawn for Missouri City, a utopian community with many parks and large public buildings where education, hospital care, and other social services would be financed with profits from the mines. Investors were promised $108 annually for every $100 invested. In 1846 it was declared that Iron Mountain and Pilot Knob contained enough ore to supply the world for a century.

Development of the ore bodies, which proved to be less rich than the first wild reports claimed, was substantial after the Plank Road to Ste. Genevieve was built and especially when the Iron Mountain Railroad reached the mines in 1858. After the Civil War, several new furnaces were built at the mines and at Carondolet near St. Louis. Of Missouri's output up to 1870, Iron

16. Hayward M. Wharton et al., *Missouri Minerals—Resources, Production, and Forecasts* (Rolla, Mo.: Missouri Geological Survey and Water Resources, 1969), p. 5.

Mountain had produced more than 90 per cent. Two flourishing towns were built: Iron Mountain and Pilot Knob. The railroad diverted commerce from Ste. Genevieve to St. Louis, and by 1875 the cost of producing charcoal from timber near the mines had led to the construction of additional furnaces in St. Louis, where they could be supplied easily with Illinois coal.

The Tri-State Lead-Zinc District

The development and decline of the Tri-State District occupied much less time than the mining cycle in the Old Lead Belt. The first record of lead in the western Ozarks was written by Schoolcraft when he visited the Indian diggings on Pearson Creek near the present site of Springfield.[17] Small mines were worked in Greene and Webster counties in the early 1840's and near Joplin in 1848. The initial discovery at Granby in Newton County was made in 1849, and the large deposits in that field were discovered in 1854. By 1857, hundreds of cabins had been built and scores of shafts had been sunk. Before the Civil War the Granby lead was hauled by wagon to Boonville on the Missouri, to Linn Creek on the Osage, and to Fort Smith on the Arkansas for shipment to outside markets.

There is no universally accepted explanation of the origin of the lead and zinc ores of the Tri-State District. How the ores were transported, concentrated, and enriched has been studied by more than a dozen eminent geologists. One view holds that the ores were concentrated into rich deposits by cold meteoric waters, which include descending groundwaters and ascending artesian waters. Another view is that the lodes were deposited by ascending hot water and gases from deep molten masses of rock material. Regardless of the theory accepted, the deposits were laid in vertical fractures and horizontal solution channels, or runs. The greatest concentrations of rich ores extend from Spring River in Missouri through Cherokee County, Kansas, to the Neosho River in Oklahoma (fig. 9-1).

In the early years, mining was carried out in a manner similar to practices established in the Mineral Area. Professional miners from the Lead Belt are known to have immigrated to the mines of southwest Missouri by 1849.[18] They were joined by local farmers. Most of the districts were regarded as poor man's camps because the ores were shallow and could be dug with little else besides a pick, shovel, and a bucket and windlass for hoisting ore.

Zinc ore frequently was encountered in conjunction with lead, often at deeper levels, but little was known of its value. Huge quantities of sphalerite (zinc ore) were thrown onto debris piles. The accumulated zinc at Granby was used to construct a stockade for protecting the women and children against Civil War raids.[19] After the war, this mineral was removed from the stockade walls and marketed at three dollars a ton.

In the early days each camp had its own smelter. Kennett and Blow were at Granby, Mosely at Neosho, and the Harklerode Company smelted for the Turkey Creek mines.[20] Marketing lead posed a difficult problem in prerailroad days. The common method of transporting it to market was to haul pigs by wagon to Spring River and Cowskin Creek, load them onto flatboats, then float them to the Grand River in Indian Territory, from there to the Arkansas, and finally to New Orleans via the Mississippi.

The Atlantic and Pacific Railroad's arrival at Joplin in 1870 coincided with the discovery of superb mineral deposits in that district. In 1870 there was not a house in Joplin, but by 1874 it had become a city of three thousand people, one-third of them miners, and thirteen furnaces. Rich lead deposits caused the settlement of Oronogo, Webb City, and Carterville in quick succession. By 1872 a process for treatment of zinc blende had been discovered, and almost immediately zinc production became more important than lead. Zinc and

17. Henry Rowe Schoolcraft, *Journal of a Tour into the Interior of Missouri and Arkansas in 1818 and 1819*, in *Schoolcraft in the Ozarks*, ed. Hugh Park (Van Buren, Ark.: Press-Argus Printers, 1955), p. 113.

18. Arrell M. Gibson, *Wilderness Bonanza: The Tri-State District of Missouri, Kansas, and Oklahoma* (Norman: University of Oklahoma Press, 1972), p. 20.

19. Ibid., p. 21.

20. Ibid., p. 24.

lead were discovered in 1886 at Aurora and on Pearson Creek at Springfield.

Not only was the geology of the Tri-State District a controlling factor in mining and milling methods and land use, it also exerted much influence in the founding, growth, and longevity of mining camps and towns. The miners needed places to buy equipment, food, and clothing and also shelter and entertainment. Limited means of transportation required them to live adjacent to the workings, which in turn gave rise to a large number of mining camps. If the ore bodies were large, the camp became a town; if deposits ran out quickly, the camp folded and the merchants moved on.

Gibson has divided the Tri-State camps and towns into four stages of urbanization.[21] First came the mining camp, usually short lived if the ore deposits in the vicinity were limited. In the second stage, the mining town miners still lived in the area and worked its deposits. Soon the economy of the town became more diversified because it had to supply the smaller outlying camps. In the third stage, workers lived in the larger towns and commuted to the mines by electric trolley. The fourth stage was a time of long-distance commuting, first by trolley and later by automobile. In this stage, when 90 per cent of the mining was carried out in the Picher, Oklahoma, field, some of miners lived in Picher or Cardin, but many resided in Miami, Commerce, Galena, and Joplin. Many camps failed to pass the first test, so that today only about thirty urban centers from the original array of camps remain.

At one time or another, there were eighty-one camps in the Tri-State District:

WE-TAK-ER Mine, showing hand jig and picking shed. Granby, Missouri, area, *circa* 1905. (Reproduced from Ernest R. Buckley and H. A. Buehler, "The Geology of the Granby Area," *Missouri Bureau of Geology and Mines*, 2d. Series, 4 (1905): ix.)

In southwest Missouri these included Lehigh, Wentworth, Pierce City, Carthage, Neosho, Grand Falls, Dayton, Scotland, Leadville Hollow, Chitwood, Carl Junction, Thurman, Webb City, Carterville, Oronogo (Minersville), Smithfield, Waco, Thoms Station, Four Corners, Blende City, Duenweg, Prosperity, Porto Rico, Fidelity, Diamond, Murphysburg, Joplin, Blytheville, Stephens Diggins, Sherwood Diggings, Cox Diggings, Pinkard Mines, Leadville Mines, Carney Diggings, Tanyard Hollow, Taylor Diggings, Belleville, Jackson Diggings, Central City, Saginaw, Swindle Hill, Parr Hill, Lone Elm, Moon Range Diggings, Spring City, Racine, Seneca, Alba, Lawton, Granby, Bell Center, Central City, Asbury, Burch City, Klondike, Georgia City, Stark City, and Cave Springs. Southeast Kansas produced Galena, Badger, Peacock, Emire City, Crestline, Baxter Springs, and Treece. In northeast Oklahoma were Tar River Camp, Picher, Commerce (Hattonville), Douthat, St. Louis, Hockerville, Quapaw, Cardin, Lincolnville, Peoria, and Century.[22]

21. Ibid., p. 27.

22. Ibid., p. 28.

The origin of their names is conjectural. Geographical and mineralogical factors were important, as in the case of Grand Falls, Blende City, and Galena. Many settlements were named after prominent individuals: Picher, after the mining family responsible for its development; Joplin, after the Reverend Harris Joplin; Webb City, for the owner of the land where the mineral was found. Other names sprang from the whimsy and imagination of the miners; such are typical of all mining camps. A few of the more productive mines were Poor Boy's, Big Run, Klondike, Bonnie Belle, Elta May, Betsy Jan, Mary Gibson, Sunflower, What Cheer, Mahutaska, and Never Sweat.

Although basic operations in the early years of the Tri-State Mining District were not dissimilar from those in the Lead Belt, the nature of the ore deposits and long-established practices mitigated against the large-scale development typical of the eastern Ozarks. Hired labor was seldom used before 1885, but two-man operations were very common. The major mining tools were a double-pointed pick, a square scoopshovel for loading the ore can, and a round-pointed shovel for digging. The windlass, equipped with rope and bucket, was operated by a hand crank. Animal and steam power were used as the deeper mines were worked by larger companies.

As in the Old Lead Belt and other Ozark lead-zinc mining districts, the principal underground mining operations used the room-and-pillar method, whereby columns of bedrock were left undisturbed to support the roof. In this way the need for mine timbers was eliminated. In some places, large open-pit mines were developed, notably the Oronogo Circle Mine, noted for the production of some thirty million dollars worth of lead and zinc.

Because of the scattered nature of the deposits, centralized milling did not develop until late. By 1905 there had evolved a definite system that became recognized nationally as the Joplin Mill Practice. The cost of erecting a Joplin mill was low, and when a deposit was exhausted, the mill could be dismantled and moved to a new location. Concrete foundations were erected at the new mine and the mill was set up once more.

The scattered deposits led to land-leasing companies and independent miners who paid royalties according to the amount of ore that was produced. Royalty payments to the landowners ranged from 5 to 5.9 per cent, depending on the cost of mining, whether the area was in a proven field, whether expenses were shared, and other related factors. The landowner usually surveyed his tract into lots of about an acre each and leased them on the basis of one man to an acre. Gradually, the best mineral lands became consolidated under a few mining and royalty companies. Among the larger ones were Granby Mining and Smelting Company, which held large tracts of Atlantic and Pacific Railroad land under lease; Thompson and Graves Mining and Royalty Company; A. B. Corn Mining Company; Thurman Company; Chapman and Riggins Land and Smelting Company; Jasper Lead and Mining Company; Picher Land Company; East Joplin Mining and Smelting Company; and Moffet and Sergeant Mining Company.[23] The leasing-and-royalties system became so well established in the Joplin area that as mines in Missouri closed and new mines in Kansas and Oklahoma opened, it was used in these areas as well.

Foreign capital was attracted to the Tri-State District in the 1890's when English and Swedish investors purchased mining property near Joplin.[24] Even earlier, in 1882, the stage had been set for the concentration of lead smelting in the hands of a single firm, Picher Lead Company. Through a series of consolidations and transactions, this firm secured the exclusive use in the United States of the process for converting lead fumes into white lead. From 1886 on, Picher Lead Company controlled most of the smelting in the Tri-State District.

Charcoal was the chief fuel until the 1880's, when coal from the nearby Kansas fields succeeded it. After 1900, natural gas was imported into the district for lead smelting. In fact, because natural gas was so effective in the smelting of zinc blende (sphalerite), most of the Tri-State zinc ores were smelted on the fringe of the district in the Kansas, Oklahoma, and Arkansas natural-gas fields.[25]

23. Ibid., pp. 147–48.
24. Ibid., p. 165.
25. Ibid., p. 123.

From 1930 to 1955, most of the mining was in the Kansas and Oklahoma fields, but Joplin continued to be the leading supply and financial center of the mining district. By 1930, most of the mining and smelting had been concentrated in the hands of the Eagle Picher Mining and Smelting Company. Wildcat shafts were practically unknown. The ore bodies were explored systematically by core drilling, and the estimated tonnage of concentrates was computed beforehand. In the 1950's the Eagle Picher West Side Mine near Treece, Kansas, was operating at the 428-foot level in a huge gallery, with a 125-foot ceiling, containing a tool and welding shop and a vehicle maintenance center.

In the final days of the Tri-State District in the 1950's and early 1960's, there were serious labor problems and prolonged strikes. After the war-years flurry of activity brought on by high prices for lead and zinc, mining operations settled into established patterns. Three-fourths of the production was by the large operators. Gougers, usually an association of four to six miners, leased mined-out and abandoned properties and worked small pockets of ore, which they sold to Eagle Picher. A few small mining companies opened new mines in shallow grounds in the tradition of the poor man's camp.[26] Finally, in 1967, when Eagle Picher closed its facilities, mining in the Tri-State District ceased.

The impact of mining in shaping the cultural landscape hardly can be assessed in its entirety. More than thirty permanent settlements have persisted from more than eighty mining camps once established. A large network of railroads, including switching yards and sidings, was established by three major lines: the Missouri Pacific, the St. Louis–San Francisco (Frisco), and the Missouri-Kansas-Texas (Katy). One of the largest interurban railways in the United States, the Southwest Missouri Electrical Trolley, connected Tri-State towns, from Carthage, Webb City, and Carterville in the north to Miami and Picher in the southwest. This system also carried passengers to Pittsburg, Galena, and Columbus in Kansas. An extensive network of modern roads was constructed. U.S. Highway 66 was a major east-west highway connecting Chicago and the West Coast, while U.S. Highway 71 linked Kansas City and the Gulf States.[27]

26. Ibid., p. 99.

General view of the concentrating and smelting plant of the Granby Mining and Smelting Company, Granby, Missouri, *circa* 1905. (Reproduced from Ernest R. Buckley and H. A. Buehler, "The Geology of the Granby Area," *Missouri Bureau of Geology and Mines*, 2d. Series, 4 (1905): 111.)

A major development was electrification of the mines and mills. In 1890 the Southwestern Power Company built a hydroelectric station at Grand Falls on Shoal Creek, the first power plant in the Tri-State. Several other generating plants soon were established, including the Lowell plant on Spring River near Galena and the Riverton, Kansas, thermal plant two miles upstream. In 1913 the Ozark Power and Water Company completed Powersite Dam and its hydroelectric plant on White River in Taney County to produce additional power for the Tri-State mines. In 1922, the Lowell, Riverton, Grand Falls, and White River power plants were combined into the Empire Electric Power Company, with headquarters in Joplin.[28] Powersite Dam formed Lake

27. Richard S. Thoman, *The Changing Occupance Pattern of the Tri-State Area of Missouri, Kansas, and Oklahoma*, University of Chicago Department of Geography Research Paper no. 21 (Chicago: 1953), p. 82.
28. Gibson, *Wilderness Bononza*, p. 81.

Taneycomo, and because it was the first of the large Ozark lakes, it is a landmark in the development of the Ozarks region. In the 1920's, Union Electric Supply followed Empire's lead and constructed huge Bagnell Dam on the Osage River, forming Lake of the Ozarks, to supply power for the mines in the Old Lead Belt and for the St. Louis area.

Because of the power required by the mines, smelters, and mills, natural-gas service and electric utilities were available in Tri-State towns long before other sections of the Ozarks were reached. City water mains and sewage facilities often were installed as adjuncts to mining operations.

On the negative side, the Tri-State landscape remains pockmarked by shallow diggings, gaping water-filled open pits, and huge chat piles, many three hundred feet high, formed by waste rock from milling operations. The former mining areas, strewn with abandoned car bodies, castaway refrigerators, and other household dump material, create a forlorn and blasted landscape, a constant reminder that mineral resources are, after all, limited and nonrenewable.

Other Historic Lead-Zinc Districts

The Central Mining District, centering on Morgan, Miller, and Camden counties but including much of the Osage-Gasconade Hills, was never as important as the Lead Belt or the Tri-State District. The mines were smaller and more scattered, and consequently they were not consolidated and mechanized. By 1910 the district was essentially defunct, although some mining continued as late as World War II, when lead and zinc prices were high.

Lead and zinc mining in the North Arkansas Mining District was very similar to that of the Central District. The deposits were small and scattered, and mining and milling operations were never consolidated and developed to a degree anything like that of the two major lead-zinc mining districts. Mining was especially concentrated in Marion County, although there were scattered lead and zinc mines in several surrounding counties in north-central Arkansas. At one time or another, there were more than fifty mines to the north and southeast of Yellville. There were many near the mouth of the Buffalo River and the town of Rush. As in other districts, the mines had colorful names: Cook, Last Chance, Columbia, Morning Star, Red Cloud, Full Moon, Sam Peel, Lone Pilgrim. The last mining in the region was done in the Rush Creek area in Marion County from 1959 to 1962. Today the town of Rush, a cluster of a dozen or so weather-beaten and empty houses and sheds, resembles a western ghost town.

The New Lead Belt

Since the mid-1950's there has been extensive exploration and rapid development in the New Lead Belt in Reynolds and western Iron counties. The ore, primarily lead with some zinc, copper, and silver, lies in flat beds some 900 to 1,000 feet beneath the surface. In some areas the ore bodies are 140 feet thick and 3,000 feet wide. Geologists believe the ores were deposited in and near a buried offshore reef that meanders from southwestern Washington County through western Iron County and across the northern half of Reynolds County to a few miles north of Ellington.

Indian Creek, situated about thirty-five miles northwest of Bonne Terre, was the first major ore body to be discovered outside the Old Lead Belt. This mine, operated by St. Joe Mineral Corporation, produced some 4.5 million tons of ore in its first nine years of operation, 1954 to 1963.[29] It has been developed through two concrete-lined circular shafts. The mine and modern 2,500-ton mill is a prototype of St. Joe's Viburnum, Fletcher, and Brushy Creek operations. Similar mining and milling facilities have been built in the New Lead Belt by Cominco, Amax, and Ozark Lead Company.

Mining is by the room-and-pillar method, with twenty-five-foot supporting pillars at intervals of about thirty-five feet. The mines, opened in the 1960's, use diesel-powered rubber-tired trucks to haul to underground crushers. Repair and maintenance shops are located beneath the sur-

29. "Indian Creek—The Prototype Operation," *Engineering and Mining Journal* 165 (April 1964): 89.

face. After primary crushing, the ore is hoisted to the surface, where lead and zinc concentrates are separated from the powdered ore by flotation, a seemingly unlikely operation whereby tiny lead and zinc particles become attached to bubbles and are floated off the rock waste. The lead concentrates are trucked or railed to smelters at Glover, Buick, or Herculaneum. The zinc concentrates go to St. Louis or Europe to be smelted.

Hoist house and mill buildings at the Amax Homestake Lead Mine in the New Lead Belt, Iron County, Missouri.

Economic Effects

The economic effects of mining today are substantial. Except for management and technical personnel, the mines employ people who commute from farms and surrounding towns. They have helped to stop the population decline that has been so characteristic of interior Ozark counties. Census data show that the population of Reynolds County, Missouri, declined from 8,923 in 1930 to 5,161 in 1960, but with the development of mining during the 1960's, the population rose to 6,106 by 1970.

Income from mining has had a salutary effect on the regional economy. By 1969 lead and zinc valued at $51,058,000 had replaced livestock raising as the leading industry in Reynolds County. Farmers who have turned to the lead mines can earn as much as $12,000 per year, nearly twice their former income in many instances. In 1976 the New Lead Belt produced 504,095 tons of lead worth $252,892,000.[30] Zinc, copper, and silver amounted to more than $75,000,000.

Perhaps the most unique geographical feature of the New Lead Belt is the new town of Viburnum. Planned by Bartholomew Associates of St. Louis for St. Joe Mineral Corporation, the former crossroads settlement, consisting of a general store and a house or two, had blossomed into a modern town of six hundred residents by 1979. It had a shopping center, four or five new churches, the Viburnum Inn, a new consolidated school, an airfield, and a new multisided office and research building belonging to the Missouri Division of St. Joe Mineral Corporation. An air-pollution conference at the Viburnum Country Club drew meteorologists, geologists, mining engineers, and air-pollution consultants from such distant places as San Francisco and Colorado. Viburnum, formerly served by a logging railroad taken out in the 1920's, now has a new railroad, this time a heavy-gauge system built by the Frisco to haul lead concentrates and pigs. Modernity has come to the remote Courtois Hills, and it is well financed. Remarked a mining executive: "The county court of Iron County spends most of its time figuring how to spend tax money from the mines."

30. *Missouri's Environment* 3 (March 1977): 4.

The Sink-Fill Iron Districts

A second iron smelting district grew up around sink-fill iron deposits in Phelps, Crawford, and Dent counties in Missouri (fig. 9-1). Apparently, the first bloomery was founded in 1819 or 1820 at Thickety Creek in Crawford County and operated until about 1830. The Maramec Iron works, or Massey's, was the next to be founded. Thomas James and Samuel Massey of Ohio established the

Cherry Valley Mine No. 2, Crawford County, Missouri, *circa* 1912. A filled-sink iron ore deposit. (Reproduced from G. W. Crane, "The Iron Ores of Missouri," *Missouri Bureau of Geology and Mines*, 2d. Series, 10 (1912): 1.)

ironworks at Meramec Spring, about six miles southeast of St. James, in 1827. The site offered the advantages of good hematite ore, water power from Meramec Spring, limestone for use as a flux, and an adequate supply of hardwood timber for charcoal. The remote location was not a serious disadvantage at first because the demand for iron was local. A second furnace at Moselle in Franklin County, Missouri, was constructed and financed by the James family in 1846.

The Maramec Iron Works was organized as an iron plantation similar to those of eighteenth-century Pennsylvania. All lands, building, and equipment belonged to the partners, and the establishment had many of the characteristics of a feudal manor. Operation of the plant required about one hundred men, of whom about seventy-five were married and lived near the furnace. Men employed as woodcutters and charcoal burners often lived at some distance from the smelter. Before the Civil War, slaves were leased from plantation owners in the Missouri River valley to do the heavy work.

Charcoal was made by the old method of piling oak and hickory cordwood on a level piece of ground 40 to 50 feet in diameter, covering this with earth and allowing the wood to char in a low-oxygen environment. Wood was cut in the winter, and the crude ovens were operated during the summer and fall. Approximately 500 acres of timber were cleared each year to supply the charcoal required for the ironworks. The Maramec Iron Works owned approximately 10,000 acres, which made it nearly self-sufficient in timber resources. Unlike the furnaces at Pilot Knob and Iron Mountain, which employed a permanent force of choppers, the Maramec Iron Works employed area farmers as woodcutters in their slack season, thereby reducing the cost of wood by twenty cents per cord.[31]

The practice of cutting all timber (clear cutting) subjected charcoal iron producers, and lead smelters as well, to charges of exploiting the country's natural resources. Many people mistakenly blame the demise of Ozark iron smelting on destruction of the forests that provided fuel. In fact, however, the ironworks never experienced a shortage of timber for charring. Unlike a sawmill the ironworks required a heavy plant investment and could not easily move its equipment. Thus the iron and lead smelters had a natural incentive to preserve the forests and were among the earliest leaders in fire prevention. It was self-interest that prompted Samuel Massey, superintendent of the Maramec Iron Works, to ask Missouri Governor John Miller to punish the Indians for firing the woods near the ironworks.[32] Fires near an iron or lead smelter could easily destroy the fuel supply for the coming year.

Hematite was dug from a sinkhole west of the ironworks and hauled to the furnace in wagons. Water from Meramec Spring provided power to operate the blowers, which forced air into the smelter and the several forges on the property, and to operate the huge trip-hammer that was used to pound out impurities. The settlement included a store, gristmill, and a collection of

31. James D. Norris, *Frontier Iron: The Story of the Maramec Iron Works, 1826–1876* (Madison, Wis.: The State Historical Society of Wisconsin, 1964), p. 45.

32. Ibid., p. 46.

miners' cabins on a ridge, overlooking the Meramec River valley, known as String Town.

Iron was sold in various forms. Bars, blooms, and pigs were shipped to St. Louis by way of the Old Iron Road to Hermann or via the Springfield Road to the Gasconade River. Kettles, ovens, stoves, cannonballs, and railroad equipment could stand the charge of direct shipment to St. Louis by wagon. Company stores, which had exclusive rights to market Maramec iron, were established at St. Louis, Hermann, Jefferson City, Boonville, Brunswick, Independence, Warsaw, Lebanon, and Springfield. Efforts were made to use the Meramec, Gasconade, and Osage rivers to ship iron, but they were largely unsuccessful. Hermann and St. Louis were the chief ports through which Maramec iron found its way to markets as far east as Pittsburgh.

The closing of the Maramec Iron Works in 1876 resulted from the financial problems of William James rather than depletion of the iron or timber resources. The shutdown was caused by the Panic of 1873, coupled with James's heavy investment in a new furnace, the Ozark Works, located on an 8,000-acre tract on the Atlantic and Pacific Railroad near the point where it crossed the Little Piney River ten miles west of Rolla. Although the Maramec furnace produced 4,500 tons of iron during 1875, none of it was sold because the price of cold-blast iron would not cover the cost of production. Today the site of Maramec Iron Works is owned and operated by the Lucy James Foundation as a historical park in conjunction with the Missouri Department of Natural Resources.

Often, small manufacturing concerns fail because they do not keep up with advancing technology. The fact that some charcoal furnaces continued production fifty years after the closing of the Maramec Iron Works indicates that technological change alone cannot explain the failure of individual ironworks. Even William James's bankrupt Ozark Iron Works operated under receivership until 1890. The Sligo Iron Furnace, a charcoal ironworks in eastern Dent County, was not constructed until 1880, and it operated successfully until 1921.

Sink-fill iron deposits, on which the early iron furnaces in Franklin, Phelps, and Dent counties were based, are widely distributed in the interior Ozarks. Mining was carried out at one time or another in Crawford, Franklin, Gasconade, Maries, Miller, Phelps, Dent, Texas, Howell, Reynolds, Carter, Oregon, and Ripley counties. Most of the ore mined far from the smelters was shipped to smelters in the East. Iron mines were operated near Poplar Bluff and West Plains as recently as the 1950's.

Ore washer at the Orchard Mine in Carter County, Missouri, *circa* 1912. (Reproduced from G. W. Crane, "The Iron Ores of Missouri," *Missouri Bureau of Geology and Mines*, 2d. Series, 10 (1912): 82.)

In recent years the Ozarks again has become a major producer of iron ore, but none of it is smelted in the region. In the 1960's, Hanna Mining Company, which took over operations at Pilot Knob after a series of ownerships changes, opened new hematite deposits nearly 900 feet beneath the base of Pilot Knob. Previously, the ore had been mined in an open pit atop the mountain and through a shaft sunk in the west slope. The ore is milled at the mine and shipped in pellet form. A second major ore deposit was discovered south of Sullivan by means of magnetic measurements, followed by core drilling. The mine, located not far from the old Maramec Iron Works, is operated by Meramec Mining Company, a joint venture of Bethlehem Steel Company and St. Joe

Charcoal ovens of the Sligo Iron Furnace at Sligo in Dent County, Missouri, *circa* 1912. (Reproduced from G. W. Crane, "The Iron Ores of Missouri," *Missouri Bureau of Geology and Mines*, 2d. Series, 10 (1912): 3.)

Mineral Corporation.[33] There is no geologic relationship between the ores that were mined for the Maramec furnace and the ores at Pea Ridge. The new mine, opened in the 1960's, is in magnetite ore imbedded in igneous rocks approximately 900 feet beneath the surface. The ore is hoisted to the surface, milled, roasted in pellets, and shipped to various places. The rising cost (as much as five million dollars per year) of pumping water from the mine, coupled with low iron prices caused in part by foreign competition, caused the Pea Ridge Mine to close in January 1978.

Other Ozark Mining Operations

Tripoli, a porous, decomposed siliceous rock, has been mined near Seneca and Tiff City in Newton County, Missouri, since 1869. It was used first for scouring lint and proved to be an excellent filter for city water systems. In 1919 the Seneca deposits were purchased by the Barnsdall Tripoli Company, which began to market tripoli as an admixture in concrete. Tripoli, known as tiff (not to be confused with barite), is a soft, friable, porous silica of the chalcedony variety.

The terms *silica sand* and *glass sand* are applied to sand and sandstone having chemical and physical properties that can be used for a number of industrial purposes. The prime requisite is that the sand be essentially pure. Most of it is used in the glass industry. Glass sand is mined in the Ozarks in two widely separated districts. The largest production comes from the St. Peter sandstone along the Mississippi River Border. It was first mined in large quantities when the Pittsburgh Plate Glass Company plant was founded at Crystal City in 1874. The sandstone is soft and easily quarried, and most of it comes from Jefferson and Ste. Genevieve counties.

There are hundreds of millions of tons of glass sand in thirteen northern Arkansas counties, primarily along the White and Buffalo rivers. However, present exploitation is limited to Izard County, where only two firms are mining the sand.

In the early 1880's, manganese mines were opened in Independence County, Arkansas, northwest of Batesville. In 1881 the Keystone Mining Company of New York and Pennsylvania began buying rights to mineral deposits around Cushman, Pfeiffer, and Sandtown. Manganese in pebbles and boulders could be dug from shallow deposits in a relatively soft sandstone. Some of the boulders were reported to be as large as cotton bales.[34] Operations remained small and were similar to the system used in the Tiff Belt in Washington County, Missouri. In 1889, Keystone paid only ten thousand dollars in wages to miners who worked in the shallow pits.

From the early years of the twentieth century to the 1930's, W. H. Denison was the biggest operator in the manganese district. The mining

33. "Meramec Iron Ore Project Starts Production at Pea Ridge," *Engineering and Mining Journal* 165 (April 1964): 93–108.

34. William D. Spear, "Farming and Mining Experience: Independence County, Arkansas, 1900–1925," (Ph.D. diss., Washington University, St. Louis, 1974), p. 81.

was carried out on a contract basis whereby Denison provided the tools and the mining property and purchased the ore that was produced. The system was not designed to afford large profits for the miners. Because the rewards were low, the mining was often seasonal, and workers drifted in and out of the nearby communities. The mines were closed during the Depression years in the 1930's but were reopened during World War II and operated until the mid-1950's. It is reported that when manganese ore prices were high in the 1940's, one man came to the area with a bulldozer and took out fifty thousand dollars' worth in two weeks.[35]

Granite is quarried at Graniteville in Iron County, Missouri, near Elephant Rocks. The first quarries were opened in 1868 by B. G. Brown, who was governor of Missouri from 1870 to 1872, and T. A. Allen, founder of the St. Louis and Iron Mountain Railroad. The stone, marketed under the trade name *Missouri Red Granite*, became a popular building and paving material. It was used extensively for construction in St. Louis, and the waterfront docks there and at Cape Girardeau were paved with Missouri Red. Only one quarry is operating now, and production is restricted primarily to monuments. As the quarries closed, the population of Graniteville declined from 600 in 1940 to 140 in 1970.

Limestone and dolomite are abundant in the Ozarks. One of Missouri's first industries was the manufacture of lime from stone quarried from a number of formations bordering the Mississippi and Missouri rivers and, in southwest Missouri, in the vicinity of Springfield. The lime was manufactured in the rudest manner: logs were heaped and blocks of limestone were thrown on them and burned. Later the lime was burned in small kilns, a few of which are still standing in various states of delapidation. Two of the larger companies operating in 1978 were among the earliest processors of lime: the Ash Grove Lime and Cement Company at Springfield and the Mississippi Lime Company at Ste. Genevieve.

Sligo Iron Furnace at Sligo in Dent County, Missouri, *circa* 1912. (Reproduced from G. W. Crane, "The Iron Ores of Missouri," *Missouri Bureau of Geology and Mines*, 2d. Series, 10 (1012): 3.)

At present, limestones and dolomites are quarried mainly near the major population centers, where they are used for building-stone, lime, cement, and refractory purposes. They are mined primarily in a belt paralleling the Mississippi River, in counties bordering the Missouri River, and in several counties in southwest Missouri and northwest Arkansas. Some of the limestones and dolomites have outstanding qualities of beauty and strength. Among the better known as building stones are those from Carthage, Missouri; the Beaver quarries (no longer operating) at Beaver, Arkansas, from which many of the large buildings in Eureka Springs were constructed; and the so-called black-marble limestones quarried at Batesville, Arkansas, which were used in the construction of many public buildings in the Arkansas Valley, including the state capitol.

Mineral Legends

Legends of rich deposits of precious metals and of lost mines, mainly gold and silver, have been

35. Ibid., p. 111.

passed down from the earliest European settlers and have become part of Ozark folklore. Perhaps people who are poor and who remain poor through several generations have a fascination for wealth that comes easily and quickly from hidden sources beneath impoverished rock-rubble soils. It is clear that the Ozarks has great mineral wealth, and fortunes were made as large mining combines were established. However, this wealth is founded on the base metals (lead, zinc, and iron) and not on the precious metals, such as gold, silver, and platinum. Ozarks geology does not portend the discovery of great riches in the latter metals, nor is it to be found in the new wealth producers: petroleum and coal. Modern prospecting for mineral deposits is scientific business, and there is no active search for precious metals in the Ozarks at this time. But this was not always the case; local histories and folklore are replete with attempts to discover and mine silver and gold.

A few examples of mineral folklore will acquaint the reader with the nature and repetitiveness of the stories. This one, from a recent history of Baxter County, Arkansas, is told with minor variations in several parts of the Ozarks:

> Looking back, it seems strange that a student of our county's history could so easily forget that it was the lure of precious metals that brought the first Europeans to our region. De Soto's men camped for a while on the banks of White River at the mouth of Bruce Creek in 1555 and prospected in the surrounding hills. The slag piles from their crude mining operations are mute testimony of their visit here. Evidently they did not find their gold and silver, although the legend of a lost Spanish silver mine guarded by the skeleton in Conquistador's armor still persists. Not many years ago, a stranger appeared in the Monkey Run community, discreetly asking several boys if they could guide him to a certain cave in the Bruce Creek Hills, and the almost forgotten legend was revived.[36]

It is doubtful that De Soto's men ever penetrated Arkansas as far as Baxter County, and as for the slag heaps, they are more likely the product of a more recent venture, when lead and zinc smelting was done in north Arkansas after the Civil War.

Another common Ozark lost-mine story focuses on an eccentric or recluse who discovered a silver or gold mine but used the ore only when in need of ready cash. The whereabouts of the mine was never divulged:

> There is a legend of a lost silver mine on either Hightower (now Carson) or Lithia Creek. Some versions say a lost lead mine, but I prefer the shinier story. The story goes that a Mr. Hightower used silver bullets in his pistol and hunting rifle. Whenever his supply would run low, he would disappear, and in a few days would be back home with a new supply of silver bullets. He promised his sons that he would reveal the location of his secret mine to them before he died. But, alack, Mr. Hightower died with his boots on, accidently killed by a silver bullet from his own pistol. For many years his sons and neighbors hunted in vain for his secret vein of silver. As with all legends, this story is based on facts. And if the silver bullets were fact, then this man was the original "Lone Ranger."[37]

Then there is the more factual folklore of a persistent breed of prospectors with entrepreneurial talents. One of the more interesting stories concerns the Splitlog Silver Mining Company:

> In 1887, a group of men posing as mining promoters, interested Matthias Splitlog in financing a McDonald County gold and silver mining venture. Splitlog was a Wyandotte Indian who had made a fortune in Kansas City real estate, although unable to read or write. "Pay dirt" was reportedly found some four miles northwest of Anderson, Missouri. With Splitlog's financial backing, events moved fast. The Splitlog Silver Mining Company was organized, the city of Splitlog laid out, and a daily stageline begun to Neosho. Assay reports claiming heavy deposits of gold and silver threw the countryside into a fever of mining excitement. Roads were reportedly lined with white-topped wagons labeled "bound for Splitlog." A railroad company was capitalized at $3,000,000, and Splitlog was made treasurer of the construction company. He drove the first spike—a silver one—with appropriate flourish, "after music by the Indian band from the territory."[38]

36. Mary Ann Messick, *History of Baxter County, 1873–1973* (Mountain Home, Ark.: Mountain Home Chamber of Commerce, 1973), p. 291.

37. Ibid., p. 291.

38. *Missouri: A Guide to the "Show Me" State* (New York: Duell, Sloan, and Pearce, 1941), p. 507.

This mining venture flourished until it was discovered that there were no ores. When Splitlog's lode of cash petered out, the mining boom and railroad venture collapsed. The promoters fled in time to escape punishment, but Splitlog was ruined. The railroad became part of the Kansas City Southern's holdings.

While in full bloom, the Splitlog venture caused heavy mineralization in formerly barren limestones and dolomites in adjacent parts of northern Arkansas. Prospectors from Benton County soon discovered these deposits, but only a few mining ventures were established. The amazing good fortune and skill of Arkansas prospectors reported in local newspapers is recorded in a recent history of Benton County:

> The biggest interest in mining came in 1887. At this time they were working the Split Log [sic] mine northwest of Bentonville in the Indian Territory (actually the mine was in Missouri). The stories of the great wealth to come must have got to people for every week's newspaper would carry a new article on someone who had found some rich ore while digging a well, or just laying on top of the ground in their back 40.
>
> "Mr. James Nees, who was digging a well in the northwest part of Bentonville last week, found some of the richest specimens of Jack or zinc ore we have ever seen. It would go 90 percent zinc.["]
>
> "Col. Albert Peel of Avoca came by with a fine specimen of copper ore. He said there were strangers in his area locating mineral claims on Government land.["]
>
> "The Bentonville Mining Company was formed in 1887 with a capital stock of $1,000. The company struck ore in their mine on Pea Ridge that indicated exceeding richness. It is a mineral of some kind, as it melts readily, and has the appearance of silver. Specimens have been sent to different points, and a report of its value is daily expected.["][39]

One of the most colorful Ozark mining stories concerns the Kruse Gold Mine near Rogers, Arkansas. The mine originated as a vision and was established by the Kruse family as instructed in the vision. The mining venture began auspiciously on January 27, 1903. That day, some fifty people in Rogers received telegrams from W. H. Kruse of Chicago saying, "Ten million dollars for all the people of Rogers." No one knew what it meant, but most were interested. It seems that sometime around 1900, W. H. Kruse, a successful businessman in Le Sueur, Minnesota, began having visions, which he would write down on paper with his eyes closed. In one of these visions, Kruse was told about a gold mine on his father's farm in Arkansas. He was told that under the roots of an old wild apple tree he would find a gold mine so rich that he could reconstruct the economy of the world after the ravages of a great war that was coming.

Not satisfied when members of his family in Arkansas could not find the tree, Kruse journeyed to Benton County and, after some looking, found a wild apple tree. He dug at its roots and found loose and crumbly "ore," which assayers said contained only the faintest traces of gold. Not satisfied with the assayers' tests, Kruse conducted his own and found the ore to contain $425 worth of gold per ton. The improved assay reports led to digging in 1905. A rustic 100-foot tower of logs and boards was built, and a shaft was sunk a few feet. However, the tower was blown over in a high wind a few months later and never rebuilt. Work was resumed from time to time, but no pay dirt was ever taken out.[40]

The story of a lost silver mine of Shannon County, Missouri, is told in several versions. If we are to believe them, at least two people spent their lives searching for the mine. Dr. Abijah Tyrell, who bought the site near the Sinks on Singing Creek, spent his last days searching for the mine, and his son Frank spent a lifetime hunting for it. The story goes like this:

> In 1873, Dr. Tyrell of St. Louis treated a man who was injured who related a story about a lost silver mine and claimed he knew where it was. Dr. Tyrell immediately bought 900 acres surrounding the Sinks and organized a mining company. He moved to the sinks and with him came his 10-year-old son, Frank. Frank studied at the Missouri School of Mines in Rolla. Despite the failure of organized searches and an expensive shaft sunk into the hillside and despite scoffing of unbe-

39. J. Dickson Black, *History of Benton County, 1836–1936* (Little Rock: International Graphics Industries, 1975), pp. 69–71.

40. Ibid., p. 74.

lievers, Frank Tyrell hunted for the silver mine off and on all his life. He believed, and said his studies supported his belief, that the granite porphyry of the sinks contained sulphite of silver. Frank Tyrell died at 1955 at the age of 90.[41]

Sometimes similar characters and incidents appear in the tale of the Old Slater Copper Mine, located southeast of Eminence.

There are many more stories of lost mines and rich mineral strikes, but these will serve to illustrate their nature. It is certain that legends of mineral wealth are firmly entrenched in local folklore. A recent county history stated that no fewer than seven valuable minerals could be discovered in the subsurface bedrock:

> We know it's here and where it's at . . . lead, zinc, marble, rich soil, field stones. And probably, silver, gold, oil, and platinum . . . though we don't know exactly where. But isn't it comforting knowledge? These metals are here, for the future use and economy—if we need them.[42]

41. Margaret Ray Vickery, *Ozark Stories of the Upper Current River* (Salem, Mo.: Salem Publishing Company, n.d.), p. 71.

42. Messick, *History of Baxter County*, p. 295.

Selected References

Black, J. Dickson. *History of Benton County, 1836–1936*. Little Rock: International Graphics Industries, 1975.

Bradbury, John. *Travels in the Interior of America*. London: Sherwood, Neely, and Jones, 1817.

Buckley, Ernest R. "Geology of the Disseminated Lead Deposits of Washington and St. François Counties," *Missouri Bureau of Geology and Mines*, 2d. Series, vol. 9 (1908).

———, and Buehler, H. A., "The Geology of the Granby Area," *Missouri Bureau of Geology and Mines*, 2d. Series, vol. 4 (1905).

Carrière, Joseph M. *Tales From the French Folklore of Missouri*. Northwestern University Studies. Evanston, Ill.: Northwestern University Press, 1937.

Charlevoix, Pierre Francis Xavier de. *Letters to the Duchess of Lesdiquières, Giving an Account of a Voyage to Canada, and Travels through that Vast Country, and Louisiana, to the Gulf of Mexico, Undertaken by Order of the President King of France*. London: R. Goadby, 1763.

Columbia. Missouri State Historical Society Archives. "A Summary Description of the Lead Mines in Upper Louisiana, a report to Captain Amos Stoddard, first Civil Commandant of Upper Louisiana in 1804," by Moses Austin.

Crane, G. W. "The Iron Ores of Missouri," *Missouri Bureau of Geology and Mines*, 2d. Series, vol. 10 (1912).

Du Pratz, Le Page. *Histoire de la Louisiane*. . . . Paris: De Bure, l'Ainé, La Beuve Delaquette, et Lambert, 1758.

Gibson, Arrell M. *Wilderness Bonanza: The Tri-State District of Missouri, Kansas, and Oklahoma*. Norman: University of Oklahoma Press, 1972.

Gist, Noel P. *Missouri: Its Resources, People, and Institutions*. Columbia: Curators of the University of Missouri, 1950.

"The History of St. Joe," *St. Joe Headframe*, Special Edition. Bonne Terre, Mo.: St. Joe Minerals Corporation, fall 1970.

Houck, Louis. *A History of Missouri*. Vol. I. Chicago: R. R. Donnelly and Son, 1908.
"Indian Creek—The Prototype Operation." *Engineering and Mining Journal* 165 (April 1964): 89.
Johnson, Hugh Nelson. "Sequent Occupance of the St. Francois Mining Region." Ph.D. dissertation, Washington University (St. Loois), 1950.
Jones, J. Wyman. *A History of the St. Joseph Lead Company*. Published for private circulation. New York: St. Joseph Lead Company, 1892.
McMahon, David F. "Tradition and Change in an Ozark Mining Community." Master's thesis, St. Louis University, 1958.
Megee, Mary C. "The Geography of the Mining of Lead and Zinc in the Tri-State Mining District." Master's thesis, University of Arkansas, 1953.
"Meramec Iron Ore Project Starts Production at Pea Ridge." *Engineering and Mining Journal* 165 (April 1964): 93–108.
Messick, Mary Ann. *History of Baxter County, 1873–1973*. Mountain Home, Ark.: Mountain Home Chamber of Commerce, 1973.
Missouri Department of Natural Resources. *Missouri's Environment* 3, March 1977.
Missouri State Highway Commission and the Writers' Program of the Works Progress Administration. *Missouri: A Guide to the "Show Me" State*. The American Guide Series. New York: Duell, Sloan, and Pearce, 1941.
Norris, James D. *Frontier Iron: The Story of the Maramec Iron Works, 1826–1876*. Madison: State Historical Society of Wisconsin, 1964.
Prospectus of the Missouri Iron Company and Missouri and Iron Mountain Cities. Hartford, Conn.: P. Canfield, 1837.
Rafferty, Milton D. "Persistence Versus Change in Land Use and Landscape in the Springfield, Missouri, Vicinity of the Ozarks." Ph.D. dissertation, University of Nebraska, 1970.
———, Gerlach, Russel L. and Hrebec, Dennis. *Atlas of Missouri*. Springfield, Mo.: Aux-Arc Research Associates, 1970.
———, William H. Cheek, and David A. Castillon. *Economic and Social Atlas of Missouri*. Springfield,
Roome, Charles C. "Selected Aspects of the Southeast Missouri Mining Region." Master's thesis, University of Missouri-Columbia, 1962.
Sauer, Carl O. *The Geography of the Ozark Highland of Missouri*. The Geographic Society of Chicago Bulletin no. 7, Chicago: University of Chicago Press, 1920.
Schoolcraft, Henry Rowe. *Journal of a Tour into the Interior of Missouri and Arkansas in 1818 and 1819*. In *Schoolcraft in the Ozarks*, edited by Hugh Park. Van Buren, Ark.: Press-Argus Printers, 1955.
———. *A View of the Lead Mines of Missouri. . . .* New York: C. Wiley and Co., 1819.
———. *Scenes and Adventures in the Semi-Alpine Region of the Ozark Mountains*. Philadelphia: Lippincott, Grambo and Co., 1853.
Schroeder, Walter A. *The Eastern Ozarks*. National Council for Geographic Education Special Publication no. 13. Normal, Ill.: Illinois State University, 1967.
Shumard, Benjamin F. *Report on the Chouteau Tract or Spanish Mineral Land Grant*. St. Louis: St. Louis Lead Mining Co., 1873.
Spear William D. "Farming and Mining Experience: Independence County, Arkansas, 1900–1925." Ph.D. dissertation, Washington University (St. Louis), 1974.
Statement Concerning the St. Francis Lead Company. St. Louis: St. Louis Lead Co., 1867.
Thoman, Richard S. *The Changing Occupance Pattern of the Tri-State Area of Missouri, Kansas, and Oklahoma*. University of Chicago Department of Geography Research Paper no. 21. Chicago: University of Chicago Press, 1953.
Thompson, Henry C. *Our Lead Belt Heritage*. Flat River, Mo.: News-Sun, 1955.
Vickery, Margaret Ray. *Ozark Stories of the Upper Current River*. Salem, Mo.: Salem Publishing Company, N.D.
Wharton, Hayward M., et al. *Missouri Minerals—Resources, Production, and Forecasts*. Missouri Geological Survey and Water Resources Special Publication no. 1. Rolla: 1969.

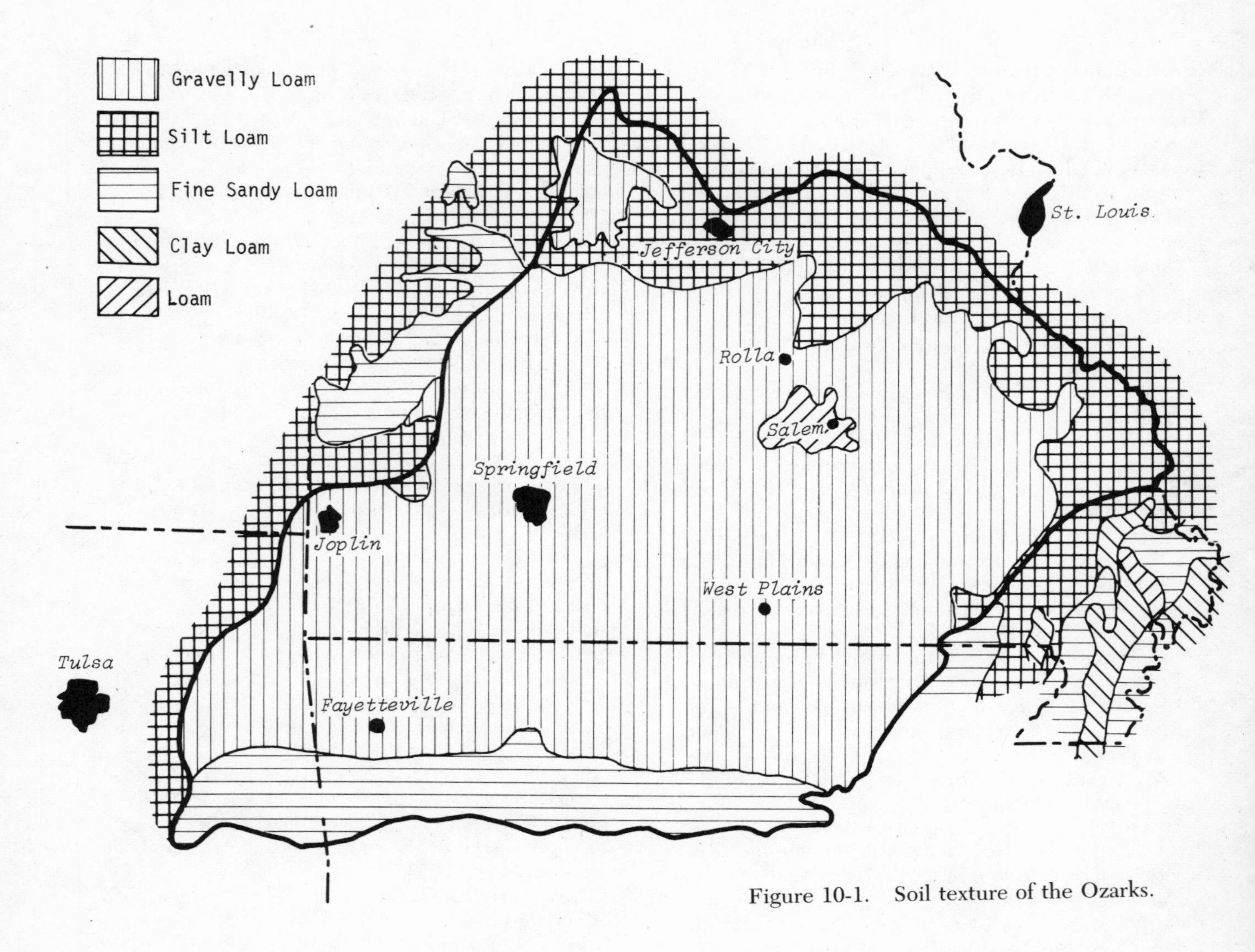

Figure 10-1. Soil texture of the Ozarks.

10. Ozark Agriculture: Patterns of Trial and Error

For the pioneers who settled the Ozarks, the single most important factor in the economic development of the region was the quality of soil resources. Today, after more than a century of agricultural settlement, the well-being and prosperity of the people is dependent on the continued use of the soil, although perhaps less so than in former times. Nevertheless, of the three groups of renewable natural resources—soils, plants, animals—used by man through the ages, soils are perhaps the least understood by the average person. The primary reason for this is that soils are covered by vegetation, and to examine a soil therefore requires special effort. The significance of the various soil features, such as color, depth, texture, structure, and tilth, is understood by few.

Soil is complex. It is composed of weathered rock material, decayed and partly decayed organic matter (humus), air, and water in various conditions. The soils of the Ozarks are diverse in physical properties and fertility. The variations result from the several factors that effect soil formation, including the parent, or geological, material from which the soils were derived, climate, topography, drainage, natural vegetation, and the length of time the soils have weathered. Physical features that give diversity to Ozark soils include color, topsoil depth, texture, subsoil, subsoil pans, underlying material, and tilth. Each is significant in identifying soils and interpreting their fertility levels. Soil profiles—the succession of layers, or horizons, in the soil—reflect the diversity of Ozark soils. The chief parent materials of Ozark soils are loess, limestone and dolomitic limestone, shales, and alluvial deposits. Sandstone and granite are of minor importance.

Most of the soil in the Ozarks was formed by the decay of rock formations (fig. 10-1). On upland flats and gentle slopes, most of the surface materials are derived from the underlying rock, and formation contacts commonly correspond with sharp differences in soils. On steep slopes, more-resistant beds of rock, particularly the cherty limestones and dolomites, dominate the soils as well as the topography. Because of their resistance, the cherty limestones form the summit elevations; accordingly, their weathered products mantle the lower slopes, which are occupied by less-resistant rocks. This, coupled with their extensive distribution, makes the soils derived from cherty limestones by far the most extensive type in the Ozarks.

In cherty soils, the residual chert (flint) is the most conspicuous feature. It is present in the topsoil, the subsoil, at the surface, or in all of these positions. In some localities fences are built with chert that has been taken from farm fields.

Abandoned farm, Ozark County, Missouri, 1976. Note cherty soils.

In some places the soils are free of chert and are quite fertile. Those of the Springfield Plain and the upland prairies and flats in the interior are generally the best of the upland soils derived from limestones and dolomites. Basin soils also are known as fertile soils; some of the better-known soils of this type are in the Belleview, Arcadia, Farmington, and Fredericktown basins of the St. Francis Mountains. The coves, or pocket valleys, in the Boston Mountains, such as the Richwoods, Wiley's Cove, and the Limestone Valley, were known as garden spots in former times. The latter valleys are now largely abandoned and little used for agriculture because of the limited amount of fertile land and their distance from suitable markets.

On the northern and eastern borders of the Ozarks are rather deep and fertile soils derived from wind-deposited loess. These are undoubtedly the most fertile of all upland soils in the Ozarks; their long history of cultivation is testimony to this and their natural resistance to erosion. In sharp contrast are the thin, droughty soils of the glade lands in the White River basin. These soils, and those derived from the resistant felsites and granites in the St. Francis region, are largely useless for purposes of cultivation.

Bottomland soils always have been the most sought after. They are well distributed throughout the Ozarks; even the most rugged hill districts of the Gasconade and Eminence dolomites contain many spacious valleys. Some of the most prized alluvial land is on the lower courses of creeks flowing into larger rivers; it is usually very rich, heavy alluvium and is less subject to flooding. Land like this was the first selected for settlement.

The natural vegetation of the Ozarks has been an important agricultural resource (fig. 10-2). Surveyors' reports and accounts of early settlers agree that the amount of forested land is greater today than it was when the region was first settled. Apparently, the distribution of prairie and woodland was much the same as at present; that is, grasses grew on the undissected plateau, and forests occupied the hilly regions.

Forests covered as much as three-fourths of the Ozarks in its primeval condition. The other quarter was tall-grass prairie, with big and little bluestem especially prominent. Virtually all of the prairie land has been plowed and converted agricultural uses. Most of the forested land is privately owned, and the average holding is small. There are some large private holdings, but they represent only a small part of the total forest land. The Mark Twain and Ozark national forests occupy approximately 20 per cent of the forested area.

The reports of pioneers and the field notes of the men who made the first land surveys indicate that trees on uplands often were stunted. Hard, cemented fragipan layers under level upland tracts may have retarded penetration of tree roots and caused slower growth. Many forested tracts had a parklike appearance, and young trees and brush were not as widespread as they are now.

Although small prairies such as the Barrens in Perry County were common in the eastern Ozarks, the western part was about 50 per cent parklike grasslands. The Springfield Plain had especially luxuriant bluestem grasses that were reported to have grown as high as a man on horseback (fig. 10-3). In Greene County, land was divided about equally between prairie and woodland; the prairies occupied uplands, and timber covered valley floors and slopes.

The practice, used by Indians and other hunters, of burning prairies to drive buffalo, deer, and elk is believed to have been important in retarding tree growth on the uplands. Sprouts and seedlings were killed, and the grasslands profited at the expense of the forests. According to old settlers many prairies grew over with timber after the Civil War. Not infrequently the name *bald* applied to heavily wooded knobs, singularly inappropriate today, is a relic of the early days when it had real meaning. Steyermark has suggested that soil factors may have been at least as important as fire in limiting tree growth on the uplands in some locations.[1] The practice of burning was continued by settlers for many years to provide grazing for their stock. With settlement and fencing, the forest began to claim burned-over tracts. Maintenance of pastures with fire is still practiced, even though "brush hogging" of persimmon sprouts, scrub cedar, and other "increasers" is the more common method of holding down growth of undesirable plants.

Small grassy areas occur on hilltops where there is a deficiency of soil and groundwater. These areas, which typically contain interspersed red cedar (juniper), prickly pear, and scruboak, are known as glades when they occur on hillsides or cover large areas. Cedar trees that line fence rows in the vicinity of the glades, given every appearance that they were planted by industrous farmers, are more likely to have been seeded by birds that fed on juniper seeds and then stopped for a rest on nearby fences.

Although they are distributed most widely in the White River Hills, there are glade lands along the Gasconade, Niangua, and other north-flowing streams where the Jefferson City dolomite outcrops. Thin soils and southern exposures account for the dry conditions and the peculiar vegetation association. There are glades in the vicinity of the St. Francis Mountains where the Potosi formation provides similar conditions.

The Ozarks is one of the northernmost regions for the southern pine forest. Extensive stands of short-leaf pine were found in early years on the Piney Fork of the Gasconade River and in Ozark, Douglas, Reynolds, Carter, and Washington counties in Missouri. Such forests also were found in the White River country of Missouri and northern Arkansas. In the Boston Mountains, pine forests were found in the eastern part and on the south slope in the central section.

Aerial view of a portion of Perry County, Missouri. This area of fertile loess soils is populated heavily by people of German ancestry.

Among the hardwoods there is sharp contrast between upland and lowland types. The upland forests consist almost exclusively of oaks, generally 90 per cent or more of the total timber. White oak, post oak, black oak, and blackjack are the main varieties. On the ridges, black oak and white oak are common; on the hillsides, post oak and blackjack do well. Chinquapin oak, like the softwood cedar, is a bluff tree. Hickory and walnut do well on better upland soils.

In the valleys, because of better soil and water conditions, there is a greater variety of species and individual trees grow much larger. Sycamore occupies stream-bank locations, often forming canopies that nearly cover small streams. Cottonwood, maple, black walnut, butternut, hackberry, tulip, and bur oak were most abundant originally. In the southeastern Ozarks, bordering

1. Julian A. Steyermark, *Vegetational History of the Ozark Forest*, University of Missouri Studies no. 31 (Columbia: 1959).

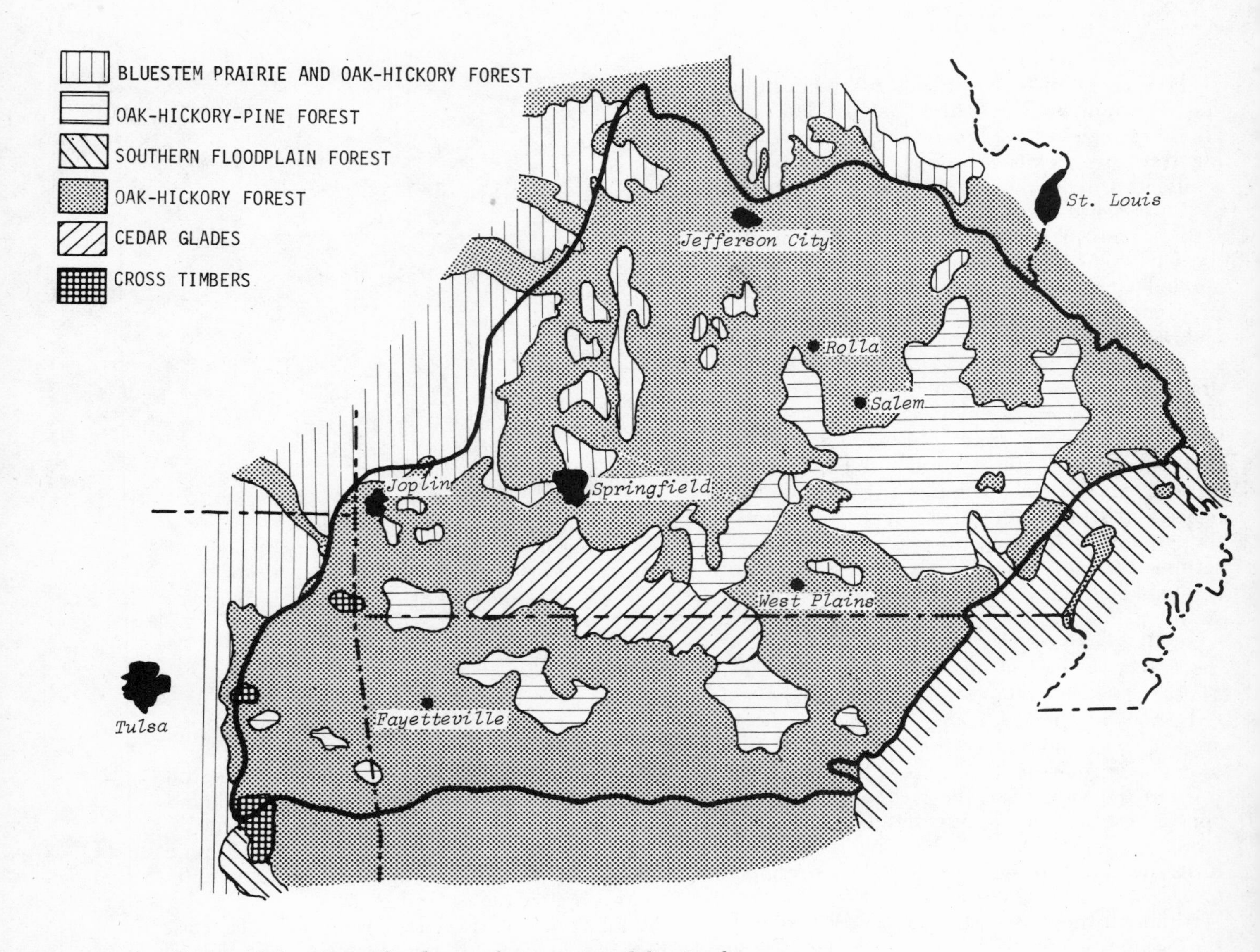

Figure 10-2. Generalized natural vegetation of the Ozarks.

the Mississippi embayment, cypress, gum, and birch are present.

The understory has great variety. Flowering redbuds and dogwoods are harbingers of spring, while blackberries, currants, dewberries, and huckleberries are gathered in season.

In the western Ozarks the Osage orange, also known as bois d'arc and hedge apple, has become widespread in pastures and fence rows. It is hardy, thorny, and resistant to drought. Posts made from the bois d'arc are nearly indestructible. In early days, Osage orange seeds were shipped from East Texas, Arkansas and western Missouri to Kansas and what is now Oklahoma, where they were planted as fences in the treeless plains. The seeds brought as much as forty dollars a bushel in the 1870's.

The prairies, even more than the forests, have been modified by man. Most of them, consisting of bluestem and other tall grasses, were plowed

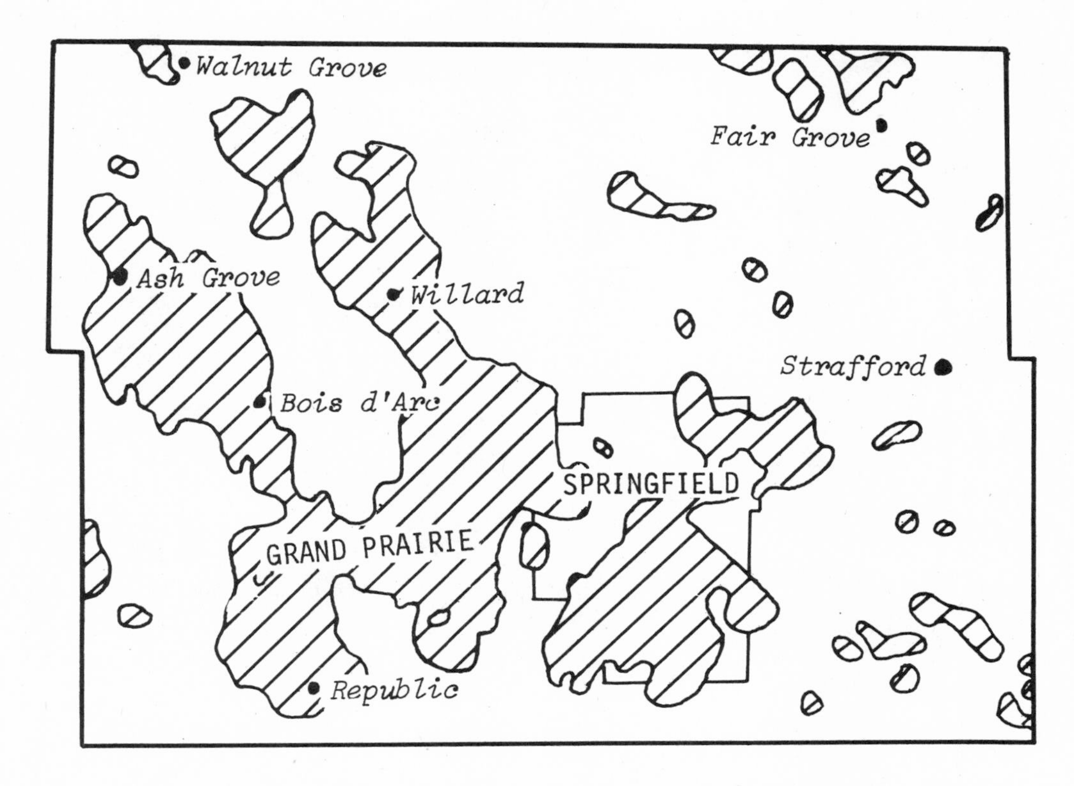

Figure 10-3. Distribution of natural prairies in Greene County, Missouri. Source: United States Land Survey, *Plats and Field Notes*.

when agriculture became more intensive. In the Ozarks, bluestems gave way to Kentucky bluegrass, which now grows wild wherever soil conditions are good. Most pastures presently are of highly mixed varieties of grass including lespedeza, clover, orchard grass, and fescue. It is winter-hardy fescue, which has been planted throughout the Ozarks in recent years, that has revitalized the range-cattle industry. The practice of clearing land of trees and scrub by bulldozer or by aerial application of herbicides is a controversial issue. Critics of the practice maintain that the Ozarks is being converted to a "fescue desert."

Trial and Error

The Ozarks lies in the General Farming and Forest Region of the United States. Because of physical conditions, accessibility, and marketing, agriculture there has been marginal, and many experiments have been tried. Although an unusually large number of agricultural systems have been used, it is apparent to even the casual observer that there have been great strides toward standardization and the elimination of many specialty crops.

The new settler in the Ozarks had several options in obtaining land. As a squatter, he could choose a likely plot of unsold government land and live on it in the expectation of buying it later. Or he could claim the land and purchase it at auction for a minimum sum of $1.25 per acre. The sale price, depending on the location of the land, was frequently two or three times the minimum. A third way to obtain land was through acquisition of New Madrid certificates, issued by the federal government after the earthquakes of 1811 and

TABLE 10-1
Crops and Livestock in the Eight-County Area, 1850

Crops		Livestock	
Wheat (bushels)	115,383	Horses	12,688
Rye (bushels)	1,144	Asses and mules	2,651
Indian corn (bushels)	2,126,089	Milk cows	11,352
Oats (bushels)	633,721	Working oxen	9,457
Barley (bushels)	231	Other cattle	29,436
Buckwheat (bushels)	122	Sheep	45,401
Flax (bushels)	45,257	Swine	78,163
Tobacco	78,614		
Wool (pounds)	88,796		
Hemp (tons)	125		
Maple sugar (pounds)	1,075		
Beeswax and honey (pounds)	166,362		

Source: U.S. Department of the Interior, *The Seventh Census of the United States: 1850* (Washington, D.C., 1953), 675, 682.

1812. The certificates, intended to assist persons whose land had been ruined in the cataclysm, were issued fraudulantly and totaled more than five times the number of heads of families in the earthquake region. Many were used in the settlement of Howard County on the northern Ozark border. A fourth way to secure land was to purchase property, at prices that ranged from eight to twenty dollars an acre, that had already been claimed and improved.

Pioneer Agriculture

The first settlers from east of the Mississippi occupied the leveler lands and better soils. Most of the agriculture was for subsistence, although some surpluses were shipped from the more accessible settlements. The fertile basins in the St. Francis Mountains produced surpluses for the workers in the nearby lead and iron mines. Nevertheless, commercial agriculture in the pioneer stage developed slowly, partly because the markets were inaccessible and partly because the first settlers were as much woodsmen as cultivators. In forested areas the cultivation of crops was supplemented by hunting, fishing, and the gathering of honey, berries, nuts, fruits, and greens from the forest.

Compared with the hardships of pioneer life on the plains, the life of the Ozark pioneer must have been relatively easy. A log house could be erected in a very few days. An unlimited supply of game and fish was close at hand; pigeon, wild turkey, and deer were plentiful. An abundance of mast and prairies of bluestem grass provided for the cattle and hogs, so it was unnecessary to cultivate more than a few acres of basic crops. Statistics for the very early years are not available. As for the number of livestock, a farmer's own account would have been an approximation, for most of it ran loose on the open range. Hogs in particular were killed for meat according to the need, with no accounting expected. Gradually, livestock came to be marked, usually with a cut in the ear, to denote ownership.

Corn, a staple for man and beast, became the most important crop grown by the first settlers. Table 10-1 shows the early farm produce for eight counties in the Springfield Plain. Because of the

Cultivating with a double shovel in the Missouri Ozarks, 1969. A rare sight.

Sorghum-molasses mill and cooker, Stone County, Missouri, 1975.

isolated area and the primarily subsistence economy, nearly all the pioneer farms produced some wheat, tobacco, flax, hemp, and cotton for domestic use. The women spun wool or cotton for clothing. As late as 1868, farmers as far north as Lawrence County, Missouri, grew sixty-six bales of cotton.

Unlike the French, the American frontiersman did not live in a community but set up a farm of his own in an isolated place. Using well-established practices, he promptly killed the trees on approximately five-acre plots by girdling, or removing a ring of bark. Since the dead trees dropped their foliage, the sun could reach the earth and the field could produce crops the first year. In the second year the trees were cut, the stumps rooted out, and the underbrush removed.

Fields were broken with a bull-tongue plow, the single blade of which was preceded by a sharp steel prong, or colter, which either cut the roots or caused the plow to jump over them. It was very suitable for use in rough land and for opening new fields. In the first years it was drawn by oxen, later by horses or mules. The land was leveled by harrowing or by dragging heavy brush over it. After harrowing, the land was laid out in squares with a bull-tongue plow and corn was dropped in at the intersections by hand. The seed was covered either with a hoe or by dragging a rock or log down the rows.

Corn was the favorite crop. It could be fed to stock, sold, or turned into whiskey in a still. The shucks were useful material for chair bottoms, horse collars, mats, brooms, or mattress stuffing. Cobs were used for fuel, pipes, or dolls for the little girls in the family. Wheat was raised for white bread and biscuits. Garden crops, consisting of the vegetables most popular today, except tomatoes, were of great importance in adding variety to the diet. Cotton and flax were raised for the home production of cloth, and maple sugar and honey served as the main source of sweetening. Sorghums for molasses were introduced later.

Hemp and tobacco farms were established before the Civil War in the Missouri River valley. Many slaves were brought in to cultivate these crops; both were grown in the remote areas for local needs and in the Missouri River valley as commercial crops. Before the age of wire cables, hemp ropes were much in demand. The crop was well established in Kentucky and Tennessee, and settlers from these states planted large fields of hemp in the Missouri River bottoms in the vicinity of Lexington, Rocheport, and Glasgow. Tobacco could be grown in commercial quantities along the Missouri River, where transportation costs were lower. Cotton, the chief commercial crop of the Arkansas River valley, was farmed commercially in the lower White River valley, where there was reliable river transportation.

General Farming

General farming began about 1870 in the better farming areas, notably the river border areas and the Springfield Plain. By that time much of these areas had become well settled and the native grass, which had been an important factor in the early agriculture of the western Ozarks, began to disappear. Before this, it had been the custom to burn over the prairies and woodlands each spring. As the country became more heavily settled and fenced, this practice had to be abandoned. A thick growth of underbrush, which had been kept down by the annual fires, sprang up in the open fields and choked out the grass. At the same time, settlement and cultivation began to reduce the acreage of the natural range to a marked degree.

Another aspect of general farming, comparatively cheap railroad transportation, became important after 1870. Before that time the only feasible commercial agricultural product was livestock, which could be driven north to markets on the major rivers. Railroad transportation meant that wheat, corn and other grains, as well as livestock, could be produced for market.

The transition from subsistence and livestock farming to general farming occurred quickly, as indicated by the rapid adoption of improved machinery for cultivation. In 1868, for example, the firm of McGregor and Murray in Springfield sold more than seven hundred turning plows.

The rapid shift toward general farming was most pronounced in the areas that were settled early because of the smoother topography, better soils, and better transportation facilities. Grain growing proved profitable, especially on the red soils of the Springfield Plain, the Fredericktown soils of the Arcadia, Belleview, Farmington, and Fredericktown basins, and on the loess soils of northern Missouri. In the interior of the Ozarks, residents practiced general farming in the valleys, where conditions were favorable, but in hill country the farms continued to be of the subsistence or livestock types. Many of the interior districts did not develop general farming practices until the turn of the century. As late as the 1930's the farms in the headwater valleys in Reynolds County, Missouri, were noticeably less progressive than those of the lower valleys.[2] In 1911, Marbut notes, in the Richwoods Basin near Mountain View, Arkansas, "there was no possibility of any form of specialized farming that would require frequent and rapid marketing of products. The basin lies too far from a shipping point when both distance and character of road are considered."[3]

By 1900, general farming dominated the agricultural system in the Springfield Plain and the Missouri and Mississippi borders. It was regarded as a desirable and secure form of agriculture, as is attested by an observer's remarks:

> Greene County is especially blessed in not being a region where the farmer has to place his reliance almost wholly on any one particular crop. He can choose for his speciality, if he so wills, almost any standard crop of the temperate zone. Or he can have crops of any and all grains, fruits, and vegetables. Thus, with more than one string to his bow, he can feel sure that if disaster befalls one or two of his crops, the others will hold him safe from harm.[4]

General farming and its diversity of crops and livestock led to smaller farms, especially in the areas near Springfield, Fayetteville, Springdale, Cape Girardeau, Perryville, Hermann, Washington, and in the Caledonia, Belleview, and Farmington valleys in the St. Francis Mountains. A 1917 county history stated that "small

2. Margaret Riggs, "Valley Contrasts in the Missouri Ozarks Region," *Journal of Geography* 35 (December 1936): 351–59.

3. Curtis F. Marbut, "Soil Reconnaissance of the Ozark Region of Missouri and Arkansas," in *Field Operations of the Bureau of Soils, 1911* (Washington, D.C.: Bureau of Soils, U.S.D.A., 1911).

4. Johnathan Fairbanks and Clyde E. Tuck. *Past and Present of Greene County, Missouri* (Indianapolis, Ind.: A. W. Bowen and Company, 1915), p. 198.

General farm scene including varied crops, orchards, and livestock. (Courtesy Missouri State Historical Society.)

farms and diversity of crops" well could be adopted as the motto of Greene County. Another commentary noted the extent to which this subdivision of land had progressed by 1917.

> Take a late map of the county, which shows the names of each land owner, and the size of his holdings, and you will be surprised to see how far this subdividing of land has already gone. In one government township, taken haphazardly from the map, I fine one hundred and forty-four farms. Of these, ninety-six, exactly two thirds of all, are tracts of eighty acres or less. Fifty-one are forty acre tracts.[5]

Of course, there were a few large farms at that time and some very large timber tracts were held by individuals and lumber companies, but the tendency toward smaller farm units is evident. As the land was used more intensively, there was a natural increase in land values.

Between 1890 and 1900 the number of farms in the eight-county area around Springfield increased from 13,540 to 23,311, an addition of nearly 10,000 farms. For the next twenty years the number remained fairly stable, but a marked decline occurred after World War II. This pattern of development is typical of the better agricultural lands in the Ozarks.

As in pioneer days, the chief field crops throughout the Ozarks were corn and wheat. Corn, used primarily as livestock feed, at all times exceeded other grains in acreage. The soil of the river bottoms and the upland prairies were re-

5. Ibid.

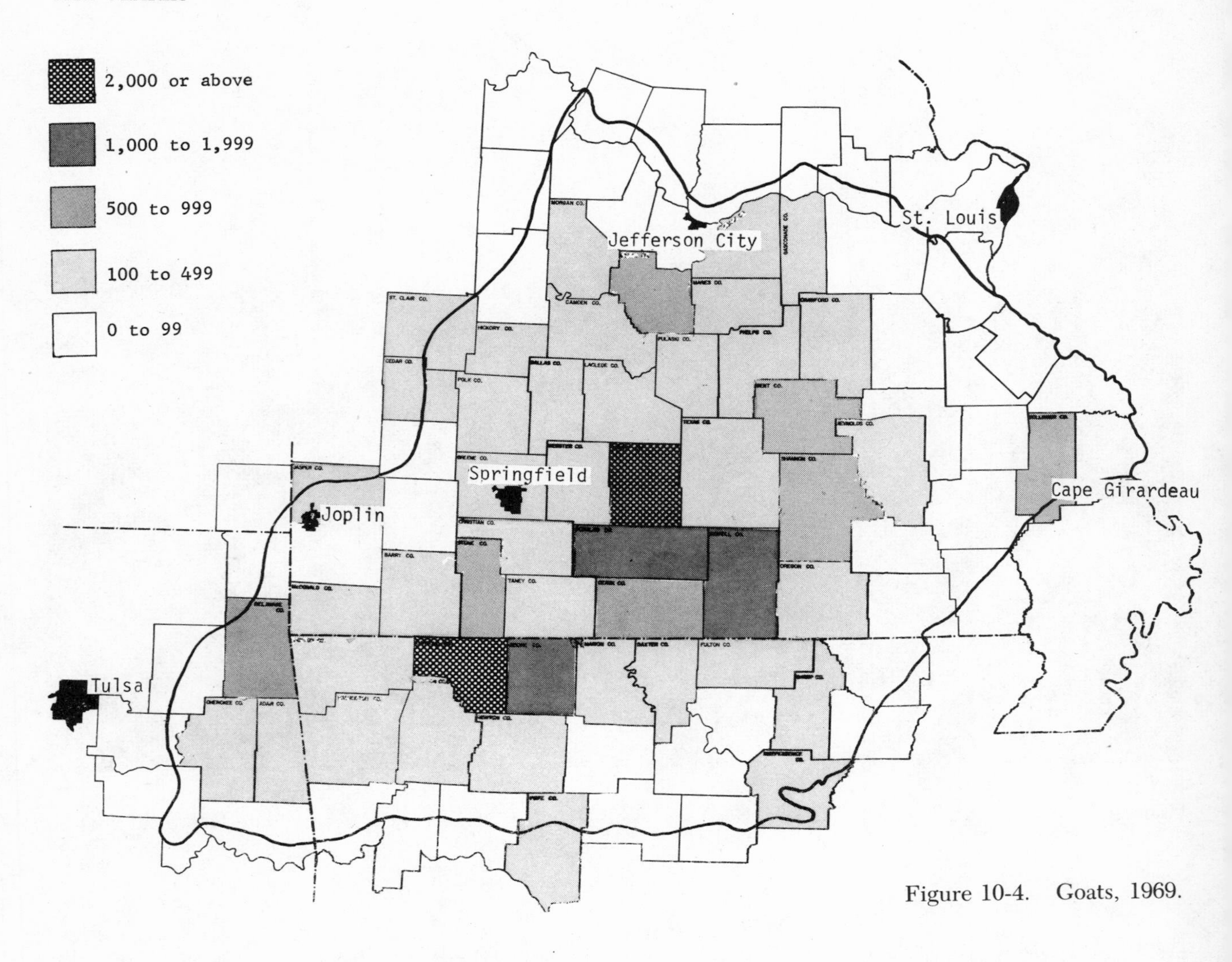

Figure 10-4. Goats, 1969.

garded as emphatically corn land. Wheat was the standard cash crop, although unusual weather conditions, chinch bugs or Hessian flies sometimes caused reduced yields. Oats, barley, feed sorghum, and forage crops provided livestock feed.

Cattle and hogs, along with horses and mules, were raised widely, but sheep were not as popular as in earlier years, when they supplied wool for homespun clothing. The general farmer usually kept two types of cattle: those raised for meat and those raised for milking purposes. In the cream-can stage of dairying, the general farmer could obtain a profit from a few dairy cows, and by stall-feeding a few head of beef stock, he could add to his income. Hogs, raised in large numbers for a time, were fattened for market and sold profitably. Milk goats and Angora goats were introduced in part because their habit of eating brush helped in maintaining pastures. The huge Scottish-owned Missouri Land and Livestock Company, based at Neosho, Missouri, successfully used goats to manage its experimental farm, Sandyford Ranche. This company purchased

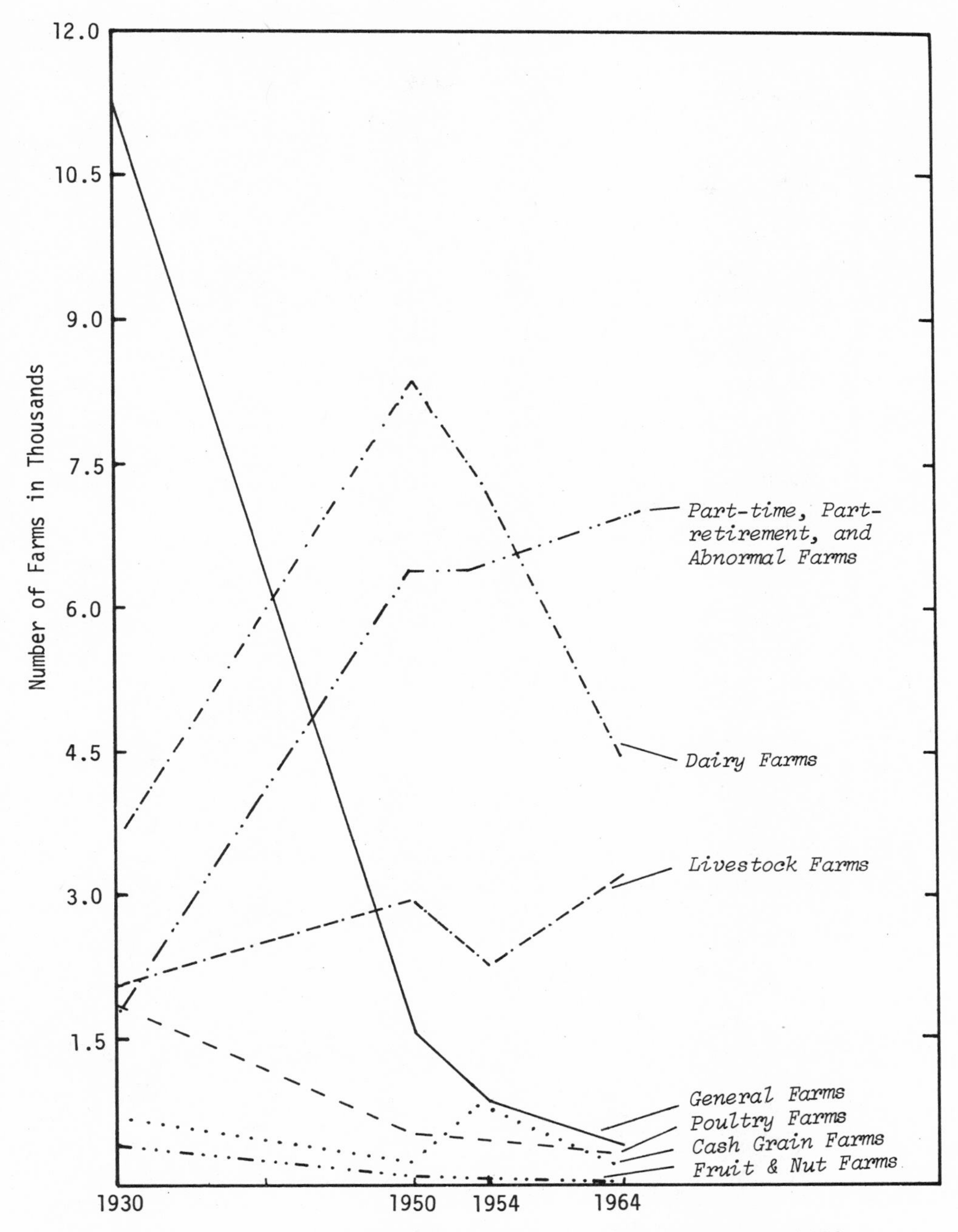

Figure 10-5. Types of farms in the Springfield vicinity. Source: U.S. Census of Agriculture, 1930, 1950, 1954, 1964.

goats in Texas and sold them to farmers in the western Ozarks.[6] "Goating down" pastures became an established practice that persisted until the large tractor-powered rotary "brush hogs" became common in the 1950's (fig. 10-4).

There was considerable improvement in production methods during the general-farming era. Smaller farms called for more care, more intensive cultivation of cropland, and improved animal husbandry. Higher land prices and smaller farmsteads required larger yields in crops and livestock.

During the pioneer stage of agriculture, when land was plentiful and cheap, maintaining fertility received little attention. It is reported that farmers would tear down log stables and move them to new locations when the accumulation of manure made it impossible to use the stable. It was easier to move the stables than the manure. With the adoption of more intensive land use, farmers hauled manure to fields to be spread as fertilizer.

Not all parts of the Ozarks participated in the progress that followed the Civil War and the construction of railroads. Some sections, notably the Courtois Hills and the Osage-Gasconade Hills in Missouri and a vast area extending southward through the White River Hills and into the Boston Mountains, languished in the pioneer subsistence phase of agriculture. In Indian Territory (Oklahoma), progress was held up by the unorganized political situation. Full-blood Cherokees of the Keetoowah Society retreated to the flinty hillsides and valleys in eastern Oklahoma, where they sought to keep alive ancient tribal traditions and by this method shut out reality. Another large nonprogressive group consisted of poor whites, commonly renters, who came to the area during the period of Cherokee government as laborers or renters on Indian land. Thus many of the elements of progress associated with the New South era failed to penetrate the Cherokee Ozarks. In the accessible and progressive sections of the Ozarks, the period 1870–1910 saw widespread adoption of scientific farming methods encouraged by colleges of agriculture at the universities and by other organizations, such as the Grange, the Agricultural Wheel, and the Farmers Alliance.

By 1900, general farming began to give way to specialized agricultural production, although it was many years before it was replaced as the principal type of farming. The general farm (fig. 10-5) retained its position of leadership in the Springfield vicinity until the 1940's, when the dairy farm became the leading type. From 1930 to 1964 the general farm fell from first place to fourth in number of farms. The decline from 11,172 in 1930 to 420 in 1964 meant the statistical loss of 10,742 general farms, a pattern that extended throughout most of the Ozarks and much of the United States as specialized agriculture became necessary.

Several factors contributed to the decline of general farming. Specialty farming, introduced in the 1890's, attracted some farmers from general farming to the production of apples, peaches, strawberries, or tomatoes. Shortly after 1900, even more turned to dairy farming. In recent years, many general farmers have switched to livestock, often in conjunction with part-time employment in nonfarm jobs. However, the overriding forces contributing to the decline of general farming have been the improvements in transportation, organization, and integration for the marketing of agricultural products throughout the United States. Increasing area specialization and the economies of scale of production have made general farming largely uncompetitive.

The decline of general farming was demonstrated by the decrease in wheat and corn acreages, which were for the most part, products of general farms. Data from the U.S. Census of Agriculture illustrate that in the entire Ozark region there were substantial declines in corn and wheat acreages by 1940, and by 1964 corn and wheat acreages had declined to insignificant levels except in the eastern and northern borders (figs. 10-6, 10-7).

Fruit Growing

As general farming began to decline in the Ozarks, fruit growing increased in importance. From the earliest time to the present, apples and

6. Larry A. McFarlane, "The Missouri Land and Livestock Company, Limited, of Scotland: Foreign Investment on the Missouri Farming Frontier, 1882–1908," (Ph.D. diss., University of Missouri-Columbia, 1963), pp. 120–22.

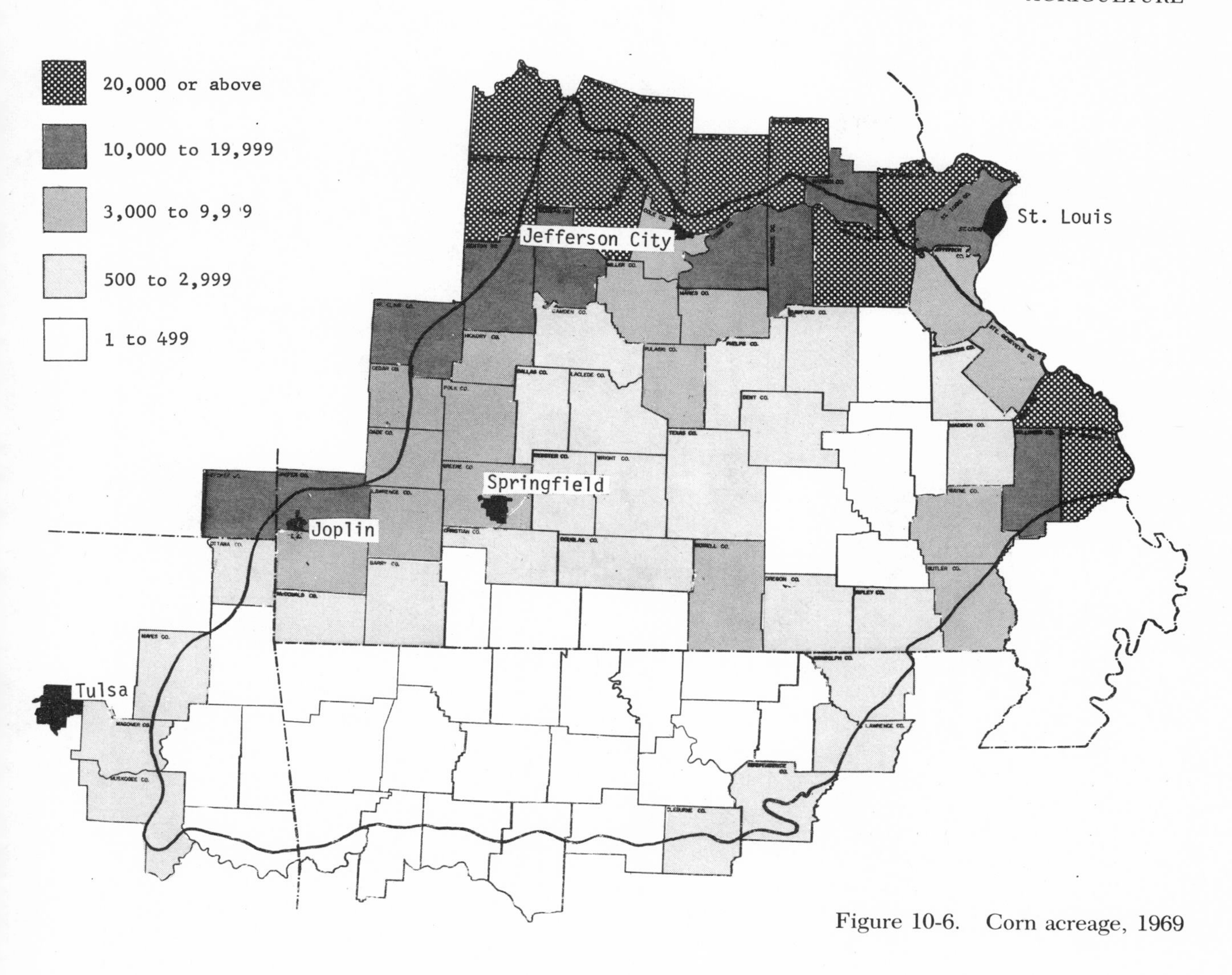

Figure 10-6. Corn acreage, 1969

peaches have been the most popular and most successfully grown fruits. Apples were grown so widely in small household orchards that the Ozarks was known as the Land of the Big Red Apple even before the coming of the railroads and the development of commercial orchards. The Knous, Huntsman's Favorite, and Ben Davis apples became popular in the early orchards. Most of the peaches were seedling or Indian peaches, the kind that come up where peach pits are dropped. Seedling peaches grew in fence rows, in roadside ditches, among apple trees, and around the back doors of farmhouses where the pits had been discarded. Seedling peaches are common today. Even though they vary greatly in size and taste, they are sometimes picked and eaten in season.

Railroad officials encouraged fruit growing. During the 1880's and 1890's, thousands of trees were planted, mainly along railways in the western part of Missouri and in northwest Arkansas. In Missouri, large orchards were set out in 1892 near Seymour in the southern part of Webster County. Howell County also was an early center for commercial orchards. Pomona, named for the ancient Greek goddess of fruits, was founded as a peach-

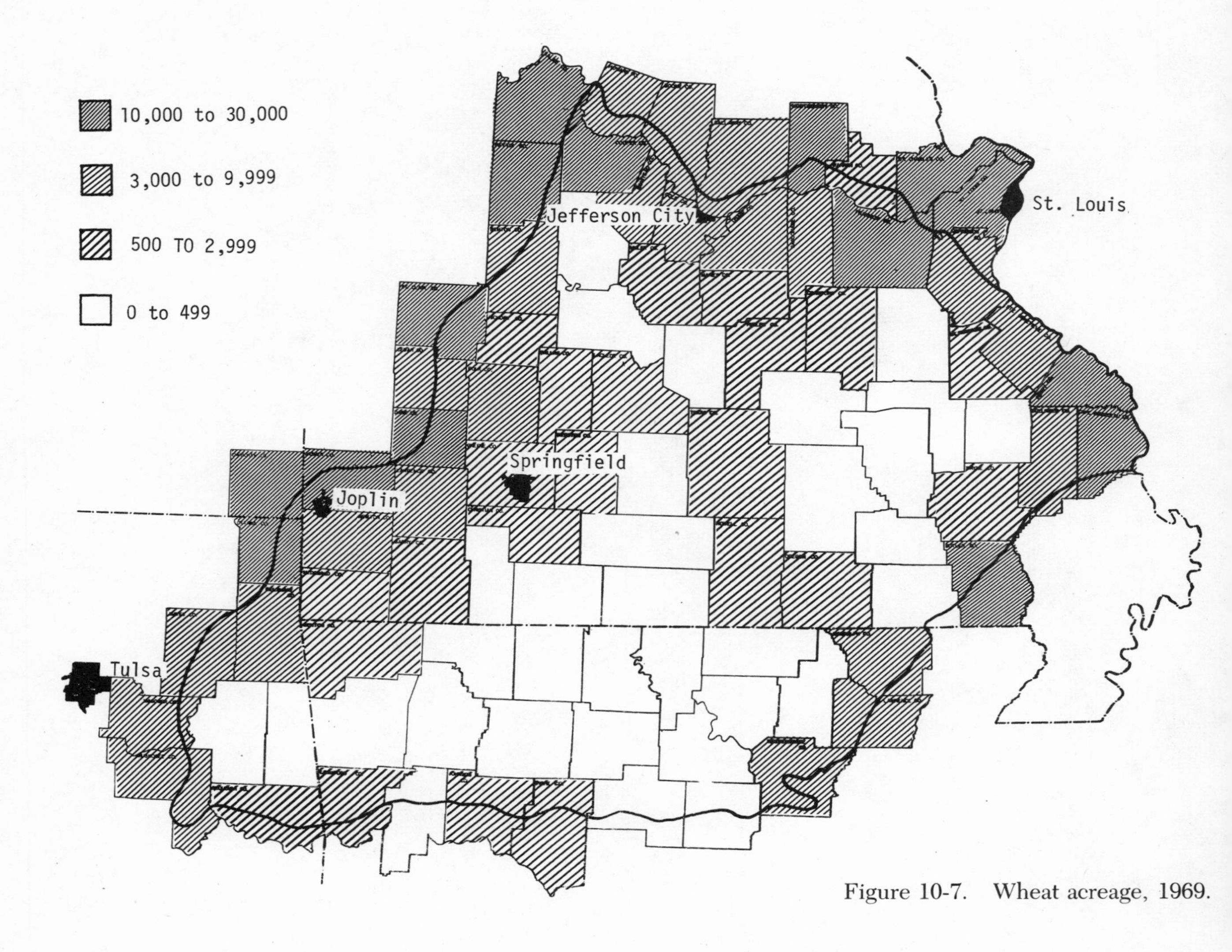

Figure 10-7. Wheat acreage, 1969.

plantation community on the railroad a few miles north of West Plains. In northwest Arkansas, orchard plantings were heavy in Benton and Washington counties, especially along the St. Louis–San Francisco Railroad. The Cherokee boundary, west of which land was owned in common until allotment (which took place in the period 1902–1910) and could not be bought by whites, effectively kept out new fruit growers, and most of the inhabitants of the area were unresponsive to the development taking place to the east. Thus a cultural fault line began to appear at the Oklahoma boundary.[7]

A major stimulus to fruit growing came in 1901 when the apple season produced an extra-good crop. Because of drought, crops generally failed that year and farmers found the small household orchards an important source of income. Interest in apple culture increased and orchard acreage

7. Leslie Hewes, "Cultural Fault Line in the Cherokee Country" *Economic Geography* 19 (April 1943): 136–42.

was expanded. By 1905, orchards of 500 to 2,000 and 3,000 trees, two and three years old, became common. Plantings were numerous near Seymour in Webster County, in the vicinity of Springfield and Republic in Greene County, and around Marionville in Lawrence County in Missouri and near Springdale, Rogers, Farmington, and Prairie Grove in northwest Arkansas. About twenty years later, in 1923, within a radius of six miles of Marionville, there were 2,500 acres in commercial apple orchards capable of producing 100,000 barrels of apples. In Greene County, orchards of 40 and 100 acres were common, and larger ones of 200 to 400 acres were not unusual.

The period of important fruit acreage and production fell between 1910 and 1940. Although large orchards were set out before 1910, most of the trees did not reach bearing age until after that time. By 1940, most of the orchards had fallen into disuse or had been cleared and the land converted to other uses.

During the apple era, much of the crop went by rail to St. Louis and points east. Apple barns were built at railroad sidings, where apples were sorted and graded before shipment. Many of the larger fruit farms operated cider presses. Commercial evaporators produced dried applies and peaches on a large scale, thereby saving year-end surpluses, just as pioneer families had saved their surpluses by sun-drying them on the roof of a shed.

Fruit growers associations were established as a means of dealing with the problems of marketing and securing labor to harvest the crop. A large production of apples around Marionville and Logan in 1914 and 1915 glutted the fruit market at picking time, resulting in low prices and losses for the growers. Faced with this condition, they organized a stock company and erected a large cold-storage building on the Frisco Railroad at Marionville. Eventually the Ozark Fruit Growers Association marketed a large part of the production from the orchards of southwest Missouri and northwest Arkansas.

Fruit growing began to decline in the early 1930's, a time of important geographic and economic adjustment in fruit growing throughout the United States. Increasing commercialization, mechanization, organization, and technology demanded greater specialization if growers wanted to maintain their individual shares of an increasingly discriminating competitive market. Gradually, the kitchen orchards and small farm orchards disappeared from the U.S. landscape and fruit growing became concentrated in scattered specialized locations. It declined in the Ozarks because of growers' reluctance or inability to make the necessary adjustments to remain competitive.

Through the developmental years, as the number of apple trees in the Ozarks increased, the orchards became infested with the codling moth, or apple worm. At first the moths were controlled by repeated treatments of lead arsenate or a mixture of lime, sulfur, and water, but gradually the sprays became ineffective.

Other factors contributed to the decline of apple growing. A depressed economy during the 1930's curtailed the market, and drought caused failure of the fruit crop in 1934 and 1936. Although the war years of the 1940's stimulated a stronger demand for apples, orchardists were beset by higher labor costs and outright labor shortages during the harvesting season. During the 1930's and 1940's fruit acreage gradually diminished; few new plantings were made, and other crops replaced the aged and less productive trees. In the outskirts of Springfield, orchards were cleared to make room for new houses as the city experienced unprecedented growth during the 1940's and 1950's. By the end of the severe drought that persisted for several years during the 1950's, virtually all of the large orchards had disappeared. Similar declines in acreage occurred throughout the Ozarks.

At present, fruit growing on a commercial basis is highly localized. The largest orchards are in areas that were formerly important for production of fruit, notably in southwest Missouri in the vicinity of Marionville, Seymour, Springfield, and Cassville; in Cooper County where loessal soils provide exceptionally good growing conditions; and in Arkansas near Bentonville, Rogers, Springdale, and Fayetteville. Rogers Orchards at Prairie Grove, Arkansas, claims to be the largest apple grower in the Ozarks.

Several factors have contributed to the persistence of fruit growing in these locations. First, orcharding reached its greatest development there during the 1920's; Marionville had adopted the title *Apple Capital of Missouri* by that time. Since there was a larger fruit acreage to begin with, more of it has persisted to the present. Second, the Orchard Growers Vinegar Company established a vinegar plant at Marionville in 1924, and plants were built at Rogers and Springdale, Arkansas, about the same time. Low-quality apples could be sold to the vinegar plants during periods of drought or heavy insect infestation. In this way, growers near the plants derived some income from their orchards, but producers in other areas became discouraged and converted orchard land to other uses. Third, the large cold-storage plants built between 1910 and 1930 continued to handle apples until they were converted to store poultry and meat during the war years. The apple-storage plants offered growers a somewhat improved market over that of other growers during the Depression years of the 1930's. Fourth, apples and peaches could be sold to canneries, which were expanding operations in Springdale. Fifth, a tradition of fruit growing became better established in the old growing areas. Knowledge concerning the care of trees and the handling and marketing of fruit has lasted over the years; most of the present-day fruit growers are old hands or are descendants of early growers. A few roadside stands have persisted up to the present.

Truck Farming

In the southwest Missouri and northwest Arkansas, raising tomatoes for canning purposes began around 1900 and expanded very rapidly. For several reasons, tomatoes were well suited to the time and setting. First, they could be grown on very rough and rocky hillside farms. Second, the whole family could help in setting plants, tending them, and picking the crop. Third, tomatoes hauled to the nearest cannery brought in badly needed cash at a time when many farmers suffered reduced income because of the decline of the timber industry. Fourth, women and girls found employment in the canning season to bolster family income.

The raising of tomatoes and truck crops rarely became the sole farming operation, but fields of one to three acres of tomatoes became common on farms near the canneries. Most of the tomatoes for a given cannery were raised within a radius of eight or ten miles. Near Springfield and Marionville, they were grown in conjunction with fruit orchards to help defray the cost of cultivation and care of the orchard until the trees reached bearing age.

Tomato farming required little investment other than labor, and the profits were at times substantial. In 1905, upland tomatoes in Webster County, Missouri, yielded an average of 72 bushels per acre for a gross return of $16.39 per acre. For this reason, they were grown widely on small upland subsistence farms in the rougher parts of southwest Missouri and northwest Arkansas.

Commercial canning continues to be important in northwest Arkansas, although the number of plants has declined since the 1950's. In 1950 the number of member plants in the Ozark Canners Association in northwest Arkansas counties looked like this: Benton, 13; Boone, 6; Carroll, 7; Washington, 21; Madison, 20. Springdale became the chief canning center as the plants there enlarged and diversified. The leading processed items are green beans, greens (spinach, turnip, poke), and tomatoes. Other products canned in Springdale at the height of the canning era were strawberries; various other berry crops, such as blackberries, boysenberries, and youngberries; and apples, grapes, and potatoes. In recent years the trend has been toward fewer but larger canneries that process a wide range of products. By trucking in produce from other growing areas, canneries can operate year round.

Apparently, many of the early Ozark canneries were no more than family enterprises that operated only when prices were high. Any favorable combination of supply and demand brought a marked increase in shade-tree canneries. Normally, the produce of these small ventures was sold to larger canneries located in a nearby town. Wild blackberries, beans, and a few other vegetables were packed, but the main product was tomatoes. The small canneries fit into an economic niche created by time and place, taking advantage of the availability of cheap surpluses from the farms and the lack of rigorous competition from other producing areas.

Economic forces and adverse climatic factors

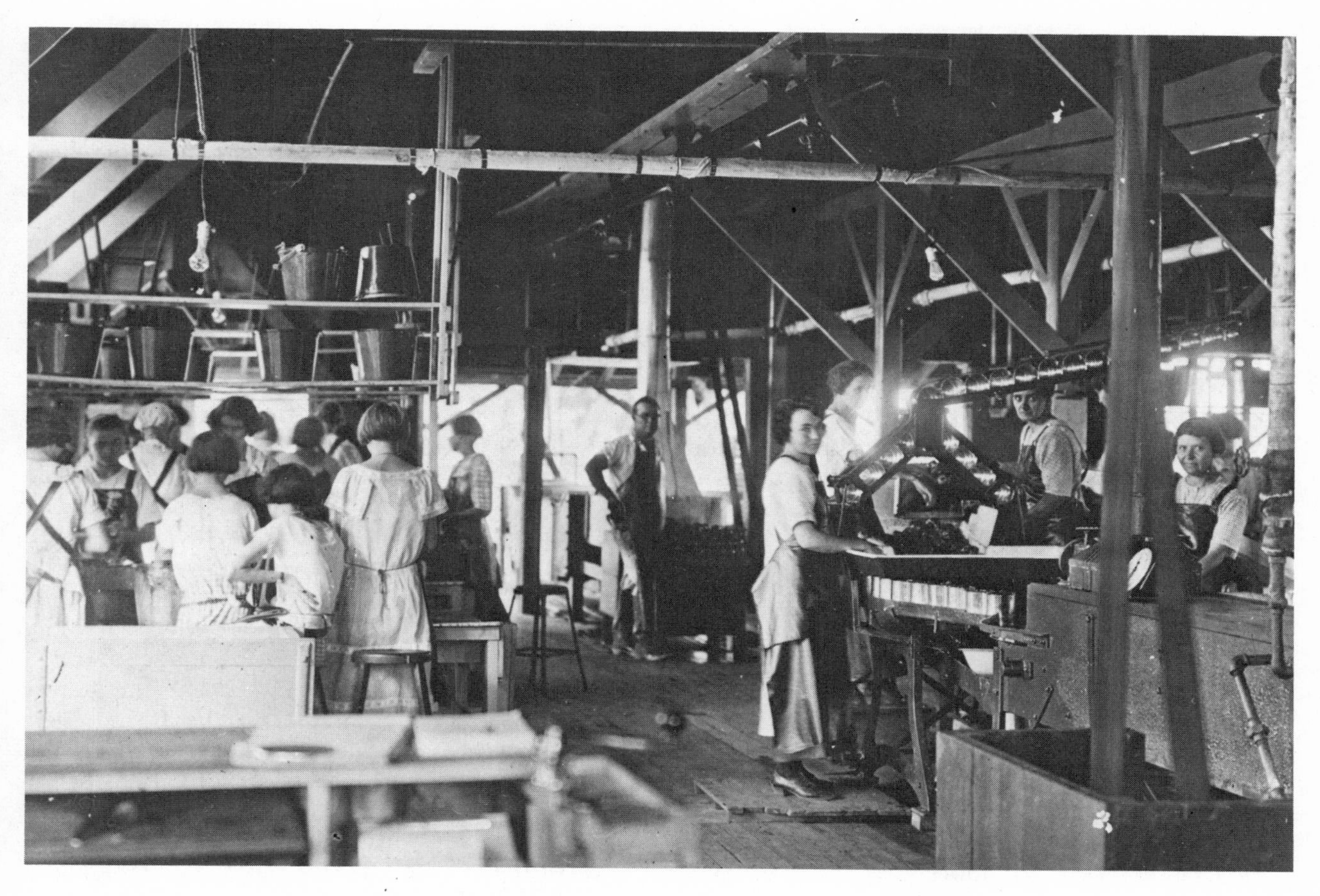

Canning factory at Billings, Missouri. (Courtesy Missouri State Historical Society.)

brought the decline of tomato farming. Droughts of the 1930's and blight in the wet years caused crops to fail and canneries to close. World War II was accompanied by a labor shortage, probably the most culpable factor in the closings. Stoop labor was almost impossible to hire when better-paying and less-demanding work could be obtained in nearby cities. Thus surplus farm labor, the main support of tomato farming and the cannery industry, was diverted toward urban employment. The products of small canneries could not match the quality and prices of larger plants in more favored growing areas. By 1955, tomato farming and the canneries it supported had all but disappeared from the landscape. Only a few small commercial patches of tomatoes are planted now near Springdale, Arkansas; the city's canning industry depends mainly on produce shipped in from the Arkansas Valley and even more distant truck-farming areas.

Strawberry growing on a commercial scale developed in the late 1890's in two Ozark localities: southwest Missouri and the lower south slope of the Boston Mountains near Van Buren, Arkansas. By the 1920's, it had spread through southwestern Missouri and northwestern Arkansas and into eastern Oklahoma.

Strawberry cultivation flourished for the same reasons that tomato farming became important. Strawberries grew well on the chert-choked soils of the hillsides; in fact, the stone covering in cherty soils provided an excellent mulch, holding frost in the ground in spring so that the plants did not bloom too early and providing a dry surface on which the berries could ripen free of mildew. Freshly cleared land was preferred because of the greater humus content. The care and harvesting of strawberries consumed much labor, a surplus commodity on the small Ozark farms of the early 1900's. Furthermore, strawberry farming required little in the way of land and capital outlay, and when they heard stories of sales exceeding five hundred dollars from patches of less than an acre, farmers quickly started setting out strawberries to bolster their income. Grown usually no more than ten miles from point of shipment, the berries were marketed through growers associations, which set up railside receiving and crating sheds at the main shipping points. Where rail facilities were not available, grocery or feed dealers purchased the berries and resold them at these points.

The picking season normally lasted five weeks, from the end of May to the first of July. Since most of the production came from family farms, where women and children could help with the harvest, little outside labor was used. In a few cases, where fields of fifty acres or more had been set out, outside laborers were brought in to help with the harvest.

During peak production in the 1920's, strawberry growing had spread throughout the area and several towns had become important shipping points. At Logan, Missouri, the most important of these, there were two large strawberry barns, and it was not unusual for 150 carloads to be shipped during a season. Ozark, Springfield, Marshfield, Aurora, and Monett were other important points of shipment in southwest Missouri. Springdale, Rogers, Bentonville, Farmington, Prairie Grove, and Van Buren were the most important shipping points in Arkansas, but many other towns shipped several carloads each season. Stillwell, Tahlequah, and Sallisaw were the chief shipping points in Oklahoma. Most of the strawberries were transported to St. Louis and other eastern cities.

The growth and decline of strawberry farming paralleled that of tomato production; the virtual cessation of strawberry growing for distant markets after World War II resulted from labor shortages. Only a few commercial growers remain today, and most of the production is in the vicinity of Stillwell, Oklahoma.

Viticulture

The growing of grapes is well suited to the climate and soils of the Ozarks. Viticulture was introduced early and was an important step toward the success of the German settlements at Hermann. In 1845 there were fifty-thousand vines in the vicinity of Hermann, and by 1849 the number had grown to seven hundred thousand. By 1850 the grape harvests rivaled hemp in value. The success of grapes at Hermann led to extensive plantings of vineyards at Ste. Genevieve and Boonville and in Franklin, Warren, and St. Charles counties. The vineyards were located on loess hillsides, which afforded warm soil, excellent drainage, and protection from unseasonable frosts. The climate was said to be better than that in the Rhine River country because of the sunny fall weather, which permitted the grapes to ripen with high flavor. Before the introduction of viticulture, Hermann had been losing population, but the excellent harvest of 1848 reversed this trend. In 1856 a yield of one-hundred-thousand gallons of wine was reported for Hermann at a profit of three-hundred dollars per acre. A large wine trade was built, the Stone Hill Winery became one of the sights of Missouri, and Hermann wines gained a wide reputation.

In the 1880's, Catholic Swiss-Germans settled near Altus, Arkansas, on the extreme southern border of the Ozarks. They planted grapes on limestone soils in the Boston Mountain foothills overlooking the Arkansas Valley. The wines became quite popular in central Arkansas, and in recent years, Wiederkehr Wine Cellars has gained a national reputation for its products.

Grapes also were grown by Italian immigrants who located in two widely separated Ozark communities. Both settlements, Tontitown in Washington County, Arkansas, and Rosati in eastern Phelps County, Missouri, were colonized in 1898 under the leadership of an Italian-born priest. The members of these colonies were fleeing from an ill-fated philanthropic colonization venture in southeastern Arkansas, where malaria had decimated their ranks. One reason for selecting the Ozarks locations was their suitability for growing grapes. Then, too, the Ozarks reminded them of their homeland in Italy, and the region was free of malaria.

The rise of the grape industry at Tontitown was rapid. The place held no importance for vineyards in 1900, but by 1920, Washington County, with 150,000 vines, had become the chief vineyard county in Arkansas.[8] Similar expansion, albeit on a smaller scale, occurred at Rosati, and wineries flourished at the two colonies until Prohibition days.

Even before the Italian immigrants began planting vineyards, the western Ozarks was known as excellent grape country. Swiss immigrant Hermann Jaeger settled in Newton County, Missouri, where in 1867 he produced a hardy new grape by crossing Virginia grapes with the wild Ozark variety. Jaeger developed a large vineyard near Neosho with his hybrid, which proved to be very successful. Later, when he learned that grape lice were causing much damage in the vineyards of France, he suggested the adoption of cuttings from the wild Ozark grapes to give more resistance to the French vines. When his suggestions were received favorably, Jaeger sent seventeen carloads of cuttings to France. Jaeger's plan proved successful and won for him the Legion of Honor for his service to French agriculture.

During the 1920's the Welch Company established several large vineyards in Washington and Benton counties to supply its new grape-juice plant in Springdale. By 1923 the company had sponsored the planting of five thousand acres, of which one thousand were along the Kansas City Southern Railway between the Arkansas-Missouri line and Siloam Springs.

During the 1930's and 1940's, grape production declined throughout the Ozarks. This may be attributed to many of the same factors that caused reduction in orcharding and truck farming: labor shortages, drought, and marketing problems. In recent years, viticulture has received a boost from the increasing popularity of wines as opposed to more robust beverages. The Stone Hill Winery at Hermann, Missouri, has reopened and the Maifest and Oktoberfest celebrated there have attracted attention to the excellent wines of the district. Plantings of Catawba and other grapes have increased, and the winery buys surpluses from the Rosati district to meet the demand for wine. New wineries have been established at St. James and Rosati. Most of the grapes in southwest Missouri and northwest Arkansas are grown under contract with the Welch Company's grape-juice cannery at Springdale, Arkansas. Grapes are grown in the vicinity of Exeter, Missouri, and at other locations near the Arkansas line.

8. Leslie Hewes, "Tontitown: Ozark Vineyard Center," *Economic Geography* 29 (April 1953): 139.

Dairy Farming

The pioneers who settled the Ozarks usually led one or more cows to their new home. Most of these animals were nondescript, largely beef cattle, but a few had been crossed with dairy breeds. These cattle supplied both milk and meat; some were used as oxen. Good-quality livestock representing the various dairy breeds did not reach the Ozarks in great numbers until after 1900.

Only a small amount of trade in dairy products was carried on at an early date. About the turn of the century, Springfield began to develop as a major dairy center. With the end of the Civil War and the coming of the railroads, Springfield grew rapidly, so that a sizable local market developed for milk, cream, and farm-churned butter. By modern standards the early trade was conducted in an extremely crude and unsanitary manner. General stores maintained cream stations that purchased cream from farmers and sent it to market in Springfield every few days. The stores bought churned butter from area farmers and dumped it into a common tub; when the butter was ready for market, the lid was nailed on and it was shipped with other products. Tuberculosis and brucellosis testing was unheard of, and dairy items were produced under any number of unwholesome conditions.

Commercial dairying began shortly after 1900. By 1905, several Springfield cream and produce dealers shipped to markets in the East and South. At that time, four creameries were established in Webster County. Lawrence County also experi-

Springfield Creamery Company, *circa* 1914. First creamery to make pickups at the farm. (Courtesy Missouri State Historical Society.)

enced a similar growth in dairying. The first large-scale dairy manufacturer in the area, Springfield Creamery Company, founded in 1910, inaugurated the practice of picking up cream at farms. Similar practices soon were established at Fayetteville and Springdale, where dairying had become established in the level upland prairies and in the valley of the West Fork of the White River.

Several factors stimulated the growth of the dairy industry. First, good markets became available in St. Louis, Kansas City, and several towns that had sprung up in the Tri-State Mining District. High prices for dairy products encouraged its extension. Second, as the area became better settled and landholdings became smaller, this required that each acre receive intensive use or that some other outlet for labor be afforded. Dairying provided a means to both ends. Third, the nature of the area's topography made it necessary to keep much of the land in pasture. Most of the grass and forage crops, such as orchard grass, bluegrass, timothy, clover, and sorghum, grew well and furnished an eight- or nine-month grazing season for stock. Innumerable springs supplied plenty of good, clear water.

At first, very few farms made a specialty of dairying, but a number had as many as ten to fifteen milk cows. Gradually, farmers began to specialize. Because dairying developed before there were large numbers of automobiles and trucks, most of the dairy farms were located close to the railroads. Springfield, with a substantial market and several railroad lines, formed a nucleus about which dairy farms were established. Thus, in the early years, commercial dairy farming tended to be concentrated around Springfield and along the railroads that radiate from the city. Each major shipping point on the railroad served as the market for a cluster of dairy farms. Later, as roads improved and trucks picked up dairy products at the farm dairy operations became more widely distributed in the interior Ozarks near railroads. However, because of poor roads, the extremely rough topography, and limited forage, it did not gain such importance in the Ozark interior.

The demand for dairy products from markets outside the area became more discriminating and competitive, requiring herd improvement, better management, and better feeding. Many herds were developed from purebred Holsteins and

Large dairy farm of the Bonne Terre Farming and Cattle Company on the property of the St. Joseph Lead Company, *circa* 1900. (Courtesy Missouri State Historical Society.)

Jerseys, but other popular dairy breeds were made up of Brown Swiss, Guernseys, and Milking Shorthorns.

Remarkable growth in commercial dairy farming occurred from its inauguration until 1940. In 1910, dairy cattle in the eight-county area surrounding Springfield totaled 64,361, but by 1940 the number had increased to 113,200. Growth during the 1920's was especially rapid. In only three years, Lawrence County rose from twenty-ninth place to third among Missouri counties in the number of dairy cattle. Between 1921 and 1924, the number of dairy cattle in Lawrence County increased from 9,640 to 14,530. By 1924, Springfield ranked fourth in the nation in churned butter, and eleven large creameries in that city employed more than 650 workers. Nearly every town of 1,500 population had creameries, and the larger trade centers began to develop more elaborate milk-processing plants. A second and smaller dairy farming area was established in Washington and Benton counties in northwest Arkansas.

A study of a farm in Logan Creek valley in the remote southern Courtois Hills (Reynolds County, Missouri) after a lapse of thirty-five years—1935 to 1970—showed remarkable shifts in land use and farming practices. The farm, operated by N. B. George in 1935, specialized in dairy cattle, but there was considerable diversity in the types of crops and livestock. In 1970 the farm was operated by George's son-in-law, Vernon Moore, and emphasis had shifted from mixed livestock–dairy farming to a specialized beef-cattle operation. Table 10-2 shows the restricted number of crops and livestock and the trend toward specialization.

Dairy farms in remote locations, such as the N. B. George–Vernon Moore farm, have been most affected by the trend toward larger, more mechanized, and more specialized dairy opera-

TABLE 10-2
Land Use and Livestock Production on the N. B. George—Vernon Moore Farm

Crop	Per Cent of Total Farm Acreage		Livestock	Number of Livestock	
	1936	1970		1936	1970
Woodland	16	24	Dairy cattle	15	0
Woodland pasture	19	26	Beef cattle	0	75
Pasture	17	32	Sheep	20	0
Grass	16	6	Hogs	35	0
Alfalfa	8	8	Chickens	large flock	0
Red clover	3	0			
Lespedeza	7	0			
Corn	4	0			
Wheat	4	0			

Source: Riggs, "Valley Contrasts in the Missouri Ozarks Region," 351–59, and personal interview with Vernon Moore, 1970. The Moore farm in 1970 included 460 acres compared to 249 acres on the N. B. George farm.

tions. The shift to larger and more efficient manufacturing plants, along with improvements in farm technology, management, and cooperative marketing, resulted in fewer but larger dairy farms with improved methods of production. In the early days, milk was separated on the farm; the skimmed milk was fed to calves and hogs, and the cream was traded for household and farm supplies. In contrast, modern dairying has been geared to cheap, fast, efficient transportation. Today, most of the cows are milked in inspected milking sheds that have the most modern equipment. Though still seen, the cream can is fast disappearing from the roadside and farmyard as it is replaced by bulk milk tanks serviced by fast and efficient tank trucks.

In recent years, milk production in the Ozarks has declined slightly. Most of this has occurred in areas outside the old, established, and highly specialized production areas. Either highly efficient production or strong market orientation seems to be required. Efficiencies of area specialization are apparently more important than cheap labor and underemployment.

Poultry Farming

Developments in poultry production over the past century have been phenomenal. There is little similarity between early-day poultry-handling methods and the increasingly footloose production methods of modern times. The pioneers rarely brought in poultry of distinct breeds. Because they allowed it to run wild in the lots around the house and barn, there was no opportunity to develop pure strains, and mixed breeds were typical. A few farmers had guineas; some had small flocks of turkeys, geese, and ducks. On most farms the chickens and turkeys were expected to find their own food. Simple poultry houses or sheds were built before the Civil War, particularly for chickens, but for many years the turkeys and guineas roosted in the trees.

Farmers raised chickens for meat and eggs. Fried chicken, mainly in the summer months, was a favorite food, just as it always has been farther south. Turkeys were eaten on special occasions, such as Thanksgiving and Christmas, as were small numbers of ducks and geese.

Certainly the methods of producing and marketing poultry and poultry products were primitive by modern standards. In the early years, eggs, incubated by setting hens, provided the new stock of fryers and laying hens. The first incubators, which appeared shortly after 1900, were the box type. They were heated with kerosene lamp and held fifty to one hundred eggs. Later, size was increased and electric incubators were introduced. Thus modern hatcheries gradually developed with great batteries of egg trays. With the introduction of the incubator, brooders succeeded the setting the hen. Small boxes kept in a warm place, often beside the fireplace or stove in the home, first served this purpose. Later brooders used kerosene, natural gas, and electricity for heat.

Ozark poultry farming developed contemporaneously with dairying. Usually the marketing of poultry and dairy products was combined; cream, eggs, and poultry were collected at produce houses and general stores in small Ozark towns for shipment to the large creameries and larger produce houses in Springfield, Fayetteville, and Springdale.

Farm women usually cared for the chickens and turkeys. Children assisted in the task of gathering eggs. Because the chickens had the run of the farmyard, the chore consisted of locating all the potential laying spots. Eggs were sold ungraded and rarely cleaned. Because they were marketed irregularly, with little protection from the heat, many of them spoiled.

Before the invention of the egg crate, eggs were hauled to market in farm wagons. A heavy layer of straw was placed in the wagon bed, and on this was placed a layer of eggs; layers of straw and eggs were alternated until the wagon was filled to the top. A layer of boards covered the whole, and a boom pole, fastened down in front and back, kept the eggs from jolting around. Almost universally, farmers exchanged poultry products for groceries, leaving few records of the magnitude of their business.

By 1920, broiler production had become widespread on general farms throughout the Springfield Plain, and poultry production assumed an important place in the agricultural economy. Each farm had at least one small shed in which laying hens or broilers were sheltered, particularly at night, when predators were on the prowl. By 1934, the production of eggs and poultry products had achieved such importance that Springfield adopted a somewhat ambitious title: The World's Poultry Capital.

Poultry farming has experienced great changes in recent years. By 1930 the semiwild and nondescript flocks that foraged for themselves and laid their eggs in the loft or in the woods, had given way to a flock of some one hundred or two hundred hybrid birds. The flocks were housed in modern poultry sheds built according to plans recommended by state experiment stations. These small family-size flocks, in turn, yielded to highly specialized production systems with flocks of twenty thousand birds or more.

Most contemporary poultry farmers specialize in one of the modern breeds or hybrids. The principal utility breeds include White Leghorn, White Plymouth Rocks, New Hampshires, Rhode Island Reds, and Inbred Hybrids. The major breeds of turkeys are Bronze, White Holland, and Beltsville. The U.S. Department of Agriculture developed the last-named breed to meet the growing demand for smaller turkeys.

Washington and Benton counties in northwest Arkansas have become the leading center for Ozark broiler production and a major broiler district in the United States. Modern poultry production under contractual agreements between the producers and the processing companies began in the vicinity of Springdale and Rogers in the late 1930's and gradually spread to outlying areas in Missouri and Oklahoma. In the valley of the West Fork of the White River, poultry farming replaced lumbering as the chief economic activity. One resident in the St. Paul, Arkansas, community pointed out that "soon after the Frisco Railroad quit hauling trees from the hills, the trucks started hauling chickens out of the valleys to processors like Campbell Soup in Fayetteville and Tyson's in Springdale." In recent years, broiler production has spread eastward to the vicinity of Huntsville and into War Eagle Valley. A second center for poultry farming has grown up during the 1960's and 1970's in the vicinity of Batesville in the southeastern Ozarks. The Banquet Foods plants in Batesville serve as the primary market for broilers and turkeys grown in this section of the Ozarks.

The changes in poultry farming are strikingly evident in the landscape. Many abandoned barns, representing an intermediate stage in the trend toward larger production units, stand in various states of disrepair and decay. This anomolous mixture of farms with abandoned poultry barns, side by side with apparently prosperous poultry farms, is repeated again and again through southwest Missouri and northwest Arkansas.

Livestock Farming

Before the railroads arrived, animal husbandry was the only feasible system of commercial agriculture. The cost of shipping grain or other bulky products over rough terrain to distant markets outside the Ozarks was prohibitive except in the eastern and northern border areas. Cattle could be driven from the western Ozarks to St. Louis and even to New Orleans. Warsaw, head of navigation on the Osage River, and Boonville, on the Missouri River, served as the main shipping points. Salt meats, cured hides, tallow, and lard were major exports via the river route. In the 1840's and 1850's, Longhorn cattle from Texas were driven northeast across the Red River, past Fort Smith, and through northwest Arkansas and southwest Missouri to Independence, Boonville, or St. Louis. After the Civil War, drovers, including James Daugherty, J. S. Hargus, and R. D. Hunter, established cattle trails to the new railheads at Sedalia and Nevada, Missouri, and at Baxter Springs in extreme southeast Kansas.[9]

In addition to the cattle and half-wild hogs than ran at large on unfenced commons, early stock farmers raised horses and mules. Horses were in strong demand both locally and in northern cities; most of the mules were sold in the southern states, where they were used in the cotton fields. The major area for mule raising was in the vicinity of the Missouri River, but a sizable number of mule and horse breeding farms were located near Springfield.

A major influence for the livestock industry in the western Ozarks was the Missouri Land and Livestock Company.[10] This company, owned by Scottish investors, purchased more than 350,000 acres in southwest Missouri from the Atlantic and Pacific Railroad and the University of Missouri. Under the management of John S. Purdy and L. B. Sidway, the company established Sandyford Ranche near Neosho, Missouri, in 1882 as a showplace to promote the region as a livestock ranching area. Blooded Angus and Hereford cattle were imported from the British Isles to stock the ranch. Bulls and blooded heifers were sold to many farmers and ranchers in the western Ozarks.

As open-range livestock farming gave way to general farming, cultivated crops, particularly corn, received more emphasis and farmers gave more attention to raising hogs and poultry. Stall-feeding cattle to produce a finished animal became more common. From about 1900 to 1940, when general farming reached its Zenith, a Corn Belt–type of livestock economy became popular. Corn was used to produce finished hogs and beef. However, beef cattle production attained its greatest importance in the loess and glacial soils of northern Missouri, where natural conditions were better suited to the production of corn and other feeds.

In the Ozarks in the years since World War II there has been a marked shift back to a livestock economy based on the production of unfinished feeder cattle (figs. 10-8, 10-9). During the 1960's and 1970's, the shift in emphasis has reached major proportions and constitutes one of the most significant economic changes in the Ozarks. As a result, land-use and landscape patterns have been altered significantly, and the changes promise to continue for some time to come. High cattle prices made conversion of timberland to pasture profitable. Between 1966 and 1969, more than 73,000 acres were defoliated and aerially seeded

9. Missouri's War Against Texas Herds," *Springfield News and Leader*, January 30, 1977, p. F1.

10. McFarlane, "The Missouri Land and Livestock Company," pp. 96–130.

Angora goats in Arkansas woodland, 1975. The Ozarks ranks second in United States Angora production.

Forest clearing for pasture in the Arkansas Ozarks, 1975.

to pasture by one southwest Missouri farmer's cooperative. In the period 1959 to 1972 in the entire Ozark region, more than 1,453,000 acres of forest were converted to other uses; 955,000 acres were converted to wooded pasture, and 377,000 acres were converted to improved pasture.

In the late 1970's, wooded land was being converted to pasture in two ways: by aerial spraying with herbicides at a cost of approximately $8.50 per acre, plus aerial seeding of fescue, lespedeza, and mixed grasses at two dollars an acre; bulldozing, cultivation, and seeding at a cost of approximately $150 per acre. In the latter case, brush is left in piles to retard water runoff and to serve as wildlife habitat.

Although the trend to beef cattle has been nationwide, the percentage growth rate in Ozarks beef-cattle operations is substantially above the national average. The numbers of beef cattle in Missouri increased 75 per cent from 1958 to 1967, considerably more than the 43 per cent increase in the entire United States. In the western Ozarks the increase in beef cattle amount to 136 per cent during the same time span. Although low beef prices in the mid-1970's caused Ozark cattlemen to reduce the size of herds, the high prices in the late 1970's stimulated another round of herd increases.

Part-Time Farming

Part-time farming has increased markedly in the Ozarks over the past few decades. This has been most pronounced in the vicinity of St. Louis, Springfield, Joplin, Jefferson City, Fayetteville-Springdale, and other larger urban areas. The number of part-time farms in the eight-county area around Springfield increased from 1,593 in 1930 (7 per cent of the total number of farms) and to 4,393 in 1964, (28 per cent of the total number of farms). The increase is contradictory to the general decline in the number of farms in the Ozark region, but typical of the situation close to growth centers.

Ozark farmers have always looked to alternate sources of income to bolster their standard of living. The early hunter-woodsman, who gained as much of his living from the wild game and the forests as from agriculture, may be considered as the prototype part-time farmer. Of necessity the first settlers were largely self-sufficient, so that in

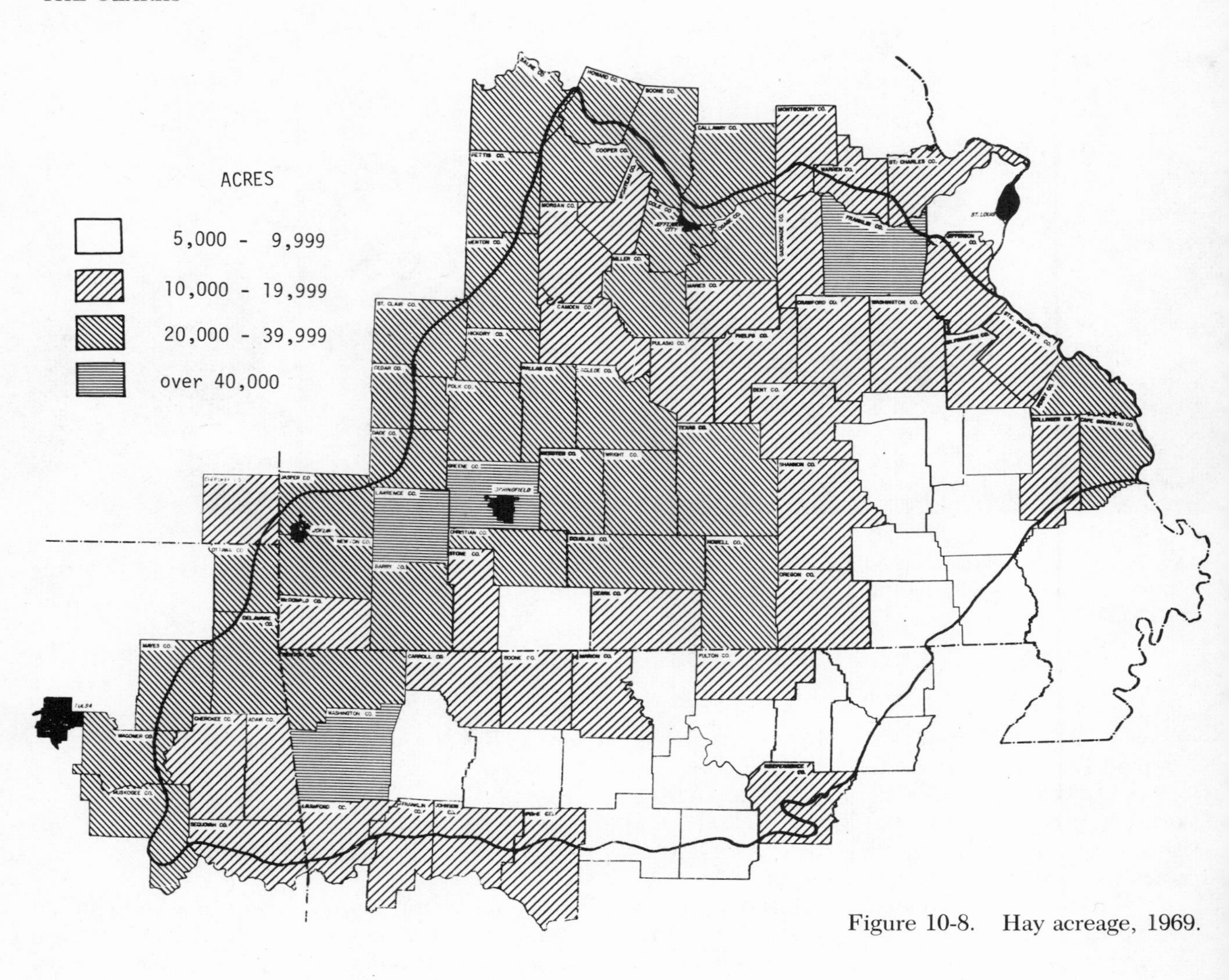

Figure 10-8. Hay acreage, 1969.

addition to producing nearly all their food and clothing, they manufactured a large part of their farmsteads' furnishings and tools. Some farmers made furniture, tools, leather products or other essential commodities to supplement their farm income. Tanyards, whiskey distilleries, stave and barrel works, ax-handle and tool works, furniture and coffin shops, sorghum mills, and gristmills were adjuncts to agriculture. In some cases, farm manufacturing persisted through several generations.

Gradually, as towns matured, capital was accumulated by the middle- and upper-income business and professional people, and this led to country-gentleman farming. Many who occupied such farms were former rural inhabitants who had made good in the city but still yearned for country living. Some of the first country-gentleman farms in the Ozarks were established in the beautiful Arcadia and Belleview valleys. These idyllic settings among the towering knobs of the St. Francis Mountains were easily accessible to residents of

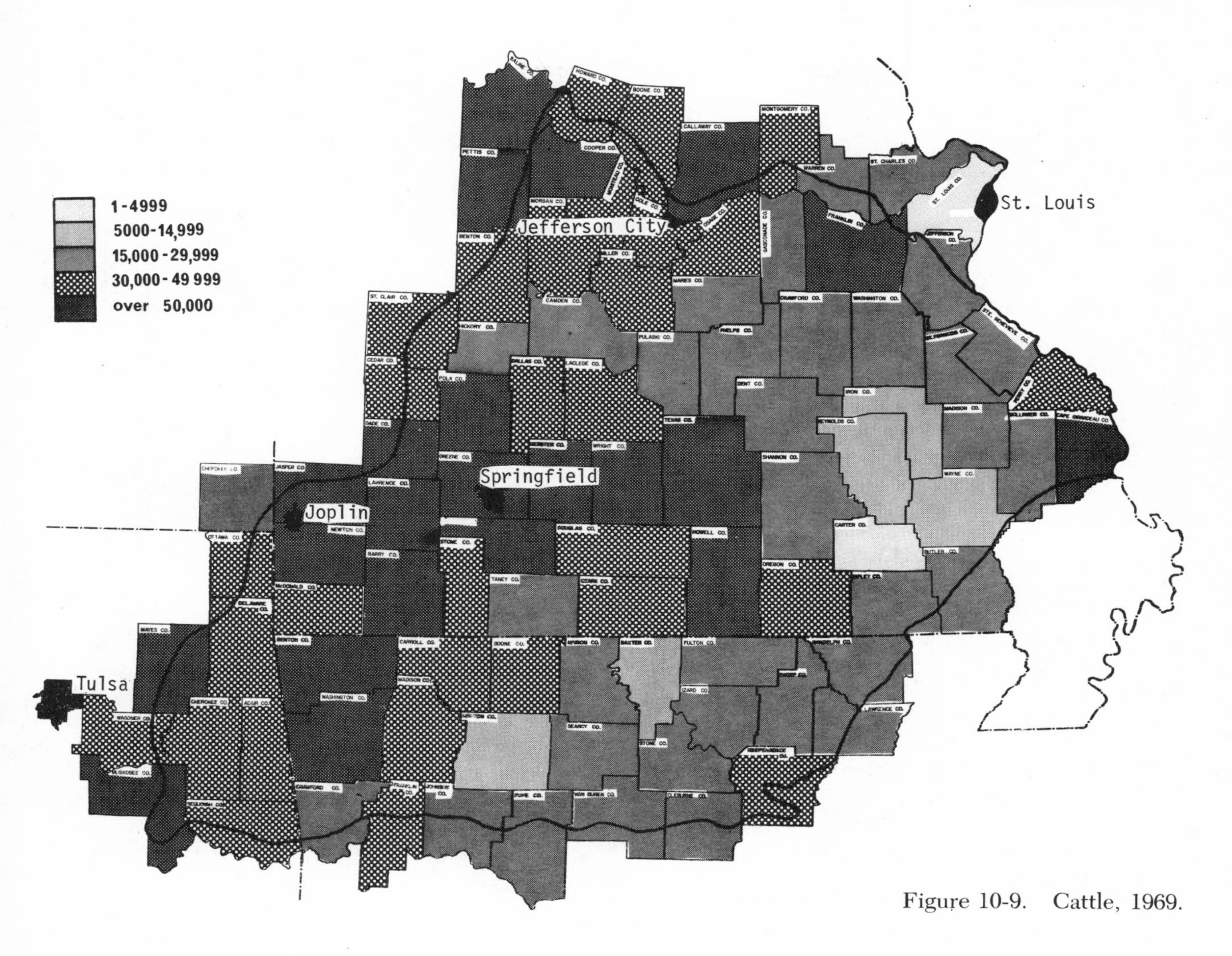

Figure 10-9. Cattle, 1969.

St. Louis, less than ninety miles to the northeast by railroad. Summer estates and substantial summer homes were built in Arcadia and Ironton as early as 1875; soon, church groups and other institutions acquired property in the valleys for recreational use. Gradually the summer homes became permanent residences or places for retirement. Improved roads and better automobiles during the 1950's and 1960's boosted the number of country-gentleman farms in the St. Francis Mountains. These well-tended estates, set in grassy valleys, have a cultured appearance reminiscent of the Shenandoah Valley and other valleys in Virginia, Maryland, and southeastern Pennsylvania. From 1900 to 1930 and after World War II, such part-time farms became common near many of the larger Ozark towns. They were used for recreation and casual living and only incidentally for agricultural purposes.

Part-time subsistence farms appeared during the Depression between 1930 and 1940. As economic activity declined, the centripetal pull of the urban centers became a centrifugal force, causing unemployed workers to seek open country where they could at least eke out a living. Because of low land prices, low-cost rural rental property, and low living costs, the Ozarks became a popular place to establish temporary subsistence homesteads. Strawberry and tomato harvesting, logging, and cannery work provided seasonal employment, which in turn provided money to purchase those things that could not be produced on the farm. In some cases, people who went back to the cities after the Depression returned to the Ozarks to reestablish part-time retirement farms.

In recent years the part-time farmer has moved to open country as the result of better roads, rural population, mobility, and the tightening cost-price squeeze in farming operations. Ozark farmers found that enlargement of the farm unit is not always easy because the conditions of slope and topography are not well suited to mechanization. The alternative to expansion has been to earn income from nonfarm employment. This has been particularly true of dairy-farm operators, who, in order to remain competitive, must have larger farm units and more—expensive—equipment.

Many dairy farms throughout the Ozarks have been converted to part-time stock farms, a transition that involves no large capital investments and allows more time to be spent off the farm. Also contributing to the increasing number of part-time farms are the farmettes established by people who work in Ozark growth centers, such as Springfield, Joplin, Jefferson City, Cape Girardeau, Rolla, Fayetteville-Springdale, and Batesville. Probably, most of these farms serve primarily as places for recreation and casual country living and only incidentally for agricultural purposes. The continued subdivision of productive farms into uneconomic farm units, coupled with increases in land prices, is fraught with risks for continued production from Ozark agricultural land. Farmers are becoming increasingly concerned that land prices are beyond the current levels of profitable economic return from agriculture.

Ozark agriculture appears to have come full circle. The original farmer was a part-time agriculturalist, keeper of livestock, and hunter. The land he plowed was safe and secure in stream bottoms. His economy was more in tune with the existing natural resources than some of the subsequent types of farming. Development of commercial agriculture in the Ozarks has been a long and sometimes destructive process replete with experimentation and constant adjustments in man-land relationships. Large-scale contemporary agriculture in the Ozarks leans heavily on livestock production. The general farm has all but disappeared, dairy farming continues under heavy pressure, and only vestiges of fruit and truck farms remain. Like his forebears, the less-progressive Ozark farmer often finds greater reward in alternate pursuits than in attempting to wrest his total livelihood from reluctant soils. One can speculate that mutual benefit may accrue to man and land.

Selected References

Fairbanks, Jonathan, and Tuck, Clyde E. *Past and Present of Greene County, Missouri*. Indianapolis, Ind.: A. W. Bowen and Co., 1915.

Gist, Noel P. *Missouri: Its Resources, People, and Institutions*. Columbia: Curators of the University of Missouri, 1950.

Hewes, Leslie. "Cultural Fault Line in the Cherokee Country," *Economic Geography* 19 (April 1943): 136–42.

———. "Tontitown: Ozark Vineyard Center," *Economic Geography* 29 (April 1953): 125–43.

Kersten, Earl W., Jr. "Changing Economy and Landscape in a Missouri Ozarks Area," *Annals of the Association of American Geographers*, 48 (December 1958): 298–418.

McFarlane, Larry A. "The Missouri Land and Livestock Company, Limited, of Scotland: Foreign Investment on the Missouri Farming Frontier, 1882–1908." Ph.D. dissertation, University of Missouri-Columbia, 1963.

Marbut, Curtis F. "Soil Reconnaissance of the Ozark Region of Missouri and Arkansas." *Field Operations of the Bureau of Soils, 1911*. Washington, D.C.: Bureau of Soils, U.S. Department of Agriculture, 1914.

Maxfield, O. O. "Geography of the Boston Mountains." Ph.D. dissertation, Ohio State University, 1963.

Meyer, Duane. *The Heritage of Missouri: A History*.

St. Louis: The State Publishing Company, 1963.
"Missouri's War Against Texas Herds." *Springfield* (Mo.) *News and Leader*, January 30, 1977.

Moke, Irene A. "Canning in Northwestern Arkansas: Springdale, Arkansas." *Economic Geography*, 28 (April 1952): 151–59.

Paullin, Charles O. *Atlas of the Historical Geography of the United States*. Washington, D.C.: Carnegie Institute of Washington, 1932.

Rafferty, Milton D. "Agricultural Change in the Western Ozarks," *Missouri Historical Review* 69 (April 1965): 299–322.

———. "Persistence Versus Change in Land Use and Landscape in the Springfield, Missouri, Vicinity of the Ozarks." Ph.D. dissertation, University of Nebraska, 1970.

———. Gerlach, Russel L. and Hrebec, Dennis. *Atlas of Missouri*. Springfield, Mo.: Aux Arc Research Associates, 1970.

———, and Hrebec, Dennis. "Logan Creek: A Missouri Ozark Valley Revisited," *Journal of Geography* 72 (October 1973): 7–17.

Riggs, Margaret. "Valley Contrasts in the Missouri Ozarks Region," *Journal of Geography* 35 (December 1935): 351–59.

Sauer, Carl O. *The Geography of the Ozark Highland of Missouri*. The Geographic Society of Chicago Bulletin no. 7. Chicago: University of Chicago Press, 1920.

Steyermark, Julian A. "Vegetational History of the Ozark Forest." University of Missouri Studies no. 31. Columbia: University of Missouri Press, 1959.

Woodward, Grace Steele. *The Cherokees*. Norman: University of Oklahoma Press, 1963.

11.

The Ozark Lumber Industry: Development and Geography

The latter part of the 1800's was a time of rapid westward expansion and homesteading as eastern settlers and European newcomers were attracted to the Middle West and the Great Plains, where land with fertile, rock-free soils could be claimed. This created a vast market for lumber to build houses, barns, and stores. At the same time, railroad construction, which required three thousand crossties for each mile of track, proceeded at an unprecedented rate. These factors, plus the general growth of the population and economy of the United States, created a strong demand for lumber and wood products and accounted for the exploitation of the vast hardwood forests of the Ozarks, as well as the less extensive Ozark pine forests.

The lumbermen who entered the Ozarks after the Civil War were pioneers, if the word's definition can be applied to the people who developed untouched natural resources, but they were primarily businessmen looking for profits. In a free capitalistic society, they bore the same relationships to social and economic development in primitive regions as the cotton farmer, the rancher, the miner, or any individual or group seeking material gain through exploitation of the natural wealth of the wilderness.

The lumbering frontier followed a definite pattern of advance from one virgin forest to another. The location of each new milling site depended upon a large number of factors, one of the most important of which was the pressing need for an increased lumber supply to meet the growing demands of a rapidly expanding nation. For the first half of the nineteenth century, the industry centered in New England, with Maine as the principal lumber-producing state. By 1850 cutting had shifted to western New York, but within ten years Pennsylvania assumed the leading position. During the next decade, penetration of the great white pine forests of the Lake States began, and by 1880 the woodsman's ax began to bite deep into the yellow-pine forests of the South. At this time, southern yellow pine began to replace northern white pine on the nation's markets, and between 1895 and 1910 the southern states produced 30 percent of all the lumber used in the United States. Meanwhile, the advance of the lumber frontier continued, and in the early twentieth century the redwoods and Douglas fir of Washington, Oregon, and California began to compete seriously with the lumber products of the Mississippi Valley.

The first important sawmill industry in Missouri was located on the Gasconade River, the nearest source of good lumber for the St. Louis district. During his journey into the Ozarks in 1818–19, Schoolcraft noted that these mills were in operation.[1] Some of them used water power, others hand power alone. During the next two decades, however, steam-powered circle mills operated in this region, and the Gasconade River valley was an important source of lumber until the Civil War. By 1880 the best timber in the Gasconade region had been cut, and St. Louis dealers were unable to meet the increasing demand for lumber products. Thus the pine stands of the Ozarks became even more important because of their proximity to the St. Louis market. Until effective transportation was available, however, these forest lands remained untapped (fig. 11-1).

The southern-pine states, including Missouri and Arkansas, played a prominent role in the phenomenal expansion of the lumber industry. As the most northwesterly extension of native southern-pine forests, the Ozarks possessed geographical advantages to tap the markets of Nebraska, Kansas, and Indian Territory.

The Ozark timber era began with the arrival of the railroads, which provided easy, low-cost transportation for bulky wood products. Two railroads were of unusual significance in stimulating interest in Ozark timberlands. By 1872 the Kansas City, Fort Scott and Memphis Railroad had begun a line southeast toward Memphis, Tennessee, through the western part of the pine forests, and the St. Louis and Iron Mountain Railroad had laid tracks southward in the eastern Ozarks through Ironton and Poplar Bluff to the Arkansas line.

Large acreages of short-leaf pine and oak were purchased by eastern investors. It was clear that the Ozark forests could supply lumber and railroad supplies for both the Great Plains and the East. The cost of stumpage was low, from a few cents to a dollar per thousand board feet, and the open winters permitted year-round logging.

Following well-established practices, lumber companies often set up complete manufacturing facilities, constructed logging railroads, and began cutting timber. Short-leaf pine forests were exploited for construction lumber, while oak was used for flooring, barrel staves, and railroad supplies. Some of the largest sawmills with the most frenzied activity were located in the southern Courtois Hills of Missouri in Shannon, Carter, Reynolds, Oregon, Ripley, Wayne, and Butler counties. Large outfits, such as Missouri Lumber and Mining Company, Cordz-Fisher Company, Ozark Land and Lumber Company, Current River Land and Cattle Company, Clarkson Sawmill Company, Doniphan Lumber Company, and Culbertson Stock and Lumber Company, were founded to exploit the timber resources of the southeast Missouri pineries. Boom towns—Doniphan, Leeper, Grandin, West Eminence, Winona, Birth Tree—grew up around large sawmills that were fed felled timber via tramways built into the forests (fig. 11-2). In the western Ozarks the Frisco built a branch line from Springfield to Chadwick in Christian County. The Hobart-Lee Tie and Timber Company operated shipping docks and company stores at both Sparta and Chadwick.

In areas outside the nearly pure stands of virgin short-leaf pine, lumbering took other forms. Chadwick, formerly known as Log Town, serves as an example. It became an important shipping point for lumber and railroad supplies when the Chadwick Branch of the Frisco Railroad was constructed in 1883. People began to move to Chadwick in larger numbers. New businesses were established—stores, boardinghouses and rooming houses, saloons, and gambling houses all flourished in the fashion of western boom towns.[2] Almost all able-bodied men in the community were earning more cash money at tie hacking or working in the sawmills than they had ever had before. Newspaper stories, verified by statements of persons who lived in Chadwick at the time, described the town as a hill-country Hell's Half-Acre. Apparently, it was as rough and lawless as some of the noted cattle and mining towns of the West.

The most important product of the hardwood forest was the railroad crosstie, which, according to specifications, was to be white oak cut six inches by eight inches by eight feet. Those of good quality brought twenty-five cents at the railhead. Many were cut by farmers from timber on their

1. Henry Rowe Schoolcraft, *Journal of a Tour into the Interior of Missouri and Arkansas*, in *Schoolcraft in the Ozarks*, ed. Hugh Park (Van Buren, Ark.: Press-Argus Printers, 1955), p. 46.

2. *Christian County: Its First Hundred Years* (Ozark, Mo.: Christian County Centennial, Inc., 1959), p. 136.

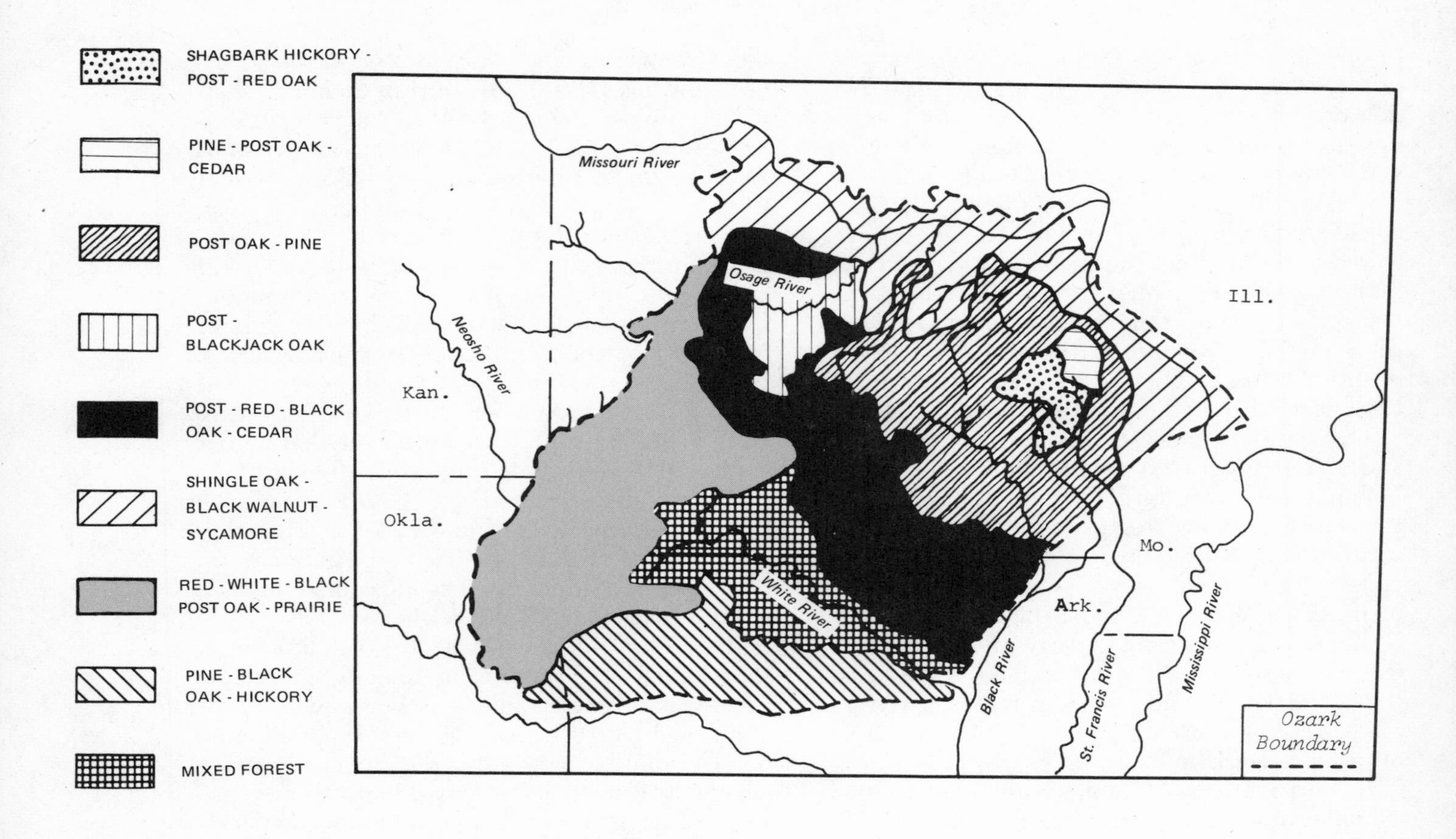

Figure 11-1. Forest-cover regions of the Ozark province.

own land, but during the most active period of forest exploitation, most of them produced by lumber companies. One of the biggest was Hobart-Lee Tie and Timber Company, which in 1890 was one of the largest businesses in southwest Missouri.

Another large concern operated on Springdale Ranch, an 8,600-acre venture that was started by a Captain Kenna in 1878 and soon was furnishing much of the timber marketed in the region. The ranch had its own tracks and train to pull carloads of logs across Bull Creek and up Happy Hollow to the foot of Mill Ridge Hill, where a steam hoist lifted the cars to the mill at the top of the hill. Lumber and ties were hauled from the mill to Chadwick in horse-drawn wagons. In later years, strings of wagons were pulled by crawler tractors.

At one time, Springdale Ranch sustained a settlement of 125 people. The property changed hands several times during the timber boom, but the ranch continued to produce important amounts of lumber and ties until the last mill burned in the 1920's. This marked the end of the boom, for most of the good timber had been cut by then. By 1930, Chadwick offered so little trade that, it was reported, the crew of the *Chadwick Flyer* had begun to stop off to shoot quail or pick blackberries along the right-of-way. In 1934, service to Chadwick was discontinued and the tracks between Chadwick and Ozark were taken up. However, the lumber industry has continued lethargically up to the present.

Likewise in Arkansas and Oklahoma the ax men followed the railroads into the best stands of pine

Figure 11-2. Ozark lumber mill towns.

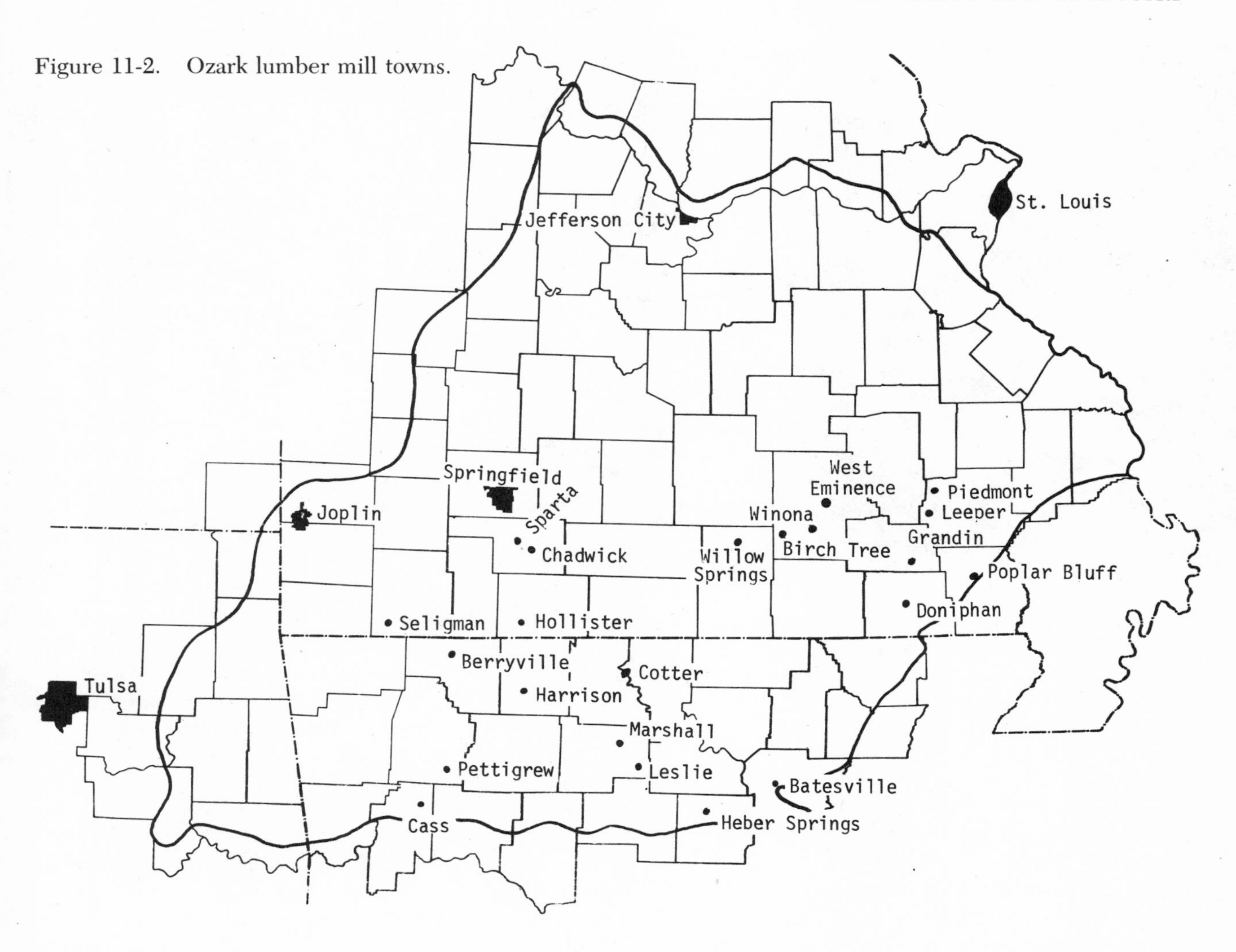

and hardwoods. The Frisco line through Fayetteville on its way from Pierce City, Missouri, to Fort Smith opened new timberlands in the early 1880's. With the railroad came Hugh F. McDaniel, construction man and tie contractor. The railroad had to have ties, hundreds of thousands of them, and McDaniel was the man who supplied them. A branch railroad was constructed into the timber on the Upper White River in Washington and Madison counties.

Growth began almost immediately. During 1887, the first year of operation, McDaniel shipped two thousand dollars worth of white-oak crossties over the Fayetteville & Little Rock Railroad. Soon new stations were established: Baldwin, Harris, Elkins, Durham, Thompson, Crosses, Delaney, Patrick, Combs, Brashears, and, later, Dutton and Pettigrew. When the railroad was extended to Pettigrew in 1897, more than a dozen lumber and stave mills were built there. Included were the American Land, Timber and Stave Company; Chess and Wymond; Pekin Cooperage Company; J. M. Bryant Company; Kentucky Stave and Heading Company; and W. L. Hillyard Stave Company. Phipps Lumber Company, the largest in northwest Arkansas, also

Making whiskey barrels at the Independent Stave Company, Lebanon, Missouri.

had a mill there. Pettigrew billed itself as the Hardwood Capital of the World.

As the timber was depleted, railways were driven even farther into the remote hill districts. By 1915, Phipps Lumber Company had cut over thousands of acres in Madison County and new timber supplies were needed. It constructed its own railroad, the Black Mountain and Eastern, into its large land holdings in the Black Mountain area of Franklin County. The line ended at Cass, which served as the shipping point until logging was completed and the rails were taken up in 1924.[3]

The Missouri and North Arkansas Railroad, which linked Joplin, Missouri, and Helena, Arkansas, cut through the rugged timberlands of the White River Hills and the Boston Mountains. Lumber and railroad ties were cut and hauled to sidings at Seligman, Missouri, and several Arkansas towns, including Beaver, Freeman, Berryville, Harrison, Pindall, Marshall, Leslie, Edgemont, Heber Springs, Pangborn, and Searcy.

Among the larger lumber dealers were Heber Springs Milling Company, Pangborn Lumber Company, and H. D. Williams Cooperage Company. The last-named furnished employment for nearly everyone in the town of Leslie. The barrel factory there was reported to be the largest of its kind in the world. It was moved from Poplar Bluff, Missouri, to Leslie in 1907, and tramlines were built back into the hills to portable "green mills" that supplied staves to the factory. In full operation the mill employed more than a thousand men. Another major producer, Doniphan Lumber Company, owned eighty-five thousand acres of timberland in Cleburne County and operated several mills in that area.

The Missouri Pacific's White River Line, constructed between 1904 and 1908, opened large acreages of timberland and spawned a host of lumber towns, including Branson and Hollister in Missouri and Cotter and Batesville in Arkansas. Because cedar grows profusely in the glades of the White River drainage basin, a number of wood-products manufacturers specializing in red cedar were established. Hanford Cedar Yard at Batesville was one of the largest markets of its kind. Much of the virgin cedar on the Upper White River was purchased by Eagle Pencil Company of Branson.[4] Cedar logs by the thousands were bought and processed into rectangular slats measuring about three by three by eight inches; these slats were shipped elsewhere to be manufactured into pencils.

Railroads were essential for profitable lumbering; where rails led, lumberman followed. Sometimes, Ozark streams were used for transportation of crossties and small timber, but only where conditions were favorable and usually only for short distances from forest to mill. Cedar logs and railroad ties were floated down the White River to Batesville and later to Cotter, Arkansas, after the railroad reached that point. Smalley Tie and Timber Company, a subsidiary of Missouri Lumber and Mining Company, floated railroad ties regularly on the Current River. The affairs of

3. Clifton E. Hull, *Shortline Railroads of Arkansas* (Norman: University of Oklahoma Press, 1969).

4. Elmo Ingenthron, *The Land of Taney* (Point Lookout, Mo.: The School of the Ozarks Press, 1974), p. 193.

Railroad-tie raft below Mill Dam, Camden County, Missouri, *circa* 1906. (Courtesy Missouri State Historical Society.)

this company did not always run smoothly. The ties usually were made in the woods during the winter and early spring, then hauled to the river and stacked to dry, out of reach of high water. They were run down the river in the fall when the threat of flash floods was minimal. The ties were either run loose in the water or fastened together in small rafts operated by two men. During the fall of 1902 the holding boom at Chicopee broke under the pressure of thousands of ties and about five thousand went downstream. Losses to the swift current in the river were frequent, and John Barber White, president of Missouri Lumber and Mining Company, doubted that he ever profited much from the tie business.[5]

For two generations, from 1880 to about 1920, railroad ties were floated down Ozark streams to railheads, where they were loaded on flatcars to be hauled away. Several large contracting companies were engaged in the business, but the Hobart-Lee Tie and Timber Company of Spring-

5. Leslie G. Hill, "History of the Missouri Lumber and Mining Company, 1880–1909" (Ph.D. diss., University of Missouri, 1949), p. 259.

field probably was the largest and had the most far-flung operations.

Along the Niangua River, contractors leased large tracts of land and set up tie camps until the timber was used up, then moved the camps to new locations. Such camps hired as many as two hundred to three hundred men. The ties were hauled to "bankings" on the Niangua, where they were branded. Contractors usually built stores to supply food and clothing near large tie bankings. There were many bankings, but three were very important: the one at Roach, now on U.S. Highway 54; the one at Mosier Hollow; and the one near Ira close to the Dallas County line.

There were three things to consider in selecting banking sites. First, the steepness of the chute had to be such that ties would not bounce and endanger the raft makers below. Second, the landing had to be shallow enough for men to work in but deep enough to float the rafts. Third, the banking, or bank, had to hold enough ties in storage to keep the crews busy.

The men who nailed the tie rafts together worked in the water winter and summer, protected by hip boots. The ties were fashioned into blocks or sections one tie wide and about sixteen feet long, holding about twenty ties. A white-oak pole was split into strips, and the strips were nailed on top as binders. These blocks were joined lengthwise with a larger white-oak strip to form a hinged "snake raft" that could negotiate the sharp bends in the river. The rafts, containing 300 to 700 ties and manned by two men, were floated to old Linn Creek at the mouth of the Niangua, where they were made up into larger rafts of 2,000 to as many as 4,500 ties before they were floated down the Osage River to the railhead at Bagnell.

The Missouri Lumber and Mining Company

The biggest timber cutter in the Ozarks was the Missouri Lumber and Mining Company. Its operations were larger and probably better financed than many similar companies, but its organization and purposes will serve to illustrate the character of large-scale lumbering during the era of forest exploitation.

As were most of the lumber companies, the Missouri Lumber and Mining Company was organized by investors from outside the region. In this case, like that of the Maramec Iron Works near St. James, the capital, management experience, and model of operation came from the forested plateau country of western Pennsylvania. By the late 1860's, O. H. P. Williams, a lumberman from Pittsburgh, had cut over most of his timber holdings in Pennsylvania and had begun to look further afield for more timber lands. He heard of the yellow pine in the Ozarks and wrote letters of inquiry to the officers of several southern Missouri counties. Williams purchased tax-delinquent timberlands in the Beaver Dam section of Ripley County for as little as $6.90 a half-section. In 1871 he and his son-in-law, E. B. Grandin of Tidioute, Pennsylvania, toured Iron, Reynolds, Shannon, and Wayne counties; Williams purchased thirty thousand acres of timberland in Carter County at an average of a dollar per acre. This became the nucleus of the Missouri Lumber and Mining Company's holdings.

The company's business connections and activities are highly significant. Grandin, its actual founder, had experience in the lumber industry, but Pennsylvania oil was the foundation of his fortune. J. L. Grandin, his brother, was treasurer and manager of the Tidioute and Warren Oil Company. These two men had organized a bank at Tidioute and were in an excellent position to furnish the capital needed for any new business venture. Another early member of the firm, John Hunter, had a merchandising background and had assisted in establishing the Tidioute Savings Bank. Hunter's son, L. L. Hunter, was a retail lumber dealer and operated a sawmill. The last member of the board of directors was H. H. Cumings, another Pennsylvania oil man. This combination represented a concentration of wealth unusual at the time. They selected J. B. White, an aggressive young lumberman, to establish and manage the Missouri Lumber and Mining Company.

Although land was purchased in the 1860's and 1870's, there was no immediate effort to exploit its timber. The successful operation of a sawmill depended on several factors. Even as late as 1880 the population of Carter County was only 2,168, an average of slightly more than three per square mile, but fortunately, it was concentrated in a few river valleys, a distribution that made it possible

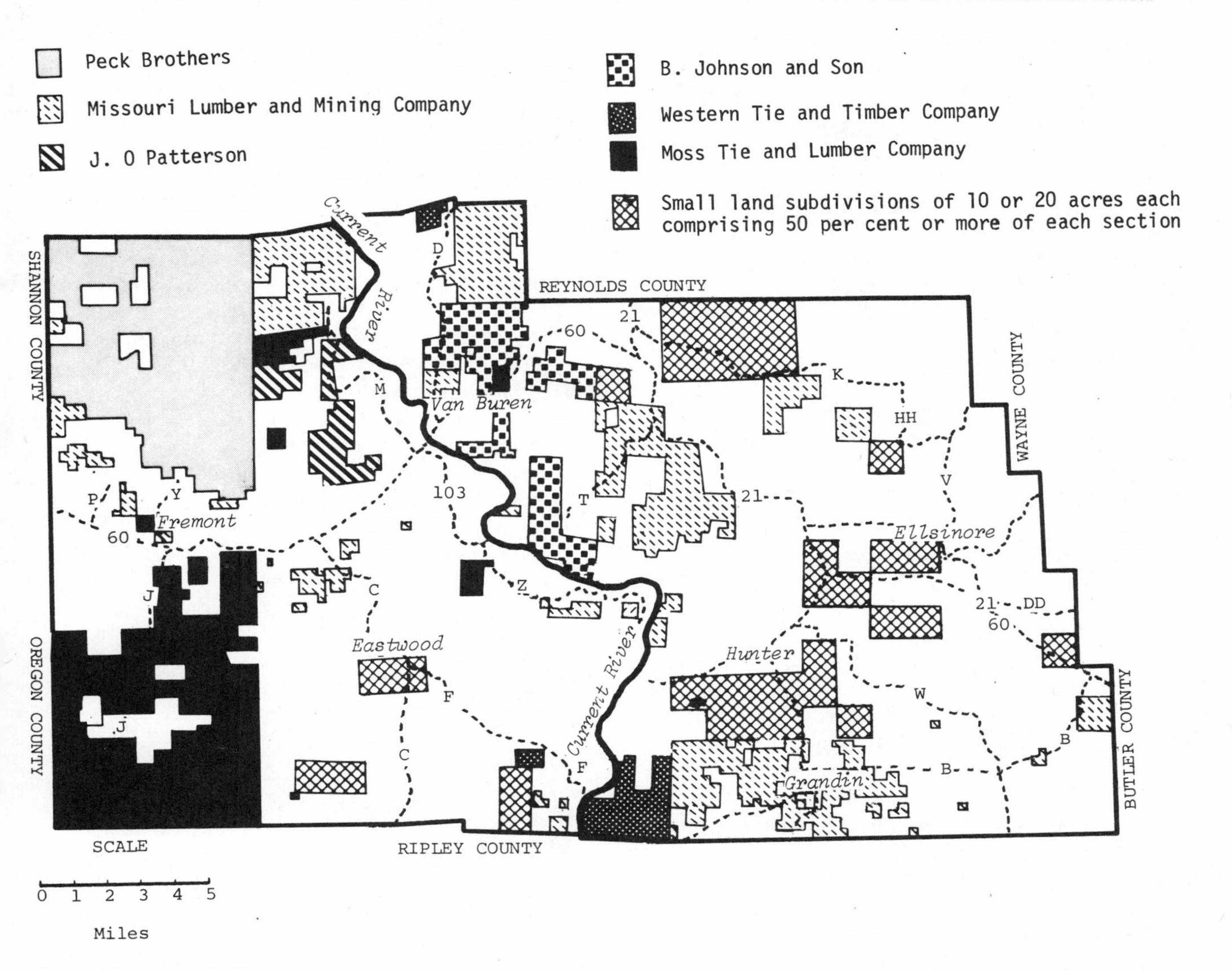

Figure 11-3. Large landholdings in Carter County, Missouri, *circa* 1920. Source: Plat Book of Carter County.

for the company to place some dependence on a local labor supply.

Of equal importance with labor supply as a locational factor were transportation facilities. Local sales of lumber products would be of only slight importance, so there had to be railroads to carry the finished product to market. Thus feeder lines to the St. Louis and Iron Mountain line and the Kansas City, Fort Scott and Memphis were needed. The closest shipping points in the early 1880's were Piedmont and Williamsville on the St. Louis and Iron Mountain, Doniphan on the Doniphan and Neelyville Branch of the St. Louis and Iron Mountain, and Willow Springs on the Kansas City, Fort Scott and Memphis. Until these railroads were built, land held for speculation purposes remained tax delinquent or of low market value.

Another factor that influenced the Pennsylvania capitalists to locate their sawmill in southern

Missouri was the low cost of stumpage for standing timber in the area. The *Fourteenth United States Census report* estimated the average price of stumpage in the nation at $1.89 per 1,000 board feet as late as 1899. During the same year, white pine stumpage in Michigan and Wisconsin cost more than $3.00 per 1,000 board feet; the pine of Missouri averaged $1.22 for stumpage. The timberlands purchased by MLMC cost much less than the estimated average. The first purchases made by O. H. P. Williams were about $1.00 per acre. This would average about $0.25 per thousand stumpage, since pine in the central Ozarks cut about 4,000 board feet to the acre. Some of the land was purchased at higher prices, but a great deal of stumpage was picked up at tax sales for an average price of $0.25 an acre. This meant a cost of only $0.085 per thousand for stumpage. In 1879 and 1880, J. B. White managed to buy, at a sheriff's sale in Carter County, two sections of land for $0.125 an acre.

The Ozarks had become a land of opportunity for lumbermen who were wise enough to get in on the ground floor. Native Ozarkers who had patented the timberland from the government were unable to use it effectively. The soil was rocky and unproductive. The only marketable resource on their property was the standing timber, and the only way to reduce it to a salable commodity required an outlay of capital that the ordinary farmer did not possess. Consequently, a large acreage of fine timberland became tax delinquent and ready to be purchased by speculators or lumber manufacturers (fig. 11-3). The old adage "It takes money to make money" fit the situation.

Often the title to land was cloudy, and it was recognized that once the timber was cut, the land was worth very little. Therefore, it was considered a good business practice to remove the timber from land of unsure title as quickly as possible. One of the most important legal cases in which the Missouri Lumber and Mining Company became involved was the suit involving the B. R. Noble lands, 15,000 acres of pine timber west of the Current River in northern Ripley County. There is probably no better example of the struggle for the big pine in the entire Ozark region. The lands were first purchased by Melvin J. Clark in 1888 as tax-delinquent property. Clark sold the timber to John R. Cook in 1890 and gave a quit-claim deed. B. R. Noble purchased the tract in 1895 and also received a quit-claim deed. Noble sold the lands the same year to Hunter and Grandin, directors of the Missouri Lumber and Mining Company, on a stumpage basis and made a written guarantee of seventy million board feet. Timber cruisers employed by Grandin and Hunter found that the Doniphan Lumber Company, which also claimed the tract, had already begun to remove the timber; when titles to much of the land proved defective, Grandin and Hunter sued Noble. J. B. White, impatient of waiting for legal action, offered to cut the timber if Grandin and Hunter would give the Missouri Lumber and Mining Company a quit-claim deed. The general manager further advised the immediate construction of a tram road directly southwest across Current River because the timber was being cut by rivals. He said:

> They [competitors] have no title and on much of this land our title is so technically imperfect that we could not make ours a basis of action in a suit for damages. The fellow that gets the timber gets it at little or no cost, for not in more than one half the cases will we be able to show up such a title as the court would require, for we cannot stand upon the weakness of their title, but have to stand upon the strength of the perfectness of our own. Carter and Culbertson [Doniphan Lumber Company and Culbertson Stock and Lumber Company] are going into this and won't compromise. . . . We should push energetically ahead into that territory quick. . . . We can get into the best body of timber before they can.[6]

Meanwhile, the Doniphan Lumber Company had ousted Culbertson from the disputed timber and decided to build a tram road from Current River into the heart of the tract. The Missouri Lumber and Mining Company then bought a farm on the proposed route of the tram and refused to grant the Doniphan concern a right-of-way. Finally a compromise was arranged by forming the Missouri Tie and Timber Company, organized by the Missouri Lumber and Mining Company and the Doniphan Lumber Company, which cut the timber. Matters of title to the land were con-

6. Ibid., pp. 282–83.

Mills of the Missouri Lumber and Mining Company at Grandin in Carter County, Missouri.

firmed many years later, long after the last virgin pine had been removed.

The impact of the large lumber companies on the economy, politics, and social life of the region was substantial. The Missouri Lumber and Mining Company built its mills at Lakewood, later renamed Grandin. Land purchases were made in several surrounding counties including, Reynolds, Butler, Carter, Ripley, Shannon, and Wayne. Grandin was selected as the site for the mill because of Tolliver Pond, a large natural body of water that proved to be a perfect place to preserve the logs until they could be sawed in the huge mill. Grandin was also near the center of the vast amount of land MLMC purchased as a cutting area. The first mill was set up in 1880 and put into operation immediately to cut the lumber for a larger mill and to provide the materials for buildings in the town.

The company built about 475 houses just west and north of the mill site, some of which are still standing. Workers could rent a house in Grandin for a very reasonable fee, a dollar a room per month, and it has been said that the houses were very nice for that particular time. In 1906 the company collected $11,836 in rent for one month.

Most of the tools used in the logging operations were made at the company-owned blacksmith shop. J. C. Thompson was boss of the shop, which turned out cant hooks, boomers, and various other tools which were needed. He is reported to have patented several pieces of equipment, including an instrument known as a sheep's foot, which was used to bind the logs down in such a manner as to make it easier to unload the railroad cars when they arrived at the mill. The store at Grandin was owned by the company and employed six to eight clerks on a full-time basis. Almost anything that was needed could be purchased at the commissary. Wild turkeys sold for $0.15 a pound, potatoes were $1.25 a bushel, and other articles were priced accordingly. The store also sold kerosene, the principal use of which was to provide light for the loggers' homes. There were two prices for kerosene, $0.10 and $0.15 per gallon. A logger finally discovered that the only difference in the kerosene was the price. The fuel flowed down a long pipe from a tank on the hill. The pipe forked when it reached the commissary, and the same quality kerosene came from both spigots. From that day forward, even the best kerosene sold for $0.10 per gallon.

The Missouri Lumber and Mining Company inaugurated its medical service in 1890. The facilities consisted of a central dispensary at Grandin, which was staffed by six doctors, a druggist, and two nurses. Field chests, filled with surgical dressings and medicines, were placed with the foremen of small camps so that when the doctor made his regular rounds, usually three times a week, he would have at hand such remedies as were necessary to treat the men. The medical service had the effect of reducing the number of accidents in the outlying camps and the mill area to a mere 10 per cent of the former level in just two years. This dramatic decrease may or may not have been due in part to the following slogans: "Unavoidable accidents rarely occur"; "If a man does not look out for himself no else can do it for him"; and "The over use or abuse of hog meat, hot biscuits, black coffee, tobacco and whiskey are precursors of nearly all disorders of the human system." Needless to say, these sayings gave the men something to think about. The charge for the medical service was rather small. Each family was treated for $1.25 per month, regardless of the number in the family. Single men were charged $0.75 per month, and independent boys and girls were charged $0.40 and $0.25, respectively. These amounts included all medical care; there were no additional charges. In November, 1906, about $800 was collected for medical services.

When the Current River Railroad reached Grandin, it helped to open a whole new aspect of lumber production. The company expanded its own railroad system, which was made up of tramlines. These short lines were used to haul timber from seventy-five acres of land each day. The logs moved from the tramlines to the main line and then to Tolliver Pond at Grandin to await the sawyer's work. Many men and mules were needed to haul the logs to piling areas near the tramlines, where they were then loaded on the log cars. There were usually ten or eleven wagons in each group, and each wagon was pulled by a four-mule team. Each group had approximately one hundred mules in its string so that the animals would not be overworked.

The logging crews went to areas where cutters had felled trees. They carried tents, food and supplies, a portable barn, and hay and grain for their work animals. The Grandin log haulers were hardy and tried to get as much enjoyment from their work as possible. Many of them vied with one another, on various occasions, for the title *Champion Log Hauler*. Firmin Sanders of Van Buren claimed to hold the record for hauling the most board feet in one day. The feat was accomplished in 1904, when Sanders hauled 22,744 board feet of logs in nine hours and forty-five minutes.

After the logs were skidded and hauled to the tramlines, they were loaded onto flatcars and taken to Tolliver Pond at Grandin. A track encircled most of the pond, and the trains unloaded their logs directly into the water. A large sluice ran to the mill from the pond below. The logs were headed into the sluice by lumberjacks, who used pike poles to guide them into the hooks that carried them up the incline to the mill.

The combined capacity of the two mills at Grandin was 220,000 board feet of lumber per day; it was reached by running two ten-hour shifts. Ninety carloads of logs a day were required to keep the mills going. The plant consisted of two sawmills, four planing mills, fourteen drying kilns, and about thirty warehouses. Herman McKinney of Grandin said he took inventory at the plant one Sunday and tallied 30 million board feet of stockpiled lumber.

The pay at Grandin was $1.50 a day, or $0.15 an hour, but some of the men made as little as $1.35 daily. The highest wages were paid for toploading, and people on that particular job received $2.50 a day. The men received their pay on the fifteenth of each month, provided the payroll was not stolen by outlaws along the way. Each worker was paid in cash. Coupons (script) were used only in the event a worker needed to borrow money before payday. He could then go to the company store and draw either a $2.00 or a $5.00 coupon.

Loading logs, Ozark Land and Lumber Company. (Courtesy Missouri State Historical Society.)

He received his merchandise, was given his change, and the total amount was charged against his next paycheck.

In 1900 the company employed approximately 1,200 persons, and Grandin's population was about 3,000. The boom continued until September, 1910, when the mill whistle blew for the last time. By 1911 all the equipment had been moved to West Eminence and J. B. White started selling land and houses. The houses fetched fifty dollars to one hundred dollars each. By 1938, Grandin had shrunk to about 300 persons. In that year Missouri Highway 21 was built through the area, providing a better means of travel and helping to connect Grandin to the outside world; however, the Frisco found it unprofitable to continue rail service to the town. But Grandin survived. Today the mill site shows but few vestiges of a lost past. One can no longer hear the buzz of the huge saw, the shouts of the workers, the roar of the locomotives. It could well be said of those men in Grandin's past: "They came, they worked, they left their mark."

As 1979 began, Grandin had about 250 residents, many of whom were engaged in small-scale timber or farming operations. If one lounges on the store porches today, he may well hear the old men talk of the great boom, or hear of the fire that burned constantly for thirty years. The fire is extinguished now; the boom is no more.

The life of the Grandin mills was extended in 1901 through the acquisition of nearly forty thousand acres of land in Shannon County from J. H. Berkshire.[7] The price of $1.50 per acre was the highest ever paid by the Missouri Lumber and Mining Company, but it added much territory to the firm's holdings. In 1909, Missouri Lumber and Mining built a new mill and the town of West Eminence in Shannon County. A hub mill and a shingle mill were added.

Many camps were established to cut, turn, and load timber to be hauled to the mills. Among those in Shannon County were Angeline, Camp Ten, Camp Twelve, Bert George Camp, Camp Five, Camp Six, and Hartshorn-Bryant Camp. Camp Twelve was the largest; it included a grocery store, a doctor's office, a barn, and several houses.[8]

The company operated large stores at Grandin and West Eminence. The latter was particularly striking for the time and place. It had several departments, including dry goods of all kinds, groceries, hardware, a shoe shop, and a butcher shop. One of the main places of entertainment was the ice cream parlor next to the general store. Prices and commodities reflect the time and pattern of life: sugar, a nickel a pound; flour, thirty-five cents for a twenty-four-pound bag; work overalls with bib, fifty cents; blue chambray shirts, fifteen cents and twenty-five cents each; good work gloves, twenty-five cents; and the best calico was six cents a yard, gingham ten.

Land Disposal

The lumber companies brought people and temporary prosperity. Towns grew up around mills, flourished for a time, passed into rapid decline, then slow attrition. In 1903, Winona, Missouri, had between one thousand and one thousand two hundred people, about two and a half times its present population. In 1903, people were confident that there would be a Winona long after the Ozark Land and Lumber Company had passed on, and the mill was expected to live at least ten more years because the company was at that time still buying more land.

The principal owner of Ozark Land and Lumber Company was Benjamin Hershey, a successful businessman, lumberman, and land speculator from Muscatine, Iowa.[9] This breed of investor expected high profit margins, from $5.00 to $5.50 per 100 board feet. The overall logging cost per 1,000 board feet in 1892 was $2.66, and that year the Ozark Land and Lumber Company sawed 55,529 logs, which gave the mill a tally of 6,454,560 board feet. Considering the large volume of lumber and the low cost of production, profits were large. When cheap stumpage was no longer available, the mills were closed, the machinery sold, the rails taken up and sold as scrap. Investment capital was withdrawn from the Ozarks for more lucrative ventures in other areas; much was used to purchase timber properties in Louisiana and in the Douglas-fir country of Washington and Oregon.

By 1915 the Ozark Land and Lumber Company had completed the removal of timber from its holdings and had changed its principal business from making lumber to selling real estate. The disposal methods varied, but the most common was selling through the mails. A nationwide advertising campaign describing the Ozarks as sheep and cattle country and as a fruit-growing region was used to good advantage. Large amounts of land were sold, sight unseen. The Missouri Lumber and Mining Company not only placed newspaper ads widely but published booklets and brochures and employed the services of a land agent. A few examples from an advertising booklet for a 28,000-acre tract in Ripley County, Missouri, will serve to illustrate one way in which Ozark imagery was created:

> The land is to be sold in blocks of 80 to 1,000 acres at $3.50 to $12.50 per acre on terms of one-fifth down, the remainder in four equal annual installments. Those who first come to see the land will have choice selections.
>
> The owners of this vast tract of virgin land offer it to

7. Ibid., p. 259.

8. Judy Ferguson, *The Boom Town of West Eminence and Its Lumbering Days* (Rolla, Mo.: Rolla Printing Company, 1969), p. 37.

9. James W. Martin and Jerry J. Presley, "Ozark Land and Lumber Company: Organization and Operations" (unpublished manuscript, School of Forestry, University of Missouri, January 31, 1958), p. 8.

those who will develop it. After studying the resources of the country for 25 years, and witnessing many experiments, they can unhesitatingly recommend this for stock and dairy farms, with small family orchards, vineyards, some alfalfa and forage crops. We sincerely believe that these will make an ideal money making combination and that the buyers will succeed beyond doubt. We do not cater to the land speculator, because we wish to see this country developed.

This is a fertile virgin land. It contains limestone. It has produced trees of wonderful size. It now produces a rank growth of blue stem grass. The rainfall averages 40 inches, the country is not very rough or mountainous, but is undulating, with some high plateaus. There are numerous creeks, springs, small lakes, and one stream of considerable size, the Current River.

Everywhere through the countryside you find peace, happiness, independence and contentment. "It is the country of the little red hen and the much read Bible," said a prominent statesman who spent a vacation on Current River.

Think of getting enough timber on the land to make most of your improvements. Think of having the eternal springs gush forth for your livestock, of not having to erect big barns to protect your stock, of being able to raise just as much on this land, with almost as little labor as on land ten times as valuable.

It will be the means of founding your fortune.

Five hundred acres costs you, say $3,000. In five years you have it developed and paid for. You sell for $25,000. Can you beat it elsewhere? This is our first land opening. The prices are LOW. They will be increased. Terms are EASY. Titles GOOD, your treatment will be FAIR and SQUARE.

Come; let me show you.

Native Ozakers no doubt scoffed at the land agents' claims, particularly the descriptions of the inherent fertility of the soil. Remarked one Ozarker when he was asked if the lands measured up to the claims: "Yes, and you can go to hell for lying the same as stealing." Yet it is interesting that sixty years later these lands are selling for $250 to $500 an acre and are becoming scarcer each year because people are reluctant to sell as land prices continue to increase. Ozarkers consider themselves to be sharp traders in land, and it is a face-losing thing to have sold out too cheap.

Sometimes the land was divided into lots and sold as such. The Ozark Land and Lumber Company even went so far as to lay out a town and sell lots for homes. A few demonstration farms were established to grow wheat, rye, livestock, and fruit, but these were mainly half-hearted efforts designed to dispose of land.

Eventually much of the cutover land became tax delinquent and was purchased by the U.S. Forest Service in the 1930's. Ozark National Forest in Arkansas included mainly cutover lands in the Boston Mountains. In Missouri the eastern cutover land became Clark National Forest; such land in southwest Missouri formed Mark Twain National Forest. The Peck Brothers holdings in northwest Carter County and adjacent parts of Shannon County was the first large purchase by the newly formed Missouri Conservation Commission to be developed as the Peck Ranch Wildlife Area.

The Effects of the Lumber Era

The timber boom resulted in a seriously depleted resource base and a greatly increased population, which, in order to sustain itself, continued to strain the natural resources of the area. Because many of the people who came to exploit the timber had established close ties in their neighborhoods, they were reluctant to move away when the timber was gone. Many of them remained, purchased cutover tracts, and began farming.

As was noted earlier, most of the large holdings that had been cut over were subdivided and sold off as farms. The effects of this subdivision in the timbered areas may be seen in census statistics. Stone County, Missouri, had a net loss of only seven farms in the decade 1910 to 1920, and Christian County, where more cutover land was sold, experienced a moderate gain in the number of farms. Most counties outside the timber area had decreases in number of farms. Many of the large properties were eventually broken up and sold, mainly to former "tie hackers" who had been thrown out of work by the closing of the mills.

Contributing to the rapid sale of cutover land were stories that a good living could be made raising strawberries and tomatoes on the ridgetops that had been cleared. For a time during the 1920's, strawberry growing became so popular that newcomers lived in tents and raised strawberries at Logan's Ridge, a community in Christian County, Missouri, However, the demand for tomatoes and strawberries declined when more favorably situated areas came into production, and after other crops were tried and proved unsuccessful, the emphasis shifted to livestock operations. Open-range grazing on cutover lands became common, and timber burning to increase forage was practiced extensively. Both of these practices delayed restoration of the timber.

As crop agriculture proved unprofitable and as forest resources were depleted even further, people began to move away. Most of those who remained suffered a reduced standard of living. The overall economy became stagnated and largely subsistence in type. The farm supplied milk, meat, and vegetables for the table, but little else, while money for those things that could not be produced on the farm sometimes could be earned through part-time employment in the small canneries or in the stave mills, ax-handle factories, or small sawmills that were sustained by timber left behind in the more inaccessible places.

The destruction of the forest cover caused serious depletion of related resources. The journals of early travelers and settlers contain many references to the plentiful supply of wild game. By the mid-1930's the populations of many wildlife species had been seriously depleted, partly because of the destruction of their natural habitat and partly because the low level of living encouraged the residents to engage in unrestricted hunting to supplement their food supply. In 1937, when the Missouri Conservation Commission was founded, the deer population of Missouri had been reduced to an all-time low of three thousand five hundred. Many other species of wildlife experienced similar decreases in population.

Soil erosion was accelerated by destruction of the forest cover and by attempts to convert steep slopes and rocky ridges to cropland. The soils of the hillier timber areas are shallow to begin with, being no more than four to eight inches deep, and those of the level areas are only slightly deeper. Destruction of the forests and the successive burning of the woods destroyed the leaf litter and organic matter, which acted to absorb rainfall, prevent excessive runoff, and retard the rate of soil erosion.

By 1935, soil erosion had become serious on much of the cutover lands. The severity of erosion depends primarily upon the degree of cultivation of the land and the extent to which the woodland has been burned over. Where burning was practiced repeatedly, appreciable erosion has occurred, and where the land has been cultivated, serious sheet and gully erosion has occurred. In places where a fair stand of timber remained, erosion was moderate; probably, slightly more than one-fourth of the original soil has been lost. The unprotected slopes have lost about half of their soil.

Reduction of forest cover and organic material that mantled the soil caused many springs to go dry. In the early days, springs were so plentiful that there was little need for dug wells. Almost without exception, homesteaders carried water from nearby springs. In the vicinity of Chadwick, Missouri, where lumbering was very active, many of the large springs went dry. One was Bubbling Spring, which supplied water for the settlement and lumber mill on Springdale Ranch. Today it is so choked with rocks, clay, and debris washed from the adjacent slopes that it is hardly visible.

The Era of Forest Management

The era of forest management dates from the 1930's, when national forests were established in the Ozarks and the Missouri Conservation Commission was created. Progress in management and improvement has been continuous, and today national forests in Missouri and Arkansas comprise approximately twenty per cent of the Ozark Upland.

The two national forests of the Ozarks—Ozark National Forest in Arkansas and Mark Twain National Forest in Missouri—are made up of several separate districts. They were designated respectively in 1908 and 1933. They contain much private land. Usually, private owners hold the cleared valleys and the land along the well-traveled roads that follow the ridges, and the U.S. Forest Service controls most of the upland area, especially away from the better roads. The forests and related natural resources have benefited in two ways: the condition of the forests on federally owned land has been improved significantly by the multiple use–sustained yield principle of Forest Service management; private owners have, in some cases, begun to adopt some of the management practices used by the Forest Service. And the privately owned land has benefited from technical assistance and fire protection provided by the Forest Service.

The purchase of forest land, which began in 1934, reduced its population. In Linn Township, Christian County, Missouri, where approximately half the land is federally owned, the population declined from 527 in 1930 to 382 in 1960, a decrease of 45 per cent. Although a few residents stayed on the land for a time under special-use permits, most were required to move. The decrease in population resulted in a reduction of pressure on the depleted resource base, for many of these people had operated general farms at or near the subsistence level and had relied on the forest to produce a small amount of cash income. At near-subsistence levels of living, proper forest management was impossible. Posts, firewood, and stave bolts were cut from immature timber to provide money for necessities.

Fire control proved to be an especially difficult problem. The traditional practice of burning the woods to green up the grass hampered early fire-control efforts. This was especially true in the Pine Ridge community in Christian County, where the number of incendiary fires was so high for a time that the area became known outside the Ozarks as a fire-control problem area. Twain National Forest records show that two hundred to six hundred fires occurred annually in the Ava District until about 1960. Some of these fires were incendiary, set by individuals to obtain work as firefighters. Probably, improved economic conditions and the availability of employment in nonfarm jobs has contributed to the reduction in the number of forest fires. Also helping have been educational efforts promoting forest conservation and opposing woods burning. By 1968 the number of fires in the Ava District had been reduced to only twenty-three.

A new experimental fire-control program, Operation Outreach, has been inaugurated. It is designed to give farmers U.S. Forest Service technical advice on the use of fire as a forest and grassland management technique. In particular, the Forest Service provides meteorological and climatological information, as well as data on soils and plant life, so that prescribed burning can be undertaken safely and at times when results will be the most beneficial. In general, fall burning is preferred, since there is less damage to trees and the humus layer than would occur in a spring burn. Certainly it is paradoxical that firing the woods, which has retarded restoration of Ozark forests and long has been the enemy of the Forest Service, must be taught to the Ozark farmer. This is especially true when the education program is being undertaken in a former fire-control problem area.

Open-range grazing was practiced throughout the Ozark region, but laws requiring confinement of animals were gradually voted in over the years, either by countywide election or piecemeal, by townships. Often, laws requiring confinement of small animals were enacted, but because larger tracts of land had to be fenced to confine the larger animals, the latter were allowed to forage freely several years longer. The first stock-confinement law in the western Ozarks was voted in Greene County, Missouri, in 1890; confinement of hogs, goats, and sheep passed 3,364 to 1,980, but confinement of horses, mules, asses, and cattle passed by the narrower margin of 3,095 to 2,164. The last county stock law to be passed in Missouri was enacted in Stone County in 1960. This marked the end of open-range grazing except in some parts of Mark Twain National Forest. Open-range grazing is now prohibited throughout Missouri; the local-option stock laws were repealed, effective January 1, 1969, by the Seventy-fourth General Assembly.

The decline of open-range grazing has followed the development of commercial agriculture, especially livestock farming. Well-informed livestock farmers know that open-range grazing and good forage management are incompatible. However, it should be noted that the livestock-confinement laws are not always enforced rigidly in the interior Ozarks.

Open range in the national forest has been made illegal, although it has not been widely prac-

Cracking black walnuts by hand at Fordland, Missouri, 1931. (Courtesy of W. A. Hagel, Kansas City, Missouri.)

ticed for some time. Since January 1, 1969, stray cattle on Forest Service land have been impounded and the person who claimed them has been subject to fine. Because the national forest contains rocky balds and glades and grassland tracts where the forests have been cleared, the Forest Service leases land to individuals for summer and winter pasturage. Income from this helps support fire control and forest management, but one-fourth of it reverts to the county governments for construction and maintenance of roads.

Several timber-management practices are used on the Forest Service lands. Because most of the timber is slow growing and in some places commercial timber production is not possible, much of the land is managed for aesthetic and recreational purposes. Only on the better land is timber-managed for commercial lumber production.

Salvage and improvement cutting are used in commercial timber stands. Fire-damaged and diseased trees are removed to make room for new growth; many contain usable wood. In the case of short-leaf pine, reforestation on favorable sites is used. This tree has a faster growth rate than the hardwoods, but it will grow well only where conditions are favorable.

Many small sawmills continue to be active. They produce stave bolts, pallet lumber, oak flooring, posts and poles, and a small amount of dimension lumber, including some timber from the national forests, sold on the stump to the highest bidder. Much of the timber is hauled considerable distances to be milled. Pulp timber is hauled out of the eastern Ozarks by rail, truck, and river barge to paper mills on the Lower Mississippi. The Independent Stave Company at Lebanon, Missouri, the largest manufacturer of whiskey barrels, purchases high-quality white-oak stave bolts from widely scattered green mills.

The glade lands, a natural environment distinctive of the Ozarks, require special management, and the Forest Service has conducted research to determine the best long-range management practices for them. They are managed primarily for watershed protection, grazing, and aesthetic purposes. Management of red cedar for market purposes was under intensive study in 1979.

The wildlife and recreational values of the national forests cannot be calculated precisely, but the forests are free for public use and the paved roads are traveled heavily on weekends and holidays by people from the Springfield vicinity and from Kansas City, Tulsa, Memphis, St. Louis, and places even more distant. This is especially true in the spring, when the new foliage appears and the dogwood is in bloom, and again in the fall, when the autumn colors are fully developed. Additional paved roads undoubtedly would facilitate fuller use of the more inaccessible parts of the forests for recreational purposes, but there would be a corresponding loss in aesthetic values. The steep, forest-crowded hillside trails, which cross clear streams on gravel bars, are unquestionably rough and require slow travel, but they offer some of the least disturbed natural scenery in the Ozarks.

On the whole, a rather low level of management is applied to privately owned forest lands. The prospects for quality timber are not good in many parts of the Ozarks; in the southwest they are poorer than anywhere else. Forty per cent of the trees are cull, and another thirty per cent should be harvested soon because they are too old or defective to manage for commercial products;

only thirty per cent are suitable for future management.[10]

Cutting practices are not conducive to sustained-yield timber production. The volume in small trees continues to increase; larger timber of preferred species, both hardwoods and pine, is being cut at a faster rate than it is growing. The supply of high-quality timber has declined steadily over the years, and unless this trend is reversed, local timber industries may encounter shortages of good-quality timber.

Most owners do not expect to gain sustained revenue from woodlands. They regard the occasional receipts from the sale of stave-bolt-quality oak, veneer-quality walnut, or the sale of black walnuts for hulling purposes as windfall money or perhaps as a reserve source of income in times of emergency.

A small number of private owners are vindictive toward the national forest. Often the low regard for the U.S. Forest Service springs from ignorance of the benefits that can accrue through good management techniques, and from misinformation concerning the operations of the Forest Service. One property owner whose land borders on the national forest remarked that he was inclined not to like the Forest Service because "they pay no taxes to keep up the roads." He also expressed the belief that forest management, as practiced by the Forest Service, was unprofitable, and he did not like the fire control crews "to come running every time I burn." He indicated that he recognized that burning in the spring is not considered a good forest- and range-management practice, but he felt the losses were small and believed burning the woods helped to control ticks, chiggers, and copperheads. Attitudes like this represent an element of persistence, a traditional, if not pioneer, concept of man-land relationships.

Forest management on private lands has been aided by the state conservation departments. The conservation departments were founded in all of the Ozark states in the 1930's to promote wildlife and forest conservation and to furnish fire protection and technical advice to property owners.

10. David A. Ganser, *Timber Resources of Missouri's Southwestern Ozarks*, University of Missouri Bulletin B845 (Columbia: January, 1966).

Walnut huller at a crossroads store, 1972.

Throughout the heavily forested parts of the Ozarks, the commissions maintain a network of fire towers backed up by trained fire-control crews.

Technical advice on timber management is provided through the Farm Forester Program. State forestry laws provide incentive for long-range management of farm woodlands. Woodland tracts that meet certain qualifications may be declared forest cropland and are thereafter subject to minimal property taxation until the timber is harvested. When the timber is harvested, a yield tax, based on the value of the stumpage, is applied. These acts grant the state additional powers in assisting landowners in the enforcement of state laws on timber theft, a continuing problem on both public and private land.

Solutions to the problems of managing forest resources and producing and using wood products lie with timber owners and the industries that harvest and process these products. Nonfarm ownership of forest land is increasing steadily. Frequently, this land is purchased for purposes other than timber production; probably, most urban buyers expect higher recreational value in addition to capital gain as land values increase. Much land is advertised in the newspapers of Springfield, St. Louis, Joplin, Kansas City, Little Rock, Tulsa, and even more remote places as country recreational estates or potential homesites of ten to forty acres. Unless changes in ownership result in consolidation of some of these holdings, the management decisions made by owners of small tracts of timber will largely determine the future of the forest resources of the area.

Recent forest-management trends that promise increased returns from forest land include: *Establishment and management of planted and mature stands of black walnut*. The rate of planting has increased sharply during the past ten years. Many thousands of seedlings are planted each year in Mark Twain and Ozark national forests as part of a twenty-year improvement program. Improvement and management of seedling walnut is becoming more common on private lands. *More plantings of short-leaf pine*. Nearly all have been on public lands. In Mark Twain National Forest, more than a million pine seedlings are planted each year and another one thousand two hundred acres per year are direct-seeded to pine. *Conversion of unproductive timberland to grass through aerial spraying and bulldozing.* Aerial spraying has been used successfully at Union Gap Experiment Station in Mark Twain National Forest to convert unproductive timberland to pasture. Spraying and bulldozing of wooded areas on private land, practiced widely, were discussed earlier.

Selected References

Baver, L. D. "Soil Erosion in Missouri," University of Missouri Agricultural Experiment Station Research Bulletin no. 349, 1935.

Britton, Wiley. *Pioneer Life in Southwest Missouri*. Kansas City: Smith Grieves Co., Publishers, 1929.

Christian County: Its First Hundred Years. Ozark, Mo.: Christian County Centennial, Inc., 1959.

Cole, Lela. "The Early Tie Industry Along the Niangua River," *Missouri Historical Review* 48 (fall 1953): 264–72.

Ferguson, Judy. *The Boom Town of West Eminence and Its Lumbering Days*. Rolla, Mo.: Rolla Printing Co., 1969.

Ganser, David A. *Timber Resources of the Missouri Prairie Region. Bulletin B797*. Columbia: University of Missouri, July 1963.

———. *Timber Resources of Missouri's Southwestern Ozarks. Bulletin B845*. Columbia: University of Missouri, January 1966.

———. *Timber Resources of Missouri's River Border Region. Bulletin B846*. Columbia: University of Missouri, 1966.

———. *Timber Resources of Missouri's Northwestern Ozarks. Bulletin B847*. Columbia: University of Missouri, 1966.

Garland, John H., ed. *The North American Midwest: A Regional Geography*. New York: John Wiley and Sons, 1955.

Hill, Leslie G. "History of the Missouri Lumber and Mining Company, 1880–1909." Ph.D. dissertation, University of Missouri-Columbia, 1949.

Hull, Clifton E. *Shortline Railroads of Arkansas*. Norman: University of Oklahoma Press, 1969.

Ingenthron, Elmo. *The Land of Taney*. Point Lookout, Mo.: The School of the Ozarks Press, 1974.

Martin, James W., and Presley, Jerry J. "Ozark Land and Lumber Company: Organization and Operations." Unpublished manuscript, School of Forestry, University of Missouri-Columbia, January 31, 1958.

Myers, J. K., and R. C. Smith. "Wood Products and Missouri's Forests," Missouri Economic Study no. 6. Columbia, University of Missouri School of Business and Public Administration Research Center, 1965.

Rafferty, Milton D. "Persistence Versus Change in Land Use and Landscape in the Springfield, Missouri, Vicinity of the Ozarks." Ph.D. dissertation, University of Nebraska, 1970.

Schoolcraft, Henry Rowe. *Journal of a Tour into the Interior of Missouri and Arkansas in 1818 and 1819*. 1821. In *Schoolcraft in the Ozarks*, edited by Hugh Park. Van Buren, Ark.: Press-Argus Printers, 1955.

12. Recreation and Tourism

It is difficult to separate the booming Ozarks tourist-recreation industry into its component parts. Recreation and tourism go hand in hand, and the growing second-home and retirement-home industry is part of the same package. When all the ancillary services and multiplier effects on employment are considered, it is a multibillion-dollar industry in the Ozarks.

Considered in its popular sense, recreation includes all the leisure-time activities that people pursue for their own pleasure. In all periods of history, men and women probably have spent the greater part of their leisure in informal talk, in visiting and entertaining friends, in casual walks and strolls, and sometimes in reading for their own amusement. These simpler activities are hidden in the obscurity that shrouds private lives, however; organized public recreation consciously has been adopted as the basis for this account.

Before we progress into discussion of the historical geography of Ozark tourism and recreation, it will be helpful to review the factors that have influenced the development of these industries in the United States. First is the continuing influence of inherent puritanism, which, even today, insists that amusements should at least make some pretense of serving socially useful ends: to keep fit; for education; to promote higher cultural standards; to recapture one's inherited past. Second, our economy has been transformed from the simplicity of the agricultural era to the complexity of the machine age. Concomitantly, cities have grown and the machine has increased the leisure of the laboring masses, simultaneously making life less leisurely.

The forms of traditional entertainment practiced by Ozarkers will be discussed in a later chapter, but at this point we can state that in the years before the Civil War the first Ozark settlers shared a common heritage with most of their fellow countrymen in the remainder of the rural United States. Dancing and "frisking together" was discouraged, as were gaming, cockfighting, and horse racing. Hunting and fishing were very popular, as were camp meetings and the usual church services. In the cities, organized sports became popular, and theatre forged ahead. Circuses were very popular. Horse races, foot races, rowing and sailing, and prizefighting became important spectator sports for the masses. If women had any leisure time, they sometimes took up embroidery, quilting, painting on glass or china, and waxwork—with commendable perseverance—and sometimes devastating results.

By midcentury pleasure travel had been well established, and the first summer resorts had been built. The new trend had been signaled in 1825 with the appearance of a little booklet called

The Fashionable Tour. The establishment of summer resorts in the East came as a direct result of improved transportation. New York had the most fashionable of all: Saratoga Springs. In the South, White Sulphur Springs was the place where wealthy plantation owners made their hegira. Many of these visitors were seeking not so much rest or amusement as the establishment of their position in the social world. Wrote one astute observer:

> Hundreds, who, in their own towns could not find admittance into the circles of fashionable society came to Saratoga where . . . they may be seated at the same table, and often side by side, with the first families of the country.[1]

The deep verandas of huge, sprawling Congress House and United States Hotel and the neat gravel walks cutting across Saratoga's spacious, well-mowed lawns served as models for accommodations at resorts that sprung up throughout the United States. The style and grace of the great resorts, with their courting yards, frock-coated gentlemen, and modish ladies in billowing hoopskirts, has never been equaled in the history of American recreation and tourism.

Probably more than any other single factor, the automobile and construction of good roads revolutionized American tourism and recreation. At first automobiles were for the rich, not so much because of the initial cost, but because of the cost of upkeep. In the early days of auto touring, vast preparations were made for a day's run. Among the items of necessary extra equipment were a full set of tools, elaborate tire-changing apparatus, a pail of water for overheated brakes, extra sparkplugs, tire chains for muddy roads, and a rear basket with a concealed reserve gasoline supply. Special motoring clothes were both functional and stylish. A hundred miles was considered an excellent day's run, and even then there had to be a lot of "sprinting" at thirty miles an hour to get over such a long distance.

By the 1930's the total number of automobiles on the road had reached twenty-five million, enough that two-thirds of the nation's families had one. The automobile of the 1930's was longer and lower, showing a definite trend toward streamlining, and with a larger more powerful engine it could pull a trailer, which by now had made its appearance as a further boon to vacationists.

After World War II the Sunday-afternoon spin, which had become so popular before the war, was replaced by a weekend trip; the vacation tour could easily span the continent. Apart from the new freeways, turnpikes, throughways, and interstate highways (to say nothing of the new cars themselves), there was a spectacular development in tourist accommodations. Primitive overnight cabins gave way to the luxurious motels demanded by an increasingly affluent society.

At the same time, the automobile continued—in what has been called Operation Outdoors—to encourage camping in national parks and forests. Hundreds of thousands of vacationing families in heavily laden sedans, pickup campers, vans, and motor homes set out intrepidly every summer to explore the wilds. Because of the large number of lakes that have been built in all sections the country, a large share of the vehicles now pull boats of assorted types. In short, the automobile has given an entirely new dimension to recreation life, which could hardly be more universal in reaching all strata of the nation's population.

Tourism and Recreation in the Ozarks

From a geographic standpoint, the Ozarks possesses unusually good resources for recreation and tourism. It is the only major upland area in the midsection of the country west of the Mississippi River. For people traveling by automobile, it is the principal hilly region for many who have only a three- or four-day weekend to spend. Des Moines, Omaha, St. Louis, Kansas City, Memphis, Little Rock, Dallas, Fort Worth, Tulsa, Oklahoma City, Wichita, and Topeka are all within an easy day's drive of some part of the Ozarks. In a long day's drive, tourists from Chicago can reach the Ozarks. It is from these large cities and their environs that most of the visitors to the Ozarks are drawn.

The region has tremendous variety in scenic beauty. The landscape is remarkably picturesque, with uplands broken into hills by beautiful water courses. Bedrock limestones have been carved

1. Dixon Wecter, *The Saga of American Society* (New York: C. Scribner's Sons, 1937), p. 437.

into sharp relief by rivers and small streams that flow into the branching arms of more than a dozen large reservoirs. Most of the hills are covered with hardwoods, mainly oaks, but with scattered clumps of maple, sycamore, and sumac that lend brilliant color to fall scenery. Cedar glades, stands of pine, and grassy balds add scenic variety to panoramic views. The climate is mild compared to that of the middle western states, and many of the region's attractions are related to the seasonal change in climate. Automobile touring is especially popular in April, when the dogwood is in bloom, and in late October, when the varied hardwoods produce their flaming fall review. Nevertheless, the chief disadvantage for the tourism-recreation businessman is the fact that winters are too cold for outdoor activity and there is not enough snow to support winter sports. Many tourist-recreation attractions shut down four or five months and use the slack season to make repairs, build additions, and prepare for the next summer season.

For many the culture and history of the Ozarks is a major attraction. The so-called hillbilly culture, whether real or imagined, has gained wide reputation, and thousands of men and women with hideaway tendencies and a preference for casual living have found the Ozarks a pleasant refuge. Furthermore, compared to many other recreation areas, the cost of an Ozarks vacation is usually less.

For purposes of discussion, I have divided tourism and recreation in the Ozarks into five sections: Health Spas and Springs; Rivers and Float Trips; Hunting and Wilderness Sports; The Lakes; and Promotion and Development.

Health Spas and Springs

The growth of health spas in the Ozarks was part of the economic development that followed the Civil War and the modification of the more severe aspects of Reconstruction. The whole country was experiencing prosperity, and money was becoming more plentiful. The taste for travel had revived, and mountain resorts, mineral springs, and waterfront resorts were serving large crowds. The arts of healing—spiritual, mental, and physical—were influenced by movements never felt before. Faith cures became popular, and in Boston, Mary Baker Eddy published the textbook *Science and Health, with Key to the Scriptures*, which was gaining adherents to the Christian Science movement. In Europe and in the East, thousands made pilgrimages to the various spas where curative properties of water were claimed. In retrospect, it is no surprise that the spring water that came out of the ground in such abundance in the Ozarks also healed. Of particular importance to the health spas that sprang up there was the yellow-fever epidemic that claimed hundreds of lives in the Mississippi Valley during the 1880's. Many people searched out more healthful locations, high and away from the swamplands along the river.

The mineral waters of the Ozarks may be classified into four major categories: muriatic, containing as their main constituents sodium chloride, or common salt; alkaline, containing sodium carbonate with or without magnesium carbonate; sulfatic, containing one or more sulfates as their main constituent; and chalybeate, which contain ferrous (iron) carbonate, magnesium carbonate, and sodim carbonate.

The mineral springs of the Ozarks were used to treat a wide range of diseases. Testimonials told of cures, and frequently a particular spring was singled out as having peculiar qualities for a specific disease. Both internal and external use of the water was recommended in most cases, but usually no specific quantities were mentioned. A report of the time suggested how to drink it:

> As to the manner of drinking a mineral water, much depends on time, circumstances and individuality. Quantity, it must be borne in mind, is an important factor, but a just measure of moderation is here likewise necessary. The time-honored custom of rising early and taking before breakfast one to four glasses of water, amounting to not more than a quart in all, is to be recommended. The water should be taken slowly, glass by glass, allowing an interval of a few minutes between the first and second and between the third and fourth glasses, and from ten to twenty minutes between the second and third; this latter interval should be passed in walking and a walk of a half mile or a mile at the end is recommended. In the case of the stronger mineral waters this morning potion is sufficient and is preferable to taking the water at any other time of the day. Chalybeate and other less potent

> waters may be taken differently and in larger quantity. The time which experience has set for a "cure" with these latter waters, under ordinary conditions, should be reckoned at not less than four weeks; a shortening of this period by greater daily consumption of water is unwise and sometimes even dangerous.[2]

The most well known of Ozark spas was Eureka Springs, Arkansas (fig. 12-1). Not only did development proceed so rapidly that Eureka Springs took on the trappings of a boom town, but the construction of hotels, bathhouses, and summer homes proceeded in a more substantial and complete manner than at any other place. The pattern was not unlike that at other large resorts: first, a remarkable healing of a well-known figure, in this case Judge L. B. Sanders of nearby Berryville, Arkansas; next, word-of-mouth advertising of the healing powers of the waters; then the attraction of large crowds, who camped out or lived in temporary shelters; and, finally, the establishment of grocery stores, hotels, bathhouses, livery stables, and all other necessary conveniences.

Judge Sanders visited the springs in 1879, and by July 4 of that year, four hundred people had been attracted to the waters that had rendered a remarkable cure to the judge's chronic case of erysipelas. Soon, four communities had grown up around the main springs: Basin Spring Community, Harding Spring Community, Evansville, and South Eureka Community. By April, 1880, the population of the town was estimated at various numbers, even as high as fifteen thousand. A federal decennial census taken that year recorded three thousand residents who could claim permanent residence for voting purposes.

By the early 1880's, Eureka Water from Basin Spring was being bottled and shipped in all directions. As early as 1881 the temporary business buildings and boardinghouses were being replaced with more permanent structures. Several promoters helped to publicize Eureka Springs and to develop hotels and businesses. Foremost among them were the members of the Eureka Springs Improvement Company, some of whom have been mentioned as leaders of the progressive movement that swept through the Ozarks after the Civil War. The company's directors were headed by Powell Clayton, former governor of Arkansas, president; A. H. Foote of St. Louis, secretary; and Logan H. Roots, a prominant Little Rock financier, treasurer. These men were instrumental in promoting the Eureka Springs Railroad Company in 1882 and constructing the elegant Crescent Hotel in 1886. Built of native Ozark stone in American Gothic style, the Crescent was the showplace of northwest Arkansas.

June Westfall and Catherine Osterhage in their book, *A Fame Not Easily Forgotten*, tell of the Crescent's gracious southern hospitality:

> An army of white coated servitors catered to the slightest whim of each guest. Meals featured the true Southern cuisine and tall frosty mint juleps were to be had at all times, served on the shady porches and walks.

The Crescent put on gala balls in its elegant ballroom, and picnics, streetcar rides, horseback riding, carriage rides, and hiking were pleasant diversions.

After 1908 the hotel was operated as a college and for a period in the 1930's as a hospital operated by Norman Baker, a flamboyant protégé of the notorious Dr. Brinkley of Kansas. In recent years the Crescent has been restored and its popularity is increasing because of its connection with the past splendor of Eureka Springs.

Altogether, more than fifty hotels of various sizes appeared in Eureka Springs during its first fifty years. Only the Crescent, Basin Park, and New Orleans survive. The hotels and bathhouses here and at other springs in the Ozarks were built at the end of the era when "taking the waters" was popular. Mental attitudes throughout the United States changed soon after the springs first received publicity. Mandatory free education helped to widen mental horizons and led to critical examination of the actual healing value of the spring water. By the end of World War I the medical profession had a firm hold on the minds of most people, and medicine and surgery seemed the most legitimate means to alleviate pain and suffering. Many visitors continued to return to Eureka Springs out of habit, but as the following passage notes, the scene changed rapidly:

2. Paul Schweitzer. "A Report on the Mineral Waters of Missouri," *Geological Survey of Missouri*, 1st. Series, 3 (1892): 30.

Crescent Hotel, Eureka Springs, Arkansas. (Courtesy Arkansas History Commission.)

As for the scene in Eureka Springs, the newspapers began to omit the many letters written by grateful people healed by the water from the springs, and in their place appeared what was considered more lucrative advertising. Nationally advertised pills and nostrums were advocated over and over again until they gained a kind of universal acceptance. The water never changed but the acceptance of its therapeutic qualities almost completely died out.[3]

No doubt the success of Eureka Springs contributed to the establishment of resorts, hotels, and bathhouses at many other Ozark springs, particularly those in northwestern Arkansas and southwestern Missouri. In the period 1880–85 a surprising number of springs that had served as sources of water for people and livestock for years were discovered to have amazing health-restoring qualities that had gone unsuspected for years.

One of the largest hotels in northwest Arkansas was the Park Springs, constructed close by springs at the northeast corner of Bentonville. The huge, rambling two-story brick building with verandas on all sides was served by its own railroad line, which connected with the Frisco in Bentonville. The hotel was purchased by Ozark Christian College in 1940.

3. Jane Westfall and Catherine Osterhage, *A Fame Not Easily Forgotten* (Conway, Ark.: River Road Press, 1970), p. xii.

In 1885, when the Kansas City, Fort Smith and Southern Railroad was built to nearby Splitlog, Missouri, the town of Sulphur Springs was laid out. A large hotel and several cottages were built around the springs and run by Charles Hibler and his wife. When the railroad was extended to Sulphur Springs in 1889, several additional hotels were built. When it was constructed in 1909, the Kilburn was said to be the largest hotel in northwest Arkansas.

The town of Siloam Springs in Benton County, Arkansas, developed around twenty-seven springs in the valley of Sager Creek. A number of lots were sold between 1879 and 1883 when stories of cures at some of the healing springs in the area had people talking of what a great place it would be for a health resort. Most of the development occurred after the Kansas City, Pittsburg and Gulf Railroad was built in 1894. In 1915, well after the mineral-water rage had passed, there were three hotels in business.

Eldorado, seventeen miles west of Bentonville on Spavinaw Creek, was the first health resort in Benton County. A large three-story hotel was built beside several springs in the 1870's, but after a disastrous flood in 1883, there was little growth. In the 1920's a restaurant, dance pavilion, and several summer cabins were built.

East of Eureka Springs in the Arkansas Ozarks, only a few springs gained other than a local reputation as picnicking and camping areas. The healing power of Ravenden Springs in Randolph County, according to local legend, was first revealed about 1880 to the Reverend William Bailey, who was suffering from a stomach ailment. Three times in one night Bailey dreamed that he had drunk from the waters and had been cured. The next day, he went to the springs and began his treatment. Apparently the waters were helpful, for the minister lived until 1909. During the flush times at the springs, the grand Southern Hotel was built. It was a forty-room frame structure with a double gallery across its wide facade. Wooden stairs led from the hotel down a steep hill to the springs.

Heber Springs, located on the edge of the Ozarks at the foot of Round Mountain, takes its name from the mineral springs in a ten-acre municipal park. During the spa era, each spring—sulphur, magnesia, and arsenic—was said to have special curative powers. Even today some of the older residents swear by the health-restoring qualities of the springs, and visitors from Batesville and other nearby towns come to the springs to fill empty milk containers and bottles with the mineral waters.

In the Missouri Ozarks, Eldorado Springs commanded the widest reputation. In 1892, when Eldorado Springs was a flourishing town of one thousand five hundred inhabitants, it was reported:

> Less than ten years ago this spot was a perfect wilderness. A remarkable cure was effected in 1881 by the use of waters issuing from a crevice in the rock at the bottom of a pretty valley, the renown of which spread so rapidly that a town was laid out forthwith and actually built within a very few years.[4]

As was generally the case, Park Spring, the one that effected the above-mentioned cure, became public property and its rights were jealously guarded. There were other springs in the vicinity, including those at West Eldorado, known as the Nine Wonders. A rival establishment was started at West Eldorado, but by 1892 it had become a deserted village. On the other hand, things were flourishing at Eldorado at that time:

> A number of hotels, the largest of which is the "Forest Grove" have been built in the past few years at an aggregate cost of $50,000. Several bathing establishments with hot and cold water facilities, a Casino hall and similar attractions bring up the total money spent to $80,000. Guests and patients are well taken care of and receive the comforts they have the right to expect. No bottling establishment exists yet on the ground, though a very considerable trade is carried on from the sale of the water. Pamphlets, descriptive of the place, are printed every year, and may be had on application to Mr. W. P. Cruce.[5]

As at many other locations, the mineral residue at the springs was used to manufacture soap so that after departing the resort visitors could continue treatment until they returned.

The waters of Jerico Springs in southeastern Cedar County, Missouri, heavily chalybeate,

4. Schweitzer, "Mineral Waters of Missouri," p. 155.
5. Ibid.

were recommended for rheumatism, kidney and stomach diseases, and other ailments. The springs were on the property of M. J. Straight, owner of the bathhouses erected nearby. The spa never attracted large crowds because of scant accommodations and difficulty in reaching the place. The main spring was not large and a pump was used to supply water to the bathhouses.

One of the largest resort hotels in the Ozark region, the Gasconade Hotel in Lebanon, Missouri, was erected shortly after a deep well was drilled. Several months later it was discovered that iron pipes, which exhibited no unusual property while lying in the yard, became strongly magnetized when placed in the well or connected with those previously put down. It was found that a pocket knife rubbed on the well pipe would pick up a nail weighing eighty grains and that a compass in the vicinity of the well would be powerfully deflected within a radius of three feet. Although it was widely believed that the waters from the well were magnetic, they were the same waters that are now being pumped from the sandstone aquifers throughout southwest Missouri. Paul Schweitzer, who carefully studied the mineral waters of Missouri in 1892, explained the magnetism of Lebanon Magnetic Well:

> It is a well known fact, however, that an iron bar or tube held in a certain position, to be fixed for each place, becomes a magnet; it is further possible that a tube, sunk to a great depth, may reach rock formations that are magnetic and will communicate their magnetism to the tube. Such facts have been observed in a number of instances and are not remarkable, because not rare; but even a strong magnet, such as the iron tube of the Lebanon well doubtless is, cannot influence the water flowing through it, to either become magnetic itself or to exhibit by virtue of it any unusual properties; it is a matter of interest, and will remain so, but not one of weight from a medical point of view.[6]

It is interesting to note that the magnetic surveys conducted by the Missouri Geological Survey in the 1930's and the 1960's identified several magnetic highs in the Ozarks, One such location, first discovered with sensitive magnetometers and later core-drilled, proved to be a valuable

Gasconade Hotel at the Lebanon Magnetic Well, Lebanon, Missouri, *circa* 1892. (Reproduced from Paul Sweitzer, "A Report on the Mineral Waters of Missouri," *Geological Survey of Missouri*, 1st. Series, 3 (1892): 142.)

iron-ore deposit. In the 1960's it was developed as the Pea Ridge Mine in Washington County. Even more interesting (but not a likely explanation for the magnetic well) is the fact that a magnetic high was identified in the vicinity of Lebanon.

Although the reputation of magnetic water undoubtedly was a factor in the development of the resort, Lebanon had several geographical advantages. Its elevation of 1,280 feet established its advantages as a sanatorium as regards pure air and freedom from malaria, prevalent in the lower-lying country. It was only 180 miles from St. Louis on the main line of the St. Louis–San Francisco. The hotel, an imposing structure operated by R. C. Beaty, was described by Schweitzer:

> A large hotel has been erected at a cost of $100,000 in the usual summer hotel style, with verandas and pleasant nooks and corners, three stories in height, and altogether of striking appearance. Bath houses for men and women, with sitting and dressing rooms, bowling alleys, billiard halls, an opera house, and other attractions are provided. More than $200,000 may safely be estimated as having been spent on improvements inci-

6. Ibid., p. 143.

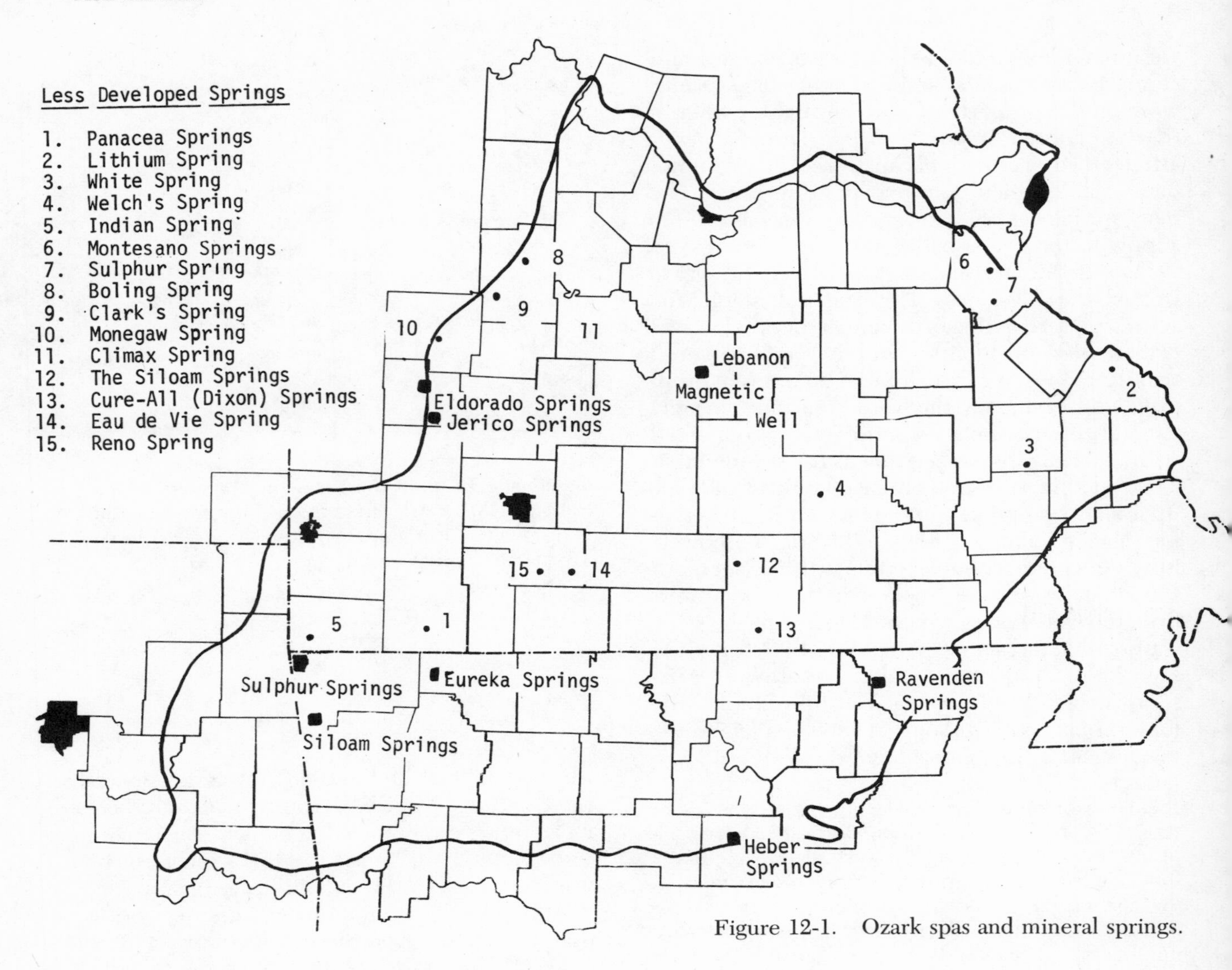

Figure 12-1. Ozark spas and mineral springs.

dental to developing the place as a health resort; pamphlets, descriptive of it, to be had on application to the manager.[7]

In 1892 a medical staff was appointed, with Dr. Paquin as superintendent and physician in charge. The bathing facilities were remodeled and enlarged so that, in addition to the ordinary cold and hot baths, "turkish, russian, and electric, besides sea-salt baths, with or without massage treatment, and medicated vapor baths, are constantly accessible."[8]

By 1892, other springs (fig. 12-1) were noted as resorts or places where summer cottages were built: *Indian Spring* in McDonald County "six miles west of Wade on the Splitlog Railway." A

7. Ibid.

8. Ibid.

hotel and private residences were built there, and the water was recommended for rheumatism and kidney disease. *Lithium Spring*, about nine miles north of Perryville in Perry County. *White Spring*, some six miles south of Fredericktown in Madison County on the St. Louis and Iron Mountain Railroad. Accommodations consisted of a few cottages and a boardinghouse that opened during the summer to serve people from neighboring river counties. Apparently, many of the visitors came from the Mississippi River bottoms because the waters had a reputation for curing malaria in addition to the usual dyspepsia and stomach troubles. *Montesano Springs* and *Sulphur Spring* in Jefferson County. The Montesano waters issue into a marshy valley where a resort hotel, built sometime in the 1880's, was in business for about ten years before it burned down. Sulphur Spring was never developed, being used instead as a casual visiting place by excursion parties from St. Louis. *Boling Spring* and *Clark's Spring* in Benton County, though never developed, have muriatic waters that reportedly were used by picnic parties and by families and visitors who for health reasons sometimes stayed there several weeks. *Monegaw Spring* in the Osage River valley was the major mineral-water resort of St. Clair County. In the 1880's a twenty-seven-room hotel and a number of bathhouses were built to serve visitors, who could reach the place from either Osceola or Clinton. *Climax Spring* in extreme western Camden County was owned by an Indianapolis group that built a small hotel and tried to make a summer resort of it by advertising but failed because of the inaccessibility of the place. *The Siloam Springs* (Sulphur, Keystone, Rheumatic, Iron, Norman, Siloam, Crooked Ash) of Howell County, about eighteen miles northwest of West Plains, were improved by the owners and managed by John Johnson, one of the partners. Two hotels and a bathhouse for hot and cold baths were erected. The springs were reached over a very rough road from West Plains. *Cure-All (Dixon) Springs*, some fifteen miles south of West Plains, could be reached only over very rough roads. The site, consisting of five springs (Electric, Eagle, Sore Eye, Potash, Iron), flourished briefly in the 1880's. The waters of *Panacea Springs*, about seven miles east of Cassville, Missouri, were discovered to be useful in treating rheumatism, kidney diseases, dyspepsia, and bowel troubles. The Springs were unimproved in 1892 and were used mostly by area residents. Two springs in Christian County, Missouri—*Eau de Vie* and *Reno*—flourished as summer resorts during the 1880's. Hotels were built at both places.

It is interesting that the very large springs of the Courtois Hills region, such as Big Spring and Alley Spring, were never developed, nor did they receive much publicity during the heyday of the health spas. No doubt the reason for this was that to command anything more than area trade it was necessary for a resort to be located no more than a few miles from a railroad over rather easily traveled roads. By the time railroads had penetrated the remote sections of the Ozarks, the spa era had passed. Perhaps one of the last efforts to establish a health resort in the Ozarks was the small sanatorium built by Dr. C. H. Diehl of Roxanna, Illinois, at Welch's Cave and Spring in Shannon County, Missouri. He envisioned a resort for asthma sufferers to breathe "the mineral laden air" that came up through the cave tunnel. In 1916 a large native-stone building was erected at the entrance to take advantage of the cool air wafting from the cave and the spring pool. He was unable to attract enough patients or picnic parties to the remote area, and in 1933 the property was sold at a tax sale in Eminence.

As a direct result of the days when taking the waters was popular, many Ozark springs became public property, and many of those that were in private hands were developed and preserved. During the past forty years, most of the very large springs have been acquired by the state or federal governments. Several of the larger springs serve as state parks or trout hatcheries. One who stands for a moment on a hot summer day under the overhanging alcove of limestone and experiences the cool air rising from water issuing from Meramec Spring (or one of the Ozarks' other large springs) can appreciate the springs' intrinsic value before the advent of air conditioning.

Rivers and Float Trips

One of the first attractions for vacationers in the Ozarks was the fishing on clear, spring-fed rivers

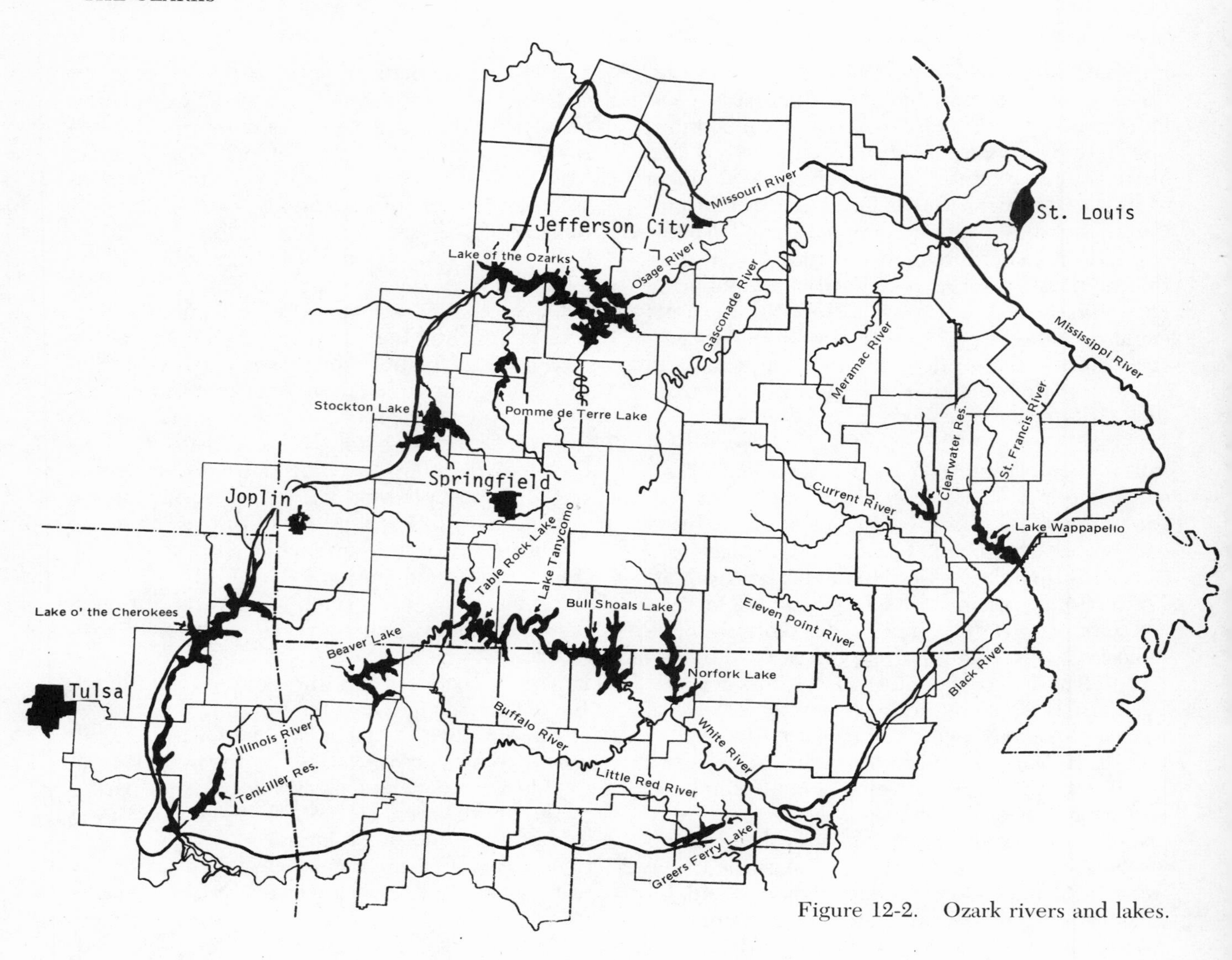

Figure 12-2. Ozark rivers and lakes.

and streams (fig. 12-2). Hunting parties and float trips became popular at about the same time the health spas were built. Undoubtedly, many of the visitors to the spas organized some of the first of these excursions. The most popular floats were on the White and Current rivers, but many other streams also were popular.

Perhaps the most important single event to popularize float fishing in the Ozarks was the Current River excursion of Missouri Governor Herbert S. Hadley in 1909. Hadley was the first Republican governor since Reconstruction, and many people wanted to see "the Mysterious Stranger." The expedition was organized by Congressman W. P. Elmer; John M. Stephens, Frisco agent at Salem; Sam Hughes, Frisco immigrant agent; and John Curran, head of the Missouri Immigration Commission. The purposes of the jaunt were to publicize the Ozarks and to let the people of the Missouri Ozarks see their governor. The trip, which included a banquet at Salem, the railhead, and a float from Welch's

Governor Herbert S. Hadley with party on a float trip on the White River, 1909. (Courtesy Missouri State Historical Society.)

Spring to Round Spring, received wide publicity in the large state and regional newspapers. Representative Elmer wrote of it:

> We blazed the event in the local newspapers, all done free, and soon had $1,000, with which to stage the supper, build ten flat bottomed boats to carry our crowd, and one to carry provisions and equipment, hire river guides and transport the crowd to Welch's Cave.

A banquet, which included baked opossum, was served in Salem for $1.50 a head. It was the first time a Missouri governor had visited Salem, and more than three hundred fifty tickets were sold. The next morning, the governor and his party of about forty persons, including several state officials and distinguished businessmen from Missouri, traveled by "hacks, buggies, and surries" to Welch's Cave, where they boarded the boats:

> Hadley's boat led the parade and the "grub" boat brought up the rear. He had sandwiches and coffee ready at the Spring. Everybody was in a good humor except a couple of newsmen to whom the trip was a bore and arduous. . . . Not a mishap all the way. About 4:30 the guides said "camp" and we did. A tent was provided for the governor and a few others, but most of us slept on the ground in the open.

At Round Spring a panoramic photograph of the group was made and later published all over the United States. A great deal of national attention was drawn to the "discovery" of the Ozarks by Governor Hadley.

The float-fishing trip has changed considerably

over the years; guides are only rarely used, the canoe has become popular, and the automobile has opened more streams to floating. Sauer provides a description of the Ozark float trip of the early 1900's:

> At some convenient point the party, usually accompanied by a guide, starts down the river in flat-bottomed boats, which are rowed or poled when desired. The canoe, although well suited to Ozark streams, is almost unknown. The trips are usually taken in a very leisurely fashion, numerous stops being made to fish. Camp is pitched on a gravel bar or at a spring.[9]

Among the more popular floats were the one from Round Spring to Van Buren on the Current River, which was approximately fifty miles long and required nearly a week. The float from Alley Spring to Eminence could be accomplished in one day, but fishing parties often continued downstream past Two Rivers Landing to float the Current River. There was a float from Galena to Branson on the White River. The whole White River below Powersite Dam in Taney County, Missouri, was used for float trips, and Spring River below Arkansas Power and Light Company's Dam No. 3 was a good one. Some of the floats were made popular by a few outfitters who provided equipment and guides. Bales Mercantile and Boating Company in Eminence, Missouri, and Jim Owen's Float Service at Branson were among the larger and better-known outfitters.

Float fishing was at first a pastime of the well-to-do vacationer; it was relatively costly, even at reduced Ozark prices, to mount a float trip complete with boats, tents, fishing gear, food, and guides to steer the boats, point out likely fishing spots, and make camp and cook. Area residents had always float-fished, of course, and for many families the catch provided a welcome relief from a monotonous diet of pork, corn bread, beans, and garden produce.

In the years since World War II, particularly the 1960's and 1970's, Ozark river floats have been transformed from a semiwilderness sport for the more fortunate to a family activity. Several factors are responsible for this change. Better roads and increased use of the automobile have opened nearly all of the floatable Ozark streams. Any location on a stream where the public may enter is a potential put-in or take-out spot. First fiberglass and then aluminum boats replaced the heavier wooden flat-bottomed johnboats. The aluminum johnboat continues to be popular among fishing enthusiasts, but canoes are favored much more today. Two books have helped to make the Ozark float trip popular. The first, *Stars Upstream*[10] by Leonard Hall, is an appealing description of the natural beauty and simplicity of life along the Current and Jacks Fork rivers. The second, *Missouri Ozark Waterways*[11] by Oscar Hawksley, provides specific instructions and detailed maps on how to gain entrance to and run almost every Missouri Ozarks stream capable of floating a canoe or johnboat. Canoe rental businesses have sprung up rapidly to supply the demands of floaters from outlying cities, including Kansas City, St. Louis, Springfield, Tulsa, Little Rock, and Memphis. It is not unusual to see several vans, pulling specially designed trailers loaded with as many as a dozen canoes, pull up at a put-in spot, such as Hammond Camp on the North Fork of the White River, and disgorge several Boy Scout troops. Even short-term residents of the Ozarks can feel a bit chagrined and quite nostalgic about the good old days when one could float for a day and encounter only a handful of canoes. It goes without saying that guides are seldom used these days; even a novice would feel a bit out of place with a guide among a pack of canoes carrying inexperienced paddlers less than sixteen years old.

Hawksley cites the prime reason for the change from float fishing to pleasure canoeing:

> The special attractiveness to families cannot be overemphasized. Most Ozark rivers, in summer, are so mild that even the family with small children need not fear travelling by canoe. The few places on the average river run which could cause difficulty for the inexperienced paddler occur at places so shallow that the stern paddler can step out and lead the canoe around the

9. Carl O. Sauer, *Geography of the Ozark Highland of Missouri* (Chicago: University of Chicago Press, 1920), p. 230.

10. Leonard Hall, *Stars Upstream* (Columbia: University of Missouri Press, 1958).

11. Oscar Hawksley, *Missouri Ozark Waterways* (Jefferson City, Mo.: Missouri Department of Conservation, 1965).

trouble spot. . . . The gravel bars are nearly all potential campsites and Ozark gravel bars are nearly devoid of noxious insects. To top it all off, no license is required for paddle craft.[12]

Unfortunately, many of the most popular stretches of floating water have been destroyed. The James River, once one of the favorite float-fishing streams, is severely polluted. Downstream from Springfield, it drains the streets and parking lots of the city and receives the treated but odoriferous sewage water that is pumped into Wilson's Creek. Long stretches of other float streams, including the Osage, White, Little Red, Illinois, and Grand rivers, have been flooded by the construction of large dams. The float-fishing stream par excellence was the White River, but its shoals and pools have been inundated by waters from several large lakes.

The sport involved in floating consists especially of the successful running of a shoal. Where streams cut into a particularly resistant layer of rock, a series of rapids, a shoal, is the result. Most Ozark streams consist of series of pools with normal water flow broken by shoals in between. The large reservoirs interrupt the flast-flowing water and submerge the shoals. The construction of Bull Shoals Dam destroyed several of the best shoals on White River. Schoolcraft provided what is probably the first written record of a troubled but successful run down the Bull Shoals. Reading it helps us to understand what was lost under the waters of the reservoir:

In our descent this day, we have passed several hunters' cabins on both banks of the river, but met nothing worth particular note until our arrival at the Bull Shoals, situated twenty miles below M'Gary's. Here the river has a fall of fifteen or twenty feet in the distance of half a mile, and stands full of rugged calcareous rocks, among which the water forms and rushes with astonishing velocity and incessant noise. There are a hundred channels, and the strange navigator runs an imminent risk of being dashed upon the rocks, or sunk beneath the waves, whose whirling boiling and unceasing roar warns him of his peril before he reaches the rapids. There is a channel through which canoes and even large boats pass with a good depth of water, but being unacquainted with it, we ran the hazard of being sunk, and found our canoe drawn rapidly into the suction of the falls, apprehensive of the results. In a few moments, not withstanding every effort to keep our barque headed downwards, the conflicting eddies drove us against a rock, and we were instantly thrown broadside upon the rugged peaks which stand thickly in the swiftest part of the first chute or fall. Luckily it did not fill, but the pressure of the current against a canoe thirty feet in length, lying across the stream, was more than we could counteract, and we had nearly exhausted our strength in vain endeavors to extricate and aright it. For all this time we were in the water, at a depth of two, three, and four feet, at a cool January temperature, but at length succeeded in lifting it over a ledge of rocks, and again got afloat. We now shot down the current rapidly and undisturbed for 600 yards, which brought us to the verge of a second chute, where we twice encountered a similar difficulty, but succeeded, with analogous efforts, in passing our canoe and effects in safety.[13]

Johnboats on the Jacks Fork River, 1970. Johnboats are popular for river fishing.

12. Ibid., p. 7.

13. Schoolcraft, *Journal of a Tour into the Interior of Arkansas and Missouri*, in *Schoolcraft in the Ozarks*, ed. Park, pp. 136–38.

Dam and power plant of Ozark Power and Water Company forming Lake Taneycomo at Forsyth, Taney County, Missouri. (Courtesy Missouri State Historical Society.)

Hunting and Wilderness Sports

Hunting continues to be as popular in the Ozarks as it was for the first settlers. There is ample written record that they practice it for sport. During his three-month journey in the Ozarks in 1818 and 1819, Schoolcraft and his companion killed nine deer, twenty-five turkeys, three wolves (coyotes), one prairie hen, and one goose. Bear were seen frequently, and deer herds were large. On Christmas Day, 1818, while Schoolcraft was staying with settlers on Beaver Creek, the hunters killed fourteen turkeys in a matter of two hours. Friedrich Gerstäker's journal gives ample evidence of the variety and abundance of wild game.[14] Only once, while in the Upper White River country and because of the game, was Gerstäker tempted to settle in America.

Through the efforts of the state conservation departments and the U.S. Forest Service in regulating hunting activities and managing habitat, wildlife populations have been restored from the low ebb of the 1930's. Deer and wild-turkey seasons attract the largest number of outside hunters. Often they come prepared to rough it in the woods for a week or more. They are sometimes equipped with any number of expensive weapons, including newfangled muzzle-loaders; camouflaged clothing; tents or camping vehicles; cooking equipment; and, in one instance reported in a newspaper, an ample supply of beer and spirits and a gasoline-powered electric generator to provide power for a television set so that the group of lusty hunters would not miss the Monday night football telecast.

Other wild game and fish are hunted enthusiastically—rabbit, quail, squirrel, bullfrogs, etc.—in almost every conceivable fashion: bows, muzzle-loading rifles, gigs (sharp-pointed spines attached to a pole and used in taking frogs and rough fish), and shotguns ranging from .410's to 12 gauge. Various illegal hunting methods are used, including such things as spotlighting and baiting deer (with salt or feed) or noodling (feeling by hand) for fish along stream banks.

14. Friedrich Gerstäker, *Wild Sports in the Far West* (Durham, N.C.: Duke University Press, 1968).

TABLE 12-1
Corps of Engineers Lakes

Lake or Reservoir	Completion Date	Estimated Cost	Visitors, 1976
Lake o' the Cherokees	1941 (WPA project)	9,372,960	. . . .
Norfork	1944	69,390,000	3,842,398
Clearwater	1948	10,527,000	946,049
Wappapello	1941		1,825,000
Bull Shoals	1951	93,400,000	3,885,447
Tenkiller Ferry	1953	23,713,000	5,668,200
Fort Gibson	1953	42,494,000	3,570,200
Table Rock	1958	70,382,000	6,379,163
Pomme de Terre	1961	17,129,820	1,380,811
Greers Ferry	1962	51,174,000	4,224,088
Beaver	1963	49,403,000	3,842,398
Webbers Falls	1969	83,688,000	863,600
Robert S. Kerr	1970	93,387,000	1,054,900
Stockton	1974	75,531,000	1,785,247

Hunting and fishing are becoming more and more organized and commercialized. There are bass derbys, fishing for prizes, and specialized gear, including such things as special gigging boats equipped with reflected lights and powerful bass boats designed for competitive fishing. Even the dog men, who are among the most traditional of hunters, are well equipped with citizens band radios as they follow their dogs through the night in search of fox or raccoon.

Many Ozarks residents resent outside hunters. Landowners are likely to allow local boys to enter their property, but it is heavily posted for anyone with whom they are not acquainted. Frontier attitudes regarding wildlife and hunting are slowly waning, but many native Ozarkers consider it their right to take game wherever it may be, even if it means entering posted land.

Private hunting lodges have always been popular, but until recently they were reserved for people who could afford to purchase wild land and use it only for recreation. In recent years, several cooperative hunting lodges have been established, and memberships are sold for as little as ten dollars per month. Such lodges are not popular with most residents. One Ozarker put it this way: "Those fellas from St. Louis and Memphis and even Springfield come down here and tear hell out of things with their fancy four-wheel-drive pickups and kill our deer and turkeys. A lot of them do more boozin' than huntin'."

The Lakes

The first of the great Ozark lakes was built by Ambussen Hydraulic Construction Company for the Ozark Power and Water Company. Congress authorized the project on February 4, 1911, and in the fall of that year, Ambussen began to bring in men and machinery. The dam was to be 70 feet high and 1,063 feet long and eventually would create a lake covering 2,080 acres of land, with 52.9 miles of shoreline. It was a small project by modern standards, and the approximate cost of construction and land acquisition amounted to only $2,250,000. But the impact of the Powersite Dam project, which created Lake Taneycomo in Taney County, Missouri, both immediately and future, was monumental.

Some two hundred to eight hundred men were used to build the dam, and a little town, called Camp Ozark, grew up near the construction site. The payroll ran about one thousand five hundred dollars a day, a large sum considering the time and place. Land was acquired without undue resistance, except for a tract owned by Missouri Cook Casey, a widow who had raised eight children, who held out for a higher price than the appraised value. On March 24, 1912, the Ozark Power and Water Company paid the full price for the Casey land, but then the dam had been completed and the lake was filling up, leaving no time to clear the timber from the Casey property. For many years a sunken forest stood in the lake as a memorial to the widow Casey's persistence.

By 1916, power transmission lines had been built to Joplin, Springfield, Monett, Carthage, and Webb City, and soon after that, lines were strung to the towns in the White River valley. Thus modernity, in the form of electrical power, came to the wild White River Hills many years before it reached seemingly more accessible areas. The geographical disadvantage of rugged hills and remote location had been transformed by the advantage of a favorable site for the development of hydroelectric power for the growing markets in Springfield and the Tri-State Mining District.

The recreation potential of the lake was recognized immediately. Four resort towns grew up on its shores: Rockaway Beach, Branson, Hollister, and Forsyth. Two of the towns, Hollister and Forsyth, had been established much earlier, but the new lake had a major impact on their economy. Each of these resort settlements offered its own brand of diversions for vacationers.

Hollister is one of the most unusual towns in the Middle West, since its buildings were constructed to conform with an Old English architectural pattern. As early as 1914, there were already several boats on the new lake:

> Tucked away on the shores between Branson and Hollister is a "shipyards" where boats are being built entirely of native material. Others are shipped in "knockdown" from factories. A forty-footer known as the "Sammy Lane" was launched only a few days ago. "The Shepherd of the Hills" is another boat well known. The "Sammy Lane" is a mail boat. Sail boats for pleasure are also to be found on the lake.

Lake Taneycomo was praised for working "marvelous" changes in the White River region of the Ozarks, which had so far been devoid of any water impoundments. Even as early as September, 1913, Robertus Love, writing in *Technical World*, called attention to the wave of optimism in the vacation resort area in the hills:

> The thrill of the new day is felt everywhere. New hotels have been going up all summer. Fishing and hunting clubs are going up all along the lake. And the good roads boosters are seeing to it that a fine drive will have been finished by the end of the season. This lake is going to make that section of the Ozarks the principal vacation mecca within a few years. Shut in by mountain fastnesses, this land has been, until a few years ago, a little empire to itself. It has lived its own life and gone its own ways. It has had its tragedies and comedies, its thrilling days of feudists and Baldknobbers, bushwhackers and mountain adventures.
>
> But now a change has come and who knows but in a few years electric cars will run up and down the shores of this new lake that promises to revolutionize the entire Ozark region. Already the people of the Ozarks are adapting themselves to the new conditions, which promose not only to attract thousands of sightseers, summer visitors, and permanent residents, but also to develop industries undreamed of in this hitherto sequestered region of romance and mystery, illicit distilling, and honest hillside farming.

Willard and Anna Merriam founded Rockaway Beach. Originally, the town was named Taneycomo, but Mrs. Merriam renamed it after visiting Rockaway Beach in New York. The red Oriental peaked roofs on the Taneycomo Hotel, which burned recently, were her idea. The old hotel had pillars of cedar trees, little changed so that their branches interlaced, reaching to the ceiling. Although on ground level, each room was elevated because the hotel was built on the hillside. This style of multilevel architecture continues to be popular for resorts and housing developments around Ozark lakes.

The resort town of Hollister was platted by William J. Johnson, a landscape architect, whose plan drew upon the natural beauty of the limestone hills by means of terraces, parks, and supporting walls of stone. The commercial buildings are of the English half-timbered type and are constructed of wood, stone, and stucco. A report written in 1940 characterized it as a planned village "often referred to by sociologists as a good example of the possibilities of the American rural town." Whether Hollister was a rural town then is conjectural, but certainly today it is in the midst of a booming tourist-recreation region.

Lake Taneycomo has undergone continuous change since it was formed by the completion of Powersite Dam in 1913. It was a warm-water lake until the 1950's, when Table Rock Dam was built. Rockaway Beach and other resorts underwent certain changes as a result. The traditional style of vacation, which included visits lasting from two weeks to a whole summer, were popular before water from Table Rock entered Lake Taneycomo. The temperature of cold water feeding from the bottom of Table Rock is less than 60° Fahrenheit at all times. This discouraged swimming and proved fatal to many kinds of fish. Fortunately, as a cold water body, Lake Taneycomo proved to be good trout habitat. As a result, Rockaway Beach became a trout fisherman's resort and a home base for vacationers who like to tour the region.

In 1929, construction on the second major dam in the Ozarks was begun. Bagnell Dam, built on the Osage River by Union Electric and Power Company, was completed in October, 1931, becoming the largest hydroelectric plant in the Ozarks and impounding one of the largest manmade lakes in the United States. The dam was constructed by Stone and Webster Engineering Corporation, cost thirty million dollars, and created Lake of the Ozarks. This large lake, sometimes called the Ozark Dragon because of its unusual shape outlined by the S-shaped meanders of the Osage River, has one thousand three hundred miles of shoreline. It is said to be the last of the major lakes built by private capital in the United States. A rail line was extended to the site and, as was the case at Lake Taneycomo, a workers camp, known as Bagnell, was established nearby. Skilled workers were brought in from outside, but many of the laborers were hired locally, providing an opportunity for outside corporations to see that the Ozarker's image as a listless worker was more fancy than fact.

This time, there was considerably more resistance to those responsible for purchasing the property in the river bottoms. The entire town of Linn Creek, the county seat of Camden County, had to be moved from its site on the Osage River near the mouth of the Niangua. Powersite Dam was small, mainly a river-channel dam that flooded a relatively small acreage, but Bagnell Dam was built from bluff to bluff, backing water across the fertile Osage River floodplain and into tributary valleys.

Among the foremost opponents of the dam was the Snyder family, owners of the Hahatonka Castle, a summer place built by R. M. Snyder of Kansas City. On a 3,500-acre estate, a gray limestone 3-story, 28-room mansion of modified Late English-Renaissance design was built. The structure, begun in 1905 and completed in 1922, was erected on the flat summit of a crag known as Deer Leap Hill. At the base of the hill was Hahatanka Spring which was partly flooded by the lake. The estate was used little by members of the Snyder family, who contended before the Missouri Supreme Court that the construction of Bagnell Dam caused extensive damage to the property.

Located in the northern Ozarks, the recreation potential of Lake of the Ozarks was recognized immediately, and elaborate plans were laid to develop resorts and summer homes. Camdenton, built on the upland and established in 1929 as the seat of Camden County, is by virtue of its youthfulness something of an anomaly in Camden County. The business buildings define a large landscaped circle and are of the modern English half-timber design. Near the dam a community, Lake Ozark—composed of a single row of one- and two-story buildings, cabins, restaurants, dance halls, taverns, and shops—grew up to cater to vacationists. Osage Beach, a tiny resort village, was one of the earliest projects planned by real estate promoters in connection with Lake of the Ozarks. A town was platted and a few lots sold when Bagnell Dam was first proposed in 1928. However, the Depression halted development, and many lots remained unsold until prosperity resumed during and after World War II.

It is interesting that in the midst of the current controversy over the proposed U.S. Army Corps of Engineers dam on the Meramec River near Sullivan, Missouri, one can read in a recent history of Baxter County, Arkansas, a chapter titled "The Dreams Come True–Norfork and Bull Shoals Dams." Attitudes toward harnessing the power of rivers have changed in the years since

Ben Kantor of the Peer International Corporation wrote this ditty about man and Nature:

You've all heard the story, that's covered with glory.
A story about Uncle Sam.
How old Mother Nature was challenged and changed
By the building of Boulder Dam.[15]

By 1938 the Federal Power Commission had rescinded the rights of all private power companies, including Dixie Power Company and White River Power Company—which dated back to 1916—pending the determination of projects to be undertaken by the United States in the White River Basin. In 1941, construction began on Norfork Dam on the North Fork River in Baxter County, Arkansas. The result was one of six reservoirs that were authorized for construction in the White River Basin by the Comprehensive Flood Control Act of 1938. It was rushed through to completion during World War II for its electric-power production, although generation facilities were not included in its authorization.

Community groups met at Harrison, Arkansas, in 1940 in an attempt to get hydroelectric power included in the project purpose. The reasons were rather basic:

> Those areas were not adequately served at the time and the sparseness of population could not justify any expansive companies. On the other hand, the population growth which usually came with the construction and completion of the dams and reservoirs could make it feasible for private power companies to move in. Some feared the cost-benefit ratio would not justify Congressional expenditure unless hydroelectric power was included. Privately, most citizens would have accepted any government project with open arms. . . . Depression gripped the communities. Farms were being abandoned and communities were drying up. . . . Even a partial solution to their economic problems was met with hopeful enthusiasm.[16]

The Corps of Engineers established its headquarters at Mountain Home to administer the affairs of Norfork Dam and to begin the construction of Bull Shoals Dam. Construction villages, similar to those at Powersite and Bagnell dams, sprang up around Corps of Engineers dams built before the mid-1950's. When Norfork Dam was under construction, many area residents quit their low-paying jobs to work at the dam for thirty cents an hour, "a fabulous common labor wage for the area." The social impact of the two dams was substantial as men sought to learn new jobs and work habits and as new machinery and materials were introduced. Even the children were influenced by the glamour of the projects:

> Remember those orange colored "hard hats" the workers wore? How I secretly envied the children of our neighborhood when he [one of the fathers] swaggered into the Monkey Run Store wearing his hard hat. The roads leading to the dam site carried a constant stream of trucks laden with strange looking machinery and material.[17]

As soon as construction began, Norfork Dam became an attraction. The Morrison-Knudsen Company, principal contractor, built an overlook that became a popular Sunday-afternoon sightseeing stop until the site was closed in January, 1942, because of the "fear of war sabotage." Spencer, the main boom town adjacent to the dam, was promoted by Charles Bivan, who promoted Disney, Oklahoma, on Lake o' the Cherokees. Mary Ann Messick's recollection of Norfork Dam's impact vividly describes the dramatic changes in land and life:

> Actually there was not one-but three boomtowns. Spencer, at the dam site, Salesville [also known as Ellis] on Highway 5, and in between the two false front towns was Hutcheson. In all three towns, businesses sprung up overnight—lumberyards, hotels, boarding houses, trailer parks, rent houses and cabins, stores, department stores, garages, cafes, pool halls, beauty shops, and a restaurant. In March, '41, even before the contract was let, the Arkansas Employment Service opened an office in Spencer. One thousand people applied for jobs the first week. Since local people were to have first chance at the jobs, applicants had to show a Baxter County Poll Tax Receipt.

15. Mary Ann Messick, *History of Baxter County*, 1873–1973 (Mountain Home, Ark.: Mountain Home Chamber of Commerce, 1973), p. 291.

16. Ibid., p. 320.

17. Ibid.

Hahatonka Castle, Camden County, Missouri. Country estate of the Snyder family of Kansas City. (Courtesy Missouri State Historical Society.)

The building of Norfork Dam was our first mass encounter with the outside world—including the gaudy, bright-light world of dance halls, scantily clad show girls, and gamblers. Sheriff Harvey Powell and his deputies had their work cut out—but before long they had Spencer "cleaned up." The Chef—a cafe featuring beer, wine, and illegal gambling—was closed and padlocked.[18]

18. Ibid.

On May 23, 1941, a celebration was held at Norfork Dam, it attracted twelve thousand people. Special trains were run from Springfield and Little Rock, and a parade, including bands from Springfield, West Plains, Little Rock, Harrison, and Cotter, wound from the Salesville junction to the dam. There were few critics of the U.S. Army Corps of Engineers in those days.

By 1970, however, in the midst of the national environmental movement and after completion of a dozen Corps of Engineers dams in the region, a more affluent Ozark population paused to reflect and to criticize proposed corps projects. The large lakes seem to have spawned the doom of future impoundments. No doubt the corps dams promoted much of the Ozarkers' prosperity and attracted many of the new people who are among the opponents of future peojects.

Norfork Dam was completed in 1944, the first of a series of large Corps of Engineers reservoirs that eventually would amount to more than an investment of more than one billion dollars when all of the power installations, boat docks, public-access roads, and parks were constructed. Table 12-1 lists the Corps of Engineers lakes and reservoirs in the Ozarks along with the dates of completion, cost, and the number of visitors in 1976.

Promotion and Development

As is the case with most business enterprises, promotion and development of Ozark tourism and recreation have progressed hand in hand; it is a cumulative process whereby development begets promotion and additional promotion leads to further development. The early health spas were first, and, as we have seen, they published brochures and placed advertisements in newspapers. The railroad companies also were important promoters of the Ozarks as a place for recreation. Construction of Lake Taneycomo was a landmark event; as the first of the Ozark lakes, it opened a whole new aspect of recreational development.

One of the milestones in the promotion of Ozark tourism was the founding of the Ozark Playgrounds Association on November 25, 1919. This organization, the first of its kind in the United States, carried on national and regional promotional campaigns for the recreation and tourism industry of northwest Arkansas and southwest Missouri until 1979. The 1977 *Official Directory of the Ozark Playgrounds Association* consisted of 101 pages of color advertisements, descriptions, and maps from hundreds of businesses, including motels, resorts, marinas, historic attractions, caves, fishing docks, and canoe rentals. The Ozark Playgrounds Association sprang from an automobile tour to Eureka Springs, Arkansas, in the fall of 1919 by the Rotary Club of Joplin. The ninety-mile trip required a full day. After the tour, it was decided to establish an association to promote Ozark attractions, the foremost of which were Eureka Springs; Monte Ne, a resort near Rogers, Arkansas; Bella Vista, a resort near Bentonville, Arkansas; Springfield, Missouri; and Lake Taneycomo.

With the construction of the large lakes in the 1950's the Ozark Playgrounds Association grew rapidly as more water sports and lake-front attractions were developed. A perusal of the back issues of the *Official Directory* is a good way to assess the evolution of the tourism and recreation industry. Advertisements in the 1930's and 1940's emphasized scenic drives, historic attractions, caves, overnight and weekly cabin rentals, and fishing. From the 1950's to the present, the *Official Directory* carried, increasingly from year to year, advertisements related to water sports, resort ads, motel accommodations, convention activities, country-music presentations, and second-home and retirement-home developments. There has been an increase in advertisement and recreation services that appeal to the whole family. Increasing emphasis is placed on activities for women and children. As one informant put it, "the only thing that has gotten smaller in this business are the bathing suits."

The Ozark Playgrounds Association served as a model for state tourism commissions in Missouri, Arkansas, and Oklahoma. These agencies became especially active in publicizing the Ozarks in the 1970's. At the local level, each major lake or reservoir has its own promotional association. In the case of the larger lakes, various clusters of attractions, usually along a developed stretch of highway or an arm of a lake, have their own promotional associations intended to attract visitors. When combined with chamber-of-commerce advertising in most of the nearby lake towns, the result is an intricate geography of tourism and recreation promotion that is well designed to attract the visitor to the Ozarks and then direct him to various attractions.

A complete historical geography of current tourism-recreation attractions of the Ozarks would be most useful and interesting, but it is beyond the immediate purposes of this account. However, it is useful to sketch briefly the development of selected tourist-recreation businesses in order to provide historical perspective.

Monte Ne

One of the most interesting stories, not just because of the colorful background of its builder, but because of its size and influence, concerns the resort built by Coin Harvey near Rogers, Arkansas. Monte Ne was constructed at what was formerly called Silver Springs, where Coin had retired after an active life in the real estate business and politics.

William Hope Harvey was born in 1851 in Buffalo, West Virginia. A child prodigy in matters of finance, he was admitted to the bar at the age of twenty-one. In 1884 he opened real estate offices in Denver and Pueblo, Colorado, and in a relatively short time amassed considerable property and other wealth. He returned to Chicago, where he had practiced law, and immediately entered the political brouhaha over free coinage of silver. His lectures in favor of free coinage of silver were published in a book called *Coin's Financial School*, which sold more than a million copies. It was from this book that he got his nickname. Harvey became a close friend of William Jennings Bryan, the champion of free silver, and was a close adviser when Bryan ran for president in 1896.

Coin Harvey's retirement was brief. By 1901 he had become actively engaged in the construction and promotion of Monte Ne, and in 1902 the railroad was extended to the resort from Lowell. Bryan and U.S. Senator Ben ("Pitchfork") Tillman of South Carolina were on hand for the dedication:

> The little one- or two-car trains arrived at the impressive log station with a reverberating blast from the engine's whistle and a tolling of its bell. Passengers alighted from coaches and were met with a royal welcome. Upon naming their destination, they were escorted to the near-by lagoon, where deep blue-green waters from Big Spring reflected stately trees of the forest. At the lagoon visitors were ceremoniously ushered aboard a long, low Venetian gondola in which they were leisurely transported to the hotel or cottage of their choice. The gondoliers were dressed in colorful costumes, and the final minutes of the journey were made as pleasant and inviting as possible.[19]

The resort was impressive. In 1904 the Monte Ne Club House, Hotel and Cottage Company, Inc., was formed to build a hotel 220 feet long and four stories high. The "cottages" constructed of logs for a rustic effect and were between 300 and 350 feet long. They were known as Arkansas, Texas, Louisiana, Missouri, and Oklahoma rows, no doubt a fairly good identification of the home states of most of the visitors. In 1904 a newspaper and a bank were established. A splendid golf course was available to guests, and there was an enclosed swimming pool and a rustic pavilion at which many grand balls were held.

Reportedly, Harvey had considerable trouble with organized labor and stopped construction on the large stone hotel. It seems strange that organized labor was strong enough at that early date to influence his decision, but perhaps his national reputation in politics had some influence in the matter. In any case, Coin's untiring efforts to develop the resort and to promote tourism—in 1913 he started promoting The Ozark Trails, an association devoted to acquiring more and better roads in the four-state area—were doomed to failure.

> Coin was born thirty years too soon as a developer of the resort trade. Two teams of the Western Baseball Association were brought to Monte Ne aboard a special train for an exhibition game. Again the good people frowned upon such goings—on Sunday. The attraction was not repeated. Then Harvey and the Frisco agreed to disagree on several problems, whereupon the Frisco refused to handle the special excursions.[20]

By 1920 the summer resort at Monte Ne had become a lost dream to Coin. He lost the railroad, bank, and newspaper. There had been trouble with the stockholders, and people just did not come to Monte Ne as they once had. The financial loss and the loss of his eldest son a few years earlier apparently drove Coin into retirement again.

Harvey spent his last years attempting to build a pyramid at Monte Ne to house the secrets of "our civilization." Work was started in 1925, but

19. Clifton E. Hull, *Shortline Railroads of Arkansas* (Norman: University of Oklahoma Press, 1969), pp. 244–45.
20. Ibid., p. 245.

the project was never completed. A metal plate on top of the pyramid was to read, "When this can be read, go below and find a record of and the cause of the death of a former civilization." Several items were to have been placed in the pyramid, including a 400-page book telling of "our civilization."

The last big event held at Monte Ne was the national convention of the Liberty party in 1932. Coin Harvey helped launch the party and served as editor of the *Liberty Bell*, its newspaper. Its slogan, "Prosperity in Ninety Days," was to be realized by initiating many of Coin's old free-silver ideas. In many ways the convention was a gathering of political eccentrics. Plans were laid for a crowd of 10,000, but only 390 voting members were on hand for the nomination:

> The crowd and delegates were made up with a sprinkling of Reformers, Socialists, Populists, and disgruntled Democrats and Republicans. Many of them were selling books and giving out tracts with their own beliefs.[21]

Among the delegates aspiring for nomination were the likes of Dr. John Brinkley of Milford, Kansas, he of goat-gland rejuvenation fame, and Alfalfa Bill Murray of Oklahoma. Nevertheless, Coin Harvey, at the age of 82, was nominated as the standard-bearer of the Liberty party.

The party was badly defeated in the fall election, and Coin spent the last four years of his life attempting to raise money to build the pyramid. He died in 1936 at age 85 and was buried in a mausoleum beside the lagoon at Monte Ne. When Beaver Lake was filled, the mausoleum was moved to higher ground as the lake waters encroached on the old resort.

Bella Vista

The development of Bella Vista in extreme northern Benton County, Arkansas, is one of the most significant stories related to the Ozark tourist-recreation industry. Many of the innovations that have proved successful at other locations were developed at Bella Vista. Much of what is included in modern second-home and retirement-home development was tried at Bella Vista many years ago.

The story of Bella Vista began on November 11, 1918, when two large touring cars drove into Bentonville. The drivers were two brothers from Dallas, Texas, one with his wife, the other with his wife and small son. The end of the war could not have been a better omen for the two brothers, F. W. and C. A. Linebarger, for the year before, with a third brother, C. C. Linebarger, they had invested three thousand one hundred dollars in six hundred acres of land in Sugar Creek Valley seven miles north of Bentonville. This purchase included bluff-rimmed East Mountain and spectacular Big Spring. The three Linebargers had been engaged in the real estate business in Texas, townsiting they called it. At Bella Vista they planned to build a resort.

The idea of building a resort on Sugar Creek actually was the idea of another owner, William Baker, a Presbyterian minister. He had already built a small dam, forming a lake on the creek, and had named the spot Bella Vista. In spite of his selling a few lots to local people, financial difficulties set in and the Baker-Smith Land Company sold the property to the Linebarger brothers.

In contrast to the former owner's policies, the Linebargers immediately set out to gain regional sales. They spent the first year selling Bella Vista lots to families from such centers of new oil prosperity as Dallas, Fort Worth, Bartlesville, and Tulsa. The Linebargers were soon joined by their most successful salesman, Dallas Rupe of Dallas. Rupe sold the "staggering amount of $80,000 worth of property" to Tulsa families in the spring of 1918, resulting in the first row of cottages at Bella Vista: Tulsa Row. When oil was discovered at a new place, the Linebarger salesmen were not far behind. By 1926 the sales booklet *Bella Vista, Nature's Gem of the Ozarks*, enticed oil men with the assurance that "Bella Vista, on account of its nearness to the Midcontinent Fields, is properly called the Summer Capitol and Playground of the Oil Men of the Southwest."

Among all the oil families at Bella Vista were some of the Osage Indians, who made a lasting impression on the people of Bentonville as they

21. J. Dickson Black, *History of Benton County, 1836–1936* (Little Rock: International Graphics Industries, 1975), p. 151.

drove about in their big cars, sometimes bedecked in traditional dress. There were as many as forty or fifty Osage families at Bella Vista in the 1920's.

The Linebargers used a technique long practiced by real estate promoters: sell property to prominent citizens and use their inherent prestige to sell additional lots. One of the most appealing aspects of living at Bella Vista was the opportunity to rub shoulders with the very rich or socially prominent. Doctors, bankers, university presidents, ministers, and businessmen were especially sought after by Bella Vista salesmen. A list of Bella Vista owners and their occupations indicates who was making money in the Southwest: W. W. Patterson, coal-mine owner, Pittsburg, Kansas; T. E. Braniff, insurance, Oklahoma City; Walter Harrison, business manager of the *Daily Oklahoman*, Oklahoma City; T. S. Terry, wholesale and retail jewelry, Bartlesville, Oklahoma; Mrs. Camilla Davis, Texas Farm Loan Mortgage Company, Dallas. Most of the Bella Vista owners were wealthy enough to have servants, almost all of whom were Negroes. Among the property owners of national prominance were Congressman Sam Rayburn and Will Rogers. Will Rogers' wife's parents lived in nearby Rogers, Arkansas.

The lots were priced modestly, considering the wealth of many of the purchasers. Original terms were "$300 or $250 Summer Homesite, $15.00 cash, $15.00 per month. $200, $150, or $100 Summer Homesite, $10 cash, $10 per month. No interest, discount 8 percent for all cash." By the mid-1920's, prices were no longer advertised in *Nature's Gem*, Bella Vista's newsletter, but were referred to as reasonable. In the summer of 1926, 600 cottages were occupied and there were 4,700 registered guests. By 1928, there were 700 cottages owned by people from ten states. Most of the guests came from Oklahoma, Texas, Mississippi, Louisiana, and Kansas.

The Linebargers were innovative, to say the least. Each year, new improvements were made to extend the line of services. Perhaps the most popular entertainment was dancing. The dances were held every night except Sunday. Music was played by various bands, including Doc Miller and the Quadrangle Orchestra, Marshall Haynes' Bella Vista Orchestra, Ockly Pittman's Bella Vista Blue Bonnet Orchestra, and Carl Wortz's Ozark Smile Girl Band. C. A. Linebarger watched every person, every night, for infractions of the posted rule: "Anyone dancing with heads together or doing 'shimmy' or like dancing will be ejected from the floor. Polite dancers welcome." The Wonderland Cave nightclub opened in May, 1930. For opening night, it had a top band, and more than eight hundred people came. This cave became very famous as one of the top night spots in Arkansas. For a time, in the 1920's, Bella Vista's dances were broadcast several nights a week by radio station KVOO in Tulsa.

Bridge was popular for the wives, but hiking, tennis, horseback riding, fishing, and swimming were popular with almost everyone. In 1919 a cornfield in the Sugar Creek bottoms was converted into a nine-hole golf course. The swimming pool was equipped with electric lights in the 1920's. Special events were arranged nearly every week: air shows, pony races, fireworks displays, bucking-horse contests, boxing matches, and open-air theatre.

The Linebargers participated enthusiastically in another hallmark of boosterism. Beginning in the 1920's, the Ozarks was promoted as the Land of a Million Smiles, which gave rise to the popular "Smile Girl" contest. Bella Vista, a flourishing Benton County city, always sponsored a candidate for the contest.

Bella Vista was the Ozarks' most advanced pioneer second-home and retirement-home development. Eventually, nearly all phases of the present system were established at Bella Vista. Purchasers of lots had the privilege of using the facilities at Bella Vista whether they built a home or not. Most buyers preferred to let the Linebargers build for them rather than exercise their option to build their own cottages. Because most cottages were built on steep, narrow lots, they were frequently extended out from the hillside on open foundations enclosed with lattice work. Lattice work, widely used in India, had become popular in England in the 1800's and was used much in the United States in the 1920's in the construction of summer resorts. The cottages built by the Linebargers compared favorably with city dwellings of that time. They had hardwood floors, plasterboard ceiling, stone fireplaces, kitchen with sink and cabinets, servants' room, and "Holy of Holies" (a bathroom with tub, shower, lavatory, and toilet).

After a time, many owners found that they could not use their cottages as frequently as they wished to, so many of them were empty much of the time. The Linebargers provided a rental service whereby, for a fee, they would rent the cottages to visitors for periods ranging from a few days to several months. They also engaged in reselling cottages and lots for those who wanted to divest themselves of their holdings at Bella Vista. Thus by 1930 most of the administrative, organizational, and operating procedures of modern second-home and retirement-home developments had been fairly well explored at Bella Vista.

To continue the story of Bella Vista, one must begin at West Memphis, Arkansas, and then follow the career of John Cooper from West Memphis to the Spring River country near Hardy, Arkansas, and finally to Bella Vista. John Cooper was born in Earl, Arkansas, in the delta country and after attending Vanderbilt University at Nashville, Tennessee, and Cumberland Law School at Nashville, he entered practice in West Memphis. Cooper's career as a practicing attorney lasted only one year. Very soon he was engaged in several enterprises, including farming; trading in cotton, soybeans, rice, and cattle; selling farm machinery; heavy construction; sawmilling; cotton ginning; and banking.

As a young man, Cooper had made several trips to the southeast Ozarks in the Spring River country. As his business ventures prospered, he was unable to forget the Ozark hill country, and in 1943 he went by boat from Hardy up the South Fork of Spring River to Otter Creek. This particular spot intrigued him so much that in 1948 he purchased four hundred acres and named it Otter Creek Ranch. A small house on the river bank was enlarged as a summer home for the Coopers. A portion of the tract was subdivided into lots to be sold to others who wished to build a weekend cottage. There were already several camps and inns in the area, including Ravenden, the elegant old health resort some twenty miles east. Many of the summer places had Indian names, so the Coopers decided on the name *Cherokee Village* for their new development.

In 1953, at a time when Sharp County, Arkansas, was down to about six thousand five hundred people—or about half what it was in 1940—the Cherokee Village Development Company was formed for the purpose of subdividing the tract into smaller lots and selling them. From the beginning it was a family corporation, with all the brothers and sisters of John and Mildred Cooper as stockholders.

The first property was sold in the summer of 1954. Governor Orval Faubus, Burl Ives, and an obscure Cherokee Indian chief were invited to the dedication of the village on June 11, 1955. The ceremony was arranged to attract attention to the new development and to assist in the sale of lots. The major amenities with the early properties were all-weather roads, electricity, man-made Lake Cherokee with three parks, and access to the river for swimming and fishing. Cooper Communities, Inc., was one of the first second-home developers to invite prospective buyers to view the properties with all expenses paid.

In 1960 the concept of the village changed from weekend place to year-round residence. The goal was now to be a recreation and retirement community. At this time the company employed land planners to make a thorough study of the situation to determine the village's growth pattern and its needs for recreation, businesses, schools, churches, and utilities. This plan has been followed since then with very little variation.

In 1977 the village consisted of fifteen thousand acres and approximately twenty-five thousand lots. By 1979, more than 95 per cent of the lots had been sold, and Cooper Communities, through a subsidiary company, engages in a lively resale business of both lots and properties. There are seven man-made lakes, a town center for shopping, a community center for civic and social events, and hundreds of modern homes and townhouses to accommodate guests and permanent residents. Although houses have been built on only about 10 per cent of the lots, mainly those close to the lakes, Cherokee Village has a population of approximately three thousand five hundred, making it the largest town in Sharp County. A 1978 color map of Cherokee Village listed the following community services and shopping facilities: Village Rentals; Cooper Communities, Inc.; Chamber of Commerce; Cherokee Village Recreation Department; Cherokee Village Sanitation Department;

Cherokee Village Security Department; The *Cherokee Villager* newspaper; Quapaw Water Service; U.S. Post Office; medical clinic; Carolyn's Dress Shop; Cherokee Insurance Agency; Sitting Bull Restaurant; Thunderbird Gift Shop; Village Barber Shop; Village Beauty Shop; Village Dry Cleaning and Laundry; Village Furniture; Village Garden (garden shop); Village Liberty Supermarket; Village Mobile Service; Village Pharmacy; Village Realty; and Wigwam Gift Shop.

Cooper Communities has established similar developments at Bella Vista, where the property of the Linebarger brothers was purchased and is being expanded, and at Hot Springs Village in the Ouachita Mountains. The latter communities are larger than Cherokee Village.

Village Homes, Inc., a subsidiary of Cooper Communities, reported home construction up sharply in 1976. A report in the *Weekly Vista*, the Bella Vista newspaper, of January 4, 1977, had a thoroughly optimistic tone:

> Citing an overwhelming acceptance of the quality of construction and a close working relationship with property owners, Gene Blasi, president of Village Homes, Incorporated reported significant increases in the volume of construction in all the Cooper Communities in 1976. Final figures for the fiscal year ending September 30, 1976 indicated that Village Homes had one of the best years in its history in spite of what many have called a "continued sluggish economy."[22]

Sales volume was reported up $18,973,925, a 30 per cent increase over the previous twelve-month period. Totals for each of the Village Homes divisions were as follows: Cherokee Village, $3,388,309; Bella Vista Village, $7,796,051; Hot Springs Village, $7,689,575; Consumer Division, $1,137,697. It was reported that Cooper Communities had a net cash flow of $147,000,000, unquestionably a large part of which impacted in the Ozarks in and near Bella Vista Village and Cherokee Village.

One can only speculate about the consequences of full development of the villages into communities of forty-five thousand to sixty thousand residents if all the lots were developed and occupied. The requirements in energy would be substantial, and if on-lot sewage disposal were no longer permitted, the cost of development on the rocky hillsides would be very high. However, the village plans incorporate a number of modern subdivision concepts, including clustered services and commons that serve as buffers from continuous developed land. In all probability, the planned communities, and there are several others—Horseshoe Bend, Fairfield Bay, Holliday Island—would be, if they grew to full planned size, environmentally more sound than unplanned communities of similar size.

22. *The Weekly Vista*, vol. 12, no. 1, January 4, 1977.

The Shepherd of the Hills Farm

The cumulative effect of a variety of different types of attractions is perhaps best exhibited in the vicinity of Branson and Table Rock Reservoir. Even before nearby Lake Taneycomo was built in 1914, Harold Bell Wright's book *The Shepherd of the Hills*, which was an immediate success after it was published in 1907, had made that area in western Taney County a popular attraction. Wright, a minister-author who made his home in Lebanon, Missouri, for several years, had visited the vicinity of Dewey Bald on many occasions. While there, he wrote a fictional account about the people and the area.

As early as 1910, vacationers started coming into the area to see where the book was written and the places and people it was written about. The Matthews farm was the original setting of the *Shepherd of the Hills* story, and some of the original buildings still stand today. Shepherd of the Hills Farm and its popular outdoor reenactment of Harold Bell Wright's story has been developed into one of the prime tourist attractions in the Ozarks. Its link with history and early settlement has given it an important place in the tourist-recreation blend of the area, so much so that the Branson-Table Rock Lake area is sometimes called the Shepherd of the Hills Country.

Silver Dollar City

Only a few miles west of Shepherd of the Hills Farm on Missouri Highway 76 is Marvel Cave, which was opened to the public by William Henry Lynch. He became interested in the cave, located in Stone County, Missouri, when he helped explore its twenty-two passages and three streams. Lynch bought the cave property and devoted a large part of the remaining years of his life to it, opening it to public touring in 1894. He called it Marble Cave because he thought it contained marble; the name has since been changed to Marvel Cave.

When the Lynches opened the cave to visitors, they attracted a hardy but small clientele who had to journey to the spot from the Missouri Pacific railroad stop on Roark Creek, northwest of the cave, or make a two-day trip from Branson, staying overnight in cabins at the Lynch homestead. In 1946, Hugo and Mary Herschend of Wilmette, Illinois, visited the Ozarks country and became interested in the cave. A ninety-nine-year lease on the property, secured in 1950 from Lynch's daughter, provided the basis for what was to be the Ozarks' largest tourist attraction.

Silver Dollar City, located over Marvel Cave, opened in May, 1960, on the site of the abortive 1880's mining community of Marmaros, which was founded to exploit the bat guano in the cave. Today it is one of the nation's most popular entertainment facilities of its kind. Its distinction as an attraction lies in Mary Herschend's concept of a middle western Williamsburg, with native craftsmen demonstrating their skills. The city keeps alive more than twenty historic crafts once commonly found in the hills. Visitors are allowed to chat with the craftsman as he works and see, at first hand, the methods being used.

In 1963 the first Missouri Festival of Ozark Craftsmen marked the beginning of an activity that would eventually draw to Silver Dollar City a quarter of a million people and more than sixty craft displays yearly. At this festival, held each October, the visitor can see everything from glassblowing to log hewing to cane-bottomed chair weaving to fiddle making. Each year additional attractions, crafts, and accommodations are added to serve the ever increasing number of visitors. The concept, which involves a rather pleasant blend of commercial activities with traditional crafts and historical-cultural activities , has proved so popular that the management of Silver Dollar City opened a similar attraction near the entrance to the Great Smoky Mountains National Park in eastern Tennessee. Because of the success of the Ozarks attraction, personnel from Silver Dollar City are in demand as consultants for other theme-park developments throughout the United States.

Tourism-Recreation Regions of the Ozarks

In delimiting eight tourism-recreation regions in the Ozarks, the concentration and linkages between specific points of interest, such as lakes, caves, state parks, national forests, resorts, and historical sites, were taken into account (fig. 12-3). The regions are broadly generalized to include much open and wild land that is essential for scenic tours, but areas that are essentially undeveloped or have less potential for tourism-recreation have been omitted. In this way the regions are different from the recreation regions that are defined by the three state tourism commissions, which include, for reasons of maintaining good public relations, all sections of the respective states in the tourism-recreation regions. The names that I have applied to the various regions were taken from striking physical features, historical or cultural traditions, or they are the names that have become popular during long periods of use.

Lake of the Ozarks Region

This region, about equidistant from St. Louis and Kansas City, features 65,000-acre Lake of the Ozarks, with 1,300 miles of shoeline behind Bagnell Dam. The hills, creeks, bluffs, natural bridges, caves, springs, and the lake make this area one of the outstanding recreation regions of the Ozarks. It is heavily used, attracting vacationers not only from the large urban centers of St. Louis, Kansas City, and Chicago, but also from other areas, especially Missouri, Illinois, Iowa, and Kansas.

A resort economy prevails throughout most of this relatively sparsely populated region. Businessmen in Camdenton estimate that retail volume has increased manyfold since development of the resort began. In Eldon, another trade

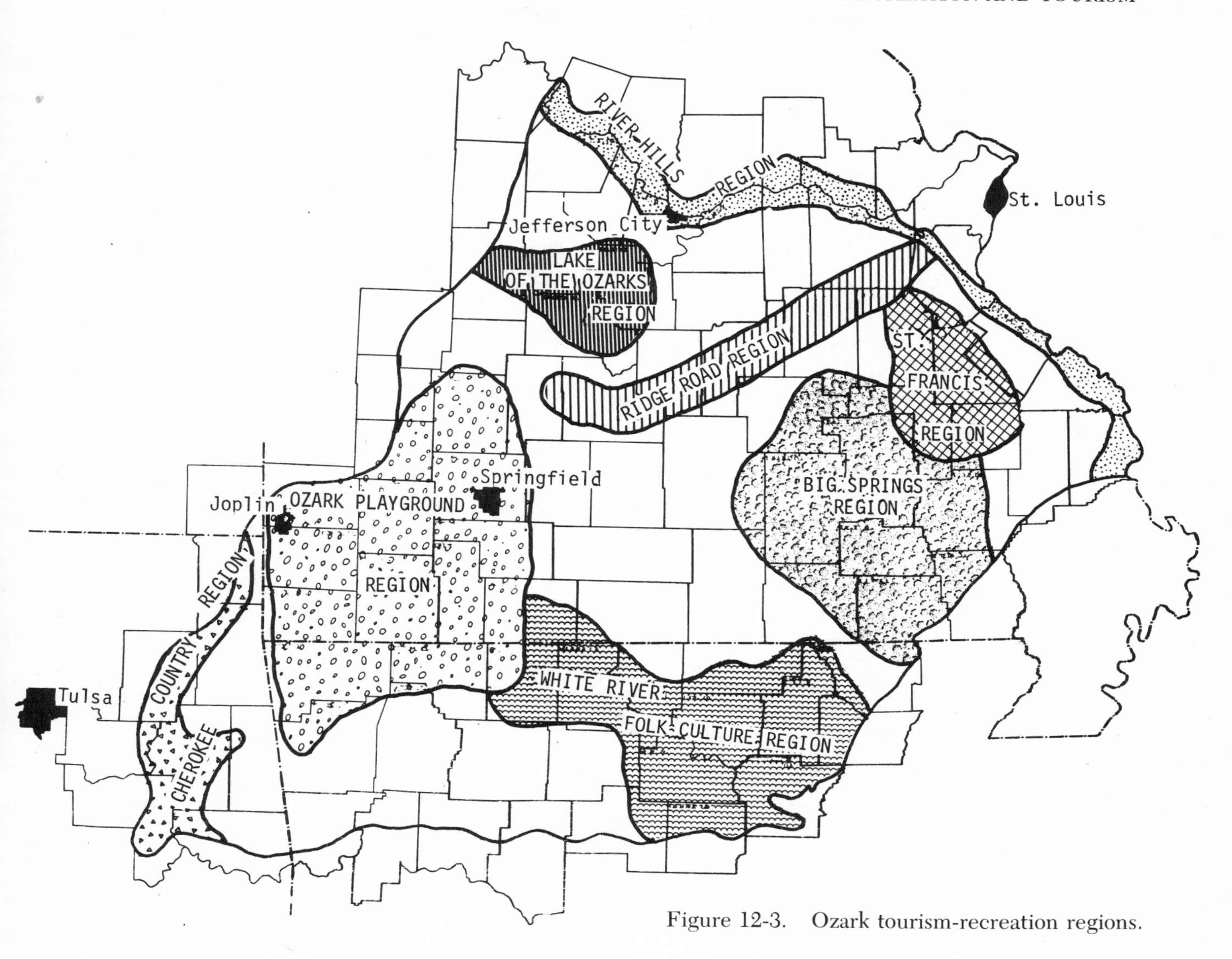

Figure 12-3. Ozark tourism-recreation regions.

center, retail volume is said to have increased four times between the completion of Bagnell Dam in 1931 and 1940 and to have expanded tenfold since 1940. Within this region is Lake of the Ozarks State Park, the largest state park in Missouri. It contains a deer preserve, beach, boat dock, and picnic, camping, and riding facilities. There are two commercially operated caves: Bridal and Jacob's. Hahatonka Spring and the ruins of Hahatonka Castle are major attractions, as are the many resorts and roadside gift shops. Second homes and retirement homes have been built in large numbers.

Probably the best-known resort on Lake of the Ozarks is Tan-Tar-A, which covers four hundred acres. Its central location in the state of Missouri makes it a convenient and popular place to hold statewide meetings. The new Windgate Center will expand convention accommodations to forty-six meeting rooms with capacities of ten to three thousand people. Over the years, increasing emphasis has been placed on sports activities. Water-sports activities continue to be popular, but the resort now advertises itself as a golf and tennis center. It is a complete resort in that it operates twelve months a year, offers package plans for guests, and provides an extensive range of activities and services. Among them are these: marina, fishing docks, swimming pools, sauna and health spa, several eating places, golf courses, bowling, billiards, tennis, ski slope, and horseback riding. A December, 1978 price quotation lists the rates for a winter package of three days and two nights, lodging, and meals at $89.00. The "honeymoon package" of five nights and six days, including luxury accommodations with a champagne cocktail party and various sports activities, sold for $366 in winter or $499 in season and holidays.

The Lake of the Ozarks region is perhaps the most maturely developed in the Ozarks. The stretch of U.S. Highway 54 from Camdenton to Eldon is a rather fully developed strip of motels, restaurants, fast-food establishments, children's rides, boat docks, resorts, country-music halls, antique shops and bric-a-brac stores, realty offices, and assorted other commercial activities that cater to both transients and residents.

Ridge Road Region

The Ridge Road Region focuses on Interstate 44 from Sullivan to near Lebanon. The existence of this well-traveled highway and U.S. Highway 66, which preceded it, have been important in developing the natural attractions of this region. In fact, the name *Ridge Road* was selected over *I-44 Region* as the proper designation for this tourism-recreation area because some of the attractions, including the once-popular Gasconade Hotel at Lebanon, were developed when most people traveled by railroad.

The hills, streams, and caves are the major attractions. At the northeast end of the region is Meramec Park and at the southwest extremity Bennett Spring State Park, two of Missouri's best-developed parks. Two of the Ozarks' most outstanding caves, Meramec Caverns and Onondaga Cave, are located near Stanton and Sullivan, respectively. The Meramec River and the lower reaches of Huzzah and Courtois creeks are popular float streams.

East of St. James is the Italian settlement at Rosati and a number of extensive vineyards. The wineries at Rosati and St. James are popular tourist attractions. At the south edge of St. James is the settlement at Yahweh City, former home of a religious sect that follows the beliefs of Joseph Jeffers, its spiritual leader and founder. The sixty or so disciples believe in direct communication with Yahweh and in the mystical power of pyramids. The compound, established in 1972, consists of a half-dozen frame houses, an office and press building, perhaps a dozen or more mobile homes, and a pyramid-shaped building where religious meetings and other events are held. Yahweh City is not open to the public, although in June, 1977, visitors were invited to an open house. In 1979 it was abandoned by the religious group and purchased by investors who hoped to develop it as a tourist attraction.

Southeast of St. James is Meramec Springs, jointly operated by the Lucy James Foundation and the Missouri Department of Natural Resources. It includes the spring and a trout hatchery, the ruins of the Maramec Iron Works, a historical museum, and inviting picnic grounds.

Other attractions include the University of Missouri at Rolla, one of the formost mining and engineering universities in the United States; Fort Leonard Wood, near Waynesville; and a number of camps and float services in the vicinity of the Gasconade River and the Big and Little Piney rivers.

St. Francis Region

This important recreation area in eastern Missouri is centered in the oldest geological formations outcropping anywhere in the Ozarks. Much of it is being preserved in a national forest, and there are five small state parks: Washington, St. Francois, Hawn, Elephant Rocks, and Johnson Shut-ins. There are many picturesque gorges cut through granite. At Graniteville are the widely known Elephant Rocks, huge boulders eroded into fantastic shapes. Also in the region are four rather isolated mountain peaks that attract tourists: Iron Mountain, Pilot Knob, Buford Mountain, and Taum Sauk Mountain. The last-named is the highest point in Missouri. At the base of the St. Francis Mountains are scenic Arcadia and Belleview valleys.

Historically, this region was one of the earliest to be settled in the entire Mississippi Valley. Place-names indicate the early French influence, and a French dialect is still spoken by a few older residents around Old Mines, a settlement north of Potosi. At Potosi, center for the mining of barite, is the grave of Moses Austin. Huge chat piles of waste rock from the lead mines around Flat River and Bonne Terre are reminders of mining's former importance. The mining museum and tours of Bonne Terre Mine are popular tourist attractions.

The tourist-recreation blend in the St. Francis region, like that of most of the northeastern Ozarks, is different from that of the bustling lake districts in the southern and western Ozarks. Camping, picnicking, horseback riding, canoeing, and touring are very popular. There is little development in the form of motels, amusement parks, or resorts.

Visitors who tour the pleasant and picturesque Belleview and Arcadia valleys find a different style and more leisurely pace than in the western lakes country. These valleys were discovered early by visitors from St. Louis. By the 1870's, summer homes were being built by wealthy families. Because the region could be reached easily on the St. Louis and Iron Mountain Railroad, the St. Francis Mountains became a popular vacation spot for St. Louisans. Tracts of the most desirable land were purchased by individuals for private estates and by churches for summer camps and rest homes. Stewardship of the aesthetic and scenic values of the land, combined with the fact that the streams are mainly small and poorly suited for large lakes, has produced a remarkable pleasant cultural landscape.

Trout fishing at Bennett Spring State Park, Dallas County, Missouri, 1973.

Big Springs Region

This rugged, forest-covered area is drained by a number of clear streams and contains many large springs. There are five state parks. Big Spring State Park contains what is said to be the biggest spring in the United States. Three other state parks, Montauk, Alley Spring, and Round Spring, also are noted for a large spring, while Sam A. Baker State Park is known for encompassing some of the wildest country in Missouri.

Not all of the large springs are in state parks. Greer Spring, north of Alton, is the most outstanding of these. There are many caves in the area, although few have been developed on any large commercial scale because of their remoteness from major highways.

The Big Springs region is in its developmental stage. Until recently, it was the retreat of the intrepid canoe enthusiast and camper. Large parties of canoes and johnboats set out from Montauk Spring or Round Spring on the Current River or Alley Spring or Eminence on the Jacks Fork and ended up at Van Buren. Rose Cliff Lodge, the decaying remains of which cling to a bluff on the Current River overlooking Van Buren, was the final destination of many of these parties. Among frequent visitors there were Leonard Hall, journalist; Julian Steyermark, botonist; Thomas Hart Benton, artist; and others interested in preserving the natural beauty of the Ozarks.

The establishment of national scenic riverways on the Current and Jacks Fork rivers has attracted national attention to the formerly isolated region. As a result, considerable development is taking place in the form of motels, camping areas, canoe rentals, and supply stores. However, development along the riverway is controlled by the federal government in order to preserve the riverfront. As yet, only a few small housing developments have been attempted near private lakes built on tributary streams.

Included in the area are large acreages of Twain National Forest. These lands and private property are mainly forested and support some of the largest deer herds in the Ozarks. Texas and Shannon counties are normally among the leaders in the number of deer killed during the autumn hunting season. There are two medium-sized reservoirs: Lake Wappapello and Clearwater Lake. They attract a large number of visitors from nearby counties in the Ozarks and from the lowlands to the southeast.

The distance to major highways is probably the most important limiting factor in the tourism-recreation development of the region. As improvements are made to roads connecting with U.S. Highways 60, 63, and 67 and Interstate 44, travel time will be reduced. However, with increased accessibility, the wilderness character of the region—its fundamental asset—will, of necessity, be changed.

Ozark Playground Region

This large recreation region covers the southwestern corner of Missouri and extends well into Arkansas. Besides the many interesting scenic features, there are major population concentrations in Springfield (140,000), Joplin (38,424), and in the northwest Arkansas counties of Washington and Benton. Much of the area is in Mark Twain National Forest. More than any other district of the Ozarks, this is the core area of tourism and recreation. It was here that the great spas were built and some of the first large lake resorts were developed.

For purposes of description, it is convenient to subdivide this region into six subregions: the Beaver Lake Area, the Eureka Springs Area, the Shepherd of the Hills Area, the Springfield Area, the Joplin Area, and the Stockton–Pomme de Terre Area.

The Beaver Lake Area features approximately 880 private and public use campsites, outstanding fishing in the 28,000 acres of lake, and the winding waters of the White River. There are a number of championship golf courses and a wide range of hotels, motels, and restaurants. Thousands of visitors with a liking for history are attracted to the Pea Ridge and Prairie Grove battlefields.

West of Beaver Lake is the Strip, nearly thirty miles of commercial establishments along U.S. Highway 71 beginning at the Missouri state line and extending to Fayetteville, Arkansas. Included in it are the communities of Bella Vista, Bentonville, Rogers, and Springdale. At Tontitown, an Italian settlement, the restaurants that serve traditional Italian food are popular, as is the annual grape festival. Bella Vista Village is the largest of the Ozark second-home and retirement-home developments. The campus of the University of Arkansas rambles over the hills of Fayetteville, which also serves as a popular jumping-off place for shunpiking into the Boston Mountains. This popular Ozark diversion consists of traveling the winding back roads to discover tiny communities and to view homes and farms in the more remote sections of the region.

The Eureka Springs Area consists primarily of the old resort town. It is billed as the Little Switzerland of America because of the stylish homes and old hotels perched on precarious ledges and hillsides. Eureka Springs is touted as "a Victorian showplace where artists and writers congregate," and it offers a wide range of attractions: Blue Spring, Onyx Cave, the Passion Play, the Christ of the Ozarks, and the Holiday Island Exotic Animal Park, Visitors find accommodations either at one of the old resort hotels—Crescent, Basin Park, New Orleans—or at one of several new motels and inns that have been built along U.S. Highway 62 at the edge of town.

In nearby Berryville, Saunders Memorial Museum offers an outstanding display of firearms. The old Grand View Hotel at Berryville still stands. Constructed in 1902, when the coming of the Missouri and North Arkansas Railroad promised a lively future for Berryville, the hotel is an imposing brick building with prominent wooden galleries, in the steamboat-Gothic style, girdling each of its three floors. It has a high-peaked roof with a pointed tower.

The Shepherd of the Hills Area has a highly developed resort economy, especially around Lake Taneycomo and Table Rock Lake. The name derives from the popularity of Harold Bill Wright's book and much-visited Shepherd of the Hills Farm and Theatre. The outstanding attraction in terms of visitors is Silver Dollar City. Trout fishing, boat excursions, and camping are the chief activities on Lake Taneycomo. Trout, stocked by the Missouri Department of Natural Resources, are taken from the bank or by drifting down the lake from the spillway behind Table Rock Dam. Table Rock Lake has many camping sites and marinas. Warm-water fish, particularly bass, crappie, and channel catfish, make Table Rock Lake one of the most popular fishing spots in the Ozarks.

Rockaway Beach, Branson, and Hollister offers individual brands of diversion for vacationers. The region adjacent to the lakes is especially desirable as a location for retirement and second homes. As seen at night, the lake district resembles a sparsely settled city.

A stretch of Missouri Highway 76 west of Branson has become known as the Branson Strip. Included in the thirteen-mile section between Branson and Missouri Highway 13 are motels, inns, restaurants, antique shops, more than twenty gift and sourvenir shops, a shopping center, four country-music halls, Shepherd of the Hills Farm, Silver Dollar City, and a collection of lesser attractions.

Roaring River State Park, near the western headwaters of Table Rock Lake, is one of the most completely developed in Missouri. Its spring supports a trout hatchery, and camping and motel facilities are available.

The Springfield Area has a number of major tourist-recreation attractions. Approximately ten miles southeast of the city is Wilson's Creek Battlefield National Park. Northwest of Springfield is Fantastic Caverns, which features a cavern tour by vehicle. To the east on Interstate 44 is Exotic Animal Paradise, which features automobile tours of the property, where various animals from all parts of the world are kept.

Christ of the Ozarks, Eureka Springs, Arkansas, 1972.

Within the city are several major attractions: the national cemetery; Southwest Missouri State University; Drury, Evangel, Central Bible, and Baptist Bible colleges; the federal medical center; and the national headquarters of the Assembly of God church. As one of the oldest towns in the Ozarks, Springfield has an interesting history and a number of historic homes and commercial buildings.

Springfield, Queen City of the Ozarks, provides an important ingredient for the tourism-recreation blend of the Ozark Playground Region. It has the most complete range of services available in the Ozark region, including two large and well-equipped hospitals; a large regional shopping mall in addition to the downtown area and other shopping centers; a wide range of motel and convention accommodations; a selection of movies; theatre; a symphony orchestra; dozens of restaurants to suit varied tastes; and many evening-entertainment and cultural attractions.

Jig dancers performing at School of the Ozarks, Point Lookout, Missouri, 1977.

The Joplin Area is particularly popular with history buffs and mineral collectors. The city has been billed as the town that Jack built because it is built literally upon the now-abandoned mines that produced the zinc ore known as jack. The mineral museum in Schiffendecker Park, walking tours among the chat piles, and shunpiking to old mining camps are popular pastimes. Probably the most elegant houses in the Ozarks were built by mining tycoons west of downtown Joplin. Many of these homes, which included servants' quarters and carriage houses, are opened during a house tour in the fall of the year.

Outlying attractions in the Joplin area include George Washington Carver National Monument near Diamond; Truitt's Cave at Lanagan; Rockhound Paradise at Anderson; Ozark Wonder Cave at Noel; the tiff mines near Seneca; and the Carthage marble quarry and plant at Carthage. Pineville, the county seat of McDonald County, Missouri, is one of the most undisturbed and picturesque towns of the courthouse-square type. Here, under storefront canopies, Vance Randolph collected from residents many of the stories he incorporated into several books on Ozark folklore. In the summer of 1938, actors Henry Fonda and Tyrone Power and a complete technical and camera crew moved in to film the movie *Jesse James*.

The Stockton–Pomme de Terre Area, compared to the other districts of the Ozark Playground Region, is in its youthful stage of development. Stockton and Hermitage are the chief towns, located, respectively, north of the dams. There are additional physical similarities: each lake has two major arms; state parks—Stockton and Pomme de Terre—are located on the point of land where the arms of the lakes meet; both lakes have a reputation for good fishing and water sports; and, finally, construction of marinas, visitor accommodations and services, and residential subdivisions is progressing rapidly at both lakes.

White River Folk Culture Region

Tourism and recreation attractions are being developed very rapidly in this region. In addition to three large lakes—Norfolk, Bull Shoals, Greers Ferry—the region possesses superb float streams, including the Buffalo, Spring, and North Fork rivers. For convenience in description, I have subdivided the region into five sections: the Harrison Area, the Twin Lakes Area, the Mountain View Area, the Hardy Area, and the Greers Ferry Area.

The Harrison Area includes the scenic Buffalo River, one of the most popular Ozark float streams and, according to residents, the last of the good warm-water float-fishing streams. South of Harrison is Scenic Highway 7, one of the most popular routes through the Boston Mountains for shunpikers. Along Highway 7 south of Jasper is the theme park Dogpatch U.S.A. Conceived in 1967 by O. J. Snow and nine other Harrison businessmen, the park, developed on an 825-acre tract known as Marble Falls, depicts Al Capp's comic strip "Li'l Abner." Visitors are welcomed by Daisy Mae, Li'l Abner, Mammy and Pappy Yokum, Marryin' Sam, Moonbeam McSwine, and other characters from the comic strip. Next door is Arkansas' only ski resort, Marble Falls Resort and Convention Center. There are accommodations at the motel or the chalets of Marble Falls and camping facilities at approximately 452 private and public use campsites in the area.

The Twin Lakes Area is centered on mammoth Bull Shoals and Norfork lakes. Canoe floats are popular on the North Fork River and trout fishing

Anchor Travel Village tourist court at Branson, Missouri, *circa* 1945. (Courtesy Missouri State Historical Society.)

is available on the river or several private trout farms at several of the large srpings that issue into the North Fork. Complementing the many resorts and marinas on the lake are a wide variety of attractions and accommodations: Bull Shoals State Park, Penrod's Museum, Mountain Village 1890, Norfork Federal Fish Hatchery, the oldest home in the White River country (Wolf House), and the resort communities of Mountain Home, Bull Shoals, and Lakeview.

The Mountain View Area has enjoyed a profitable increase in visitors as a result of the new $3.4 million Ozark Folk Culture Center and the opening of Blanchard Springs Caverns as a recreation area. Mountain music is the theme at Mountain View. Visitors at Folk Culture Center are treated to music played by area residents on the dulcimer, fiddle, or pickin' bow. The Rackensack Society musicians, including nationally known Jimmy Driftwood from nearby Timbo, Arkansas, (best known for "The Battle of New Orleans" and "The Tennessee Stud") assemble informally on Friday nights to play their music in an old store building in Mountain View. More than twenty crafts are preserved at the Folk Culture Center, and lodges are available at the park for visitors to stay overnight or for longer periods.

At Blanchard Springs Caverns, visitors are led every twenty minutes along Dripstone Trail, which leads them through three-fourths of a mile of caverns, including the giant Cathedral Room, which measures 180 by 1,200 feet and has 65-foot Giant Column. Aboveground are opportunities to hike or camp in the Sylamore District of Ozark National Forest or to float and fish in the Buffalo River.

The Hardy Area is known as "land just made for tranquility." There are excellent accommodations in motels and at the resort developments at Horseshoe Bend and Cherokee Village. Camping is available at approximately 397 private and public campsites, including those at Mammoth Spring State Park. Spring River is one of the better cold-water canoe and float-fishing streams in the Ozarks. Evening musical entertainment is lively at the Arkansas Traveler Theatre.

Much of the recent tourism-recreation development and other commercial growth has occurred along Arkansas Highway 167 between Hardy and Ash Flat. Sharp County is one of those Arkansas Ozarks counties that, because of poor roads and local politics, had two county seats. The new courthouse, a sprawling one-story structure of contemporary architectural style, is at Ash Flat, about midway between the former county seats at Hardy and Evening Shade.

The Greers Ferry Area, on the south slope of the Boston Mountains, focuses on forty thousand-acre Greers Ferry Lake. The lake is popular for sailing, water skiing, scuba diving, swimming, and fishing. The Little Red River below the dam vies with the lake for fishing trophies. Popular activities include tours of the federal fish hatchery, hikes on Sugar Leaf Nature Trail, and the Ozark Frontier Trail Festival and Crafts Show in October. The resort communities of Quitman, Clinton, Edgemont, Heber Springs, and Brownsville provide ample services and overnight accommodations.

River Hills Region The northern and eastern borders of the Ozarks were the first to be settled by whites. The history and cultural tradition include French, American, and German elements. Many of the region's attractions are based on the influence of the two great waterways, the Mississippi and Missouri rivers. For convenience of description, I have divided the region into two subregions: the Mississippi River Border Area and the Missouri River Border Area.

The Mississippi River Border Area consists of many attractions scattered along the river between Cape Girardeau and Ste. Genevieve. The river border is an important transportation corridor—water, rail, and highway—and much of the history and culture of the area is connected with commerce and trade. The most visited attraction is the historical old town of Ste. Genevieve, where elements of French culture dating back to the eighteenth century have been preserved. Points of interest at Ste. Genevieve include Ste. Genevieve Catholic Church, which casts its shadow across the square. The stained-glass windows and names of priests and important parishioners tell of the dominance of French and then German culture. Nearby is an historical museum and Old Brick House Restaurant, said to be the first brick building west of the Mississippi River. Other houses dating from the late 1700's and early 1800's, include Vital de St. Gemme de Beauvais House, Jean Baptiste Valle House, Bolduc House, Meilleur House, Francois Valle House, Green Tree Tavern, and Misplait House. In the old cemetery, weathered gravestones record, often in French, the memory of many early residents of Ste. Genevieve.

Other attractions in the Mississippi River Border Area include East Perry, a string of German communities—Uniontown, Frohna, Altenburg, Wittenburg—where descendents of immigrants who settled in the 1840's have retained their language and customs to a remarkable degree; Bollinger Mill and Covered Bridge; and Trail of Tears State Park, which overlooks the Mississippi River. A suitable base for tours is Cape Girardeau, an old waterfront town where people from the Ozarks mingle with flatlanders from the Mississippi alluvial plain. At Cape Girardeau are Southeast Missouri State University and many early nineteenth-century buildings and homes.

The Missouri River Border Area is rich in history and culture. The section between Washington and Jefferson City is known as the Missouri Rhineland because of the large number of people of German descent. The section above Jefferson City is the historic Boonslick country, where Daniel Boone and his sons first established saltworks and opened the area to settlement. At Washington in Franklin County is the Missouri

Folk musician at the Ozark Folk Culture Center, Mountain View, Arkansas, 1976. (Courtesy Arkansas Department of Parks and Tourism.)

Meerschaum Plant, billed as the world's leading manufacturer of corncob pipes. Traveling upriver, along scenic Missouri Highway 100 on the bluffs overlooking the fertile Missouri River valley, one enters the town of Hermann. Because many of the German immigrants who settled there in the 1840's and 1850's were well educated, Hermann is known as the cultural capital of the Missouri Rhineland. There are many examples of German architecture in the commercial and residential buildings. In autumn and spring, when Oktoberfest and Maifest are celebrated, the houses are opened to the thousands of visitors who crowd the streets of the town.

At Jefferson City, locally known as Jeff City, is the state capitol and the large cluster of state office buildings required to administer programs to provide services for Missouri's 6.5 million people. Other points of interest include the Executive Mansion, the Missouri State Penetentiary, the national cemetery, and Lincoln University.

Upstream in the heart of Boonslick country is Boonville, built on the crest of the bluffs and encircled by hills. In the residential section are antebellum brick residences "with generous rooms, wide halls, and modest Classic-Revival details, flamboyant houses of the 'gingerbread' era' "; and modern bungalows and ranch-style homes. Arrow Rock State Park on the hills overlooking the Missouri River is at the extreme northern point of the Ozarks. In Old Tavern at the park, built by John Huston about 1834, are many furnishings of that era, including walnut, maple, and stenciled chairs and canopied beds. The park also includes the old Arrow Rock jail, George Caleb Bingham House, and William B. Sappington House.

Cherokee Country Region The Cherokee Country Region, situated on the extreme southwest border of the Ozarks, focuses especially on water sports, canoeing on the wild rivers, and fishing in the lakes on the Neosho (Grand) and Illinois rivers. The Illinois, by far Oklahoma's most popular float stream, is convenient and commercialized—the perfect place to develop canoe skills. Spring Fork of the Neosho River, near Quapaw, offers commercial canoe outfitters, and many other streams await the aggressive canoeist. Flint and Barren Fork creeks, tributaries of the Illinois, can be floated with minimum portage during the high-water seasons, early spring and late fall.

For purposes of description, the lake areas may be subdivided into the Spavinaw–Lake o' the Cherokees Area, and the Fort Gibson–Tenkiller Area.

The Spavinaw–Lake o' the Cherokees Area includes many marinas and motel and resort accommodations at recreation areas on the three lakes. Notable concentrations are found in Twin Bridges Recreation Area, Honey Creek Recreation Area, Cherokee Recreation Area, Spavinaw Recreation Area, Upper Spavinaw Recreaction Area, and Salina Recreation Area. The communities of Grove, Jay, Spavinaw, and Salina serve the east shore, or Ozark side, of the two large lakes. Shangri-La Resort and Lakemont Shores are probably the best known of the large resort developments. As in the other Ozark lake recreation areas, the resorts advertise widely and offer package plans for visitors.

The region is rich in history: Salina was the site of Chouteau Trading Post, established in the early nineteenth century by the same French family that figured in the founding of St. Louis, Missouri; near Jay is Oak Hills Indian Center, where Cherokee artisans produce crafts; and ten miles above Upper Spavinaw Lake is the site of Fort Wayne, headquarters of Captain Nathanial Boone, son of Daniel Boone, who conducted the Indian boundary surveys. Immediately to the north are the old lead-zinc mining towns of Commerce, Picher, and Cardin, Oklahoma, and Baxter Springs and Galena, Kansas. These towns and the backwoods hills provide interesting areas for shunpiking.

The Fort Gibson–Tenkiller Area includes the two large reservoirs by the same names, the channeled and improved sections of the Grand and Arkansas rivers, including Greenleaf Lake, and the rugged Brushy Mountain section of the Boston Mountains. In addition to the various resorts, marinas and fishing docks, the region is rich in historical attractions. Resort communities include Fort Gibson, Hulbert, Cookson, and Blackgum. At Tahlequah, the capital of the Cherokee Nation, are Northeastern Oklahoma State College and the

Cherokee Museum. Southeast of the city is Park Hill, where Chief John Ross established his home in 1839 near the Presbyterian Mission. Ross Family Cemetery and John Murrell Mansion are nearby. At Fort Gibson, many of the buildings of the old army post have been restored and opened to the public.

Environmental Effects of Tourism and Recreation

The development of tourist and recreation attractions necessarily affects the landscape. Increases in population inevitably produce change. As outsiders are attracted to a region, the residents encounter different lifestyles, and established patterns of life are gradually altered. Over the years, some of the visitors have become permanent residents, so that the character of the resident population has itself evolved over time.

Many of the tourist attractions along Ozark highways give a Coney Island appearance to the landscape. Go-carts, bumper cars, minibikes, country-music halls, and other attractions designed for family entertainment are mixed with antique shops, drive-in food establishments, restaurants, gift and souvenir shops, and signs and billboards. Two notable tourist string developments have grown along the section of U.S. Highway 54 between Camdenton and Osage Beach in the Lake of the Ozarks region and along Highway 76 west of Branson in Taney County. Some observers have recommended that certain recreation services having nuisance value be grouped and located where they do not mar aesthetic values or other tourist attractions.

The development of second homes and retirement homes has progressed rapidly around the lakes. There was little nuisance, at the outset but as the development has become more intensive, several problems have cropped up. First the danger of serious pollution of groundwater supplies and the lakes has increased as more onsite sewage treatment facilities (septic tanks) have been installed without proper construction methods or inspection. In an effort to gain speculation profits, the acreage that is subdivided for homes often exceed demand. Developers are sometimes allowed to put in access roads meeting

Sequiota Cave and Spring, Springfield, Missouri. Water from the spring formerly supplied a state trout hatchery, but the water has been polluted severely by septic drainage from residential subdivisions.

minimum engineering standards and turn them over to the county for maintenance. Often this results in covering scenic hills with many crisscrossing access roads but few houses; equally important, there is little tax base for maintenance of the roads. An extra burden is placed on community facilities, such as highways, hospitals, and schools, by increases in seasonal and permanent population.

The problems created by the sale of cheap land are not new to the Ozarks. Carl O. Sauer described the basic dilemma that existed about 1920 as follows:

> The large areas of cheap land have given rise from time to time to promotion schemes. For this business the region possesses unusual inducements. The Ozarks are near large centers of population. They have an attractive climate, especially to northern people. The region delights city people who think of country

life in romantic terms. In the hands of skillful manipulators, well-selected illustrations and half-truths are elaborated artfully from these points of attraction. Visions of comfortable country homes are held out to city clerks and tradesmen who have tired of the precariousness and routine of their present occupations. Fruit orchards, chicken farms, cattle and hog ranches, are the favorite projects promoted. Usually the very poorest land, which even the natives have avoided, is chosen. This is either laid out in small tracts of five to forty acres, or a stock company sells shares in a very large tract. In either case the profits are figured on the basis of a high per acre productivensss. In this way land has been sold for fruit orchards on which trees could have been planted only by blasting holes, and chicken ranches have been promoted in inaccessible locations where the production of grain is an impossibility and even grass grows with difficulty. Some of the land which has been sold for purposes of intensive farming is so rough that it is impossible to drive a wagon over it. If properly managed, the companies clear many hundred percent, and the investor is left with a tract of land that is nearly worthless because it is poor and is too small to be put to any practical use. Much of the land is sold for taxes after the owners are disillusioned. In numerous cases the owner, who has not seen the land, has decided to quit his position and move to his "farm." By the time he is established on the place a large part of his savings is gone, and in the course of a short time the remainder is lost in the hopeless effort to produce a living there. Finally the settler is reduced to doing odd jobs in the vicinity at very low wages, or, if fortunate, returns to the city to begin over. The promotion of these schemes has not only unloaded on the region families who have become its wards, but has discredited the Ozarks entirely in the minds of many people, in spite of their not inconsiderable possibilities of successful development.[23]

The image of the Ozarks as a place for cheap retirement living is not entirely false, but certainly there have been many mistakes in land use. It behooves both the newcomer and the longtime Ozark resident to embrace a philosophy of conservation and wise use of natural resources. Even today many immigrants, particularly those who have come to gain a livelihood wholly from a small tract of land as part of the back-to-the-land movement, do not understand the limited productivity of Ozark soils. There are some who, either from their own misunderstanding or in a frantic effort to make a living or to speculate in land investment, misrepresent the region and its possibilities. The following advertisement that I picked up in a crossroads general store when the back-to-the-land movement was at its zenith in the early 1970's is interesting because of its resemblance to Sauer's remarks and to advertisements by lumber companies that were disposing of cutover land in the early 1900's.

WANTED: "NATURAL" FAMILIES

We are presently farming organically, in the heart of the Ozarks, our 600 acre farm overlooking Bryant Creek south of Mansfield, Missouri. This is one of the seven pollution free areas left in the United States. To enable us to secure a better market for our livestock and produce, we are selling 5 acre homesteads to people who want a better way of life. There is employment in Mansfield and Ava; both are 6 miles from the farm by blacktop. The homesteads are in timber because they've not been farmed for over 25 years. The ground is rock free, level, farmable, and has never been "Pesticided" or chemically fertilized. Some tracts have fruit trees.

Buy 5 acres, subdivide it into acre homesites and pay for your own land, sell retiring couples, a friend, anyone who wants to live in a clean community and have natural foods available. Choose your own neighbors, or keep and farm your own homestead. We're not selling any parcel smaller than 5 acres. Five acres of anything would support and supply a family with all produce, grain, poultry, small meats, and dairy products. What you don't want to raise, someone else can supply.

Two and three bedroom homes with full basements are available for under $20,000, 5 acres included. There are some reasonable restrictions for your own protection. Within the year, if we have enough marketables raised here, a marketing co-op will be formed to secure a steady outlet for surplus commodities.

Aerie Acres wants doers, the now people, whether you're 8 or 80. Each of us has something to offer others from apples or bees to yucca or zucchini, so extend a helping hand and be part of this composite community.

Visit us; stay for supper.

The world energy crisis casts a pall over the tourism-recreation industry, just as it does over the entire American economic system. It is impossible to predict what the future of the tourism-recreation industry will be if gasoline is

23. Sauer, *Geography of the Ozark Highland*, pp. 186–87.

rationed or its price increases to a prohibitive level. Although the higher cost of fuel might discourage some visitors, it could attract others. Some tourists, who normally might select a vacation on the East or West coasts or in Europe, might opt for a less-expensive Ozark vacation, thereby helping to offset the visitors who cancel vacation plans altogether.

The settlements scattered about the lakes and along highways are not energy efficient. It is expensive to provide services of the everyday type—health care, education, electricity, and fuel—when the houses are scattered several hundred yards or even a mile or more apart. Many of the people who live in the lake areas work in growth centers, such as Springfield, Joplin, Miami, Fayetteville, Springdale, Rogers, or Muskogee. Conceivably, the cost of transportation could become so prohibitive that such long-distance daily commuting would be abandoned.

Selected References

Arkansas State Planning Board and the Writers Project of the Works Progress Administration. *Arkansas: A Guide to the State*. American Guide Series. New York: Hastings House, 1941.

Basler, Lucille. *A Tour of Old Ste. Genevieve*. St. Genevieve, Mo.: Wehmeyer Printing Company, n.d.

Bella Vista (Ark.) *Weekly Vista*, vol. 12, no. 1, January 4, 1977.

Bird, Ronald, and Fenley, R. D. *Contribution of Part-Time Residents to the Local Economy of a County in the Missouri Ozarks, 1960*. University of Missouri Agricultural Experiment Station Research Bulletin 814. Columbia: University of Missouri Press, 1962.

———, and Miller, Frank. *Where Ozark Tourists Come From and Their Impact on Local Economy*. University of Missouri Agricultural Experiment Station Research Bulletin 798. Columbia: University of Missouri Press, 1962.

———. *Contributions of Tourist Trade to Incomes of People in the Missouri Ozarks*. University of Missouri Agricultural Experiment Station Research Bulletin 799. Columbia: University of Missouri Press, 1962.

Black, J. Dickson. *History of Benton County, 1836–1936*. Little Rock: International Graphics Industries, 1975.

Christian County Centennial, Inc. *Christian County: Its First 100 Years*. Ozark, Mo.: 1959.

Crisler, Robert M., and Hunt, Mahlon S. "Recreation Regions of Missouri," *Journal of Geography* 51 (January 1952): 30–39.

Directories of Chambers of Commerce and Lake Associations in the Ozark Region.

Duffield, Benny. "Comparisons of Float Trip Recreation Opportunities by Visitors to the Eleven Point River." Master's thesis, University of Missouri-Columbia, 1972.

Dulles, Foster Rhea. *A History of Recreation: America Learns to Play*. New York: Meredith Publishing Co. 1965.

Gerstäker, Friedrich. *Wild Sports in the Far West*. Durham, N.C.: Duke University Press, 1968.

Hall, Leonard. *Stars Upstream*. Columbia: University of Missouri Press, 1958.

Hawksley, Oscar. *Missouri Ozark Waterways*. Jefferson City: Missouri Department of Conservation, 1965.

"Historical Description of Cherokee Village." Mimeographed. Cherokee Village, Ark.: n.d.

Holmes, Benjamin F. "Recreational Occupance in the Big Springs Country of Southeast Missouri." Master's thesis, University of Missouri-Columbia, 1952.

Hull, Clifton E. *Shortline Railroads of Arkansas*. Norman: University of Oklahoma Press, 1969.

Mark Twain National Forest. *Plan for Managing National Forests in Missouri*. Rolla, Mo.: 1976.

Missouri State Highway Commission and Writers Program of the Works Progress Administration. *Missouri: A Guide to the "Show Me" State*. American Guide Series. New York: Duell, Sloan and Pearce, 1941.

Ozark Playgrounds Association. *Official Directory, Ozark Playgrounds Association*. Joplin, Mo.: 1977.

Rost, Harry T. D. "A Geographic Study of Recreational Resources and Facilities in Northwest Arkansas." Master's thesis, University of Arkansas, 1956.

Sanning, Lynn. "Bagnell Dam and the Lake of the Ozarks Region." Term paper, Department of Geography of Missouri, Southwest Missouri State University, 1977.

Sauer, Carl O. *The Geography of the Ozark Highland of Missouri*. The Geographic Society of Chicago Bulletin no. 7. Chicago: University of Chicago Press, 1920.

Schoolcraft, Henry Rowe. *Journal of a Tour into the Interior of Missouri and Arkansas in 1818 and 1819*. In *Schoolcraft in the Ozarks*, edited by Hugh Parks. Van Buren, Ark.: Press-Argus Printers, 1955.

Schweitzer, Paul. "A Report on the Mineral Waters of Missouri," *Geological Survey of Missouri*, 1st. series, vol. 3 (1892).

Simkins, Paul D. "A Study of Recreation in the White River Hills of Missouri," Master's thesis, University of Missouri-Columbia, 1954.

Vickery, Margaret Ray. *Ozark Stories of the Upper Current River. Salem* (Mo.) *News*, n.d.

Ullman, Edward L. "Geographical Prediction and Theory: The Measure of Recreation Benefits in the Maramec Basin." In *Problems and Trends in American Geography*, edited by Saul B. Cohen. New York: Basic Books, 1967.

Vogel, Robert S. "The Lake of the Ozarks Region, Missouri: A Study in Recreational Geography." Master's thesis, Michigan State University, 1957.

13. Nonmaterial Cultural Traits

Although a complete analysis of the cultural traits of an area as large as the Ozarks would require all the detail of a mail-order catalog and an organization comparable to that of the federal census, something can be done to convey the idea to the reader. In his history of pioneer life, Wiley Britton,[1] has given us a picture of the material culture of the pioneer in southwest Missouri, and Vance Randolph has elaborated on it in several books to present to the world the isolated hill man and his family. In recent years a spate of books, mainly of the reminiscent type dealing with everyday life in the rural Ozarks, has been written.

Memorabilia have been nourished by the Ozark resident's belated reflection on his past and accompanied by the national bicentennial and a host of centennial celebrations in towns founded during the railroad-building boom of the 1870's and 1880's. The telling and retelling in redundant detail of hog killings, fiddle making, moonshining, quilting bees, cabin raisings, rail splitting, tie hacking, food preserving, hayrack rides, spelling bees, party playing, long walks to rural schools in all kinds of inclement weather, revivals, fist fights, pie auctions, shootings, trials, hangings, funerals, family reunions, Fourth of July celebrations, kangaroo courts, drawing water from the well, carrying water from the spring, and churning homemade butter tell of the passing of the cultural isolation of rural America. Little of this was unique to the Ozarks; much the same rural lifestyle, with variations, once existed throughout the Middle West, the Great Plains, the South, and in virtually every other rural section of the United States. A simple subsistence lifestyle perhaps lasted longer in the Ozarks and is therefore fresher in memory. Undoubtedly the Ozark tourism industry has played an important role in preserving the country image of the region even to the point of nurturing crafts and skills that were little known by early residents of the region.

1. Wiley Britton, *Pioneer Life in Southwest Missouri* (Kansas City: Smith-Grieves Company, Publishers, 1929).

Education

Strictly speaking, the whole of the process whereby the individual becomes adjusted to his culture may be thought of as education. This naturally includes both the unconscious adjustment and that which is carried out consciously and purposely by society. Although it is probably true that the school is the most effective agency of change in an isolated area, the ability to teach culture through radio and television has removed the buffer of isolation from formerly remote sections. It is perhaps arguable whether the two media accurately reflect the existing cultural mores or encourage higher levels of cultural achievement.

In former times, education was not regarded as highly as it is now. The family-farm institution was particularly strong, and there was a feeling that very little of that taught in the schoolroom would be important in making a living. This attitude is not completely absent, but it is far less prevelent today. Farming is a vocation that offers a livelihood to fewer people each year, and successful farming, in any terms, requires many skills taught in schools.

Education in the Ozarks has lagged behind that of more prosperous sections. In the 1930's, when an eight-month session was considered minimal for elementary education in Missouri, many Ozark counties had shorter terms. In Missouri ten of the 17 districts that provided less than four months of school were in the Ozarks as were 95 of 114 districts that provided four to six months and 756 of the 875 that provided six to less than eight months. In all, 86 per cent of the school districts in Missouri that provided less than the standard eight-month term were in the Ozarks, as were only 11 per cent of those that provided more than eight months.

Although the level of education has improved much, Ozark counties continue to lag behind more prosperous regions. In only Cole, Pulaski, Greene (Missouri), and Washington (Arkansas) counties had the median school year completed risen to 12 years or more by 1972. Each of these counties has a major college or university. Still, in more than half of the interior Ozark counties, less than 40 per cent of persons 25 years old and over had completed high school in 1972. Percentages ranged from 29.1 in Gasconade County to 58.4 in Greene County. Education lagged even more in the Arkansas and Oklahoma Ozarks. Schools were established in the Cherokee Nation at an early date, but they served only a small part of the potential student population.

There continues to be substantial resistance to formal education, much of it expressed in an unconscious way. Although most natives express interest in supporting schools, those who place great store in traditional values believe that formal education draws native youth out of the shelter of families, out of churches, and out of participation in the family and community. Frequently, one hears about college-educated young people who no longer closely associate with their family because "they got ruined by too much education."

In a column in the *White River Leader* (Branson, Missouri), "Uncle Bill From Kirbyville" expressed some of the native beliefs about the nature and worth of a higher education:

> Ed ask if the government has ever given serious study to the groundhog, and nobody didn't know that either. Ed allowed that a Government that can spend hundreds of thousands of dollars on researching hawks wings, owls eyes and the navigation equipment of bats and porpuses had ought to be able to appropriate a few thousand for groundhogs. Bug Hookum has agreed with Ed that folks get too carried away with useless learning.
>
> While the schools of higher learning are doing research in pinup calenders and comic books, and the younguns is taking courses in movie appreciation and ping pong, Bug said, bricklayers and plumbers in this country get more work than they can do at $11 a hour. It ain't no wonder, declared Bug, that the educated is the ones out of work.
>
> Clem Webster was agreed with Bug that students in what they call the liberal arts has plenty to be liberal with. They got all the time in the world while they spend money their folks worked a lifetime to save up. They got no responsibility in life but to take their bodies to a room to be talked to, and if they want to take part in a riot somewhere they git excused from that. With nothing to do but look down their noses at the working world, Clem said, it ain't no wonder the students git restless and burn down the schools.[2]

For many, however, education is, first, a means of getting a job. Second, it is essential for successful interactions with non-natives. Although regional accent is of little importance, bad grammar is believed to be a distinct disadvantage in dealing with outsiders. The native Ozarker who secures a good education may attain a managerial or ownership position or gain a position in the legal and

2. "Uncle Bill From Kirbyville Says Groundhog Deserves Research?" *Branson* (Mo.) *White River Leader*, January 31, 1972, p. 2.

political system. In these situations, he is often in a superior competitive position compared to a non-native with equal talents and education.

Until the present generation, education beyond the eighth grade was not considered essential. The decision to attend high school not only had important ramifications for one's future, it also meant contact with a different lifestyle for many. Donald Holliday tells of his brother Gerald's decision to attend high school in Hollister:

> When Gerald started to high school in 1944, he started after having faced and made a serious decision—whether to go to high school, for in the community of Pine Top, the common thing for a young man to do after he finished the eighth grade, somewhere between the ages of thirteen and twenty-one or so, was to begin to farm with his father. In order to make the decision to go to high school, Gerald was forced to determine that he wanted a higher education. The younger brothers never faced that decision; it was made for them by consolidation and universal public school laws. Thus when they started to high school, they did so with their goals yet undefined. Not until they graduated and were faced with the decision to go to college or not to go were they forced to consciously consider objectives.[3]

Education is usually not a thing to be displayed. Speech habits are indicative. The configuration of dialect is both geographical and individual. In the remote sections it may yet be so pronounced that even an occasional departure from it stamps the speaker as an outsider; in the more accessible sections it is confined to the ignorant or the occasional lapse of the educated. A person of education may seem to have two languages: one to meet the formal and more stilted demands of polite society, the other for ordinary discourse with those he considers his equals or inferiors. Cralle relates an interesting example told by one of his students:

> You know, when I'm up at college I believe I can talk about as well as any of them. But let me get down here in these hills again, get on a pair of overalls and about three days' growth of beard, and I'll be talkin just like a hill-billy.[4]

A contemporary example of this dualism can be observed in the language usage of educated individuals who have joined the citizens band radio rage. The requisite singsong CB jargon sometimes becomes mixed with throwback rural colloquial expressions. While evesdropping on a CB radio, I was entertained by a real countrified dialogue between two young women, only to hear one of them suddenly speak in ordinary conversational tones, "Mary, I really can't believe I'm talking like this."

Relatively little has been written about Ozark dialect. However, Vance Randolph has suggested that the source of the unusual wealth of literary words in the Ozarks is sixteenth- and seventeenth-century English. Cralle has pointed out that the old Blue Back Spelling Book and the King James Version of the Bible are two other possible sources. A few examples of Old English words sometimes used by natives: *agile, admired, bemean, beguile, candidly, cavil, caucus, contentious, careen, dilatory, diligent, disfellowship, docile, denotes, exhort, forsake, fray, jaunt, genteel, lavish, meander, proffer, ponder, partake, peruse, rectify, reconcile, ridiculous, tragedy, warysome, wrest,* and *loiter*.

Compilation of lists of colloquial expressions is pursued furiously these days. Probably, the meaning of 80 per cent of the "pure Ozark" words would be entirely familiar to most Kansas or Iowa farmers who have reached the age of fifty. They are rural colloquialisms sometimes modified by geographic surroundings. *Afore* (before), *ary* (singular of any), *bulge* (advantage), *born days* (life), *cut the mustard* (succeed), *woods colt* (illegitimate child; this expression is rendered as *pasture colt* in the Plains States), *hear to* (to agree), *hog wild* (excited), and *honin'* (eager) are examples of relatively common rural middlewestern terms taken from an "Ozark word list."

The scholars who work with language usage put the Ozarks in the South Midland speech group-

3. Donald R. Holliday, "Autobiography of an American Family" (Ph.D. diss., University of Minnesota, 1974), p. 146.

4. Waldo O. Cralle, "Social Change and Isolation in the Ozark Mountain Region of Missouri" (Ph.D. diss., University of Minnesota, 1934), p. 64.

ing. Although there has been little systematic study of Ozark speech patterns, preliminary investigations indicate that there are important differences where Germans or people from Yankee or North Midland backgrounds settled. It was the social predominance of Yankees, or Germans, rather than numerical predominance, that influenced speech habits. Timothy Frazer suggests that the German immigrants in the Illinois counties adjacent to the Ozarks patterned their speech habits after the socially prominant northerners who settled there:

> It thus seems likely, at least from the slight amount of information available, that the Germans did adopt the Northerner as a cultural and language model, and that the Germans themselves were great enough in numbers and status to account for the spread of their adopted English to become standard for the region.[5]

Thus in the northern and eastern Ozark borders, where northern and German influences have been strongest, a North Midland speech pattern is predominant. Such phrases as *school leaves out*, *sick to the stomach*, and *quarter to* (as opposed to *school lets out*, *belly ache*, and *quarter of*) are considered indicators of North Midland dialect.

Entertainment

Traditional Ozark entertainment was much different from today's. We have seen how technological advances have worked to reshape the economy and transportation network of the region. The impact of technology, combined with constant social change, has been to modify entertainment forms. Old forms have persisted to some extent, mainly in the sections where roads and rails did not penetrate until later, but for the most part, established present-day entertainment is not unlike that of other sparsely populated rural sections of the United States.

Gilmore[6] studied the traditional entertainment in the Ozarks and compiled an interesting and surprisingly varied array of entertainment forms. He found that by 1900 fairly elaborate entertainment activities had evolved. Literary society meetings were held regularly in almost every community throughout the Ozarks by that time. These were almost always held on Friday nights at the schoolhouse. Attendance often meant an inconvenient if not hazardous trip after dark by lumber wagon, buggy, horseback, or on foot. Stream crossings could be dangerous after dark, and the roads themselves were dangerous. A correspondent in Howell County complained:

> All along one of the largest and most travelled roads in the south part of the country the large loose stones or boulders are so numerous that it is dangerous to drive faster than a walk with a buggy or carriage and also very hard on a loaded wagon as well as dangerous.[7]

Because the literaries provided something to do and a break from the work routine, they were well attended. They included debates, spelling bees, ciphering matches, and kangaroo courts. In the spelling bees and ciphering matches, the excitement of a contest was combined with tangible learning that stimulated pride in the school patron. Debates on topics of every conceivable nature, ranging from speculation about the future of the world to the universal and unresolvable problem of the relative usefulness of the broom and the dishrag, occupied the whole interest of an audience. Gilmore used newspaper accounts of debates to compile a most interesting list of topics that included whiskey and war, love, the Indian, education, personalities, the printing press, man's nature, woman, religion, morals, and prospects for the future. Even the intrepid and educated German hunter-woodsman Friedrich Gerstäker joined in a debate before a large crowd in Arkansas. Gerstäker's selected debate topic was "Which enjoys life most, has fewer cares, and lighter sorrows—a short or a long-tailed dog."[8]

The kangaroo court combined the drama of a courtroom trial with the ribaldry of a practical joke that contained for the audience "all the interest,

5. Timothy C. Frazer, "American Dialect Acquisition in Foreign Settlement Areas" (Paper delivered to the American Dialect Society, Western Illinois University, Macomb, Ill., November 1976).

6. Robert K. Gilmore, "Theatrical Elements in Folk Entertainment in the Missouri Ozarks, 1886–1910" (Ph.D. diss., University of Minnesota, 1961).

7. *West Plains Journal*, January 19, 1899.

8. Friedrich Gerstäker, *Wild Sports in the Far West* (Durham, N.C.: Duke University Press, 1968), pp. 327–29.

suspense, and humor of a stage play." Elaborate stage settings were rare at literary performances, but costuming was an important element in the presentation of many entertainments. At times, colored flash powder was fired to illuminate dramatic tableau scenes. Sometimes the performers at the literaries were schoolchildren, but often, especially in the instances of debates and kangaroo courts, the adult members of the community performed for their fellow citizens.

School closing programs were among the most obviously theatrical of all Ozark folk entertainments. The performers were the students, and their performances consisted of plays, dialogues, recitations, speeches, Delsarte drills, or whatever other mode of entertainment the particular district had come to expect. Even the drill in lessons for examination period served as entertainment for the proud parents and patrons of the school. Frequently the schoolhouse was decorated for the occasion with flowers, evergreens, and students' work. Preparation for the closing-of-school event occupied a large part of the last two months of school, and many teachers felt that their chances of being rehired for the following year depended upon their producing a program that not only would entertain their patrons but also would compare favorably with previous programs.

Religious gatherings of all kinds were extremely important in the life of the Ozarker, as they are today. When families were more isolated, religious gatherings provided people with the opportunity to "participate in fellowship with neighbors, engage in group singing, witness the emotional performances of his fellows or to participate in such performances himself, and most important, be entertained by a minister or ministers." All of these entertainments were enjoyed in the knowledge that they were part of a religious service and therefore were approved by the community. Ministers often gained reputations for their ability to preach an interesting and entertaining sermon, sometimes acquiring near-star status in the eyes of their admirers. Their messages were often emotional, lengthy, and fundamentalist, often enlivened with pantomimic action and humorous anecdotes. Camp meetings added to the usual enjoyment the extra dimension of spectacle, of crowds of people, of camping out, and of an intensified emotional atmosphere.

Religious debates usually were conducted in an atmosphere of intense partisan emotion and at times extended over several days. Baptisms drew large crowds to witness the converts filing into waist-deep water, there to be totally immersed by a minister. Although usually carried out in the spring of the year, sometimes it was necessary to break ice in order to accomplish the feat. River baptisms continue to be highly regarded and frequently used by rural churches.

Box and pie suppers were attended by those who were interested not only in the good food involved but in the entertainment aspects as well. Much of the enjoyment derived from the time-honored ritual of identifying the supposedly unmarked boxes or pies and of purchasing the desired one at the best possible price. Keen but good-natured rivalry was generated when the prettiest girl was selected in a beauty-cake contest.

Picnics were always popular, as they are today. Shady groves and cold springs were to be found in abundance, and it was a simple matter for a family to pack a basket lunch and slip away from work and worries for a few hours or for a day. There were special occasions celebrated by a large community picnic. Intense notes of patriotism and sentiment pervaded the celebration of the Fourth of July, Decoration Day, veterans' encampments, and old settlers' reunions. Attractions at the organized picnics often included balloon ascensions, orators, circle swings, lemonade stands, the popping of firecrackers, recitations, songs, and instrumental music.

Ozarkers in the horse-and-buggy era were especially fond of baseball, and the town team was cheered on win or lose. Traveling teams, such as the Nebraska Indians, provided spectacles out of the ordinary. The Sunday baseball craze was preached against zealously, but scores of 65 to 5 were proudly recorded in the newspaper of the winning town.

Court trials were attended in the fall and spring. As with hangings, their very rarity added to their desirability as entertainment. At times, the hangings took a macabre turn, with the convicted man participating to make the event a gruesomely festive occasion. On one occasion at Ava, Missouri, someone in the crowd asked the condemned man, "Is that you, Jodie?" to which he replied, "I told you I would try to be here." At Fort Smith, Arkansas on the southwest Ozarks border, nearly ten thousand persons were tried, and 168 of them were put to death in the court of Hanging Judge Isaac Parker between 1875 and 1896. Large crowds were attracted when as many as six condemned men were hanged at one time.

Political gatherings were enthusiastically attended. Band concerts were especially appealing because of the setting under the stars. The community Christmas tree, with its gaily wrapped and sometimes surprising presents, was a lure to many.

Hunting and fishing were closely tied to the real business of living. They were carried on in very much the same way as plowing the corn, simply a matter of augmenting the family larder with game and fish. Noodling (hand fishing) and gigging were popular means of taking fish, as they are even today. Dynamiting was practiced, as was the more simple expedient of mashing a sack of green walnuts to pulp, weighting it, and sinking it in one of the deep holes filled with fish. Whatever chemical action took place, it was well known that every fish in the hole came to the top of the water on his back and could easily be gathered in.

Collective work, such as road repair and threshing, provided an opportunity to socialize. When the thresher came into the neighborhood, all who had wheat met it at the first stand and followed its progress through the neighborhood until the last wheat was threshed. Hog butchering and apple peelings were likewise popular and helped to preserve the fine art of conservation.

Contemporary Entertainment

Contemporary entertainment in the Ozarks is not greatly different from that of other rural sections of the Middle West. Outdoor sports, particularly hunting and fishing, are very popular. Much of the entertainment is the canned variety: rock and country-western music are played on stereos, tape players, and radios; soap operas, charismatic detectives, news and sports events fill the prime TV slots. "Friday Night at the Movies" has replaced the Friday night "literary." "Saturday Night at the Movies" has supplanted the Saturday night band concert.

In recent years handicrafts and craft festivals have become popular, but this is mainly a nonnative thing. Many of the quilts, tablecloths, bedspreads, rugs, dolls, pots, and articles of clothing are made from craft kits. Apparently, there is little residual knowledge of native crafts, and much of the revival of native crafts can be attributed to the businesses serving the tourist trade.

Support of school activities continues to be strong. Basketball is especially popular, and a town's reputation rides on the outcome of the Christmas-season tournament and league championship. Somewhat surprisingly, girls' and women's softball and basketball have been popular for a generation or more. In recent years, as part of the national emphasis on women's activities, interscholastic women's athletics has increased. Football, which requires more players, has less of an historical tradition in the smaller Ozark schools. When a town can boast of an eleven-man football team, it is a sign of city status. Dramatic productions are mainly confined to schools, where junior and senior plays are traditional. School proms and parties are popular, but the propriety of dancing at school events is still hotly contested in many communities. Books assigned as required reading are often scrutinized carefully by school patrons to seek out profane or "inappropriate" passages. In some cases, the use of controversial books is the subject of emotional debates at meetings of the school board. School dress codes at Mountain Grove, Missouri, were the subject of discussion in January, 1976, as reported in the *Springfield Leader and Press*:

> The school board here has taken under advisement a five-point revision of the high school student dress and behavior code proposed by the executive committee of the high school Parent-Teacher Association.
>
> A group of 14 citizens, including the PTA president, submitted petitions with 955 signatures to the school board. The petitions call for five revisions of the dress code, including changes to specifically allow pantsuits, slacks, and long hair (if kept neat and clean), but that it forbid skooter skirts, shorts, cutoffs, hot pants, tank tops, sexually suggestive lettering, alcohol and tobacco lettering on clothing, and use of tobacco.
>
> Currently, the code specifies only that student dress will be "neat and appropriate for the occasion."
>
> The board concluded that if the suggested rules are adopted, they are almost certain to be challenged in

"Men Who Rode for Parker." Deputy U.S. Marshals who served in Indian Territory for the Hanging Judge at Fort Smith, Arkansas. (Courtesy Arkansas History Commission.)

court. However, at the insistence of the PTA committee, the school board agreed to ask the opinion of the legal department of the state department of education about the advisability of the suggested new rules.

Religion continues to be an important part of the Ozarker's life. Probably, a smaller proportion of the population attends church regularly than in the past because of the many outdoor activities and other alternatives. Float trips, picnics, camping out, swimming, boating, and hunting are regular Sunday fare for many Ozark residents. Sometimes, recreation activities are combined with church activities, but usually not. Revivals seem to be regaining some of their appeal, particularly the open-air brush-arbor event. Music, singing, and vigorous preaching continue to be the main attractions, as in times past. Occasionally, spectators park nearby to take in the revival, but the rowdies, imbibed with white lightning, who harassed the congregations in former times long since have found other outlets for their style of entertainment.

The number of rural churches has declined over the years, probably because of a combination of the decline of religious influence in the rural area and partly because of the decline in population below the level that can support a church.

Cralle describes the problems of maintaining churches at Birth Tree in Shannon County in the 1930's (1930 population, 505):

Six different denominations about the same time originally built churches in Birch Tree: The Methodist Episcopal; Methodist Episcopal, South; Missionary Baptist; Christian; Presbyterian, and the Roman Catholic. At this time the mills were thriving and the population was above 500. About 1925 a Pentecostal (Holiness) Church was established and they also erected a building. With the closing of the large lumber mill all but three families of the Roman Catholic faith left the town and since that time these three families have gone and by 1920 their building was sold and wrecked. The Methodist Episcopal (North) membership meanwhile dwindled and all efforts at church and Sunday School were dropped, this building finally being sold and wrecked in 1928. Some of the members have affiliated with the Methodist Episcopal Church, South. The Presbyterians abandoned and sold their church in 1914, and for a long time the Christian Church was active. A revival meeting in 1922 resulted in 50 additions to the church, and a full time pastor. Within two years the full time pastor was cut to twice a month, later to once a month, and for three years they have had no regular church service. They maintained a small Sunday School until recently. The Missionary Baptist and the Methodist Episcopal Church, South, have services twice a month. They hold an occasional union service at Christmas or Easter and arrange their regular meetings on different Sundays to avoid competing with each other. Denominational friction is breaking down: a large number of each denomination attend the services of the other when their own church has no service. Each maintains a small Sunday School. The Pentecostal seems to be the most flourishing Church remaining and their membership is gaining.[9]

Thus, except for loss in population, the example of Birch Tree in the 1930's contains most of the conditions being faced by many religious leaders in the Ozarks today: competitive denominationalism from a period of church building, the breakdown of a degree of social isolation in which the church was almost the only place to go, and half or more of the churches having given up the struggle to maintain regular services.

Although many rural churches are plagued with declining memberships, church organization continues to be strong in the growth centers of the Ozarks. In Springfield, Cape Girardeau, Joplin, Fayetteville, Batesville, in the towns in the lake districts, and in smaller towns with only modestly increasing populations, the churches are reasonably healthy, if not prosperous. The new town of Viburnum in Iron County, built to house the workers in the lead mines, has a new shopping district, a large new school, modern suburban-style houses, and no less than five new churches to meet the sectarian needs of the inhabitants. Apparently, Ozark sectarianism surfaces wherever economic conditions permit. Although churches in the population growth areas tend to prosper, those in the sparsely settled areas often hold services in a union church shared by two or more denominations.

Natives vs. Outsiders

Much is made of the native Ozarker's reluctance to accept outsiders, or furriners. Herlinger[10] has likened this to the behavior of distinct ethnic groups. It appears that about 1900 was the latest point in time that any new settlers were incorporated folklorically into the Anglo-Saxon population of the remote sections of the Ozarks. Herlinger notes that there is a clear difference in the way Taney County, Missouri, residents recount their heritage:

Natives (those who settled, or whose ancestors settled, in the hills prior to about 1890) think of heritage in terms of group survival. The past is thought to have been a physical and spiritual struggle to make a life in the frontier. Talk commonly concerns the close dependence of families upon each other, the hard work involved, the wide variety of crafts and skills natives possessed, and the community expression of Christianity at camp meetings and revivals. Commonly natives of any age are anxious to place themselves in the context of their ancestors; they were eager to show me pictures of family ancestors and of historic family outings.

Non-natives (those who settled, or whose ancestors

9. Cralle, "Social Change and Isolation," p. 236.

10. Elizabeth Herlinger, "Historical, Cultural, and Organizational Analysis of Ozark Ethnic Identity" (Ph.D. diss., University of Chicago, 1972).

settled, in the hills after about 1890) seem more often to conceptualize the past in terms of the frustrations of poverty. Settlement for these families was primarily in little towns, small settlements, or on semi-developed farm land. The emphasis in their talk today is upon past inconveniences (for example, no toilets, dirt floors, no electricity) and upon the adaptation, change, and growth that the area has experienced since 1900. These people tended to show me pictures that illustrated how roads, stores, bridges, and towns had changed. They only rarely seemed concerned with their family ancestry or their place in it (outside their nuclear family).[11]

Birthright, then, is the basis for being a native Ozarker. Time does not make one a native, though longtime association with the land and its people may make one more nativelike. The highest compliment a native can pay a non-native is that he is "really just an old hillbilly like me." There are peculiarities in the birthright that rival the complexities of claiming citizenship in the United States. The Ozarks birthright is not passed through women:

> A native's mother need not be a native. Having a native mother does not make one any more native than merely having a native father. But one who does not have a native father is "not really native." . . . Another peculiarity of individual native inheritance is that birth in the hills is not required for native status. Many young natives marry and then temporarily leave the hills to seek their fortunes elsewhere. . . . The children of native parents are native, no matter where they are born.[12]

To say that native Ozarkers refer to themselves as hillbillies and to non-natives as furriners or outsiders is too sweeping a generalization. Likewise, the distinction by natives between a stranger (a native Ozarker from another part of the region) and a furriner, or non-Ozarker, is more fancy than fact. The term *hillbilly*, which apparently came into popular use about 1900, has been much stereotyped, and many native Ozarkers object to it altogether. One's attitude toward use of the word is largely a matter of personal preference and individual situation. Some, particularly those who have acquired a good education, reject the word outright. Others of equal stature may accept it and use it themselves, so long as it is recognized that they *really* do not fit the popular stereotype. Still others have become attached to the word and use it loosely to apply to anyone who lives in the Ozarks, regardless of ancestry, circumstances, or place of residence (town or country).

11. Ibid., pp. 80–81.
12. Ibid., pp. 83–84.

Lifestyles

Except for the small amount of influence of foreign immigrants, mainly among the Germans who live in the northern and eastern borders of the Ozarks, the people of the Ozarks have a wholly American lifestyle. This is not to say that there is one lifestyle, for as we have seen, the region has experienced almost continuous change throughout its history. Although it is frequently noted that very little is known about Ozarks culture and lifestyles, there has been, actually, a not unimportant amount of research into the agriculture, economic activities, customs, beliefs, education, settlement, ethnicity, and pioneer life of the people.

Two general patterns of human behavior or lifestyle among native Ozarkers may be recognized: the traditionalist and the progressive (or, less prejoratively, nontraditional). Neither of these lives up to the aspirations of the tourists who are seeking to see the folkloric Ozarker, a type of person to whom traditional values, such as honesty, morality, purity, and closeness to nature, can be attributed.

The traditionalist believes that rural values and life are superior to those found in an urban setting. This includes, or at least it did at one time, the belief that the people who inhabit the isolated small towns that served as trade centers are less moral, less forthright, and therefore less native than rural people. To the traditionalist, the city is a place of crime and pollution, and its population is believed to be largely immoral and ungodly. Conversely, the progressive Ozarker's view of city life is more likely to be tempered by what he has read or has learned in school or from television and radio broadcasts. He is less likely to reject city life and city values out of hand.

The traditionalist views himself with high regard. His assessment of his fellow Ozark hill man is in many ways similar to those held by tourists. Herlinger found that the traditionalist characterizes himself in the pattern of the folkloric hill man, even to the point of switching verb tense: "The hill people were honest, kind, skilled craftsmen. They are goodly, pure, and live close to nature."[13] The traditionalist believes he is different from non-natives because of his heritage:

> I'm a native because I'm a descendent of a special person—a man who would subject his family to the special hardships of pioneer life in these hills, for the special reasons of freedom and independence. That makes me, or any native, different from you.[14]

This folkloric view of ancestry ignores the fact that many settlers escaped to the Ozarks as dropouts seeking a place where competition was unnecessary or at least a place where land could be obtained free or at little cost.

The traditionalist places strong emphasis on knowing family genealogy. I recall stopping at a house to inquire about directions to a place and, after a while, the conversation somehow was sidetracked into family history. A son, fortyish, recently returned from fifteen years of military service, gave a recitation on the family tree, including several divorces, stepchildren, half-brothers and sisters, cousins, nephews, and nieces while his mother looked on, nodding her head in approving fashion. In many rural areas it is common for young people to identify themselves in terms of their relatives who have a better-established community identity, but in the Ozarks it is not unusual for young and adults alike to identify themselves as "I'm Jim and Mary Mathew's boy." Knowledge of all the family names in the community is expected, and older traditionalists sometimes will be familiar with most of the family names in the county.

There is a strong traditional belief that ancestors were individualistic and self-reliant, self-sufficient, capable, well rounded, and proud. Traditionalists believe they have inherited these traits: "Natives have inherited the knack of adjusting to any hardships that come their way. That's why they're really all hillbillies just like the ones who settled these hills."[15]

The land has special meaning for the traditional Ozarker. There is a strong belief that natives are the only ones who know how to wrest a living from it. It is a place of refuge, a place to come back to. Intrinsic values are presumed to be gained from the land. Holliday speaks of growing up in Taney County's Pinetop Community in the 1940's and 1950's.

> All of the boys reaped tremendous rewards from the simple fact that they knew, intimately their woods environment. They never questioned the fact, that they could survive in the woods, because they knew well enough the various characteristics of their habitat that they could reap almost anything that nature had to offer. That they knew enough about wild animals, their skill in tracking, hunting, trapping attested. Their knowledge of trees and plants, and their uses, gave them added assurance that nature would support them.[16]

The traditionalist places great store in being handy at a great many tasks, of being self-reliant and able to do for himself what others must hire done. This is a belief they share with farm people throughout the United States. Farm life demands that a degree of skill be learned in a number of different but necessary farm activities:

> By accretion, from the time the boys were very young until they were grown, until they left home, they learned the thousand tricks of shoeing horses and breaking them. They learned how to castrate a calf or a hog without letting either bleed to death. They learned all the details of the eleven-month season of growing tobacco. They learned their father's belief in planting by signs, the hundreds of home remedies for man and animal, and many of the superstitions and potions for counteracting not-quite-physical maladies. They all sawed and hammered their way to being fair carpenters, and they mixed mortar and laid rock. Bicycles, plows, tractors, trucks, cars, hayrakes, and mowing machines made mechanics of them, capable, determined, ingenious enough to repair a machine or to get it unstuck and back on the road. Double-bitted axes,

13. Ibid., p. 120.
14. Ibid.
15. Ibid., p. 146.
16. Donald Holliday, "Autobiography of an American Family," p. 138.

cross-cut saws, and mall and wedges made timbermen of them, too.[17]

There is a belief that legal matters are best handled according to local community standards. The sheriff and deputies in nearly all the rural counties are area men from long-line families. The most common violations of the law are traffic violations, including a substantial number of arrests for drunk driving, disturbing the peace, burglary, and theft. Imprisonment in the county jail is considered ample punishment for most crimes, and penalties are usually meted out according to one's family background and past history of scrapes with the law. In the instance on July 14, 1917, at the time the United States was becoming involved in World War I, when local miners, mainly from old-line families, rounded up most of the foreign workers and shipped them out of the Lead Belt with only the few possessions they could carry, the sheriff did not make any arrests. In order to bring the situation under control, military units were brought in.

A common belief is that natives "take care of their own." Natives expect that they will be taken care of in times of physical or spiritual need. They are aware of the impersonal condition of the poor in city slums, and they regard Ozark poverty as decidedly different from slum conditions, mainly because it is not associated with lack of identity. On the other hand, some of the traditionalists believe that government assistance is a native right. In some localities where the federal government has been especially active (WPA, U.S. Army Corps of Engineers, U.S. Forest Service), it is held responsible for existing conditions today and therefore it owes certain financial support. The inflationary price rises of the 1960's and 1970's are further justification for federal assistance. Although there is a certain stigma attached to poverty, particularly when it is attributed to laziness, government assistance programs are accepted rather readily. In some cases, there are complaints that the "new people" know more about the federal assistance programs and can therefore take better advantage of them. Some administrators have asserted that the food-stamp program (for people with lower incomes) in particular has been a factor in encouraging immigration to the Ozarks.

According to the traditionalist view, the native Ozarker is sharp in land dealings. Stories are told and retold of clever farmers who have sold property at a high value to an outsider, bought it back for a song, and resold it, not once, but several times. No doubt many land contracts have been defaulted, but the story is largely apocryphal. In fact, land prices have increased so rapidly since World War II that it would be difficult for anyone to have lost money in farm real estate if he had held the property more than a few years. One informant in Shannon County near the new scenic riverways stated that landowners in the area were reluctant to sell their property, almost at any price, for fear it would be resold soon at a much higher price, thereby making them look bad coming out on the short end of a land deal. Then there is the case of a student in one of my classes who researched her family history and discovered that her grandparents, who had sold their farm for ten thousand dollars in 1947, still had the money in a *checking account*, at no interest, nearly twenty years later.

Sex roles are defined strongly in the traditional lifestyle. There is women's work, which is not to be done by a man: mending clothes, washing dishes, cooking (other than wild game for special occasions), and all the other household chores. On the other hand, there seems to be no particular aversion to women doing men's work: assisting when needed in the hayfields, working in a clothing or shoe factory, or hefting one-hundred-pound barrels in a whiskey-barrel factory. It is a common joke among Ozarkers themselves that "Ozarkers are real go-getters. They take her to work in the morning and 'go get her' in the afternoon." This image of the traditional lifestyle is not without some basis in fact. One informant, a teacher married to a traditional Ozarker but who herself would be placed in the progressive-lifestyle group, said the go-getter image is not only correct but strongly resented:

> Oh, he likes it fine. He takes me to work and then drives down to the cafe where they all sit around in their Caterpillar caps and drink coffee all day. Then when he comes to get me and we go home, I have to

17. Ibid., p. 113.

cook supper, wash the dishes, and do whatever else needs to be done. I'll tell you I'd trade jobs with him.

A final cultural trait of the traditional Ozark lifestyle is the adherence to fundamentalistic religious beliefs. The Baptist Bible, Assembly of God, Church of Christ, Full Gospel, and various other pentecostal-revivalist churches serve people of all backgrounds, but their membership is strongly weighted with those of the traditional lifestyle. Those of the progressive lifestyle are more likely to attend Episcopal, Presbyterian, Methodist, Christian, Lutheran, or Catholic churches. These churches, sometimes referred to as social-gospel Christianity, are more popular among people with middle-class values.

Although social factors, particularly family tradition, are of primary importance in determining the lifestyle of individuals, there are important geographical considerations. The most obvious geographical factor influencing lifestyle is whether one lives in town or in the country. Town life, particularly in the towns that early on received technology and ideas because of their location on railroads or the more traveled highways, has always been different from rural life. Likewise, the people in the mining districts received modernizing influences in the form of rail and road transportation, steam and electrical power, improved schools, and social services. These, plus the fact that many people found employment in the mines, mills, and smelters, influenced lifestyles. Most important, the larger towns—Springfield, Joplin, Jefferson City, Rolla, Cape Girardeau, Batesville, and Fayetteville—have been centers for diffusion of ideas and technology that have had profound influences on lifestyle.

Ethnicity has had various degrees of influence, depending on the cultural level of the ethnic group. The French of Washington County, Missouri, have clung to a close-knit traditional lifestyle that centers around the Catholic church, the extended family group, and a semifeudal existence working part-time in the barite diggings. Traditional craftsmanship, including that of constructing log cabins, persisted until the present generation. Here, too, is found one of the highest unemployment rates in the Ozarks.

The traditional lifestyle of the Cherokees, particularly those who have clung to the old ways, the followers of the secret societies, has had an adverse influence on their level of living. Longtime status as wards of the government, coupled with such income as could be gained from part-time work picking strawberries and tomatoes, working in sawmills, or, for the young men, catching on as a harvest hand in the Wheat Belt or a roughneck in the nearby oil fields, provided many families with their main income for several generations. Traditional lifestyles became fixed in the culture and even today established patterns of economic pursuits are followed, so that only slowly are the cultural barriers broken down as young Cherokee men and women find new opportunities opening up.

On the other hand, the Germans on the farms of the northern and eastern Ozarks border have practiced a traditional lifestyle of progressive small farms. The mark of successful parenthood has been to raise young men and women who are equipped with the knowledge, skills, and mental attitude to be successful farmers. This traditional lifestyle, which incorporated rather ready acceptance of new agricultural methods resulting in a successful technology and high levels of production, has, nevertheless, resulted in rather small farms which have some difficulty competing in the increasingly competitive agricultural marketplace.

Thus the traditional Ozark lifestyle is that accepted mainly by descendents of the original Scotch-Irish immigrants. Although it persists most in the rugged, wooded hill districts—the Osage-Gasconade Hills, the Courtois Hills, the White River Hills, and the Boston Mountains—it may be found near the major growth centers. Scarcely thirty miles from Springfield, in the breaks along the Burlington Escarpment, there are families who live in quite isolated valleys, where in one instance the family automobile must be parked nearly a half-mile from the house because the stream crossing is so poor. Even within the larger towns there are small neighborhoods where clusters of ramshackle houses surrounded by vintage automobiles symbolize a nonprogressive "Ozark ghetto" lifestyle.

In recent years there has been much speculation on the probable effects on politics, attitudes, and beliefs by the large number of immigrants who have become permanent residents. This is not only because the newcomers themselves comprise a large share of the population, but because they are believed to influence longtime residents through everyday contact. Most of the statements on this matter are conjectural, but there is a small amount of factual information to support the idea.

A study[18] of ten southwest Missouri counties, sponsored by the Southwest Missouri Local Government Advisory Council, produced data indicating that Ozarkers are far less conservative than is commonly believed regarding questions of land use and environmental issues. For example, more than 91 per cent of a random-sample population believed that tourism and related businesses should be promoted while maintaining and preserving the same environment that tourists come to see; 87 per cent believed that local, state, and federal agencies should be required to include affected landowners in recreational-resource expansion plans; 53% believed the Corps of Engineers should not discontinue all further development projects, while 28% believed corps projects should be terminated; more than 88 per cent believed landowners should have greater influence, by law, regarding government purchase of land for recreation use; slightly more than 50 per cent (versus 25 per cent opposed) thought government recreation developers had given insufficient consideration to the conservation of resources; substantially more than two-thirds of the respondents regarded as too stringent the state and federal government regulations regarding decisions made by private landowners; more than 70 per cent favored increased financing for sanitary landfills, sewage treatment facilities, water treatment, and extension of farm-to-market roads; there was overwhelming support for controls to reduce the threat of pollution of surface and groundwater resources; and more than two-thirds of the respondents believed that population growth and industrial and commercial development should be encouraged.

The attitudes regarding land ownership are traditional rural beliefs, but the strong support for conservation of land and water resources may reflect nationwide publicity on environmental issues. Support for population growth indicates that Ozarkers are willing to be "Californicated" at least a little bit more. Support for commercial and industrial expansion likely will continue as a natural outgrowth of desire for jobs and economic well-being. Longtime residents often accuse newcomers of wanting to be "the last person to immigrate to the Ozarks."

18. *Citizens Recommendations Regarding Formulation of Area Development Program* (Republic, Mo.: Southwest Missouri Local Government Advisory Council, 1977).

Selected References

Branson (Mo.) *White River Leader*, "Uncle Bill From Kirbyville Says Groundhog Deserves Research?" January 31, 1972.

Britton, Wiley. *Pioneer Life in Southwest Missouri*. Kansas City: Smith-Grieves Company, 1929.

Cralle, Waldo O. "Social Change and Isolation in the Ozark Mountain Region of Missouri." Ph.D. dissertation, University of Minnesota, 1934.

Dorson, Richard. *American Folklore*. Chicago: University of Chicago Press, 1959.

Dugger, Harold H. "Reading Interests and the Book Trade in Frontier Missouri." Ph.D. dissertation, University of Missouri-Columbia, 1951.

Fairbanks, Jonathan, and Tuck, Clyde E. *Past and Present of Greene County, Missouri*. Indianpolis: A. W. Bowen and Company, 1915.

Frazer, Timothy C. "American Dialect Acquisition in Foreign Settlement Areas," Paper presented at American Dialect Society meeting, November 1976, Western Illinois University, Macomb.

Gallaher, Art. *Plainville Fifteen Years Later*. New York: Columbia University Press, 1961.

Gerstäker, Friedrich. *Wild Sports in the Far West*. Durham, N.C.: Duke University Press, 1968.

Gibbs, Christopher. "The Lead Belt Riot and World War I," *Missouri Historical Review* 71 (July 1977): 296–418.

Gilmore, Robert K. "Theatrical Elements in Folk Entertainment in the Missouri Ozarks, 1886–1910." Ph.D. dissertation, University of Minnesota, 1961.

Haswell, A. W., ed. *The Ozark Region: Its History and Its People*. Vol. I. Springfield, Mo.: Interstate Historical Society, 1917.

Herlinger, Elizabeth. "Historical, Cultural, and Organizational Analysis of Ozark Ethnic Identity." Ph.D. dissertation, University of Chicago, 1972.

Hewes, Leslie. "Cultural Fault Line in the Cherokee Country," *Economic Geography* 19 (April 1943): 136–42.

———. "Occupying the Cherokee Country of Oklahoma," *University of Nebraska Studies*, New Series, no. 57 (1978).

Holliday, Donald R. "Autobiography of an American Family." Ph.D. dissertation, University of Minnesota, 1974.

Kersten, Earl W., Jr. "Changing Economy and Landscape in a Missouri Ozarks Area," *Annals of the Association of American Geographers* 48 (December 1958): 398–418.

Miller, E. Joan Wilson. "Ozark Cultural Region as Revealed by Traditional Materials," *Annals of the Association of American Geographers* 58 (March 1958): 51–77.

Monks, William A. *A History of Southern Missouri and Northern Arkansas*. West Plains, Mo.: West Plains Journal Co., 1907.

Owen, Jim. *Jim Owen's Hillbilly Humor*. New York: Simon and Schuster, 1970.

Randolph, Vance. *Ozarks: An American Survival of Primitive Society*. New York: Vanguard Press, 1931.

———. *An Ozarks Anthology*. Caldwell, Idaho: Caxton Printers, 1940.

———. *Ozark Superstitions*. New York: Columbia University Press, 1947.

Sechler, Earl T. *Our Religious Heritage: Church History of the Ozarks, 1806–1906*. Springfield, Mo.: Westport Press, 1961.

Shirley, Glenn. *Law West of Fort Smith*. Lincoln: University of Nebraska Press, 1957.

Southwest Missouri Local Government Advisory Council. "Citizens Recommendations Regarding Formulation of Area Development Program." Republic, Mo.: 1977.

West, James. *Plainville, U.S.A.* New York: Columbia University Press, 1945.

West Plains Journal, January 19, 1899.

White River Historical Quarterly. Branson, Mo.: 1955–77.

Wright, Harold Bell. *The Shepherd of the Hills*. New York: Grosset and Dunlap, 1907.

14. The Cultural Landscape

A description of the complete Ozark scene would challenge the capacity of a computer and the lucidity and expository ability of a Shakespeare. As we have seen, the region possesses a multitude of physical settings over which have been laid, layer upon layer, a century and a half of American settlement and development. To sort out the landscape milieu and to understand it, geographers have conceived a cultural landscape:

> The cultural landscape is fashioned from a natural landscape by a cultural group. Culture is the agent, the natural area is the medium, the cultural landscape the result. Under the influence of a given culture, itself changing through time, the landscape undergoes development, passing through phases, and probably reaching ultimately the end of its cycle of development. With the introduction of a different—that is, an alien—culture, a rejuvenation of the cultural landscape sets in, or a new landscape is superimposed on the remnants of an older one. The natural landscape is of course of fundamental importance, for it supplies the materials out of which the cultural landscape is formed. The shaping force, however, lies in the culture itself.[1]

The number of possible cultural landscapes that might be produced, through time, in a region—such as the Ozarks—that is so varied in physical resources and in cultural background of its people is very large. There are almost innumerable possible permutations and combinations of physical landscape features, including bedrock, slope, soils, vegetation, rivers and creeks, and of man-made landscape features, including houses, barns, fences, cultivated fields, pastures, orchards, roads, bridges, lakes and reservoirs, utility lines, and airports, as well as the complete ensemble that makes up the urban landscape.

Included in the cultural landscape of the Ozarks are the people themselves, not only the permanent inhabitants but also the seasonal or occasional visitors as well. The various physical types, their food, and their habits of dress not only add variety to the Ozark scene but tell of the style and conditions of life in the region.

Material culture consists of those things which make up the standard of life of the people, among them housing and house furnishing, together with food and habits of dress. Though broadly similar to that of rural America in general, the material culture of the Ozarks includes important differences. The true material culture probably lies somewhere between the generalized descriptions published by local chambers of commerce and

1. Carl O. Sauer, "The Morphology of Landscape," in *Land and Life*, ed. John Leighly (Berkeley: University of California Press, 1963), p. 343.

Log house in a French settlement, Washington County, Missouri, 1976. The house was constructed in the 1950's.

those of the Sunday feature writer in search of interesting material. Marked differences in material culture exist even within the Ozark region. Some of these differences are obvious and strike the eye of the visitor on his first contact with the region, while others are much less apparent.

Houses

Houses are especially rewarding objects of study for students of landscape because they provide clues to the cultural background of the people and their approximate level of technology at the time of their construction. The construction materials often provide insight into the local resource base and the level of living, and materials and form may provide some general indication of age, although the practice of remodeling and adding on rooms complicates definitive chronological classification. Study of houses and other structures can help to fill gaps in the record of culture that are not recorded in written accounts of the region. Also, for many, the houses and outbuildings of Ozark farms are picturesque and provide an additional scenic attraction.

My interest in Ozark houses began as casual observation of the differences in types from place to place as I traveled the region on field trips. The casual interest has remained, even after several years of leading field trips through the Ozarks and sharing the interest in houses with students in my classes. We have found study of houses and farmsteads to be a rewarding way to appreciate the regional variation of the Ozark landscape. Moreover, it is a pleasant pastime, and by means of a simple system of classification, houses can be observed from the comfort of a moving automobile.

With the help of students, many windshield traverses were conducted in the western Ozarks to gather information on houses and farmsteads. Four traverses over different routes extended across the Ozarks to the Mississippi and Arkansas rivers. The houses were grouped for purposes of mapping into five major categories based on size, form, construction materials, and the approximate time of construction. Some dwellings that were unique and did not fit the classification scheme were grouped as anomalous types. The five general types are: shacks, older one-story houses, older two-story houses, interwar bungalows, and contemporary houses.

Shacks include several small one- and two-room dwellings. Both the quality of construction materials and the workmanship are below those of other house types. Exterior walls are occasionally of rough, unpainted, vertically placed boards, but more frequently the walls have been covered with tar paper or composition shingles. The houses are set on simple foundations, sometimes unmortared native stone or wooden blocks. The crude shelters built by the lumber companies as housing for their workers fit this grouping. Although most log houses are quite old, it is reported that crude log houses were constructed as late as the 1930's and some of the log houses in the Washington County Tiff Belt date from the 1950's. Other kinds of one- and two-room shacks are thrown up as lake cottages or fishing shacks.

Most older one-story houses were built after railroad transportation made the production of finished lumber an important Ozark industry. However, much of the lumber for house construction probably was brought in by rail. By then, farm journals and newspapers had begun publishing house and building plans, and farms were producing cash income that could be used to construct buildings and improve living standards. One-story frame houses were popular until World War I, when bungalows built according to standardized plans became popular.

Windows were double-hung, with one to six panes of glass per window. Doors were paneled. Siding was the narrow-finished lap type, originally painted white but now frequently covered with asbestos shingles or roll-type composition siding. The houses were set on mortared native-stone or concrete foundations, and the quality of building materials and workmanship was much better than in earlier houses. The floor plans of these houses are often T-shaped or L-shaped.

Most of the older two-story houses were built during the same time span as the small traditional houses, which they resemble in floor plan. House plans published in journals and newspapers promised a certain degree of standardization. Windows, doors, construction materials, and quality of construction are similar to the older one-story houses. Like the small one-story houses, the two-story structures have large covered porches, which in former years served as storage places for firewood, tools, farm produce, and as places for family and friends to gather on summer evenings.

Bungalows were the most popular houses constructed between World War I and World War II. Porches were smaller, probably because large porches were expensive and had become, to some degree, functionally obsolete. Usually, bungalows were constructed of lap siding, but in the Ozarks, where field stones are abundant, the bungalow of rough field stones is seen often. Nevertheless, the styles were those of the sprawling 1920's suburbs, where zoning codes and mass production dictated uniformity. Mullion windows, relatively high-pitched roofs, and firm stone or concrete foundations are identifying characteristics.

Throughout the United States the shortages of material and labor during the 1940's caused a hiatus in home building. The end of World War II brought the release of materials and an increase in labor, stimulating a construction boom that has continued to the present. The post–World War II house is disarmingly easy to identify, but its identifying features are difficult to describe.

Shed-room house, one of several small-house types in the Ozarks.

Most contemporary houses are frame structures that have a certain standardized appearance in spite of a wide range of floor plans and building materials. The long facade almost always faces the road, and eave overhangs are relatively narrow, especially on the older types. Unpaneled hollow-core entrance doors, metal framed window, large picture windows, sliding glass patio doors, and attached garages are features that distinguish this group from earlier types. Siding materials include wood, vinyl, and aluminum clapboard, unfinished boards placed vertically, asbestos and shake shingles, and brick and stone veneers. In the Ozarks there are striking differences from place to place in the quality of materials and size of contemporary houses; in the isolated sections there are many boxlike two-bedroom contemporary houses copied after their betters in the cities and towns.

Some Ozark dwellings defy systematic classification or are sufficiently unique to discuss individually. Included in this category are the French Creole, the German brick, and the mobile home.

In Ste. Genevieve, Missouri, are some well-preserved houses built by the French during the Spanish regime in Missouri. Some of them are of the peculiarly French upright-log construction,

Native-stone bungalow. Many houses and public buildings are constructed with rough field stones.

now weatherboarded. Wide galleries or porches, a style believed to be of Caribbean origin, sometimes encircle the entire house. Bolduc House, dating from about 1785, is the best preserved of the houses using vertical-log construction.

The Germans who settled in and around the Missouri cities of Ste. Genevieve, St. Louis, St. Charles, Washington, Hermann, and Jefferson City often built their homes of brick. Although less frequently seen in a rural setting, the German brick house is not uncommon in the eastern and northern Ozarks. These impressive two-story structures often are embellished with ironwork, decorative brickwork, and colored shingles laid in ornamental designs. The gambrel roof is often outlined by a bell-shaped lower slope and a double false chimney at each end of the house. Mobile homes, formerly known as trailer houses, are becoming increasingly popular in the Ozarks. This is in line with the increasing mobility of the American population and the adaptability of the mobile home to the needs and levels of living of many people. Mobile homes are usually less expensive on a square-foot basis than conventional housing, and in the Ozarks they may be towed to parcels of land which are still relatively inexpensive. Inexpensive rural living holds a strong attraction for many Ozark residents.

The houses in Ozark towns and cities are even more varied than in the countryside. Larger and more elegant homes were built by the merchants and businessmen. The large Victorian homes built by the mining-rich in Joplin and in Bonne Terre included marble porticos and carriage houses. Also of note are the elegant summer homes in Ironton and Caledonia built by wealthy St. Louis families. There are antebellum houses in the river-border towns and in the Belleview and Arcadia valleys. The large brick and frame Federal-style houses at Caledonia, Missouri, are noteworthy because of their size and their location in the interior Ozarks. Bonniebrook, the elegant residence of artist Rose O'Neill, was singularly anomalous in the rugged and isolated White River country.

Geography of House Types

The maps of house types (fig. 14-1) should be read and interpreted as one would read and interpret any other map of the same scale, with recognition that the areas that have been differentiated represent generalizations of features observed in the field. Each part of the Ozarks includes some houses of almost every type, but areas where certain types of houses are most numerous have been identified on the maps. Several interesting associations are evident: recent house construction tends to be clustered near the larger towns and in lake resort areas, especially along bituminous-surface secondary roads, federal highways, and state farm-to-market roads; small, low-quality houses are associated with areas of steep slopes and stony soils; large two-story houses are associated with more level and productive agricultural land.

Rural houses, except those built by commuters and resort developers, mainly are old. Most were built before World War I, and only a very small percentage was constructed after World War II. As in many hill districts east of the Mississippi River, much of the housing of the rural Ozarks is of poor quality. Crude shacks are numerous in the more isolated sections, where rugged terrain and poor soils limit the possibilities for agriculture. They are the main dwellings in sections of the White River drainage basin, in the rugged Courtois Hills and the St. Francis Mountains, along the northern Ozarks in the maturely dissected drainage basins of the Osage and Gasconade rivers, and in the hidden coves and along isolated ridges in the Boston Mountains of Arkansas. In the Springfield Plain and the better agricultural districts of the northern and eastern Ozarks, shacks are confined mainly to hilly belts along larger streams.

Hewes's detailed study of the Cherokee country of the Oklahoma Ozarks showed that most of the houses of that district were small, unpretentious, and often in poor repair. Likewise, farm buildings in the Cherokee Ozarks are of poorer construction than those immediately to the east. The explanation for retardation lies in cultural history, rather than in deficient natural resources, since rocks, landforms, soils, hydrography, natural vegetation, and climate are much the same as they are immediately to the east. The contrasts are of sufficient magnitude to form a cultural fault line at the Oklahoma boundary.

Bolduc House, Ste. Genevieve, Missouri. This house, constructed with logs placed in the wall vertically in the French style, was built about 1785.

House Furnishings

The life of pioneers in America often has been misrepresented. Reconstructions and memorials often depict those aspects of life that, because we have lost them, we mistakenly suppose our forebears enjoyed. Historians have shown that isolation and monotony, scarcities and shortages, hard work and early death were the common fare for frontiersmen. Although the people who first settled the Ozarks no doubt were skilled in fashioning a surprising number of useful tools and household implements from the forests, they constantly endured scarcities.

As for household wares, aside from furniture, most probably were brought by the settlers when they moved to the Ozarks. As is the case today, one did not start completely anew when a move was made. What could be put away in a pack, loaded in a wagon, or stowed on a flatboat was carried along. A recent archaological dig at a cabin site in the southeast Missouri Ozarks yielded a multitude of fragments of household implements and bearing the names of manufacturers in the East or in Europe, but there were few handcrafted artifacts.

There is considerable historical record of the material culture of the first settlers. Houses were usually one-room log structures set in a clearing and surrounded by "innumerable quantities of deer, bear, and other skins" that had been stretched and hung up to dry on poles and trees. In spring a patch of corn was planted for bread and for feeding horses. "No cabbages, beets, onions, potatoes, turnips, or other garden vegetables are raised. Gardens are unknown,"[2] wrote Schoolcraft. A visitor's approach to the cabin was announced by barking dogs. Men wore deerskin garments that served as a shirt and jacket; women frequently dressed in buckskin frocks "abundantly greasy and dirty." Schoolcraft's description of the interior of a house in the White River country in 1818 points up the primitive conditions of life:

> Around the walls of the room hung horns of deer and buffalo, rifles, shot pouches, leather coats, dried meat,

2. Henry Rowe Schoolcraft, *Schoolcraft in the Ozarks*, ed. Hugh Park (Van Buren, Ark.: Press-Argus Printers, 1955), p. 86.

Bonniebrook, home of Rose O'Neill. From left are Rose O'Neill, Clarence O'Neill (brother), Vance Randolph, and Kallista O'Neill (sister). (Courtesy Missouri State Historical Society.)

and other articles composing the wardrobe, smokehouse, and magazine of our host and family, while the floor displayed great evidence of his own skill in the fabrication of household furniture. A dressed deerskin, sewed up much in the shape the animal originally possessed, and filled with bear's oil, and another filled with wild honey, hanging on opposite sides of the fireplace, were too conspicuous to escape observation, for which indeed, they appeared to be principally kept, and brought forcibly to mind the ludicrous anecdote of potatoes and point—

"As in some Irish houses where things are so-so,
On gammon of bacon hangs up for show."[3]

A generation later, in 1839, Gerstäker, the intrepid German wanderer, described the house of a Pole who had somehow chanced to settle along the Little Red River in the extreme southeastern Ozarks:

The Pole's dwelling was nothing but a simple rough log-house, without any window, and all the chinks between the logs were left open, probably to admit fresh air. Two beds, a table, a couple of chairs, one of them with arms, some iron saucepans, three plates, two tin pots, one saucer, several knives, and a coffee-mill, formed the whole of his furniture and cooking utensils.[4]

Gerstäker's account of a midnight snack at the

3. Schoolcraft, *Schoolcraft in the Ozarks*, pp. 69–70.

4. Friedrich Gerstäker, *Wild Sports in the Far West* (Durham, N.C.: Duke University Press, 1968), p. 89.

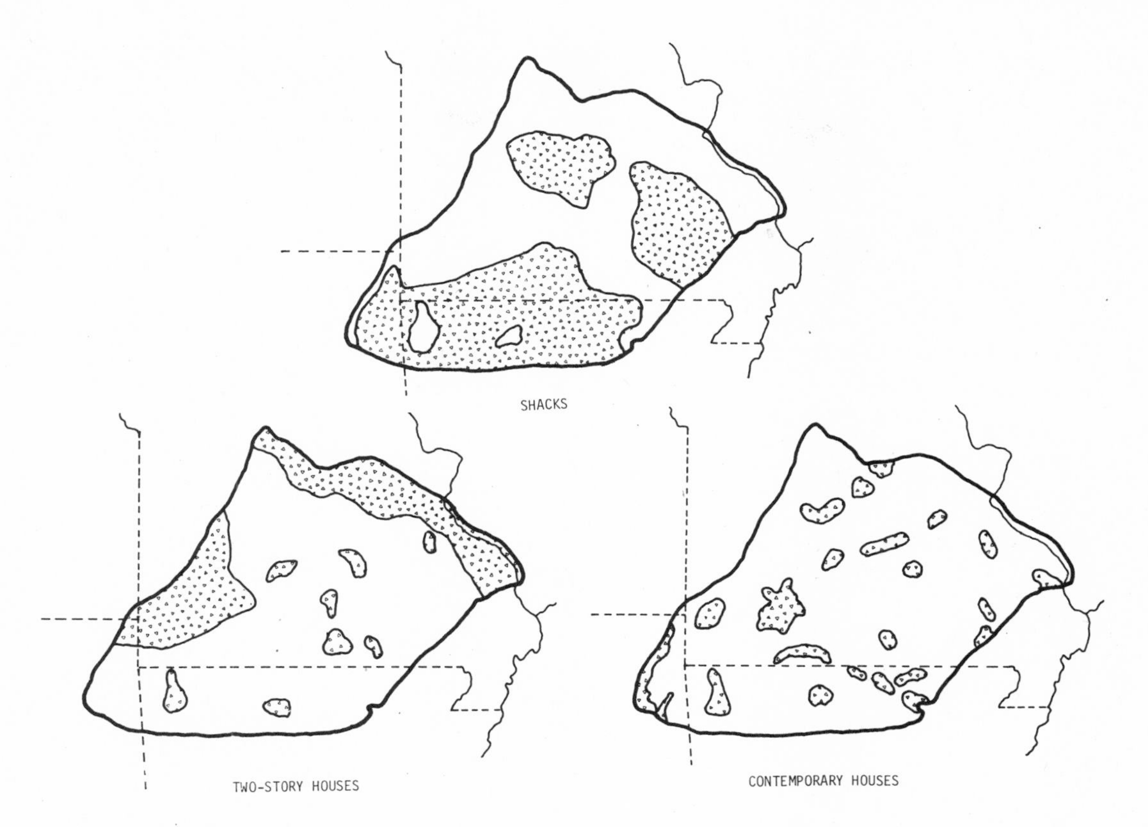

Figure 14-1. Geography of house types.

Pole's house is an amusing record of the inconveniences and work involved in preparing a meal:

Being deeply interested in our conversation, we forgot to prepare any supper, and it was not till the cold made itself felt that we went to bed. It may have been about half-past twelve, when Turoski woke up, and swore by all the saints, that he could lie no longer in bed for ravenous hunger, and that he must have something to eat, even if it were a piece of raw meat. I laughed, and told him to draw his hunger-belt tighter, but he jumped up and gave me no more rest. We made up the fire, which was nearly burnt out, and then held a council as to what we should cook. We had shot nothing, the bread was all gone, and we had eaten our last bit of pork for dinner. What was to be done? Turoski decided the point. The Indian corn of last harvest was in a small building in a field by the river; I was to go and fetch an armful, while he would prepare something in the meantime. The night was dark as pitch; I was often obliged to feel with my feet for the path like a blind man, that I might not lose myself in the forest. When, in the course of half an hour, I returned with the maize, Turoski had killed one of the fowls that were roosting on a low tree, plunged it in hot water, and while he cleaned it I fried the corn; then, while the fowl was being grilled, I ground the corn in the coffee-mill, which by no means reduced it to the consistence of flour. I moistened the grist with water, added a little salt, made a cake of it about three-quarters of an inch thick, and set it in a saucepan cover to bake. So far so good; but I wanted a couple of eggs. There was a kind of shed attached to the house, in which leaves of Indian corn, plucked green, and then dried, were kept as fodder, and here the hens came to lay their eggs. Turoski crept in, and feeling about, soon came to a nest with five, of which he brought away only two, having broken the others in his hurry. Coffee was then made

TABLE 14-1
House Furnishings, Mentor, Missouri

	Cralle Survey 1935	Wood Survey 1975
Rug on living-room floor	54%	85%
Rag carpet on living-room floor	18	13
Living-room floor bare	28	2
Windows curtained	64	100
Fireplace	6	40
Living-room stove	81	1
Furnace	3	99
Interior wall finish:		
Paint	—	20
Paneling	—	30
Wallpaper	70	50
Storm windows	—	48
Total number of houses surveyed in 1935 study: *circa* 100		
Total number of houses surveyed in 1975 study: 32		

and we had a very good supper, or rather breakfast, for it was not past two o'clock. But we were not yet to repose in safety; the monster log of hickory, that we had laid on the hearth, flared up and set fire to the chimney: Turoski mounted on the roof, while I handed him some buckets of water, and the fire was soon extinguished. At last we got to sleep, and remained so till the sun was high in the heavens.[5]

No doubt the construction of railroads was the most important single factor in bringing change in lifestyle to the nineteenth-century Ozarks. Until they were built, town life was not greatly different from living in the country. Railroads brought commerce, introduced a money economy, and brought in new people and the trappings of town life. Brick buildings replaced rough-sawed clapboard stores, and large townhouses were built by merchants who enjoyed the prosperity fostered by the railroads. In the immediate hinterland of the railroad towns, new farmhouses were built and old ones were remodeled and enlarged. Cralle[6] recorded the contrasting conditions of life and the material culture of the mid-1930's. He noted the substantial contrasts in material culture in isolated versus nonisolated communities. A recent inventory[7] of the material culture of Mentor, near Springfield, shows the striking changes in conditions of life over the past two generations. Most of the data in Tables 14-1, 14-2, and 14-3 speak for themselves. The material culture as represented in household furnishings is much improved. Houses are better painted, better furnished, better heated, and eight out of ten have air conditioning. Floors are mainly carpeted, windows are curtained, and paneling is used liberally for interior walls. The telephone, which was installed in only 16 per cent of the homes in Mentor in 1935, is now considered essential. Television, unknown in the Ozarks until the 1950's, is now in every home. Washers, dryers,

5. Ibid.

6. Waldo O. Cralle, "Social Change and Isolation in the Ozark Mountains Region of Missouri" (Ph.D. diss., University of Minnesota, 1935).

7. James Wood and Milton D. Rafferty, "Mentor, Missouri: Forty Years Later," *Missouri Geographer*, Fall 1976, pp. 21–26.

TABLE 14-2
Miscellaneous House Furnishings, Mentor, Missouri

	Cralle Survey 1935	Wood Survey 1975
Oil stove	32%	1%
Coal stove	4	—
Electric stove	—	3
Ice box	5	—
Refrigerator	—	100
Telephone	16	100
Sewing machine	53	23
Loom	1	—
Washer	—	96
Dryer	—	81
Freezer	—	30
Television	—	100
Air conditioner:		
Room	—	30
Central	—	50
Automobile	6	100
Truck	—	20
Lawn mower	—	94
Boat	—	6
Garbage disposal	—	50

Total number of houses surveyed in 1935 study: *circa* 100
Total number of houses surveyed in 1975 study: 32

TABLE 14-3
Musical Instruments, Mentor, Missouri

	Cralle Survey 1935	Wood Survey 1975
Talking machine [record player]	22%	2%
Radio	17	100
Piano	11	5
Organ	4	—
Banjo	3	—
Violin	7	—
Horn	—	2
Guitar	—	2
Miscellaneous instruments	—	2
Stereo	—	43

Total number of houses surveyed in 1935 study: *circa* 100
Total number of houses surveyed in 1975 study: 32

freezers, lawn mowers, and garbage disposals are as common in Mentor as in most cities and towns throughout the United States.

The survey of houses revealed few surprises. For example, it seems obvious that the percentage of homes with iceboxes should be greater in 1935 than at present, but in 1935 only 5 per cent of the homes in a community only ten miles from Springfield had them. Another example is the sewing machine. Not only are there fewer sewing machines today, but they are hardly the ostentatious piece of parlor furniture that they were in the mid-1930's.

Fireplaces, essential to log-cabin settlers but out of fashion by the 1930's, are now popular as aesthetic components of new houses. Possibly the most striking data are those for musical instruments. In 1935 only 25 per cent of the homes had musical instruments, and this was a time when much entertainment was of the home type. Some popular accounts of early days in the Ozarks create the impression that virtually everyone played musical instruments and sang colorful folk songs. The second and perhaps more interesting point is that only 11 per cent of the homes had musical instruments in 1975. As has been noted, much of today's home entertainment is provided by radio, television, and stereo, and if one wants to get away, the automobile provides ready access to a wide range of entertainment. Two generations of modernization, especially in the form of electrical power and the widespread use of the automobile, have eliminated most of the disagreeable aspects of rural Ozark life. Particularly among young people of high school age the automobile has become a form of entertainment in itself. Much socializing focuses on the automobile, and cruising the main drag past the drive-in, the movie, or other hangouts for teenagers is a popular pastime in small towns. Whether or not they have had a positive effect on cultural standards, these technological advances, more than any other thing, prepared the Ozarks for the modern era of immigration.

Barns and Outbuildings

The condition of barns and the number of outbuildings vary greatly within the Ozarks. In the better agricultural areas, many farms have eight or more buildings, but in areas of steep slopes and poorer soils, barns are very scarce and outbuildings often consist of a wretched shed or two. Data on Ozark barns show that most of the large barns are in the three agricultural border districts; three-fourths are constructed of sawed lumber, most of the remainder being covered with sheet metal, and only a few stone, brick, or log barns are to be found; 85 per cent have composition shingles and of those that are painted, about half are red and half are white; two-thirds of the barns need major repair and paint.[8]

The fact that barns are generally in poor condition throughout the region results from their decreasing functional utility. Mild winters make barns unnecessary for the protection of stock. In the hill country, where deep valleys and wooded slopes afford ample protection for stock, barns have never been highly regarded. Over the past half-century, the traditional frame barn with overhead loft, milking stanchions, and horse stalls has become largely nonfunctional. Farms are now less self-sufficient, and machine traction has replaced the horse and mule. If used at all, traditional barns have been renovated and equipped with modern machinery to serve as milking parlors or have been relegated to the storage of machinery or hay, functions that can be served more efficiently by the new low and spacious contemporary barns or sheds.

Silos are best represented in the more prosperous border districts, where livestock feeding and dairying gain stature. Large numbers of tall silos were constructed between 1900 and 1920, a time of rapid expansion in dairy farming. Nearly all are concrete. They are almost always located near the barn, and in about half the cases, they are attached to or built into the barn. Rotted roofs, cracked and chipped concrete, and weed-grown lots indicate that many silos have fallen into disuse as the number of dairy farms and general farms has declined. The trench silo, which is more readily adaptable to machine handling of silage, has come into wider use. Only occasionally are the older wooden silos observed. On some of the

8. Milton D. Rafferty, "Ozark House Types: A Regional Approach," *Proceedings of the Pioneer America Society* 2 (1973): 93–106.

larger and more prosperous-appearing farmsteads, metal tank-type silos are seen. These structures have the advantage of being adaptable to the storage of either dry silage or commercial livestock feeds.

The assortment of smaller outbuildings is highly variable from farmstead to farmstead. Long, low poultry barns are the largest of these miscellaneous outbuildings. Their occurrence is sporadic, except in northwest Arkansas in the counties surrounding Batesville and in Stone, McDonald, and Barry counties in Missouri, where the raising of broilers is important. Where single small poultry barns are observed, they often show signs of disuse, an indication that poultry farming is increasingly demanding larger-scale operations. The small chicken houses, which were important and functional structures when farms were more self-sufficient and when commercial poultry farming was in its infancy, are rarely used to house chickens. These small shed-type structures, now used mainly for incidental storage, are to be seen on most farmsteads, often in a pitiful state of repair.

Modern milk sheds date mainly from the 1940's. They are of quite uniform architectural style, most being patterned after plans drawn at the agricultural colleges. Typically, they are simple rectangular structures built of concrete bocks, painted white, and attached to the barn, although they sometimes stand detached from other buildings. In recent years a few more elaborate glassed-in milking parlors have been constructed.

Detached garages may be observed on somewhat less than half of Ozark farmsteads. They are typically small structures that accommodate one car. Because the newer automobiles are larger and the winters are not extremely severe, these garages frequently are not used for automobile storage but have been converted to repair shops or are used for general storage.

Grain storage bins and corn cribs are conspicuously absent. The few grain bins are small, round, galvanized sheet-metal structures with conical roofs. Even fewer corn cribs are observed, and these old wooden structures apparently have not been used for some time. Such little-used buildings are relics of a different time and a different agricultural economy. Today, little grain is raised, and most of the corn is chopped for silage. There are machine sheds and repair shops on some of the larger and more affluent farmsteads. These structures, along with assorted small sheds, round out the assemblage of farm buildings.

Fences in the Ozarks are mainly woven wire (hog wire) or barbed wire, with the former somewhat prevalent. Split-log worm fences, which were dominant shortly after the turn of the century and were still quite common in remote areas in the mid-1930's, have disappeared from the landscape except as occasional ornamental fences. Wood-panel fences are most frequently seen near the larger towns, such as Springfield, Joplin, and Fayetteville, where they add to the appearance of affluence on country estates and riding stables. Such fences serve to inform passers-by that occupants of the enclosed "farmstead" really need not farm for a living.

Because the soils are often shallow and stony, farmers in earlier times frequently constructed stone fences at the margins of the fields as they periodically cleared their cropland of chert and limestone. Today, most of these stone fences are overgrown with brush and usually are in a serious state of disrepair. Field stones are often piled at the base of trees or in sinkholes. Another distinctive and unusual stone feature is the rock crib, which is used as a corner post. It is a cylinder of woven wire, approximately three feet in diameter, filled with field stones. Cribs are usually supported with posts and girdled with discarded iron wagon tires.

Barbed-wire fences range from two to six strands, with four-strand fences the most common. Timbered land in remote areas is usually fenced poorly; two or three strands of loosely strung barbed wire is considered sufficient where free range persisted until the mid-1960's. Hog-wire fences account for three-fourths of the fencing along the highways and approximately half of the fencing along the byroads. Along the well-traveled roads, woven wire is a safety factor, protecting against straying livestock, and where persimmon sprouts and brush are still "goated down," woven wire is preferred because it is a goat-tight fence. Fence posts are mostly common split oak, but cedar, hedge, and steel posts also are widely used. It appears that steel posts are gaining in popularity. Because post holes are difficult to dig in the rocky soils, the wooden posts are sharpened on one end to be driven with a mallet.

Propane tanks, gardens, and fruit trees are associated with most rural dwellings. Propane (liquid petroleum, or LP, gas) or electricity are almost universally used for cooking purposes, even where wood is still used for heating the home. Propane also is widely used for heating purposes and has continually gained favor over wood and fuel oil because of its convenience and cleanliness. Recently the rising cost of propane has slowed the conversion from wood for heating purposes.

Wood continues to be widely used as a fuel, and woodpiles are common farmstead features. This is especially true in outlying areas, but since wood-burning fireplaces are often built in contemporary homes, the woodpile is ubiquitous. Wood-burning stoves have become popular in recent years, mainly because of rising prices for natural gas and electricity but also because of a heightened concern about energy supplies. Wide porches on the older houses, especially in the more remote locations, serve as places to keep a supply of dry kindling close at hand. Natural-gas lines serve only the larger cities in the border districts, so the interior towns depend on bottled gas, electricity, or wood for heating and cooking purposes. The restrictions on extension of natural-gas service, coupled with the rising cost of LP, has caused many rural home builders to install electric furnaces.

A rather long growing season and adequate precipitation make the production of garden truck fairly easy. Backyard gardens, although probably less popular than in earlier times, have regained stature with food cost increases. They are used mainly to produce fresh cucumbers, tomatoes, lettuce, radishes, onions, beans, and other assorted vegetables for the table. Some rather large gardens are set out to supply vegetables for home-canning purposes. The Amish families that have settled in the Ozarks during the 1970's grow especially large gardens in order to be as self-sufficient as possible. Sometimes potatoes are planted, and sweet corn is raised for both the table and the home freezer.

Fruit trees are less common than gardens, but most of the older houses have from one to half a dozen fruit trees. The few remaining large farm orchards are usually in poor condition. Apples and peaches are the most common fruits, but cherries, pears, and apricots also are grown. Grapes do rather well but are not as popular as the tree fruits. Small garden grape arbors grow beside the older-style farmhouses. They are poorly kept and may be considered relics of a time when farm families were more self-sufficient and the home canning of jams and jellies was a more widely practiced art.

Cellars are nearly always seen in farmyards where the houses are of the older types. Because bedrock is often near the surface, the cellars are usually shallow and appear as grass-covered mounds with limestone entranceways. In former times, cellars were used to store potatoes, and the walls were lined with shelves of home-canned vegetables and fruits. On the less fortunately located farmsteads where there was no spring, the cellar was the poor man's springhouse, serving as a cool place to store crocks of milk, cream, butter, and eggs. Many of the cellars were constructed shortly after the Marshfield tornado of 1880; today they serve mainly as places of refuge during storms, most of their other uses having been lost.

Windmills are rarely seen. Because springs and permanently flowing streams are abundant, windmills were never widely used except on the more level uplands. The spread of electric power service throughout the Ozarks has enabled rural residents to equip water wells with electrically powered pressure water systems. As a result, most windmills have fallen into disuse and the towers have been dismantled. Occasionally, they serve as supports for television antennas. The scarcity of windmills presented a problem for the Old Order Amish who recently settled in Webster County, Missouri. These newcomers purchased their windmills in Indiana because adequate repair parts and service could not be obtained in Missouri.

The water bucket and dipper have not passed into oblivion. Cisterns and dug wells continue to be used, although they are becoming increasingly rare. In most cases, those who continue to lift water with a bucket and rope are elderly persons who, because of the expense or because of long-established habit, have not drilled a well and installed an electrically driven pump.

Springhouses, though rarely used, are common

features of the rural landscape, because they are usually constructed of stone. Typically, they are located at the base of a hill where springs of adequate and constant flow are normally found. In former times, milk, cream, butter, meats, and other perishables were stored inside. Today, disuse is manifested by rotted doors standing ajar and muddy, hoof-marked surroundings where livestock have come to water from the springs.

Apparently, more attention is given to the beautifucation of the yard than in former times. One observer in the 1930's noted that the yard of the average farmstead was fenced to keep out livestock but was part of the accepted range of chickens or geese. Frequently the grass was completely worn away around the front of the house, and the painstaking housewife swept this area as faithfully as she swept the front porch.

Along the poorest roads, and especially in the rough land in the interior districts and in the Boston Mountains, a few poorly tended farmyards may be seen today. During the summer months, the small bench with wash basin and water bucket may be seen on the porches of some houses. A mirror is usually fastened to the wall of the house above the wash basin. Such small houses cannot easily accommodate many of the larger appliances, which rural electrification and income from off-farm employment have made available to many Ozark residents. As a result, washing machines, usually of the wringer type, often occupy a space on the back porch, and if none exists, the front porch serves as well. Occasionally a refrigerator or freezer is placed on one of the porches. Television antennas are ubiquitous or nearly so; inside, the television set has replaced the sewing machine as the most conspicuous piece of parlor furniture.

A distinctive feature of many farmsteads in the more remote areas is the assemblage of old abandoned automobiles; it is not uncommon to see as many as half a dozen scattered about a single farmyard. Apparently, the resident of the rougher parts of the region seldom purchases a new automobile, either because of the cost or because the roads are unsuited for a quality vehicle. When a car is no longer serviceable, it is abandoned on the farmstead. Frequently, the old auto bodies serve as storage or as places of shelter for hogs, goats, or poultry. On the whole, however, yards and farmyards are well tended. Yards are mowed regularly, and flowers and shrubbery are to be found around the houses. The yards along the highways are generally somewhat better cared for than those along the byroads.

Farm machinery is small, and a rather simple line of equipment is kept on most farms. Tractors are two- and three-plow types that are relatively inexpensive to operate, versatile, and well suited for powering light hay equipment. Plows, disks, harrows, drills, hay swathers, mowing machines, rakes, balers, manure spreaders, and field choppers are evidence that crop agriculture has given way to livestock farming and ranching. Combines and cultivators are restricted to the more fertile border districts.

In the border districts, where crop farming has persisted to a greater degree, the line of machinery kept on farms tends to be more elaborate and is, on the whole, newer. Dairy farms tend to have a larger line of machinery, and because milking schedules shorten the time that can be spent in the field, two or more tractors are usually kept. On stock farms, where demands on machinery are not as heavy, equipment, except for hay machinery, is often old. On many of the farms of the interior hill districts, only a tractor and mower are kept to mow weeds around the farmyard. On one large stock farm I visited in Christian County, Missouri, the complete equipment inventory consisted of a four-wheel-drive pickup and a lawn mower.

Other Settlement Features

Improvements in roads and the economies of size have virtually put an end to the country school. By 1967 the Missouri Department of Education reported only thirty-three one-room rural schools in twenty-two southwest Missouri counties. Rural residents have come to realize that schools can operate, even at minimum accepted levels, only when there is adequate financial support. Although local pride and sentiment have temporarily preserved the high school in some of the small towns, the rural elementary school has largely passed from the scene. The fate of abandoned school buildings has been variable. Some have been torn down for the lumber that can be sal-

McHaffie Church, Christian County, Missouri. McHaffies were among the first immigrants to Christian County.

vaged, others have been converted to hay barns, a few have been converted to residences, and the remainder stand empty to fall apart slowly.

A half-century of depopulation of the countryside has had less marked influence on country churches. Some abandoned churches may be seen, but most churches show signs of use. A few appear dilapidated, but in the vicinity of larger towns, where population is increasing, they are well cared for and some have recently been enlarged. Churches near cemeteries and along the better roads also have fared better. Many of the small independent churches have never placed much emphasis on the type of building used for services. Abandoned stores or service stations are considered adequate, even preferable, to big churches, which they consider showy. Many of the Pentacostal churches have colorful names, such as Church of the Bread of Life or Temple of Deliverence.

Community cemeteries have persisted, although they are sometimes poorly cared for. Some of them receive grooming only once a year, before Memorial Day, when relatives of the interred return from distant places. The small family burial plot is less well cared for, and in cases where the families have moved away, the burial plots have been abandoned to brush and weeds. Pinetop Cemetery in Taney County, Missouri, consists of a cluster of homemade and commercial headstones scattered more or less randomly among pine and oak trees, completely hidden from view of passers-by on a nearby road. Sunken spots among the trees and forest scrub attest to several unmarked graves.

Country stores and crossroads filling stations have been reduced in number. The filling station, which provided gasoline, oil, kerosene, white gas, and tire repair for the surrounding neighborhood, has fared poorly. As farm delivery of gasoline became nearly universal and as roads and automobiles were improved, rural filling stations declined in favor of centrally located major-oil-company service stations, which provide a more complete line of goods and services.

Country stores have persisted to a greater degree than rural service stations, probably because they can continue to afford some convenience to the surrounding population. Stores in sparsely settled areas usually carry a more varied line of merchandise than those in less isolated areas. Typically, the country store is housed in a rectangular false-fronted frame building with a wide veranda, which is often furnished with one or two sturdy benches so that customers may pass the time of day in a shady place. More often than not, it is a ramshackle structure accompanied by a single gasoline pump and, less frequently, by a walnut huller for the convenience of customers who gather nuts in the fall.

Inside the store, most of the shelves are filled with canned goods, packaged food, and sundry items; in a small refrigerated display case are assorted prepared meats and cheeses. A soft-drink machine just inside the front door is easily accessible to those who frequent the veranda. The remaining complement of goods—work clothing and gloves; frequently used hardware items, such as hammers, nails, nuts, and bolts; assorted pliers and wrenches; rope and barbed wire; bagged livestock feed and salt; and a small assortment of veterinary supplies—gives the appearance of having been on the shelves for a long time. Adding to the appearance of antiquity in one country store in southern Christian County, Missouri, is a potbellied stove, nearly circled by a group of rickety chairs, and on the wall, a large framed picture of

Franklin D. Roosevelt, which gives every appearance of having hung undisturbed since New Deal days. Occasionally, abandoned stores and filling stations are converted to other uses, especially when they are located on the more traveled roads. In the recreation regions, some of the abandoned buildings have been remodeled in order to house a variety of different types of retail and service establishments.

Ozark Townscapes

Transportation routes have always been paramount in the establishment of towns in the Ozarks. The earliest towns were along the major navigable streams: the Mississippi, Missouri, and Arkansas rivers. St. Louis, St. Genevieve, Cape Girardeau on the Mississippi River; Washington, Hermann, Jefferson City, Boonville, and Glasgow on the Missouri River; and Batesville on the White River are all old towns. Little Rock and Fort Smith, just beyond the Ozark border on the Arkansas River, were important river ports for the region. These towns owe their existence to favorable sites for river wharfage or crossing or to a situation that commanded a productive hinterland. The only other navigable stream of consequence was the Osage River. Warsaw was for a time a river port of some importance, and under favorable circumstances the Osage could be navigated as far as Osceola. But the Osage River was never a reliable route of commerce. Today, water-borne commerce is carried out mainly on the Missouri and Mississippi rivers. The Arkansas River Project, which recently opened the Arkansas-Grand-Verdigris waterway to the Port of Catoosa near Tulsa, Oklahoma, will no doubt be of more economic importance to the oil- and grain-rich Southern Great Plains than to the Ozarks.

Because interior Ozark streams were not navigable, most of the larger interior towns are on railroads. When railroads were built, towns were located about six to ten miles apart along the right-of-way. Many of the early railroad towns were paper towns; that is, they were planned but never built, either because the planned railroad was never completed, or because of commercial competition from adjacent towns, or, perhaps, because they were purely fraudulent real estate promotions. These early villages had two purposes: to serve as trade and service centers for the agricultural community and to serve as watering and fueling stops for the locomotives. The population during this time was mainly engaged in agriculture and was dispersed throughout the countryside. The principal transportation beyond the railroad being horseback, wagon, or shank's mare, the centers for essential services were necessarily closed spaced. Few towns have been founded since the 1850–1910 railroad construction era.

In the ensuing years, major technological changes have occurred, causing changes in settlement patterns. One of the changes is the continuing agricultural-technology revolution, which has enabled a much smaller percentage of the population to produce more than the necessary food and riber. The percentage of the population engaged in agriculture has declined continuously. A second significant change is in transportation and communication. *Time distance* is a convenient term used as a measure of the distance a man travels in one hour. On foot, men can travel four or five miles, on horseback ten or twelve, but with today's system of highways and the development of motor-vehicle transportation, it is easy to travel fifty miles in an hour. Thus today, an hour's time distance is about fifty miles. In recent years, population growth in the medium-size and larger towns has been stimulated by the industrialization of the region's economy. In combination these changes have worked to modify the region's communities. Many of the original communities have become functionally obsolete, and at the same time a few have grown into important centers of industry and population.

Construction of new highways has brought growth and prosperity to many interior Ozark towns, but at the same time highways have sometimes affected small hamlets and villages adversely. In fact, highways affect Ozark towns in several ways. Some towns formerly outside reasonable commuting distance to places of employment may be brought into range by a new highway. The location of new highways may either help or hinder a town's central business district. Towns may become more attractive as industrial locations because of improved transportation routes. Demand for additional travel-

Buffalo Shoals, Arkansas, on the White River. (Courtesy Arkansas History Commission.)

related services, such as service stations, restaurants, and motels, may be increased and centralized at preferred locations. New growth centers may emerge at highway intersections. The presence of a major highway can be expected to attract area residents to the large centers to obtain a wider selection of goods and services. Villages and small towns may suffer economic stagnation as the rural population declines and the remaining residents bypass the small places to shop in larger towns. In the Ozarks the critical population range is 500 to 1,500; that is, until about the mid-1960's, most communities under 500 tended to decline and those over 1,500 tended to have a better chance for growth. Since that time, which marks the beginning of recent immigration to the Ozarks, many of the smallest places have experienced population increases.

Ozark trade centers may be grouped according to population and the number and range of services available. Central places are usually classified into four categories: hamlets, villages, towns, and cities. According to this system, hamlets are the most rudimentary trade centers. They consist of at least five residential or other cultural or functional structures and at least one, but usually not more than nine, retail units. A regional sample of Ozark hamlets carried out by students in my classes at Southwest Missouri State University, showed that grocery stores, elementary schools, churches, service stations, and taverns are the most typical services. Unplanned in form, they occur as crossroads clusters and as sparse string agglomerations of buildings. Population of hamlets ranges from 20 to 150 with a mean of 65.

Villages are larger. The population range is 150

to about 1,000. They have commercial nuclei with a minimum of ten retail and service units. Grocery stores, taverns, service stations, elementary schools, lumberyards, auto dealers, farm-implement dealers, hardware stores, and feed dealers are typical retail outlets. Banks, telephone exchanges, and post offices are the usual services. Governmental services, personal services, professional services, and entertainment are poorly represented in Ozark villages.

Towns are more specialized urban centers that range in population from about 1,000 to about 7,000. In the Ozarks, most towns have maintained or increased their population. The greatest growth has occurred where highway improvements have been made or where tourist attractions or large-scale urbanization has taken place. Ozark towns usually have extensive commercial districts with at least 50 retail units, of which at least 30 are other than grocery outlets, taverns, or service sttions. Represented are all types of schools and professional services, such as medical, legal, and veterinary. Some warehousing, distributing, and wholesaling are usually present. The seats of county governments are most frequently (but not always) located in towns rather than in hamlets or villages.

Functional change is most notable in hamlets and villages, largely because many have regressed as trade centers. Old signs and advertisements tell of the passing of hotels, blacksmith shops, lumberyards, farm-implement dealers, automobile agencies, and so on. It is not unusual to see community libraries housed in abandoned corner service stations or restaurants or beauty shops in abandoned bank buildings. Some hamlets and villages in the tourist-recreation areas in the Ozarks have an exceptional range of services to serve the large summer population, which is sometimes several times the number of permanent residents. Likewise, regional trade towns, such as Rolla, Lebanon, West Plains, Harrison, Mountain Home, and Tahlequah, have larger-than-normal ranges of services because of the extensive trade areas they serve.

Huzzah, Missouri. Abandoned rural store and post office in Crawford County, Missouri, 1977.

Regional Growth Centers

I have said that the most striking geographic change in Ozark population during the past half-century or more has been movement of people from farm to city. Over the years, several growth centers have emerged. The influence of these cities is much greater than that of smaller places. Each commands a trade area, the size of which varies according to the range of services offered, the distance to competing growth centers, the condition of roads and required time for travel, and the density of population in the hinterland (fig. 14-2). A brief description of the historical development, chief functions, and trade areas of eight of the larger regional centers follows.

Jefferson City, the capital of Missouri and the seat of Cole County, is on the steep southern bluffs of the Missouri River. It is known locally as Jeff or Jeff City. Its location, midway between St. Louis and Kansas City on the river and a direct railroad route, has attracted a number of industries. It is, however, primarily a political city, with state government, for which it was created, its principal business.

Jefferson City was selected as Missouri's capital in December, 1821. It was one of several sites on

Main Street in old Linn Creek, Camden County, Missouri. The site of the original town was flooded by Lake of the Ozarks. (Courtesy Missouri State Historical Society.)

the Missouri River, "within forty miles of the mouth of the Osage," under consideration. In its first years, its growth was slow. After the state penitentiary was constructed in 1836 and the new capitol was finished in 1839, Jefferson City grew faster. It was incorporated in 1839, and according to the federal census, it had 1,174 inhabitants, including 262 slaves in 1840. In 1849 the steamboat *Monroe*, carrying west bound Mormons, stopped at Jefferson City and discharged cholera-stricken passengers. Sixty-three of them died, and for the next two years the plague curtailed immigration and commerce.

Railroad service to St. Louis began in 1856, but the enthusiasm brought by the railroad was soon dampened by the Civil War. Expansion of business activities did not progress rapidly until the 1880's. Three shoe factories were opened in the early 1880's to supplement an already healthy printing industry. The drawbridge built across the Missouri River in 1895 and the construction of a new capitol in 1917 helped to establish a pattern of slow but steady growth.

Over the years, the city spread inland across narrow ridges and valleys that parallel the river. High Street, following the first of the ridges east and west, became the axis of the community. The business buildings consist of blocks of brick and

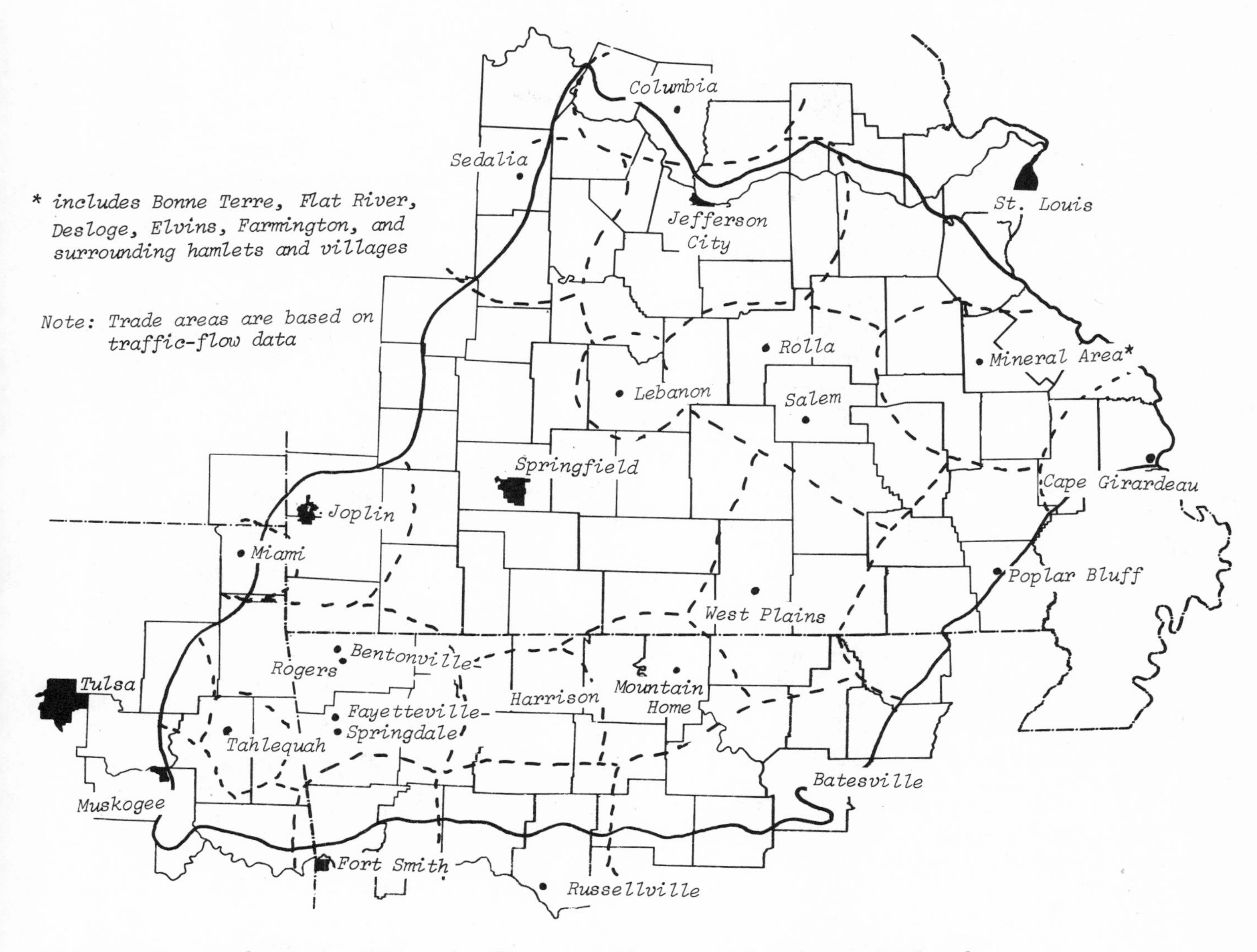

Figure 14-2. Ozark growth centers and trade areas. Trade areas are based on traffic-flow data.

stone structures. A block north of High Street, atop a bluff overlooking the river, the governor's mansion faces the capitol. The residential sections lie east, west, and south of the business district. Blacks, comprising slightly less than 10 per cent of the population, live in the southeastern portion of the city in the vicinity of Lincoln University, formerly a state-supported Negro college but now open to all races.

Compared to most state capitals, Jefferson City is small; its population was 32,407 in the Census of 1970. It is not served directly by an Interstate Highway, but I-70 is only thirty miles north via U.S. Highway 63. Commercial airlines serve Columbia–Jefferson City Regional Airport, located between the two cities. Government and finance continue to play the largest role in the city's economy.

No other place in Jefferson City's vicinity exceeds 3,500 population. California, Owensville, and Eldon are the largest of the outlying towns. The *Missouri Directory of Manufacturing and Mining* for 1976 listed the following types of manufactures employing more than 100 workers in the outlying towns: saddlery, poultry processing, shoe manufacture, clothing, charcoal briquettes, electric motors, fishing boats, wooden novelties, and aluminum and copper tubular parts. Shoe and clothing manufacturing combined make up more than half the total employment in manufacturing in the towns in the Jefferson City trade area. The pattern from town to town is similar to that of other rural trade centers: several small manufacturers or service companies that supply the needs of local or regional farms and agribusinesses, and one or two larger manufacturers of products distributed on a larger regional or national market. The latter are usually of the footloose type taking advantage of less expensive, nonunion labor in rural communities.

St. Louis lies just outside the Ozarks, but as one of America's great cities, it has always had a profound influence on the region. Although the city of St. Louis has experienced declines in population for the past three census periods (1950, 1960, 1970), the Standard Metropolitan Statistical Area (SMSA) continues to grow, and much of the growth is spreading into the northeast Ozark border. The 1970 population of the St. Louis SMSA was 2,340,400, approximately three-quarters of a million more people than lived in the entire Ozark region.

Several of the outlying towns in the Ozarks have profited from the close proximity to St. Louis. Many manufacturing plants have relocated in the outlying towns, and the larger companies have found it profitable to build small- to medium-size plants in these towns and centralize warehousing and sales facilities in St. Louis. Washington, Union, Pacific, Bonne Terre, and Farmington are the largest and most important towns from the standpoint of manufacturing employment. An inventory of manufacturers in the outlying towns shows that shoes, clothing, light metals, and mining and mineral processing are important. A complete inventory of manufacturing plants that employ more than one hundred workers includes: women's clothing, men's clothing, shoes, piston rings, vinyl advertising items, carburetor tune-up kits, aircraft parts, dairy equipment, tents and tarpaulins, lime and stone, toy telephones, electric motors, drilling mud, iron pellets, and lead smelting. An unusual product, corncob pipes, is manufactured by the Missouri Meerschaum Company at Washington. Crystal City, founded as a company town by the Pittsburgh Plate Glass Company, is on the extreme northeast Mississippi border. At Herculaneum is the massive smelter of the St. Joe Mineral Corporation.

The northeast border possesses the best transportation network in the Ozarks. In addition to good railroad facilities and the advantages of year-round navigation on the Mississippi River, both workers and manufactured products can reach St. Louis in little more than an hour from the most distant points in the trade area by way of I-44, I-55, U.S. 67, and U.S. 61.

Cape Girardeau overlooks the Mississippi from the rocky ledge that forms the Ozark Escarpment. Site of Southeast Missouri State University, the town has been the educational and commercial center of southeast Missouri for more than a hundred years. About 1720, a French soldier named Girardot, who was stationed at Kaskaskia, settled on the Cape, a rocky promontory north of the city. Shortly thereafter, maps designated the point as Cape Girardot (or Girardeau). Actual settlement did not occur until the location was discovered in the late 1700's by Americans from the eastern uplands. The growth of the town was retarded by uncertainty of land titles when the U.S. Land Commission rejected Louis Lorimier's Spanish land title. In 1815, Jackson became the county seat and Cape Girardeau languished.

Nevertheless the geographic location of Cape Girardeau pointed toward its growth as a commercial town. Its location on the first high ground above the confluence of the Ohio and the Mississippi rivers gave it strategic importance in the river trade. Logs were floated down to the sawmills, and flour mills and packinghouses were established. In 1880, Louis Houck organized the Cape Girardeau Railway Company, which eventually became the Gulf System, and placed Cape Girardeau on a main line connecting with St. Louis.

Today, Cape Girardeau is served by I-55 and

U.S. 61. Barge traffic on the Mississippi is of some importance, and the city is served by Delta Airlines. The 1976 *Missouri Directory of Manufacturing and Mining* listed 77 manufacturing establishments, of which nine employed more than 100 people. Two manufacturing plants employed more than 500 workers: Charmin Paper Products (800; household paper products, diapers) and Florsheim Shoe Company (694; men's dress shoes). Other large manufacturers include Superior Electric Products Corporation (475; household electrical appliances); Thorngate, Ltd., Division of Hart, Schaffner & Marx (400; men's clothing); Ralph Edwards Sportwear, Inc. (232; men's and boy's clothing and leather jackets); Marquette Cement Manufacturing Company (136; limestone, cement, concrete blocks), Florsheim Shoe Company plant (260; sole leather); Central Foods, Inc. (113; beef, sausage, meats); and Atlas Plastic Corporation (119; polyethylene sheets).

Poplar Bluff has a geographic site similar to that of Cape Girardeau. It is perched on the Ozark Escarpment where the Black River exits from the Ozarks onto the Southeast Alluvial Plain. The older business district lies on the floodplain, and the better residential districts stretch back across the upland to the north. A commercial strip development has grown up along the stretch of U.S. 60-62 leading north through the west part of the city. Along the strip are service stations, restaurants and fast-food establishments, motels, a shopping center, and assorted businesses that serve a vehicle-born clientele.

Founded in 1850 as the county seat of Butler County, Poplar Bluff grew slowly until 1873, when the Iron Mountain Railroad linked its trade area with St. Louis and points east. The economy of the town has been supported at various times by the lumber industry, mining of sink-fill iron deposits, trade with farms and smaller towns, employment in the Missouri Pacific and Frisco switching yards and shops, and an assortment of manufacturing plants.

In recent years, Poplar Bluff has benefited from its selection as the site of Three Rivers Junior College. Major manufacturing plants in 1976 included Florsheim Shoe Company (400; men's shoes), H. W. Gossard Company (226; lingerie), Reinell Boats, Inc. (250; boats), Rowe Furniture Corporation (350; upholstered furniture), and Smiley Container Corporation (235; candy boxes).

Springfield is Missouri's third-largest city and self-proclaimed Queen City of the Ozarks. Its population in the 1970 census was 120,000, but the estimation of slightly more than 140,000 in 1976 gives it the fastest growth rate among Missouri's large cities. Its five colleges (including Southwest Missouri State University, with 13,500 students), four television stations, several radio stations, and the widely read *Springfield Leader Press* make it the most important cultural and commercial center in the Ozarks. It has always been recognized by rural Ozarkers as an Ozark town where people are "just plain folks and are friendlier than in other big places." Much of the immigration into Arkansas and the Cherokee Ozarks in the latter decades of the nineteenth-century was channeled through Springfield. It was a jumping-off place, a trade center, and a place to conduct government business in regional offices of state and federal agencies. These functions are still assigned to the city.

In the 1820's, Delaware and Kickapoo villages were built on the present site of Springfield. The first white families, those of John Campbell, Joseph Miller, William Fullbright, and A. J. Burnett, settled in 1829 and 1830. The origin of the name *Springfield* is uncertain, but it is probably named after Springfield, Tennessee. Springfield became the seat of Greene County when the county was organized in 1833 and was incorporated as a town in 1838. In 1835 the government land office for southwest Missouri was established there, and by 1859, Springfield, with a population of 2,500, was the main trade center in southwest Missouri. In 1870 the Atlantic and Pacific Railroad built north of Springfield, and the Ozark Land Company platted a rival town, North Springfield, along what is today Commercial Street. The two towns were first linked by a trolley line, and in 1887, after the old town acquired its own rail depot (Kansas City, Fort Scott and Memphis), the two towns were consolidated.

Springfield is built around several commercial nuclei (fig. 14-3). The downtown business district is concentrated around Park Central Mall (Public Square), which is near the center of the city.

Springfield Public Square, 1879. (Courtesy Missouri State Historical Society.)

North of the square is the Jordan Creek Industrial District, which extends for several blocks east and west. North of Jordan Creek, just northeast of the intersection of Boonville and Trafficway, is a cluster of government offices, including the city hall, utilities offices, the police department, the Greene County courthouse and jail, the main library, the U.S. post office, and the Social Security office building. Farther north, Boonville Avenue intersects Commercial Street, the focus of an important commercial and industrial district, which extends east-west parallel to the Frisco tracks. The extensive Frisco shops and switching yards are located at the west end of this district.

Several outlying commercial centers have grown up over the past forty years. Small retail centers developed earlier at transfer points and terminals along the streetcar lines. Some of these small clusters of grocery stores, drugstores, and laundromats have continued in business partly

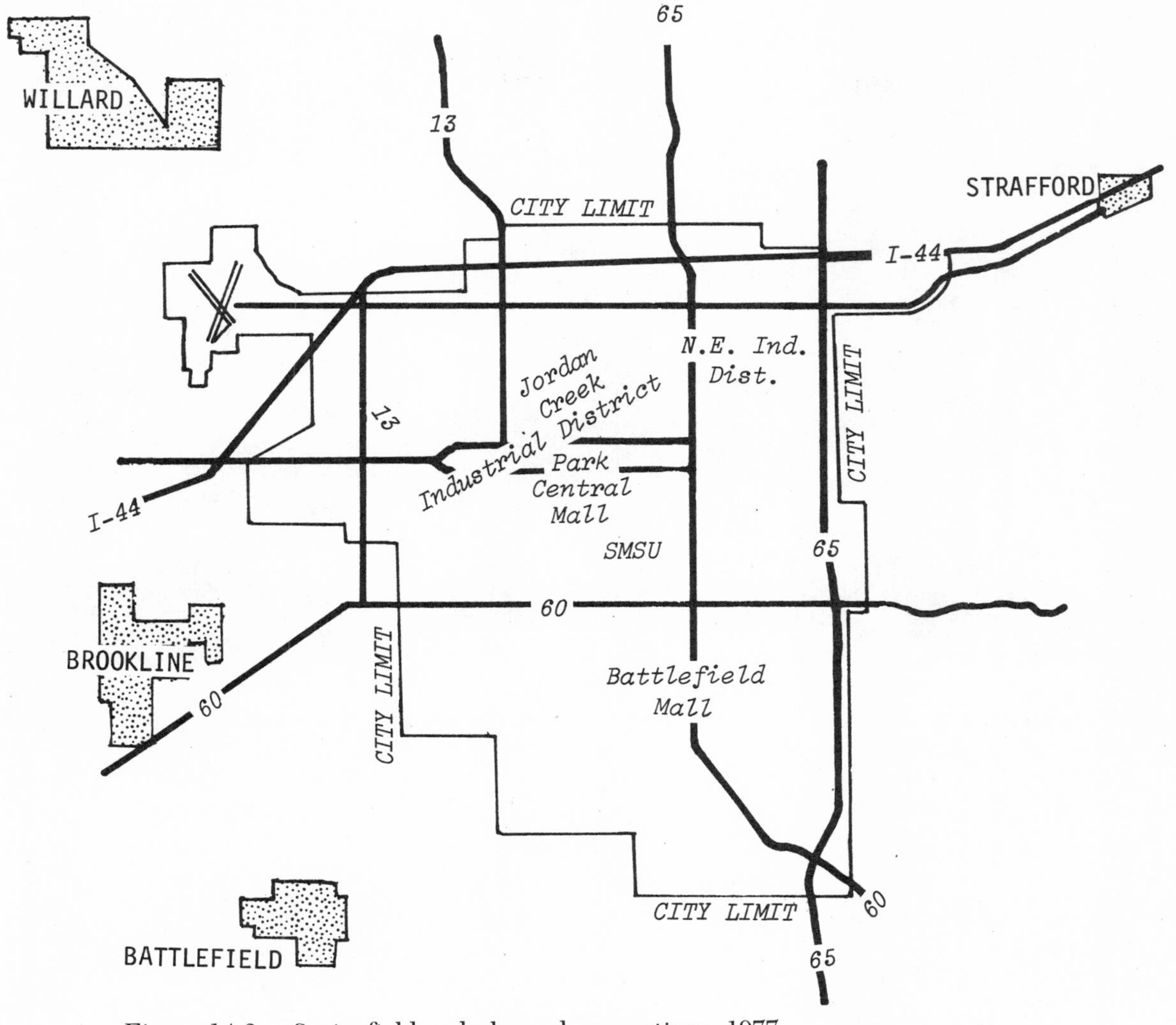

Figure 14-3. Springfield and planned annexations, 1977.

because the bus lines continued along the routes of the streetcar lines after the last streetcar ran in 1937.

In Springfield the fully developed commercial throughfares were formerly the main bypass highways. Glenstone Avenue is the most maturely developed string street: eleven miles of service stations, eating establishments, motels, grocery stores, discount stores, insurance agencies, and automobile dealerships. One major node is the motel, restaurant, and service station cluster on Glenstone between Kearney Street and I-44.

A second major commercial node is the group of off-street shopping centers developed at the intersection of Sunshine Street and Glenstone Avenue and north on Glenstone to Bennett. The Plaza on the southeast corner of Sunshine and Glenstone is the oldest; a Ramey supermarket was built there in the early 1950's. Katz City, Glen

Washington Avenue and Howell County Courthouse, West Plains, Missouri, *circa* 1890. (Courtesy Missouri State Historical Society.)

Isle, and Country Club shopping centers were developed in the late 1950's and early 1960's.

The most recent and rapid development on Glenstone is in the vicinity of the Battlefield Mall. The Mall, built in 1972 as a regional shopping center, immediately became the largest commercial cluster on Glenstone Avenue and shifted the center of gravity of Springfield's commercial structure and traffic pattern to the southeast. In 1974, there were 61 business operations in Battlefield Mall, including Montgomery Ward, J. C. Penney Company, Dillard's, Century 21 Theatre, Osco Drugs, and Piccadilly Cafeteria.

The Frisco passenger terminal was closed in 1967 when passenger service was discontinued. The shops, terminal, and most of the switching tracks in the Lower Jordan Creek Valley have been razed. Part of the land is occupied by a concrete-mix plant; a portion of the remainder is used for open storage of railroad supplies. Service on the Missouri Pacific line to Crane was discontinued, and the track was removed in 1972, thereby relegating the Missouri Pacific to switching lines serving the Jordan Creek industries. Shipments to outside destinations must go over Frisco lines.

A manufacturing directory published by the Springfield Chamber of Commerce in 1974 listed manufacturers by number of employees. Those in the over-1,000 category included Zenith Corporation (televisions), St. Louis–San Francisco Railroad, Springday Division of Dayco (V-belts), and Owens-Illinois (paper cups and food containers). Manufacturing companies employing 250 to 999 employees included: Foremost Foods Co. (dairy products), the R. T. French Co. (mustard), General Electric (electric motors), Gospel Publishing House (religious literature), Hiland Dairy, Kraft Foods Corporation (cheese), Litton Industries H. C. Division (printed electrical circuits),

Mid-America Dairymen Inc. (milk products), Mono Manufacturing Co. (chain saws), Reyco Industries (transportation equipment), and Springfield Newspapers. Other major employers included the national headquarters of Assembly of God churches; two large hospitals—St. Johns Regional Health Center and Cox Medical Center—the federal medical center for prisoners; and the U. S. post office.

There have been many developments in manufacturing in Springfield since the 1930's. The U.S. Bureau of the Census classification of manufacturing according to the Standard Industrial Classification (SIC) shows Springfield to be high in Food and Kindred Products, Fabricated Metals, Printing, Publishing, and Allied Industries, and in Chemicals and Allied Products. A telephone survey completed in 1968 by the urban geography class at Southwest Missouri State University produced the following breakdown in time of establishment of manufacturing plants: before 1900, 7; 1900 to 1909, 5; 1910 to 1919, 8; 1920 to 1929, 21; 1930 to 1939, 13; 1940 to 1949, 45; 1950 to 1959, 29; 1960 to 1967, 13. Many of the plants that have been established since World War II are large compared with older manufacturing plants.

Most of the older manufacturing plants are located in the Jordan Creek Industrial District, notably feedmills and food wholesale houses, furniture and fixture manufacture, and printing and publishing. In the 1960's, new plants began to spring up in the Northeast Industrial District and at other scattered outlying locations. Several of Springfield's long-established industries have built facilities in the new industrial parks, taking advantage of lower-priced land, better accessibility, lack of congestion, and elimination of old and obsolete buildings and equipment.

Many of the industries that were important in the 1930's have closed, and many others have moved to new locations. The Marblehead Lime Quarry is at this writing being used again as a landfill after a persistent fire that burned for several months in 1972. The Springfield Wagon and Tractor Company works has been abandoned and most of the buildings razed. The stockyards on Mill Street have been torn down; new facilities are located on Commercial Street east of Kansas Avenue.

Tower Inn, Salem, Missouri. High-rise building are landmarks in the small Ozark growth centers.

The Springfield trade area is large, compared with those of most cities its size, because it is in a sparsely settled region, a major railroad center and a focus for several major highways, including Interstate 44, U.S. Highways 60 and 65, and Missouri Highways 13, 160, and 266. The Springfield airport is served by Ozark airline. The Springfield *Leader and Press* is the major daily paper eastward halfway across the state to Shannon and Dent counties.

The Springfield trade area includes five towns with populations exceeding 5,000: Rolla, Lebanon, West Plains, Monett, and Mountain Home, Arkansas. Four towns show abnormal growth curves. Aurora and Pierce City were mining camps that followed the boom-and-bust growth pattern so typical in the Joplin area. Republic and Ozark experienced abnormally sharp upturns in the 1960's because of overspill from Springfield. In the Central Plateau, both Lebanon and West Plains have experienced steady population increases. West Plains is an abnormal town in that it is the only town of size in a large area of south-central Missouri. It has an unusually large range of services for a town of 6,500. Much of the new commercial development is along a portion of

Porter Waggoner Boulevard north of the town.

Lebanon has profited from its location on I-44, which is one of Missouri's growth corridors. Rolla is the primary city of the Osage-Gasconade Hills section. Its growth may be explained by institutional expansion (University of Missouri-Rolla, Missouri Geological Survey and Missouri Department of Water Resources), highway location, and trade from Fort Leonard Wood personnel. Mountain Home, Arkansas, owes much of its prosperity to its location in the middle of the rapidly growing lake counties.

The tourist towns of the White River Hills have only moderate growth rates, probably because much of the population increase has been outside the corporate limits of the towns. However, because of large numbers of tourists, these towns have services comparable to those in much larger towns. For example, Branson is quite similar to Neosho in the range and number of services available to permanent and transient residents.

As in other sections of the Ozarks, manufacturing employment in the outlying towns is of considerable importance. Even though the plants are small by the standards of large cities, the opening or closing of an industry that employes as many as three hundred workers can have a marked impact on a town of one or two thousand people. The 1976 manufacturing directories for Missouri and Arkansas list the following types of plants employing one hundred workers or more in outlying towns in the Springfield trade area: turkey processing, children's shoes, aluminim extrusions, prepared feeds, printing, gas and electric furnaces, women's uniforms, hospital supplies and laboratory instruments, evaporated milk, boys' clothing, electric motors, men's clothing, automotive fans, bread production, women's clothing, camping trailers, machine tools, white-oak barrels, aluminum boats, electric controls, men's shoes, truck bodies and suspensions, custom woodcarving, artificial flowers, charcoal briquettes, and women's shoes. Not only is the list of manufacturers surprisingly diverse, but there is an interesting pattern of industry clustering. For example, Brown Shoe Company, International Shoe Company, and H.D. Lee Company have several manufacturing plants that are close enough together to share warehousing and technically trained personnel.

Joplin is intimately connected with lead and zinc mining. Much of its history is captured in a mural by Thomas Hart Benton, a native son of the Tri-State District, which decorates the new municipal building in Joplin. In it are scenes of the mines and miners and the gaudy saloons, dance halls, and gambling halls that once were strung out along Main Street. The city was built, literally, upon the mines, straddling the boundary of Jasper and Newton counties.

The first settler, John C. Cox, built a home on Turkey Creek near the end of what is now Mineral Avenue. Shortly after that, the Reverend Harris C. Joplin, a Methodist minister from Greene County, settled on an eighty-acre tract. Lead is reported to have been discovered in 1849, but only a few diggings were opened before the Civil War. After the war the Atlantic and Pacific Railroad was extended to Joplin and the mining boom was on. Two towns grew up on either side of Joplin Creek: Murphysburg to the west and Joplin City to the east. In 1873 they were incorporated as the city of Joplin. As additional ore bodies were discovered, more mining camps were established so that by the turn of the century Joplin was surrounded by small mining towns.

As the mines in Joplin were worked out, the city turned to other businesses: buying and selling lead and zinc, processing and smelting ores, manufacturing explosives and mining equipment, providing services for mining companies and workers. Joplin became the primary city of the Tri-State Mining District, but, as the ores gradually petered out, the city relied increasingly on other manufactures and commerce. The abandoned tailings piles and mine shafts scattered about the town and the elegant homes just west of the downtown area are reminders of the mining era. Range Line Road, a five-mile commercial strip extending north from Interstate 44 through the east edge of the city, is a manifestation of the new Joplin. The large shopping mall and the usual assortment of restaurants, motels, service stations, and fast-food outlets indicates the city has recovered its commercial vitality. Within a fifty-mile radius of Joplin is a population of more than 350,000. Joplin has long been the marketing, commercial, and transportation hub of this area, which covers parts of Missouri, Kansas, and Oklahoma.

The growth patterns of towns in the Joplin area are some of the most distinctive in Missouri. This is in keeping with the development of the Tri-State Mining District and its subsequent decline. Only two large towns, Carthage and Neosho, both outside the main mining district, show a normal development pattern. The population trends of Webb City, Carterville, and Granby reflect the fact that these towns originated as mining camps and relied heavily on the mines. They grew fast about the turn of the century but experienced a rapid population decline between 1920 and 1940.

As is the case in most other outlying towns in the Ozarks, the chief functions are those concerned with providing goods and services to people who live in the surrounding countryside. Nevertheless, manufacturing is of considerable importance and has the same composition as in other sections of the Ozarks, namely, food processing, clothing and shoes, electronics, and light metal fabrication.

Northwest Arkansas City is a name that I apply to the Standard Metropolitan Statistical Area formed by the two counties in extreme northwestern Arkansas, Benton and Washington, that include the cities of Fayetteville, Springdale, Rogers, and Bentonville. Many residents of the communities that make up this urbanized area undoubtedly would prefer to be identified with the individual towns, but the fact that these four communities are growing into one functional unit is already being recognized in very practical ways. A recent feature story in the *Kansas City Star* described the urban development along U.S. Highway 71 in northwest Arkansas as "the Strip," and the owners of the shopping mall recently constructed midway between Fayetteville and Springdale chose to name it Northwest Arkansas Plaza.

Perhaps the best way to appreciate the dimensions of Northwest Arkansas City is to drive the length of it along its main street: U.S. Highway 71. To do this, one should avoid the rush hours, when vehicles carrying workers to their jobs in hundreds of retail stores, services, and manufacturing plants jam the highway. Unlike the flow of traffic in large cities, where the inbound lanes are crowded in the morning hours and the outbound lanes are crowded in the later afternoon, the traffic on U.S. Highway 71 through the northwest Arkansas strip has no ebb and flow but instead is the frenzied scramble of a big city string street.

The main street (U.S. 71) of Northwest Arkansas City is about twenty-five miles long. It begins just south of the Missouri state line and leads southward through the sprawling retirement town of Bella Vista, then through Bentonville, Rogers, and Springdale to Fayetteville. Except for about three miles between Bentonville and Rogers and another two miles between Rogers and Springdale, U.S. 71 is fronted on both sides by almost continuous strings of businesses in more or less random order. A windshield inventory includes the following: fruit stands, lumberyards, bowling alleys, off-street shopping centers, carpet shops, paint stores, building suppliers, antique shops, supermarkets, quick-shop grocery stores, garden shops, motels, electrical co-ops, well drillers, LP-gas distributors, a drive-in movie, automobile dealers, mobile-home dealers, savings and loans, the Daisy air-rifle plant, the J. B. Hunt Company plant, farm implement dealerships, boat sales, orchards, the Pioneer Foods plant, motorcycle sales, trucking companies, the Veterans Administration hospital, a regional medical center, and a multitude of restaurants and franchised fast-food outlets, including such familiar names as Sambo's, Pizza Hut, Bonanza, Taco Hut, Sonic, and McDonald's. There is little to distinguish the strip from scores of others that have grown up throughout the United States except that the roadsides are strewn with feathers blown from semitrailer loads of chickens that are hauled into the food-processing plants in Springdale. Nevertheless, from the heights in Fayetteville, lights on the strip present an interesting nighttime panorama.

Fayetteville, the largest of the four towns, is the seat of Washington County and the site of the main campus of the University of Arkansas. It has been the leading town in northwest Arkansas since the first lots were sold in 1828. Fayetteville became a center for education when Fayetteville Female Seminary, a pioneer girls' school, was founded in 1838. Other small colleges that were opened in the 1840's and 1850's, along with stores and most of the residences, were burned during the Civil War. Fayetteville's location midway between the Federal base at Springfield and the

Confederate encampments along the Arkansas River placed it in the midst of the Ozarks battleground.

The city of 31,915 residents sprawls across several hills that form northern outliers of the Boston Mountains. The main business district is built around the Washington County courthouse. Northwest of the courthouse and business district is the University of Arkansas campus. The most striking structure in the city is the university's administration building, a four-story brick structure with a mansard roof and dormer windows and two corner towers that are visible for miles. Many of the new businesses have been built north of the city along U.S. 71 and in the new Northwest Arkansas Plaza.

Although Fayetteville enjoys a reputation as a university town, manufacturing employment is substantial. The larger plants include Campbell Soup Company, Kearney Company (electric fuses and tools), Levi Strauss and Company (denim jackets), Ozark Forest Products, Armstrong Brothers Tool Company (hand tools), Baldwin Piano and Organ Company, Shakespeare of Arkansas (fishing reels), and several printing establishments.

Springdale is a center for canning and preparation of frozen foods. Over the years, as general farming gave way to production of small fruits and vegetables in northwest Arkansas, commercial canning prospered. Many small canneries were established in southwest Missouri and northwest Arkansas to pack green beans, spinach, poke greens, strawberries, blackberries, apples, grapes, and potatoes. Over the years, Springdale became the chief center for consolidated and enlarged canneries, and in the 1950's and 1960's plants were built to process poultry products and prepare frozen foods. Large feed companies that serve poultry farms in northwest Arkansas round out agribusiness manufacturing in Springdale. The 1976 *Directory of Arkansas Manufacturers* listed the following agrimanufacturing employers: Cargill, Inc., poultry products feedmill; Forrest Park Canning Company; Old South Foods Company; Seymour Foods, Inc.; Springdale Farms; Steele Canning Company; Tyson Foods, Inc.; Welch Foods, Inc.; and Wilson and Company, Inc.

Rogers' population of 13,189 makes it the largest town in Benton County. As in Springdale, agribusinesses are the largest employers, but metal and wood products manufacture also is important. Agrimanufacturers include Garrett Poultry, Inc.; Hudson Foods, Inc.; Pel-Freeze Rabbit Meat, Inc.; Rogers Vinegar Company; and Speas Company.

A major employer is the Daisy Division, Victor Comptometer Corporation, manufacturer of Daisy air rifles. This company, which began as the Plymouth Iron Windmill Company in Plymouth, Michigan, has manufactured air rifles since 1889. The corporation's decision to relocate in Rogers in 1957, as described by Cass S. Hough, helps to explain the increase in Ozarks manufacturing during the past twenty-five years:

> My travels had taken me to nearly every section of the country, except the far west and the far east, in search for a new home for Daisy. First, I narrowed the choice down to an area, and that was the Arkansas-Oklahoma-Kansas-Missouri one. Not only was it centrally located for the shipment of Daisy products nationwide, but in the main, people who would constitute Daisy's work force seemed to be several cuts above what I found in other areas. The time I spent in choosing *the* spot in this four-state area was spent in evaluating the people themselves. . . . The people of northwest Arkansas, by and large, are "pioneer" types, probably the last stronghold of those who want no handouts and are not only willing but eager to give a day's work for a day's pay, who take a long time making up their minds about newcomers, are cooperative and courteous.[9]

Bentonville, the smallest (population 6,391) of the four towns that make up Northwest Arkansas City, is the seat of Benton County. In addition to the normal commercial activities, clothing manufacture and agrimanufactures are the basic employers. The larger industries include Arkansas Poultry Cooperative; Kraft Foods, Inc.; Krispy Kitchens, Inc.; Bentonville Manufacturing Company (clothing); and Bear Brand Hosiery Company.

Outlying towns in the trade area of Northwest Arkansas City are mainly small, but a few are large enough to attract the familiar western Ozark In-

9. Cass S. Hough. *It's a Daisy* (Rogers, Ark.: Daisy Division Victor Comptometer Corporation, 1976), p. 159.

dustries: chickens and cheese, shirts and shoes, wood and wiring.

Batesville, the seat of Independence County, Arkansas, is the major growth center of the southeastern Ozarks. The city has grown substantially since the 1970 census reported 7,209 residents. Batesville was built on the bluffs where the White River exits the Ozarks. The red brick buildings on the new campus of Arkansas College can be seen for miles from their vantage point on the ridge north of the business district.

Batesville is sharing in the rapid growth and development of northern Arkansas. National trends account for part of this: the shift of industries to the South, faster growth of the service sector of the national economy, and the accelerated growth of population in areas that have amenities. One resident explained it this way: "It's the water, scenery, environment, and people that will work." Batesville is developing into the chief regional shopping and distribution center for the fast-growing north-central Arkansas counties.

Manufacturing is of considerable importance, particularly the two Banquet Foods plants and the Arkansas Poultry Company, which provided markets for the expansion of poultry raising in the southeastern Ozarks. Other manufacturing plants include Arkansas Eastman (chemicals), International Shoe Company, Westport Casuals, Inc. (clothing), White Rogers Company (electrical controls), and General Tire and Rubber Company.

The growth of Batesville and the Ozark counties to the north has been so rapid in recent years that some residents are beginning to express concern about its overall effects. Leo Rainey, area development agent at Batesville, put it this way:

> The things that are happening today are the things people hoped would happen twenty years ago, or even ten years ago. There were few jobs to be had then and there were political fights over committee representation on the ASCS and over who would get a $150 per month job as school bus driver. Now the people aren't as concerned about such things because there are other jobs in the manufacturing plants, in the construction business, or in the tourist business. People are now beginning to think about restraining some of this growth. We've not reached the point where no growth is the majority, but people aren't as anxious for growth as they were.[10]

Tahlequah (population 9,254) is the largest city in the Oklahoma Ozarks. Hemmed in by progressive cities—Tulsa, Muskogee, Fort Smith–Van Buren, Northwest Arkansas City—the trade area is confined mainly to Cherokee County. Tahlequah became the permanent capital of the Cherokee Nation on September 6, 1839, when the Eastern and Western Cherokees met on the site of the present square to sign the new constitution. The town was platted in 1843, and houses were removed to form the public square in 1845. In 1846 the Cherokees established two schools: the Male Seminary southwest of town and the Female Seminary at Park Hill, approximately four miles south of Tahlequah. Both schools burned, but the Female Seminary was rebuilt in Tahlequah and later (in 1909) purchased by the state of Oklahoma to form the nucleus of Northeast Oklahoma State College. The Cherokee County courthouse occupies the old Cherokee Capitol, which was built on the square in 1869.

Tahlequah, primarily a service center and college town, has remarkably little manufacturing employment. The list is short: two clothing factories, two or three wood-products manufacturers, several small printing establishments, and a ready-mix concrete plant.

People as Landscape

The people themselves comprise the final element of the Ozarks landscape. This includes all who move upon the Ozark scene, permanent residents and transients, in all their various social and economic conditions, habits of dress, and personal paraphernalia.

It is difficult to select a characteristic physical type. In the northern and eastern borders, where the German element is strongest, there are many tall, heavy-built men and women with fair complexions. In the Oklahoma Ozarks, the Cherokee bloodline may be seen in various degrees ranging from tall, copper-skinned people with jet black

10. Personal interview with Leo Rainey, area development agent, June 16, 1977.

hair and dark eyes to fairer-skinned types with dark hair and eyes. The old-line residents, descended from Scotch-Irish stock, are most often medium to tall in stature, usually slender when young, fair-skinned, blue-eyed, and often with hair that is sandy or reddish-tinged.

Although the region is not known for producing men of importance, more than a few, either natives or longtime residents, have achieved a measure of fame. Edwin Hubble, a native of Marshfield, Missouri, graduated from the University of Chicago and made outstanding contributions in the study of the universe. His observations with the 100-inch telescope at Mount Wilson Observatory led him to classify the nebulae and to confirm the theory of the expanding universe. Curtis F. Marbut grew up on a farm near Monett, Missouri, and later studied under eminent geologist Milliam Morris Davis. Marbut achieved recognition as a geologist, but he is best known for his monumental work in the study and classification of soils. Carl O. Sauer, a native of Warrenton, Missouri, on the northern Ozark border, achieved wide renown as a geographer. His publication's on geographic methodology, historical geography, and the origins of domestic grains are landmarks in the profession. As chairman and professor in the department of geography at the University of California at Berkeley, Sauer spawned a genre of geographic inquiry known as landscape geography, or the Berkeley School, which focuses on the form and function of landscape. John S. Phelps of Springfield and Phil M. Donnelly of Lebanon served as governors of Missouri. Richard P. Bland of Lebanon was a contender for the 1896 Democratic nomination for the presidency. William Fullbright of Fayetteville, Arkansas, was an influential member of the U.S. Senate until his retirement in 1974.

Several Ozarkers have attained recognition in art, literature, and music. Rose O'Neill gained attention for her designs, the most important of which, the Kewpie doll, became a national rage. Her elegant home, Bonniebrook, in Taney County, Missouri, was a showplace of style and comfort in its day. A native of Neosho, Missouri, Thomas Hart Benton, achieved international acclaim for his vigorously realistic paintings of Missouri and Ozark life. Vance Randolph, a native of Kansas but a longtime resident of Fayetteville, Arkansas, is the best-known collector of Ozark folklore. More recently, Jimmy Driftwood, who lives on a farm near Timbo, Arkansas, has achieved national fame for his folksongs, particularly "The Battle of New Orleans" and "The Tennessee Stud." Driftwood was instrumental in obtaining federal assistance to establish the Ozark Folk Culture Center at Mountain View, and he continues to be active in the Rackensack Society, an informal gathering of folk musicians who play traditional music in an old store building in Mountain View.

The foregoing list of notables is by no means complete, but simply serves notice that the Ozarks has produced talented people. Nevertheless, the character of a population can hardly be identified by examining its celebrated. There is no single Ozark type that represents a median or mode, just as there is no typical New Yorker. Ozarkers are as varied as middle westerners can be. One who moves about the region at various functions and meetings will gradually accumulate a memory full of bits and pieces from which, ever so slowly, emerges an image of the fabric of life.

A Sunday drive on a highway leading to one of the Ozark lakes provides a view of a cross-section of permanent and transient residents. Out-of-state tourists may be recognized by their vehicle license plates. A bit more can be surmised from their baggage and gear. A young couple in a Volkswagen with a canoe on top and the rear seat loaded with camping gear are headed for one of the float streams. A Winnebago motor home with motorcycle, lawn chairs, and water skis tied on wherever possible, driven by a fiftyish man, will seek out a lakeside camping spot where all the requisite utilities are available. A new automobile pulling an eight thousand dollar bass boat weaves through traffic in a hurry to get to a boat dock in time to allow its occupants to spend a few hours on the lake before returning home. An old auto with no hubcaps and blue smoke pouring out of the exhaust pipe, loaded with inner tubes, fishing poles, and youngsters, is headed for a nearby river or creek where the occupants will spend an afternoon wading, swimming, and fishing. The new four-wheel-drive pickup equipped with West Coast mirrors, buggy-whip citizens-band radio antenna, heavy mudflaps—and with a lever-action .30-30 carbine and a coiled bullwhip displayed in the rear-window gun rack—is occupied by a pleasant-looking couple who appear to be thirtyish. He wears a medium-brimmed cowboy hat, Levis and a western-cut shirt; she wears a stylish pantsuit. They are just out for a ride in what one of my Ozark friends calls a genuine Ozark convertible, otherwise known as a pickup truck.

Country music, the Nashville sound, popular with a wide cross-section of Ozarkers, attracts a cosmopolitan crowd. Large audiences are attracted to concerts featuring popular country-music entertainers, such as Buck Owens, Tammy Wynette, Johny Cash, Johny Rodriguez, or Merle Haggard. Capacity crowds are attracted to the Shrine Mosque or Hammons Center on the campus of Southwest Missouri State University in Springfield for such events. Represented in the crowd are middle-age farmers in overalls and bright young college girls in the same apparel; men dressed to the teeth in pale pastel leisure suits with white trim and wide-brimmed cream-colored cowboy hats and hand-tooled cowboy boots; women in evening gowns and stylish coiffures to match; and a multitude of men in blue jeans and open-neck shirts accompanied by women in ready-to-wear pantsuits or dresses. It is a crowd that is on hand wherever country music is played in the United States. But, lo and behold, where but in the Ozarks could an observer spot amongst the crowd a matronly woman wielding a 10X rifle scope as an opera glass?

The stereotyped postcard hillbilly is a caricature of a lifestyle that sprang from poverty, lack of skills and education, and underemployment rather than inherent laziness or lack of ambition. There is ample evidence that Ozarkers readily accept assistance from state and federal agencies and most of the material goods of modern America. The image of the region as a backwater area isolated from the mainstream of society overlooks the fact that some sections of the Ozarks had electrical power a generation before it came into common use in the Corn Belt or in the Plains States. The image of the carefree woodsman-farmer living in peaceful bliss in the midst of the Ozark forest is equally erroneous. Little about poverty is picturesque.

It is the persistence of fragments of departed lifestyles that holds intrinsic fascination for visitors. Traditional speech patterns, habits of dress, agricultural practices, family ties, and community social bonds have persisted a little longer in some Ozark communites. This peculiar resistance to change reminds one of the little patches of snow that linger, protected by the shade of rocks and overhanging banks of the north slope of a hill, long after spring has come to the southern slopes. And like the little drifts of snow, it seems unlikely that even this is retained in its original purity, but is more probably colored by experiences that have transpired since it was laid down. Thus the attraction of the Ozarks lies in its superlative scenic beauty and its cultural tradition. It is one of the few remaining places where one can not only view but also can participate in selected fragments of America's past.

The Ozarks has been washed over by several waves of immigration and change. Some sections were better suited to receive the benefits of the forces of change at various stages of time. Some individuals have succeeded more than others, and some give better promise than others. But all the land and people of the Ozarks are worth knowing, and in all cases an understanding of their history and geography goes far toward explaining their contrasting conditions. My earnest hope is that this volume will contribute to the understanding of a region that I have learned to appreciate in the same way I do my own homeland in the plains of Kansas.

Selected References

Arkansas Industrial Development Foundation. *Directory of Arkansas Manufacturers, 1976.* Little Rock: 1976.

Arkansas State Planning Board and the Writers Project of the Works Progress Administration. *Arkansas: A Guide to the State.* New York: Hastings House, 1941.

Cralle, Waldo O. "Social Change and Isolation in the Ozark Mountain Region of Missouri." Ph.D. dissertation, University of Minnesota, 1934.

Gerstäker, Friedrich. *Wild Sports in the Far West*, Durham, N.C.: Duke University Press, 1968.

Hart, J. F. "The Changing American Countryside." In *Problems and Trends in American Geography*, edited by Saul B. Cohen. New York: Basic Books, Inc. 1967.

Hewes, Leslie. "The Oklahoma Ozarks as the Land of the Cherokees," *Geographical Review* 32 (April 1942): 269–81.

———. "Cultural Fault Line in the Cherokee Country," *Economic Geography* 19 (April 1943): 136–42.

———. "Tontitown: Ozark Vineyard Center," *Economic Geography* 29 (April 1953): 125–43.

Hogg, Virginia. "Urban Pattern of Springfield, Missouri." Master's thesis, Washington University, 1934.

Kansas Department of Economic Development. *Directory of Kansas Manufacturers and Products, 1976.* Topeka: 1976.

Kniffin, Fred. "Folk Housing: Key to Diffusion," *Annals of the Association of American Geographers* 55 (December 1965): 549–77.

Maxfield, O. O. "Geography of the Boston Mountains." Ph.D. dissertation, The Ohio State University, 1963.

Meyer, Duane. "The Ozarks in Missouri History," *Missouri Historical Review,* 73, January 1979.

Midwest Research Institute. *Missouri, Its Business and Living Environment.* Kansas City: Commerce Bancshares, Inc., 1971.

Missouri Economic Development Commission. *Missouri Directory of Manufacturing and Mining, 1976.* Jefferson City: 1976.

Missouri State Highway Commission and the Writers' Program of the Works Progress Administration. *Missouri: A Guide to the "Show Me" State.* New York: Duell, Sloan and Pearce, 1941.

Springfield (Mo.) *Leader and Press.* "Amish in the Ozarks: The Old Days Returneth." February 29, 1968.

Oklahoma Industrial Development Department. *Oklahoma Directory of Manufacturers and Products, 1976.* Oklahoma City: 1976.

Rafferty, Milton D. "Persistence Versus Change in Land Use and Landscape in the Springfield, Missouri Vicinity of the Ozarks." Ph.D. dissertation, University of Nebraska, 1970.

———. "Ozark House Types: A Regional Approach," *Proceedings of the Pioneer America Society* 2 (1973): 93–106.

Ruth, Kent, et al. *Oklahoma: A Guide to the Sooner State.* American Guide Series. Norman: University of Oklahoma Press, 1941.

Sauer, Carl O. *The Geography of the Ozark Highland of Missouri.* The Geographic Society of Chicago bulletin no. 7. Chicago: University of Chicago Press, 1920.

———. "The Morphology of Landscape." In *Land and Life*, edited by John Leighly. Berkeley: University of California Press, 1963.

———. "Status and Change in the Rural Midwest—A Retrospect." In *Mitteilungen der Österreichischen Geographischen Gesellschaft.* 105 (1963): 357–65.

Schoolcraft, Henry Rowe. *Schoolcraft in the Ozarks.* Edited by Hugh Parks. Van Buren, Ark.: Press-Argus Printers, 1955.

Schroeder, Walter S. *The Eastern Ozarks.* National Council for Geographic Education Special Publication no. 13. Normal: Illinois State University, 1967.

Self, Burl, and Jackson, Philip. *Citizen Recommendations Regarding Formulation of Area Development Program.* Republic, Mo.: Lakes Country Community Advisory Council, 1977.

Sissel, Randy. "Concern Found on Land Use, Pollution." *Springfield* (Mo.) *Leader and Press*, July 28, 1977.

Thomas, Lewis F. "A Geographic Study of Greene County, Missouri." Master's thesis, University of Missouri, 1917.

Wecter, Dixon. *The Saga of American Society.* New York: C. Scribner's Sons, 1937.

Whittlesey, Derwent. "Sequent Occupance." *Annals of the Association of American Geographers* 19 (September 1929): 162–65.

Wood, James, and Rafferty, Milton D. "Mentor, Missouri: Forty Years Later." *Missouri Geographer,* fall 1976, pp. 21–26.

Index